P9-DFW-607

EVALUATING CHICAGO SOCIOLOGY

THE HERITAGE OF SOCIOLOGY
A Series Edited by Morris Janowitz

LESTER R. KURTZ

EVALUATING CHICAGO SOCIOLOGY

A Guide to the Literature, with an Annotated Bibliography

Foreword by
MORRIS JANOWITZ

THE UNIVERSITY OF CHICAGO PRESS
Chicago and London

The University of Chicago Press, Chicago 60637
The University of Chicago Press, Ltd., London

© 1984 by The University of Chicago
All rights reserved. Published 1984
Paperback edition 1986
Printed in the United States of America

95 94 93 92 91 90 89 88 87 86   6 5 4 3 2

Library of Congress Cataloging in Publication Data

Kurtz, Lester R.
Evaluating Chicago sociology.

(The Heritage of sociology)
Bibliography: p.
Includes index.
1. Sociology—United States—Bibliography. 2. Chicago school of sociology—Bibliography. I. Title.
II. Series.
Z7165.U6C474 1984   016.301   84-53
[HM22.U5]
ISBN 0-226-46476-8 (cloth)
ISBN 0-226-46477-6 (paper)

CONTENTS

FOREWORD

The growth, transformation, and decline of intellectual and academic institutions makes for fascinating reading. During the past decade, studies of various institutions of higher learning and research have helped to prevent a narrow, "cultist" perspective in sociological analysis. A well-done study of this kind, Lester Kurtz's survey of publications, with annotated bibliography, presents relevant critical sources dealing with sociology at the University of Chicago.

During the years of intellectual dominance by the Department of Sociology at Chicago, only a handful of sociologists were involved; yet their productivity remains outstanding in both quality and diversity. Kurtz, while selecting and commenting on the enduring materials, does not limit his survey to the contributions of the members of the Chicago department and includes literature critical of Chicago sociology. The result is a volume which will greatly assist the search for the origins and growth patterns of American sociology.

For the first sixty years of Chicago sociology, more than one thousand references are included and annotated in Kurtz's bibliography. More recent writings are also covered as works dealing with the Chicago school continue to appear. The few sociologists who were the core of Chicago sociology before 1950 believed that their task was mainly to break new empirical ground and to attend to the interplay of theory and research. Synthesis of existing knowledge was an important goal. Members of the Chicago school had differing theoretical orientations but broad converging elements. Even in the post–World War II period, as the organization, prestige, and status of the Chicago school were shaken, adherents continued to make ever more explicit the empirical basis on which their doctrines rested. They did not want to lose direct contact with their subject matter.

With the passage of time, codification and synthesis gained importance. Paradoxically, a Canadian historian, Fred H. Matthews, made the most pointed and relevant attempt to integrate the manifold themes of the Chicago school in his book *Robert E. Park and the Chicago School: Quest for an American Sociology*.* But even this broadly based study omits many of the Chicago school's concerns. I would like to see a comprehensive and integrated study of the Chicago school. A step in this direction is being taken by Martin Bulmer of the London School of Economics, whose forthcoming book** offers deeper understanding of the institutionalization of sociological research—the shift from individual to group effort.

The kind of grand study needed would, in my judgment, best be accomplished by the joint efforts of a sociologist and a historian. Until such a volume is prepared, however, Kurtz's bibliography and overview will serve the researchers who have an interest in the key figures of W. I. Thomas, Robert E. Park, William F. Ogburn, and their disciples.

MORRIS JANOWITZ

*Montreal: McGill-Queen's University Press, 1977.

***The Chicago School of Sociology: Institutionalization, Diversity, and the Rise of Sociological Research* (Chicago: University of Chicago Press).

PREFACE

Although much has been written about the Chicago school[1] of sociology, as this study demonstrates, and there is much on the history of the Chicago department, there has been no detailed critical effort to evaluate the entire range of Chicago sociology and its impact on the discipline.[2] That is my purpose here—to provide both a critical analysis of sociology at Chicago and a research guide for those interested in examining further the rich sociological tradition that emerges from the Chicago school. The annotated bibliography in this volume includes material published through 1982, focusing on the department's history from its founding in 1892 until 1950, by which time Chicago's dominance in sociology had waned.[3] Included are books, articles, reference materials, memorial comments, Ph.D. dissertations, and other published materials which discuss the Chicago sociology department, its faculty and research traditions. Items treating persons associated with Chicago sociology are included, among them works about important graduate students and nonsociologists such as Dewey, Mead, and Veblen who had an impact on sociological theory and research.

This project emerged out of Morris Janowitz's seminar on the history of American sociology, and it is to him I am most indebted. His encouragement and guidance throughout the entire process has been invaluable. I am obviously responsible for the final outcome, but I owe a great debt to the efforts of a number of individuals who have contributed in a number of ways, especially Herbert Blumer, Martin Bulmer, Mary Jo Deegan, Steven Dubin, David Miller, Edward Shils, and Gideon Sjoberg. Important research and clerical assistance was provided by Eloy Cazares, Rebecca Cobos, and Laura Moore.

Finally, I am grateful for the financial assistance provided by the Albion Small Fund of the University of Chicago's Sociology Department, the University Research Institute of the University of Texas at Austin, and Linda Scherbenske Kurtz.

1

THE PEOPLE BEHIND THE MOVEMENT

Every historian of the social sciences and every sociologist has at some point encountered the work of Chicago sociologists. The ideas and methods of W. I. Thomas, Robert Park, and Ernest W. Burgess, of John Dewey and George Herbert Mead, have pervaded sociological thought. Sociology as the scientific study of society became institutionalized, in large part, because of the efforts of the University of Chicago sociologists who, beginning in 1892, created a research and teaching program around the study of the problems of modern, urban society. The results of their enthusiastic efforts set the agenda for much of American sociology, particularly in the areas of urban and community studies, social organization, race and ethnic relations, symbolic interactionism and social psychology, and social change.

Chicago sociologists inspired research, sparked controversies, and created a body of literature and a set of traditions that have been praised and criticized in every corner of American social science and throughout the world. It is impossible to understand the development of sociology as a discipline without understanding the contributions of the Chicago sociologists and the debates that their work engendered. Despite the deliberate diversity present in the department from its creation by Small in 1892, the sense of common purpose and the high visibility of work done at Chicago resulted in the formation of an image of a "Chicago School." As Morris Janowitz has suggested, "The image was fashioned by other centers of sociology that competed on both academic and professional grounds. This image was also created by the other disciplines responding to the innovation of their sociological colleagues. And there was an image that emerged in the outside world among journalists, authors, and public leaders who were attracted and repelled by the substantive findings and the social pronouncements of these scholars" (1966, pp. vii–viii).

Efforts to fashion that image have never been entirely successful because of the broad range of theoretical and methodological approaches within the department. The most consistent thread running throughout the work of Chicago sociologists is the continued effort to integrate sociological theories with empirical investigation of the social world. That agenda reflects the influence of Dewey and Mead's pragmatic philosophy which insisted on the unity of thought and action, of theory and the real world.

One might speak of three generations of Chicago sociology during the period examined here. The first generation consisted of Albion Small, George Vincent, W. I. Thomas, Charles Henderson, Graham Taylor, Charles Zueblin, Ira Howerth, Jerome Hall Raymond, and Clarence Rainwater.[4] Important students during the first decades of the department's history included—in addition to Thomas—Vincent, Howerth, Raymond, and Rainwater, who became part of the faculty, Charles Ellwood, Annie MacLean, John Gillette, Edward C. Hayes, Luther L. Bernard, Emory Bogardus, Jessie Steiner, Stuart Queen, and Charles S. Johnson. Other significant figures on the scene at the time, but not in the sociology department, were Dewey, Mead, Thorstein Veblen, and Jane Addams. Marion Talbot was associated with the department, as was anthropologist Frederick Starr. Edith Abbott, who had strong ties to Hull House and later headed the Social Service Administration (the university's social work school), taught part-time in the department. Edward A. Ross and Lester Ward both lectured at Chicago during the first summers of the department's existence.

In the 1920s the faculty consisted of Small, Robert Park, Ernest W. Burgess, Ellsworth Faris, and an instructor, Scott Bedford. Students trained during that period included Robert McKenzie, Nels Anderson, Floyd House, Ernest Mowrer, Ernest Krueger, Walter Reckless, Frederic Thrasher, Ernest Shideler, Robert Redfield, Willard Waller, Fay Karpf, and Ruth Shonle Cavan. Others in the university who were linked closely to the department included L. L. Thurstone, Charles Merriam, Harold Lasswell, and Shailer Mathews.

The third generation included students from the second generation: Herbert Blumer, Everett C. Hughes, Louis Wirth, and Samuel Stouffer, as well as Park and Burgess. A Columbia graduate who studied under

Franklin Giddings, William F. Ogburn, was added to the faculty, and Clifford Shaw and Henry McKay of the Institute for Juvenile Research were closely associated with the department. Students of that period included E. Franklin Frazier, Howard P. Becker, Paul Cressey, Carl Rosenquist, R. E. L. Faris, Andrew Lind, Vivian Palmer, Leonard Cottrell, Helen MacGill Hughes, Philip Hauser, and Edward Shils.

Albion Small, W. I. Thomas and Robert Park were obviously at the center of Chicago sociology (Hughes 1964, 1979a, 1979b, 1979c; Janowitz 1966; Park 1939; Shils 1970;). As department founder, Small helped to set the stage for what was to follow.[5] Small's vision of sociology as a science (Dibble 1975) and his background in classical European social theory and philosophy (Herbst 1965; Hayes 1926, 1927) were important influences on the kind of sociology that evolved under his administrative leadership. He played a mediating role between the "systematizers" of his time like Giddings and Ward and the more empirical sociological specialists of the generation of sociologists that succeeded them (Barnes 1948a; R. Faris 1970 [1967]; Hughes 1956a). Herbst (1965, p. 156) suggests that Small's achievement "lay in his demonstration of a logical connection between the empiricism of the historical school and therefore activities of the *Verein für Sozialpolitik*."

Small's administrative role as department chair and the founder and editor of the *American Journal of Sociology* (*AJS*) may have overshadowed his intellectual contributions (Barnes 1948). He facilitated the early movement from abstract speculation to rigorous examinations of interpersonal and intergroup relations (Wirth 1953) and from moral philosophy and speculative idealism to empirical investigation (Herbst 1959) so characteristic of sociology at Chicago.

W. I. Thomas, however, was more responsible than any other individual for the development of the so-called "Chicago school." He was a pioneer in the effort to link theory and research in a comprehensive approach that encompassed both macrosociological and microsociological analyses.[6] His chief contribution, according to Park, was a new approach to sociological problems and a system of concepts (Park 1931).[7] "It is in the work of W. I. Thomas, I believe," Park wrote (1939), "that the present tradition in research at Chicago was established." Thomas brought Park to the Chicago faculty (R. Faris 1967, p. 29), and was essential to Park's development as a sociologist (Park 1939; Park and Burgess 1921; Burgess 1948, 1953).

Following Thomas's unfortunate dismissal from the university,[8] Park became the organizing force in the department.[9] His research efforts, in collaboration with Burgess, motivated research at Chicago throughout the 1920s and 1930s (Hughes 1964, 1979; Matthews 1977; Raushenbush 1979). Burgess went to Chicago as a graduate student, completing his degree in 1913, having studied under Vincent, Thomas, Henderson, and Small (Bogue 1974; Burgess 1948). He joined the faculty in 1919 and remained an integral part of the department until his retirement in 1957. Park and Burgess, who shared an office in the Social Science Research Building, inspired an entire generation of graduate students to comb the city and its institutions, looking for patterns of social organization within natural areas of Chicago, the "sociological laboratory."

As founding fathers, Small, Thomas, and Park were not sociologists by training. The boundaries between sociology and other disciplines at Chicago during those first years are not easily discernible. While consciously building the discipline of sociology, they were not building walls around it. There was a remarkable degree of interdisciplinary cooperation among social scientists as well as people in other disciplines (see Lasswell 1971; Marvick 1977; Mathews 1936; Park 1937; L. White 1929a, 1929b, 1930).[10] That cooperation was especially exemplified by the work of the Local Community Research Committee which provided the locus of much of the urban research carried out by the Chicago department (Bulmer 1980; Burgess 1929b; Smith and White 1929). Anthropology was taught in the sociology department until the creation of a separate department in 1929 and continued to be closely linked to sociology, especially through anthropologist Robert Redfield, Park's son-in-law (Leslie 1968).

Dewey's influence on Chicago sociology, although now somewhat less obvious than Mead's, can be seen in the pragmatic underpinnings of sociological theory and research at Chicago (see Lewis and Smith 1980).[11] Because of their importance to the Chicago sociologists, interpretations of the sociologically relevant work of Dewey and Mead must be understood. Efforts by Dewey and Mead to rid modern thought of metaphysics and replace it with scientific research (Lee 1945; Hook 1950; Miller 1967; Reichenbach 1939), and their emphasis on the importance of the social (Mitchell 1930, Murphy 1939), can be seen in the sociology developed at Chicago.

Another scholar who had a significant impact on sociology was Veblen, who taught at Chicago for fourteen years. One of his students claimed that "from his philosophic view of social institutions and social theories a straight path led to John Dewey's lectures" (Mitchell 1930).[12] Although not a "Chicago sociologist," Veblen is included in this work because of his impact on the discipline, the importance of the Chicago years to his career, and the fact that he is often viewed as a sociologist; his institutional analysis is in the spirit of the work done in the social sciences at Chicago.

Evaluations of Veblen's work are generally replete with superlatives, either of an emphatically negative or enthusiastically positive character.[13] An example of the enthusiasm with which Veblen has been received is C. Wright Mills's comment that he is the "best social scientist America has produced" (1960; cf. Sweezy 1957; Dowd 1966). He has been referred to as "one of the great sociologists of our time" (Hobson 1963) and by one of Parsons's students as "the most original and prophetic figure in American academic circles" (Davis 1957c). His detractors, on the other hand, were equally convinced in their assessment; H. L. Mencken claimed that his thinking was "loose, flabby, and preposterous" (1919).

Although there is some debate over whether Veblen was an economist or a sociologist (cf. Hobson 1963; Johnson 1934; Davis 1968; Nabers 1958), and he founded no school in either discipline, the impact of his thought was widespread. He wrote his most famous work, *The Theory of the Leisure Class* (1899), during his Chicago period. According to Coser (1977, p. 282), "the influence of such Chicago men as Jacques Loeb, Franz Boas, and William I. Thomas could be traced on virtually every page." What differentiated him from other sociologists at Chicago was his radical social criticism. He was highly praised by a number of American radicals and his works were reviewed in radical and socialist publications (see Huberman and Sweezy 1957). Despite his criticisms of Marx and many of his disciples, and his contemptuous attitude toward most radicals (Hill 1958), Veblen was influential in radical circles and, according to one of his students, William English Walling, provided the philosophical backbone for the American socialist movement (Dorfman 1958, p. 237; Corey 1937).

Faris obtained a Ph.D. in psychology under Dewey, Mead, Angell, and others and joined the sociology faculty after Thomas's resignation, becoming chair of the department in 1925 and later taking over the editorship of the *AJS*. It was Faris who provided the major link between

Mead and the sociologists at Chicago (Strauss 1964). Ogburn taught at Chicago from 1927 until 1951, serving as chair from 1936 to 1951. Although his major accomplishment was the championing of quantitative methods of social research, along with Thurstone and Stouffer (Bulmer 1981b), he had broad interests and made substantial contributions in a number of areas.

Others playing central roles in Chicago sociology include Blumer, who developed and elaborated Mead's social psychology (Shibutani 1970; Fisher and Strauss 1978a, 1978b); Hughes, who combined interactionism with the Chicago interest in social organization (Faught 1980; Burns 1980); Shaw and McKay, who applied theories of human ecology and social organization to problems of crime and delinquency (Burgess 1930a, 1942; Burgess and Bogue 1964); and Wirth (Fischer 1972, 1975; Blumer 1956), who fashioned an influential theory of the nature of urban life. In examining biographical data on Chicago sociologists, Carey found that, compared to most academics of the period, more were born in cities over 100,000 in population (40% compared to 16.6% of all college professors), more were likely not to have a high degree of religiosity, and they were more heterogeneous ethnically (Carey 1975, pp. 44–48). They tended to be more liberal politically than the founders of sociology in general, and had a higher proportion of women than other groups examined.

The role of those women who helped to shape sociology at Chicago, most notably Addams, Edith and Grace Abbott, Breckenridge, and their colleagues, has been underestimated (see Deegan 1978b, 1981). Burgess argues that "It would be correct to say that systematic urban studies in Chicago began with these Hull-House studies. Edith Abbott and Sophonisba Breckenridge, in what was then the Chicago School of Civics and Philanthropy (later the School of Social Service Administration of this university), had carried on a series of studies of the immigrant and of the operation of Hull-House. They began these studies as early as 1908" (Burgess and Bogue 1964, p. 4).[14] Addams's settlement house was the center of many reform activities, and a number of Chicago faculty were closely linked to the Hull House, especially Dewey, who was a champion of Addams's work and was influenced by her writings (Levine 1971; Mills 1966; cf. Addams 1929), and Burgess, who lived for a time at Hull House (Hughes 1979). The Hull House group pioneered early community studies (Addams 1889), and Addams herself was offered an appointment in the sociology department by Small (Diner 1975, p. 536).

Despite the fact that Small and others were often creatures of their time who failed to recognize the full professional potential of women (Deegan 1981; Schwendinger and Schwendinger 1974), a number of women played important roles in the Chicago department, including Talbot, who taught in the department and wrote about a protest by women faculty members (Talbot 1936). Helen MacGill Hughes worked for the *AJS* for seventeen years (H. M. Hughes 1973). Fay-Cooper Cole taught anthropology in the department, and several women, including a number of graduate students, made significant contributions to Chicago research projects. In addition, other faculty spouses played invisible, but influential, roles, including Eileen Znaniecki's participation in research on *The Polish Peasant in Europe and America* (Lopata 1965).

Despite their divergent approaches and occasional conflicts, those involved in the sociological enterprise at Chicago formed a unique community of researchers. Underlying much of the effort was the Chicago school of philosophy, and many of the debates over the results of Chicago sociology are rooted in the philosophical foundations of their scholarship (Rucker 1969, pp. 132–57).

2

PHILOSOPHICAL FOUNDATIONS

I. The Influence of Pragmatism

Chicago sociologists had strong theoretical interests and were aware of major movements in social thought. Those who criticize Chicago sociology for what some have called its atheoretical "dust bowl empiricism" fail to take into account the close relationship between the Chicago sociologists and the Chicago pragmatists, with their emphasis on experience, social processes, and social action. Pragmatic influences run throughout the various traditions of research established at Chicago. It is quite clear that Dewey's work stands at the center of American social science (Shils 1963; Janowitz 1978), and Mead's work has undoubtedly made its mark on Chicago sociology and its successors.

There has been a recent resurgence of interest in the classical philosophical issues which covered the early pages of the *AJS* (Shanas 1945; Huber 1973b; Goff 1980; Lewis and Smith 1980; Johnson and Shifflet 1981). Of particular importance was the pragmatic insistence on the dialectical relationships between theory and practice, thought and action, and the self and society. Dewey and the other Chicago pragmatists believed that the task of philosophy should lie in the application of human knowledge to social problems (Durant 1926, pp. 565–75). With its dual emphasis on research science and the practical application of knowledge, pragmatism provided a natural underpinning for the development of a sociology in the midst of a rapidly changing urban environment. Dewey and Mead were naturalists with a faith in the scientific method of inquiry and problem-solving (Lee 1945; Brotherston 1943; Moore 1961). Consequently, their influence was often more profoundly felt among American jurists, sociologists, psychologists, and educators than among professional philosophers (Hook 1950).

The Chicago school of pragmatism was first developed by Dewey, Mead, James Tufts, and James R. Angell. The philosophy department was initially headed by Tufts, who had been at the University of Michigan and later recommended that Dewey be brought from Michigan to head the department. Dewey did so, in 1894, on the condition that he could bring Mead with him. The philosophy that the Chicago pragmatists developed was influenced by the evolutionary naturalism of Darwin, by Hegel,[15] and by the American philosophers William James,[16] Josiah Royce, Charles Peirce, and George Santayana (Rucker 1969; Mead 1917, 1930; H. Mead 1931; Morris 1938, 1970; Miller 1973; Lewis and Smith 1980; Lewis 1976; Feibleman 1945). Considerable debate has emerged from a distinction between the nominalism of James and Dewey, on the one hand, and the realism of Peirce and Mead on the other. Although the debate is not a new one, it has taken on a new significance within the context of recent debates over the symbolic interactionist perspective and its roots in Mead and Dewey (see Lewis and Smith 1980).[17]

II. Fundamental Tenets of Pragmatism

The diversity within the Chicago school of pragmatism was pronounced, but not at the expense of an underlying unity. A number of their essential tenets were quite amenable to the sociology that developed at Chicago. Both the sociologists and the pragmatists were responding to the reality of the industrialization and rapid growth of the dynamic city in which they were living and thinking. That context clearly had a profound impact on their thought (Kallen 1956; McCaul 1959; Diner 1980). Chicago was a city in constant flux, with continual waves of new immigrants, rapid industrialization, and ubiquitous transformations of social life. An explanation of social life in such an environment required a dynamic, processual social theory that was compatible with pragmatism.

The turn-of-the-century optimism about the eventual perfection of human life, with its roots in Enlightenment philosophy, pervaded efforts of the Chicago pragmatists. Mead, for example, felt that the very task of philosophy, since the Renaissance, was to interpret the results of research science, the fundamental development in modern social thought (Mead 1936, pp. 258–59, 343, 353). The pragmatic insistence on the intimate relationship between thought and action (Mead 1930; McGill

1939; McKenzie 1972; Moore 1961; Ratner 1939), and the instrumentalism of Dewey and Mead (Russell 1945; White 1947, 1957; Dicken 1971) were important factors in the general orientation of Chicago sociologists.

Thomas claimed that he was not influenced significantly by Dewey (Thomas 1973). His approach, although much more empirical, was compatible with Dewey's, however, and he was influenced by Mead, who was one of his graduate instructors and later a close friend when they were both on the Chicago faculty (Miller 1973, p. xxvii). Although Dewey and Mead may have been somewhat different in their orientations, both emphasized the importance of the social in their philosophical orientation. One of Dewey's favorite sayings was that "there is no psychology but a social psychology" (Mitchell 1930).[18] Chicago sociology was criticized by many who objected to pragmatism. Whereas some observers have disliked its relativistic implications (e.g., Crosser 1955), others have argued that it is a reflection of middle-class ideology (Herman 1944) or even, as one Marxist critic put it, of a "bankrupt capitalist class" (Wells 1954).

It is inappropriate, however, to apply ex post facto political categories to the pragmatists, as is sometimes done. Pragmatism, and to a large extent the social theories of Chicago sociologists, are no doubt rooted in the middle class American experience of the early twentieth century.[19] It therefore benefits from the insights of that period, but is at the same time somewhat bound by its prejudices. The impact of pragmatism on sociological theory construction at Chicago can especially be seen in efforts to integrate sociological theory construction with empirical research.

3

SOCIOLOGICAL THEORY CONSTRUCTION

I. Sociological Theory and Research

Throughout most of the earlier period, and especially in the 1920s and 1930s, sociological theories developed at Chicago were all closely integrated around the problems of urban life. Theories of human ecology, social psychology, and social organization were all developed by a relatively cohesive group of sociologists working together in close proximity. Chicago sociologists used rather diverse methods and focused on different social phenomena and institutions, but shared a self-conscious attention to the close connection between careful on-the-spot observation and the broader development of a theoretical framework.

The most abstract ecological treatises focused not only upon broad patterns of social organization, but upon the attitudes, motivations, and definitions of the individuals affected by "natural areas" within the city. Such studies were not simply carried out in the "map room" of the Social Science Research Building, but in the neighborhoods, settlement houses, playgrounds, and places of work where individual actors responded to broad historical changes. In 1892, sociological theory was usually identified as a branch of philosophy, on the one hand, and as social politics and reform, on the other, rather than as a separate intellectual discipline. Theory construction at Chicago was distinguished primarily by efforts to combine it with empirical research and a concern with social problems, but as an effort to go beyond the speculation of earlier social theorists (Oberschall 1972), the applied research of social reformers and the unsystematic observation of journalists (Park 1973; Raushenbush 1979; Hughes 1964). Despite a general absence of systematic theory construction, Chicago sociologists made major theoretical contributions, especially in the areas of human ecology, social organization, social psychology (especially symbolic interactionism), and social control. There were deliberate efforts in all substantive areas to develop sociology as a scientific discipline.

From Philosophy and Reform to Science

What distinguished early American sociology from European sociology, Shils has suggested, was "its immersion in the first-hand experience of concrete situations." The broad systematizing efforts of Ward and Giddings played an important role in their day, but their influence has not persisted. Rather, it was the following generation of sociologists whose influence is still felt and whose work is still cited. Park, Thomas, Cooley and Ross "stood midway between the sociology of the library and learned meditation on the one hand and the increasingly circumspect research techniques of the present day on the other" (Shils 1948, p. 6).

There is considerable consensus that Thomas and Znaniecki's classic work, *The Polish Peasant* (1918–19) was a watershed in the shift from speculative philosophy to grounding sociological theorizing in empirical research.[20] That movement was present from the early years of the department's history. Thomas's *Source Book for Social Origins* (1909) played a significant role in the development of sociological theory based upon empirical research, and in breaking away from the identification of sociology with either research limited to immediate policy matters or speculative philosophy (Park 1939).

Earlier Chicago faculty had established the context within which sociology was to develop at Chicago, with Small championing the move from abstract speculation to the development of sociological theory out of actual research (Hughes 1956, p. 255). Henderson and Small attempted to create a program of research at Chicago in 1902, and Henderson proposed the creation of a "bureau of social research" in 1912 (see Lazarsfeld 1962b). A description of the department's program published in the *AJS* in 1902 demonstrates the link among sociological theory, research, and a concern for social problems that is a distinctive mark of Chicago sociology. After discussing the way in which organized charities and church enterprises of the city enlist graduate students for both employment and training, it treats the role of the university's social settlement (based "upon the plan of Hull House"). It explains how such "social endeavors" are "tributary to the training of sociological students":

> It is the purpose of this department to appropriate to the utmost every advantage afforded by the vast social laboratory within which the university is located. This purpose will be especially prominent in connection with the work of the social settlements. While the primary aim of these enterprises is improvement of the district in which they are undertaken, the settlements are social observing stations where invaluable supplementary experience should be sought by students, and where material is to be gathered by mature investigators. In so far as the work is guided by the university, it will not stop with exhibitions of altruistic sentiments. It will attempt to test general hypotheses and to establish scientific conclusion by use of the evidence which actual experiment affords. (Tolman 1902, pp. 116–17)

That explicit combination of theory and research contributed both to the success of the Chicago school and in some ways to its eventual demise.[21] Its role in transforming the discipline by providing the foundations for an empirical sociology has been widely acknowledged (see, e.g., Bulmer 1981; Lazarsfeld 1962b; Madge 1962). That emphasis was demonstrated in Thomas's research and communicated through his teaching methods, which involved an extensive use of data and the encouragement of student research "in the field" (Burgess 1948). As Edmund Volkart and others have suggested, Thomas "helped to lead sociologists out of the armchair and into the field and laboratory by establishing the tradition of empirical research for doctoral degrees in sociology" (Volkart 1968; cf. K. Young 1948).

Sociological theory was, for some Chicago sociologists, as it was for Mead, an alternative to religious and theological thinking (T. V. Smith 1932; Miller 1973; Herbst 1959). A number of commentators have noted that many of the early Chicago sociologists, and for that matter a whole generation of American thinkers (Coser 1977, p. 348), were influenced by Protestant Christianity in their early years (especially the Social Gospel movement; Levine, Carter, and Gorman 1976, p. 813), and many attempted to free themselves from that influence. Small and Vincent both had some theological training; Henderson and Faris had both been ministers, and Burgess was the son of a minister (Faris 1970, pp. 9–10).[22] Carey (1975) has shown, however, that it is inaccurate to claim that the Chicago sociologists had a strong religious orientation, or that they were all children of clergy. Some believed that sociology was a substitute for religious belief; others perceived it as an extension of their religious commitment. For Mead (1936, pp. 258–59), science was *the* major form of thought appropriate for the modern world, and it often came in conflict with dogmatic religious views of the world.

The shift from reform and philosophy to science, in the Thomas tradition, culminated in the rich empirical studies of urban life inspired and directed by Park and Burgess. Burgess contends that "by the early 1920's this 'social work' orientation had given way . . . to an ambition to understand and interpret the social and economic forces at work in the slums and their effect in influencing the social and personal organization of those who lived there. Although the objective was scientific, behind it lay a faith or hope that this scientific analysis would help dispel prejudice and injustice and ultimately would lead to an improvement in the lot of slum dwellers" (Burgess and Bogue 1964, p. 5).

Here the issue of the relationship between theory and research is brought into bold relief, because empirical investigation seemed so frequently to overshadow theoretical issues. Park claimed that his empirical efforts were always within a larger project, begun by Thomas, that would lead to systematic sociological theories (Odum 1951a, pp. 132–33). Park's theoretical contributions were related to his development of the human ecology perspective, and in the areas of social organization and race relations. Even there, however, the more systematic presentations of ecological theories were developed by others (e.g., McKenzie and Hawley). As Shils has suggested, the original vision developed by Park and Burgess "vanished and there was left behind a tendency towards the repetition of disconnected investigations." Furthermore, "From the point of view of their *direct* contribution to a systematic theory of human behavior and social organization, there is no value in them. Yet they have fulfilled a momentously important function in the development of social science by establishing an unbreakable tradition of first-hand observation, a circumspect and critical attitude toward sources of information, and the conviction that the way to the understanding of human behaviour lies in the study of institutions in operation and of the concrete individuals through whom they operate" (Shils 1948, pp. 11–12).

Similar contentions that Park's work was atheoretical have been made by others, including Kolb (1956). In responding to Kolb, Hughes contends that Park's work on cities was far from atheoretical,[23] suggesting that those who agree with Kolb should read Park's last volume of published papers (1955; see also Hughes 1955).

Later efforts to develop urban studies at Chicago along theoretical lines were undertaken by Wirth, whose theories of urban life were influenced by Park and focused on the breakdown of communal bonds (see Shils 1948, p. 10; House 1957; Fischer 1972). Despite their diversity of approaches, there is a clear line of common interest from Small through Thomas, Park, Burgess, Wirth, and Ogburn in the creation of sociological theories out of the research process, combined with a concern for social issues.

Criticisms of Chicago Theories

Two major types of criticisms have been leveled at the social theories developed by Chicago sociologists. On the one hand are criticisms that they are atheoretical, because of the focus on empirical research at the expense of social theory. On the other hand, they have been criticized for *implicit* theories and ideological assumptions. Chicago sociologists from Thomas to Park made a deliberate effort to be less ideological in their approach to social theory than were their European counterparts. Charles Tilly notes that Chicago contributions to urban research reflect both the limitations and "features that account for the great accomplishments of the Chicago school: willingness to begin with simple schemes or methods without worrying about their metaphysics, and then to apply them in detail; insistence on facts; thorough use of the most readily available laboratory; sheer doggedness" (Tilly 1964). Attention to empirical research does sometimes avert attention from larger theoretical issues raised by European social theorists (Gouldner 1970, p. 145). The lack of systematic social theory at Chicago was not, however, because of an isolation from the European masters. On the contrary, there was a strong tradition of European connections at Chicago.

Some criticisms have been directed from leftist-oriented scholars, notably in the work by Herman and Julia R. Schwendinger, who criticize Small's efforts to undermine Marx's influence (1974, pp. 280–83) and charge that a number of Chicago sociologists maintained assumptions that legitimated capitalism and systems of racist and sexist exploitation (cf. D. Smith 1965). At the core of their critique is a distrust of so-called "value-free" sociology and the effort to separate facts from values. "There is no better example of a false awareness," they write, "than the attitude taken by American sociologists toward Park and Burgess' grand theory. This theory was generally considered to be a statement of the universal processes of social interaction. But it was actually a reification and generalization of the concrete relations considered necessary for the emergence of a *stable* and *harmonious* capitalist society" (1974, p. 421).

The ambivalent relationship between the Chicago school and subsequent Marxist scholars is an important topic. There was always suspicion in some circles of Chicago sociology concerning the university's connection with John D. Rockefeller, who provided financial backing for the founding of the university (Furner 1975; Schwendinger and Schwendinger 1974; White 1929; Bulmer 1980; Wilson 1957). Ward claimed that Small was "under instructions from the capitalistic censorship that controls the University of Chicago" (Dorfman 1945, p. 210). Small was critical of Marx,[24] and was relatively moderate, but he was also a consistent critic of capitalism.[25] Shortly after the founding of the *AJS* one disgruntled recipient of a circular announcing the *Journal* wrote claiming to expect "no lasting good from a work that is conducted by an educational institution founded by the arch-robber of America." An editorial (presumably written by Small) replied that the "*Journal* will not be equivocal in exposing the usurpations of capitalism, or in explaining principles to which the people must learn to hold corporations accountable."[26]

Marxist critiques of pragmatism are also frequently applied to Chicago sociologists, such as Wells's (1954) claim that pragmatism "is the reactionary subjective idealist view of a bankrupt capitalist class." Not everyone on the left has been disenchanted with pragmatism, however. Dewey has a considerable following among progressives, in part because of his reform activities and his connections with Addams, as well as his championing of a fair trial for Trotsky (see Eastman 1941). Similarly, many on the left are influenced by both Wirth (see Braude 1970) and Veblen (Huberman and Sweezy 1957); for example, Landsman

(1957) complains that Veblen is a "museum piece" seized upon by Marxist philosophy.

Nor are all of the criticisms from the left. Crosser (1955) postulates that the extreme relativism of Dewey's approach leads to cognitive indeterminableness, sophism, and defeatism. There does seem to be more criticism from the left than from those of other political persuasions, however, in the sociological literature. That fact may be a result not only of the moderate liberal position taken or implied in much Chicago sociology, but also because of the progressive political inclinations of sociologists. Perhaps more importantly, it is because the Chicago sociologists were constantly dealing with social problems that interest progressives and they have received attention from those dissatisfied with the solutions explicit or implicit in Chicago sociology.

European Social Theory

In their efforts to develop sociological theory out of the research process, Chicago sociologists were not ignorant of European social theory. They drew upon it liberally, but did not swallow it as a whole. They drew most explicitly upon those social theorists whose work addressed the problems of the city, as well as those who were concerned with the definition of sociology as an independent scholarly discipline, especially Georg Simmel, Emile Durkheim, and Ferdinand Toennies. The image of Chicago sociologists as either ignorant of, or uninterested in, European social theory simply does not square with the facts (see Levine, Carter, and Gorman 1976, p. 813). European social thought figured prominently in their teaching and research, and in articles by Simmel, Toennies, and Durkheim translated and published in the early issues of the *AJS*. Simmel's influence was pronounced in early American sociology, thanks largely to Small's efforts.[27] Small was at the University of Berlin while Simmel himself was a student there, and the two developed a close relationship (Christakes 1978). He published fifteen papers by Simmel in the *AJS* and sent three of his students—Ellwood, Hayes, and Woolston—to Berlin to study under Simmel.

Park and Burgess's *Introduction to the Science of Society* includes ten selections by Simmel. Simmel's writings have become associated with the Chicago sociologists in many ways; Sorokin (1928), for example, criticizes Simmel and Park on the grounds that Simmel's work was unscientific.[28] In 1931 the Society for Social Research[29] published Park's

1899 notes on Simmel's lectures, and Park's students Wirth, Hughes, and Shils continued teaching Simmel's work.

Chicago sociologists drew upon a number of other Europeans, especially the Germans (Hayes 1926; Herbst 1965; Christakes 1978; Coser 1977). Durkheim's influence could also be seen in Park's synthesis of Durkheim's and Simmel's conceptions of the social (Levine 1972). Small and Park studied in Germany, and there were other significant European contacts, such as those made by Wirth, who was the first president of the International Sociological Society (Shils 1981). There were also influences from Windelband (Park's dissertation adviser; Park 1950; Levine 1972; Hughes 1964, 1979c), Toennies (Cahnman 1977), Weber (Shils 1981), and others.

In addition to the dissemination of European social theory in the *AJS*, a number of selections were included in Park and Burgess's *Introduction to the Science of Sociology*.[30] One important European influence came from Darwin's evolutionary theories, although the Chicagoans were more systematic and less evolutionary in their examination of change processes than some sociologists influenced by Darwin.[31] Some of Darwin's influence came to the Chicago sociologists indirectly through the pragmatists, for whom Darwin's theories of evolution were central (Strauss 1964, p. xviii). Other British influences include certain aspects of work by Spencer (Greer 1962), Hobbes (Meisenhelder 1977; Alihan 1938, pp. 94–98;), and the Scottish moralists (Shott 1976; cf. Stryker 1980).

There is some question about Freud's place among Chicago sociologists, especially in earlier period, although his influence was certainly felt (see G. Hinkle 1957). Burgess points out that Park and Burgess's *Introduction* was the first sociology textbook to use psychoanalytic concepts.[32] Thomas, at first interested in Freud's theories, seems to have become a critic of psychoanalysis. Chicago sociologists, although not strongly influenced by Freud, continued to demonstrate an interest in his work.[33] Ogburn, for example, was a founder of the Chicago Institute for Psychoanalysis (H. M. Hughes 1959).

Chicago sociologists, in the final analysis, were more concerned about developing their own theories of society, based upon their research, and were more closely related to the American philosophical tradition than to the European theorists. Bramson (1961, p. 17) contends that there were some difficulties in using European theory because of the tension between European sociological concepts and the liberalism that appears "dramatically in the works of such men as Robert Ezra Park and other members of the German-influenced Chicago school of sociology." On the other hand, however, the early Chicago sociologists were, in some ways, closer to the European theorists than were many of their American peers. O'Kelly and Petras (1970) argue that Small was not as individualistically oriented in viewing social reform as the other sociologists of his era. The prevailing orientation in most early American sociology, according to Hayes and Petras (1974), was toward individualistic explanation of motivation, as opposed to a relatively major role of group determinism in European theory.

One of the most significant developments in European theory, for the American sociologists, was Darwinian evolutionism, which deserves more detailed attention.

Theories of Evolution

Biological evolution played a key background role in early American sociological theory, providing a framework in terms of which early American sociologists addressed the problematics of social life and developed their sociological theories (Fine 1979; cf. Coser 1977). Dewey's "evolutionary naturalism" was outlined in his early work, *The Influence of Darwin on Philosophy* (1916; cf. Ratner 1951; Morris 1934). Social Darwinism played an important role in early American sociology, and Spencer influenced Small, Dewey, Veblen, Ellwood, and Vincent (Hofstadter 1944; Watkins 1958). Hinkle (1952) argued that the problem of the rational control of social evolution was a basic problem that pervaded Thomas's thought (cf. Bogardus 1959; Park 1939; Volkart 1953).

The impact of evolutionary theories can be overemphasized, however, and there is some evidence of ambivalence about evolution among Chicago sociologists. O'Kelly and Petras (1970) argue that Small and several other early American sociologists tended, for example, to reject Sumner's evolutionary determinism (cf. Rossides 1978). By Park's time, Spencer's popularity had already declined sharply (Levine et al. 1976), and Park was averse to Spencer's unilinear evolutionism (Coser 1977, p. 376). Radical social changes occurring in Chicago throughout much of the early decades of the twentieth century stimulated interest in social change and evolution, however.

Another area of sociological theory at Chicago which is informed by European theory is the sociology of knowledge, an important subsidiary of the Chicago traditions.

The Sociology of Knowledge

Dittberner (1979) suggests that Chicago might be called the birthplace of the sociology of knowledge in the United States. Small, Znaniecki, Wirth, Shils, and many others have attempted to develop the sociology of knowledge implicit in Mead's work. Small initiated an interest in the topic with his reviews of Max Scheler's *Wissensoziologie* in the *AJS* in 1925 (31 [September]: 262–64).

Wirth and Shils translated Karl Mannheim's *Ideology and Utopia* into English, providing the first major work on the sociology of knowledge to appear in English. Wirth's introductory essay provides a strong endorsement of Mannheim's work, placing it within the context of American pragmatism (Dittberner 1979, pp. 8, 26–27; Shils 1981). Znaniecki, however, wrote a polemic against Mannheim (Znaniecki 1940),[34] aligning himself with the antiepistemological wing of the sociology of knowledge; he regarded the attempt of the sociology of knowledge to become epistemology as an example of sociological imperialism (Dittberner 1979, p. 62).

McKinney (1955) argues that the contribution of Mead to the sociology of knowledge lies in the fact that he has supplied it with a more adequate social psychology than has been characteristic of the European efforts in the field. More recently, Farberman (1970) compared Mannheim, Mead, and Cooley, suggesting that Mead's theory of mind and self as symbolic interaction makes social factors intrinsic to mentality, providing the basis for a convergence between social psychology and the sociology of knowledge foreseen by Wirth.

Lewis (1972) argues that Mead and Peirce provide an important corrective to the epistemological individualism sometimes found in contemporary sociology. Goff (1980) develops an extensive treatment of aspects of Mead's social behaviorism relating to the sociology of knowledge, with an attempt to synthesize Marx and Mead by examining a central common issue: the relativism implied by the insight that knowledge is fundamentally social. Batiuk and Sacks (1981, p. 211) make similar observations about the relationship between Marx and Mead, arguing that, for both, "consciousness is always, at bottom, a realization of this fact: The world is a socially constituted world—the result of specific historical relationships." Although Veblen developed no systematic sociology of knowledge, he took a clear stand on his perception of the way in which knowledge was rooted in social life, particularly in his anthropological writings, and in *The Place of Science in Modern Civilization* (1919). He insisted that "habits of thought are an outcome of habits of life" (Coser 1977, p. 270).

II. Sociological Theory Construction: Human Ecology

One of the most fruitful and provocative theoretical perspectives developed by Chicago sociologists is the human ecology approach to the study of urban social organization, which provided a broad, flexible theoretical framework for most of the classic studies of urban life carried out by Chicago sociologists from the mid-1920s through the 1940s. Park, Burgess, and others developed analogies from studies by ecologists of plant and animal organization for the examination of urban social organization. The ecological approach proved invaluable in precipitating research projects and debate. It was not employed dogmatically, and was often lacking in theoretical rigor; like much of the social theory developed at Chicago, it emerged from the research itself. The pluralism of the Chicago school can be seen in the variety of applications of the perspective and the criticisms of ecological research developed at Chicago.

Human ecology views the human community as an ecological product that is the outcome of competitive and accommodative processes which affect spatial and temporal distributions. In examining those processes, attention is focused on such phenomena as natural areas, succession, symbiosis, competition, conflict, and accommodation. The impact of the approach can be seen not only in the community studies that constituted the apex of Chicago sociology,[35] but also in such disparate fields as organizational studies (Burns 1980), social psychology (Clausen and Kohn 1954; Short 1971; Komarovsky and Waller 1945), areal research (Hawley 1951, Orleans 1966), race and ethnic studies (Park 1924), and research methods (K. Young 1931b).

Sources of the Ecological Perspective

Efforts to develop a science of sociology have frequently drawn upon models and theoretical perspectives in other sciences. It is to biology that the early sociologists turned most frequently for theoretical inspiration, from Spencer's *Principles of Sociology* to Comte's and Durkheim's organismic analogies. The human ecologists turned to plant and animal ecology for a theoretical perspective to explain the processes of human social organization and social change.[36] A number of sources discuss the origins of the perspective, the most thorough of which may still be Alihan (1938) (see Burgess and Bogue 1964; Hauser 1956a; Hughes 1952, 1979; McKenzie 1924, 1934; Quinn 1940c). Shils (1970) provides a detailed summary of the origins of aspects of the ecological approach with contributions from Weber, Simmel, Toennies, and Mannheim in Germany; Durkheim in France; and the surveys of Booth and Rowntree in Britain.[37] Park (1959) locates the origins of the ecological approach in community studies, which is true of its later development. The initial formulations, however, were based upon plant and animal ecology (Hawley 1968a) and the Darwinian notion of the "web of life," as well as a number of other interdisciplinary sources (Llewellyn and Hawthorn 1945). Alihan (1938, p. 10 and passim) suggests that they include physiology,[38] economics,[39] human geography,[40] the demographic and geographic schools of sociology,[41] and rural sociological studies,[42] as well as work by regional and city planners, and real estate studies (cf. Park 1936; Coser 1977, pp. 363ff.).

Sutherland (1945) points out that human ecology theories were developed a century earlier in England and France and subsequently forgotten. Others have noted that laissez-faire assumptions are built into the ecological image and that competition, conflict, accommodation, and assimilation take place within a framework of rules similar to those advocated by Spencer.[43] Much of the theoretical impact of the approach remained implicit until it was applied.[44] Park, in his review of Alihan's work, objects to the use of the terms "school" and "doctrine" with reference to human ecology. The writers responsible for "this school and its doctrine were not aware that they were creating a school," Park (1959) insists. They were "quite innocent, in most instances, of anything that could be called a doctrine."

Some aspects of the approach were already present in Park's 1915 article, "The City: Suggestions for the Investigation of Human Behavior in the Urban Environment" (Park, Burgess, and McKenzie 1967, pp. 1–46), and in Park and Burgess's *Introduction*, with its selections on plant communities and animal societies.[45] Much of the groundwork for the Chicago ecological studies was laid by the reformers associated with Addams and the Hull House. The *Hull House Maps and Papers* (Addams 1895), for example, represent efforts by Addams, Breckenridge,

Abbott, and others, to map out the sociological and demographic characteristics found in the districts surrounding Hull House.[46] Aspects of human ecology could be seen in the work of some early Chicago sociologists as well, especially works by Mckenzie (1923) and Nels Anderson (1923). The human ecology approach came to the fore within the discipline in 1925 when Park was president of the American Sociological Society (Hughes 1979). Helen MacGill Hughes (1980–81) recalls that Park taught his first course on human ecology in the spring of 1926. Despite Park's classic statement (1936), it was McKenzie who synthesized much of what he learned from Park and Burgess to develop the human ecology approach into a more systematic theoretical perspective. As Hawley (1968b, p. xi) puts it, "The highly imaginative and restless mind of Park was impatient with details and with the rigors of closely reasoned argument. Burgess, on the other hand, was drawn irresistibly to specific empirical problems. It thus fell to McKenzie, shortly after he finished his graduate studies, to write the first definitive statements of human ecology."

Criticisms of the Ecological Perspective

Three fundamental critiques of the ecological approach have emerged: first, that it is ethnocentric, in that it is based primarily on research in Chicago and describes processes and patterns not present in other American cities or in cities in other parts of the world (Sjoberg 1959; Hauser 1965; Castells 1977). Second, some scholars claim that the perspective is deterministic. They often argue that human ecology is biased in emphasizing some facets of the growth and change of cities while ignoring others, such as sentiments, symbols, and values (Firey 1945, 1947; Kolb 1956; Wirth 1945; Engel-Frisch 1943). Finally, some critics argue that it is implicitly conservative in its orientation, positing certain patterns of social organization and change as "natural" and therefore resistant to social change (Richards 1976; Cox 1965; Myrdal 1944; Schwendinger and Schwendinger 1974).

Ethnocentrism. One of the indicators of the vitality of the ecological approach is the fact that a series of studies was inspired by an effort to disprove or to modify it on the basis of studies of other cities and other communities. Particularly controversial is Wirth's classic article "Urbanism as a Way of Life" (1938). His image of the city, although related to the ecological approach, is not inherent in the perspective and, in fact, is in some ways quite different from the image growing out of the Chicago community studies.

One of the most widely discussed aspects of the ecological approach developed at Chicago is the "Burgess zonal hypothesis," or "concentric zone theory."[47] Students in graduate courses at Chicago, even before 1920, developed maps of patterns of juvenile delinquency, motion picture houses, patrons of public dance halls, and other aspects of urban life, leading Burgess to develop his theory (Burgess 1964, pp. 5–6).

The zonal hypothesis precipitated a series of efforts to test its validity.[48] Throughout the 1920s a number of Chicago studies drew upon the perspective, including Thrasher's *The Gang* (1927) and Zorbaugh's *The Gold Coast and the Slum* (1929). Other Chicago studies found the approach valuable, including Shaw and others' *Delinquency Areas* (1929), Mowrer's *Family Disorganization*, Cavan's *Suicide* (1928), and R. E. L. Faris and Dunham's *Mental Disorders in Urban Areas* (1939). Although the hypothesis was first published by Burgess in 1923, it was not until the 1930s that significant efforts to test it were published by people outside of the Chicago department. As early as 1940, a general consensus developed "that various cities do not actually conform to an ideal circular spatial pattern," including Chicago itself, which "fits more closely into a pattern of concentric semicircles than of complete circles, and even this semicircular pattern shows important irregularities" (Quinn 1940, p. 210).

There was no consensus, however, as to whether or not the general theory of zonal development was empirically accurate. Quinn concluded, after reviewing the studies, that "although the Burgess zonal hypothesis was neither clearly proved nor disproved, it appears to possess sufficient merit to warrant the extensive research necessary for its careful testing" (1940a, p. 218); cf. Longmoor and Young 1936; Dawson and Gettys 1935; Davie 1937). A number of other studies suggest that at least substantial aspects of the Burgess hypothesis are valid, including Anderson and Egeland (1961) and O'Brien (1941). There is some support for the hypothesis in European cities, as shown in Chombart de Lauwe's (1950) study of Paris and McElrath's examination of Rome (1962).

Other attempts to apply the model to cities outside of the United States have resulted in different findings (cf. Sjoberg 1960; Gist 1957). Schnore's (1965) analysis of approximately sixty Latin American cities concludes that there are two principal urban forms: the "traditional" model of an historic center surrounded by working-class suburbs, and an industrial growth model more closely approximating that described by Burgess (see Castells 1977, p. 117).

A number of efforts have been undertaken to modify Burgess's model. Hoyt (1939) argues that social rigidity in a particular zone may result in "sectorial patterns." Hoyt (1939) argues that in some instances social rigidity in a particular zone results in "sectorial patterns." Anderson and Egeland (1961, p. 398), testing both Burgess and Hoyt, suggest that "urbanization (at the tract level) varies primarily concentrically or by distance from the center of the city, while prestige value (or social rank) varies primarily sectorially, with very little distance variation." Similarly, Harris and Ullman (1945) develop a multiple-nucleus theory which perceives the spatial deployment of different functions as a series of separate processes.

A number of people have defended the human ecology approach against charges of ethnocentrism, however. In response to that criticism with reference to juvenile delinquent studies,[49] Burgess notes that Shaw studied the spatial distribution of juvenile delinquents in other cities and found the same phenomena (Burgess and Bogue 1964, p. 7). Hughes responds to charges by Kolb (1954) about Park's ethnocentrism by saying that "it is a bit odd to read that Park was a creature of provincial knowledge of one city, Chicago, at a particular moment in its history; he was, in fact, one of the most widely read and widely traveled men of his time" (Hughes 1954).

Castells, on the other hand, claims that Burgess's model is valuable *in spite of* its ethnocentric biases. It does, he argues, account for urban development historically situated in socioeconomic conditions: "a certain degree of ethnic and social heterogeneity; an industrial-commercial economic base; private property; commerce; economic organizations functionally specialized and spatially differentiated; an effective system of transport . . . ; a central urban nucleus with high property values" (1977, p. 116). What appeals to Castells is what precipitated criticism by others: the lack of emphasis on nonmaterial factors in explaining urban growth.

Deterministic Causal Patterns. The first detailed critiques of human ecology charged that the approach was implicitly deterministic, notably those by Alihan (1938), Gettys (1940), Firey (1945, 1947), Kolb (1956),

Wirth (1945), and Sjoberg (1965). Alihan (1938) argues that although the ecologists distinguished between "community" and "society," in an effort to allow for both "that which is common to all organic life" and also "that which is strictly human" (the latter allowing for human freedom), they have failed to incorporate that distinction into the application of their perspective.

Walter Firey's (1947) *Land Use in Central Boston* maintains that cultural phenomena such as symbols and sentiments are crucial in understanding land use patterns, in contradiction to deterministic schemes formulated by Burgess, Hoyt, McKenzie, Park, Alfred Weber, and others. Firey also suggests that land use patterns in Boston are too variable to warrant forcing them into simple concentric or sector schemes (Firey 1945, 1947). Similarly, Kolb (1954) argues that anyone who believes, as he does, that value orientations have had a major part in the historical creation of urban industrial society must find the theoretical orientation of the ecologists deficient. Sjoberg (1965) points to similar difficulties in his critical appraisal of urban sociological theory.

What becomes clear as the debate emerges is that, although much was gained in theoretical precision as ecological studies developed beyond the Chicago community studies of the 1920s and 1930s, the richness of those studies was lost as the focus of research moved from "on-the-hoof" research in Chicago neighborhoods (Park 1939), to more abstract studies of quantitative data. The decline of community studies is linked to the rise of surveys which some thought would supplant them, although a recent rejuvenation of such studies has proven to be quite fruitful (see, e.g., Suttles 1968).

Other critics have called attention to the neglect of factors other than the symbolic and cultural. Willhelm (1964), for example, argues that the ecologists tend to ignore the group aspect of competition, and others suggest that the Chicago sociologists' emphasis on disorganization and the breakdown of community in the city leads them to neglect the variety of social groups in the city (e.g., Gans 1962) and alternative forms of social organization (Fischer 1972, 1975).

Perhaps the most vociferous debates surrounding the human ecology approach are charges that the perspective is inherently conservative.

Conservatism. Despite occasional rhetorical excesses, Schwendinger and Schwendinger (1974) provide the most significant critique of conservatism in the Chicago school. The most important issue is the Chicagoans' tendency to support pragmatic reforms rather than systematic rebellions against the status quo (see Gouldner 1970, p. 20). Those who believe that reform is counterproductive will find much to criticize in Chicago sociology. The Schwendingers argue that, "although not all of Park's students were ethnographers . . . some were followers of Park and Burgess's metatheory and were interested in ethnography; for them we prefer to use the phrase, the 'school of technocratic urban ethnographers'. . . . Although there are important differences between some of these studies, all of the works were within the corporate-liberal technocratic tradition. Thus, for example, Thrasher placed greater faith in neighborhood organizations for ameliorating social problems than did Zorbaugh. But both authors cast their works in the same ideological mold" (Schwendinger and Schwendinger 1974, pp. 476–77).

Park and Burgess's view of the city as an ensemble of natural areas, with natural processes of succession, conflict, accommodation, and competition, implied to some an inevitability in patterns of racial, ethnic, and class domination. Gunnar Myrdal's classic study of blacks in the United States, *An American Dilemma* (1944), for example, claims that Park's approach to racial problems is naturalistic and fatalistic, and leads to resistance of social change (cf. Chrisman 1970). Similarly, Cox (1942) criticizes Warner and the school of thought initiated by Park's student Frazier. Although they possess praiseworthy attitudes toward blacks, Cox argues, they are opposed to blacks' taking initiatives that would increase the pace of progress toward racial equality (Cox 1965).

The issue is complicated, however, and is obviously related to the basic attitudes which various critics and supporters take toward social reform. The Chicago sociologists are accused of being liberal reformers by some on the left, whereas others with similar political orientations attack the *critics* of the ecologists for being conservative. Castells, for example, argues that those who call attention to the cultural dimension of urban life develop a "common front against ecological naturalism" that is "established on the right-wing (ideological) positions, that is to say, centred on the predominance of values in social research" (1977, p. 122). Similarly, Wacker (1976) argues that the conflicting perspectives of Park and Myrdal are a consequence of the fact that Park is more pessimistic than Myrdal about the possibility of eradicating racism in the United States.

It is true, Farberman (1979) argues, that the Chicago sociologists accepted the fundamental assumptions of the intellectual climate of the era, notably to "depoliticize" knowledge. While everyone challenged certain aspects of the ecological perspective, however, such as Wirth's characterization of the quality of urban life, *"no one directly challenged the pervasive ecological paradigm itself.*[50] No superseding explanatory paradigm replaced the proposition that size, density, and heterogeneity of population caused impersonal, anonymous, segmented relationships" (1979, p. 9). Furthermore, Farberman argues, Gouldner fails to note the distinction made by Park between private and public spheres. Park's interest in discovering mechanisms of social control leads to a conclusion that in the public sphere, the individual has little control over his or her life. It is in the private sphere, however, that an individual finds ways to seek compensation. Ironically, the possibility of that freedom in the private sphere is provided by the anonymity precipitated by the ecological, demographic, and morphological processes that control the objective sphere. "Accordingly," Farberman argues, "the Chicago School killed three birds with one stone. It established the generic urban community as a unit of analysis in its own right, bounded it off from transcendent political and economic contingencies by accounting for the quality of life within it in demographic-morphologic terms, and secured the autonomy of the individual by associating that autonomy with the inevitable escalation in magnitude of demography-morphologic features" (1970), p. 16).

The Schwendingers argue that the type of sociology carried out at Chicago legitimates the development of the "benevolent technocratic analyst" and "actually masked the class nature of political power in America" (1974, p. 487). Their objection is that orientations to social change, within such a context, involve "the possibility of achieving an end to poverty on the basis of professional consensus rather than fiery conflict" (p. 489), a position which they feel is simply unrealistic.

Although there is some merit to their argument, it is too simplistic a picture of the human ecology perspective and of Chicago sociology in general, because it fails to recognize the attention to conflict among Chicago sociologists from Small (Fuhrman 1980) to Park and Burgess's text (Janowitz 1969) to the later community studies and the interactionist perspective (Kuklick 1973). Although the Chicago ecologists were sensitive toward profound barriers to social change, it is doubtful that the fatalism that Myrdal dislikes is inherent in the ecological model.[51] As Castells points out, there are some parallels between ecological and Marxist perspectives. Furthermore, the fundamental assumption lying behind the entire effort to develop sociology at Chicago is the possibility of human initiative in changing the patterns of social organization (Burgess and Bogue 1967, p. 5).

Throughout the period of classical community studies at Chicago, there was a constant attention to social-psychological factors alongside the broader ecological processes. It was perhaps inevitable that they do so, considering the fact that so much of their sociological theory was grounded in the pragmatism of Dewey and Mead, in Simmel's social-psychological essays, and in Thomas's research on attitudes and definitions of situations. As Chicago faculty and students combed the city interviewing immigrants, dance hall patrons, hobos and juvenile delinquents, they combined an interest in broad ecological patterns with the sociology of everyday life in Chicago neighborhoods.

III. Sociological Theory Construction: Social Psychology

> The human personality is both a continually producing factor and a continually produced result of social evolution, and this double relation expresses itself in every elementary social fact; there can be for social science no change of social reality which is not the common effect of pre-existing social values and individual attitudes acting upon them, no change of individual consciousness which is not the common effect of pre-existing individual attitudes and social values acting upon them (W. I. Thomas 1966, p. 11).

Theories of social-psychology developed at Chicago had a profound impact on the field, from Thomas and Znaniecki's *The Polish Peasant* through the introduction of Simmel to American sociologists and efforts to institutionalize social-psychological research by Faris and Ellwood, Thurstone's work on attitudes, to the later interactionist traditions based on the work of Mead, Dewey, Blumer, and Goffman. The interactional frame of reference quickly became the dominant form of social psychology among sociologists (Karpf 1932), despite its diverse developments. Within the Chicago department social psychology developed in several directions, despite some core problems and approaches. Fisher and Strauss (1978a) argue, for example, that the interactionist perspective has a dual tradition, one coming primarily from Mead (especially Blumer) and others whose orientation stems more from Park, Thomas, and later Hughes (cf. Stryker 1980, 1981). Those distinctions should not be exaggerated, however, nor seen as being as sharp as that between the so-called Chicago and Iowa "schools" (Meltzer and Petras 1970) developed by Blumer and Kuhn respectively, or, relatedly, that between the "Blumerian" approach and more recent behaviorist interpretations of Mead.

Much of the debate about social psychology at Chicago centers around the relative influence of Mead and Dewey, on the one hand, and, on the other hand, varying interpretations of Mead's work, a debate which I will examine in more detail later. Mead's influence was clear, nonetheless, as was Dewey's, even if it may have been embellished over the years, in part a function of the oral tradition surrounding the interactionist approach.

Social psychology was a central concern from the earliest days of the Chicago department. The subjects in the sociology department at the turn of the century were divided into three groups: social philosophy, social psychology, and social technology (Tolman 1902, p. 117). Students in the department were urged to take courses from Dewey and Mead at the turn of the century.[52]

Early Social Psychology at Chicago

Park (1929) claims that personality studies started with Simmel, whose attention to social psychological consequences of various social arrangements played a key part in the formation of the emphasis developed through Thomas, Park, and Hughes.[53] At the turn of the century, courses in social psychology at Chicago were taught by Thomas, Vincent, and Mead. Ellwood also did much to institutionalize the study of social psychology. Although he drew heavily on individual psychology, he believed the province of sociology and social psychology to be the group (Young 1927). He emphasized the intangible and imponderable factors in the human mind rather than the factors which are measurable and observable (Bogardus 1950). Thomas, however, was the sociologist who most affected Chicago social psychology.

W. I. Thomas. Thomas's contribution, like Simmel's, is both pervasive and frequently misinterpreted. Both of them resisted the formation of a systematic theoretical statement, offering instead a holistic approach to the study of sociology, a series of concepts (Park 1931), and a number of brilliant, although sometimes disjointed, insights into the nature of human life and social organization. There is considerable consensus about the centrality of Thomas's work in the development of Chicago sociology (see Park 1931, 1939; Bernard 1929; Janowitz 1966; Volkart 1968).[54] His broader influence has been widely noted, from Merton (1968) to Mills (1960), the latter claiming that Thomas and Znaniecki provide a framework for a general sociological view of "personality" which is the foremost contribution of American sociology.

Five themes in Thomas's contribution to social psychology have been emphasized by commentators: (1) his emphasis on social change; (2) the reciprocal dependence between individual and social organization; (3) his examination of "attitudes" and the "definition of the situation;" (4) his interactional and situational approaches to the study of the subjective side of social life; and (5) his empirical approach.

Thomas's emphasis on social change as the major subject of social theory (Janowitz 1966, pp. xxi–xxii) profoundly affected all aspects of his sociology. Although as Volkart (1953) points out, one cannot reduce Thomas's work to a single explanatory theory,[55] his theories of social change undoubtedly provide a key to understanding his work (cf. Deegan and Burger 1981; Coser 1977, p. 513).

Myrdal (1944) included Thomas in his critique of Park, Ogburn, and other Chicago sociologists, for their naturalistic and therefore fatalistic, view of change. Thomas's entire work, including his social psychology, is concerned with change, however, both in terms of broader evolutionary processes (Bogardus 1959), and in terms of attitudes and social change as a continuous process involving adaptation and disruption, social organization and social reconstruction (Janowitz 1966, pp. xxxii ff.; Volkart 1951, p. 11). Thomas's central substantive interests, particularly in his earlier collaboration with Znaniecki on *The Polish Peasant* (1918–19), evolved around problems of social change as they affected the subjective experiences of Polish immigrants attempting to adapt to new social organizations.

Second, Thomas's perception of social change and social control involve a recognition of the centrality of a "reciprocal dependence between social organization and individual life organization" (1918–19, 2:1128; cf. Janowitz 1966, p. xxxviii ff.). The focus on that relationship can be seen in *The Polish Peasant*, with its attention to institutional linkages for the Polish peasant in Europe and America. Thomas is concerned with identifying the formal properties of institutions and in examining the linkage among the individual, primary groups and the larger society, and particularly between the primary group and the residential community (Janowitz 1966, pp. xxxv–xxxvi). Thomas launched bold efforts to study the larger role of institutions, providing a rough outline for later efforts by Chicago sociologists in the study of institutions. As with his perception of social change, the linkage between individuals and social organization is described primarily in terms of attitudes and in terms of the interplay of the attitudes of individuals, on the one hand, and the values, mores, and folkways found in social organization on the other (see Park 1931).[56]

A third major facet of Thomas's contribution to social psychology is his emphasis on the examination of "attitudes," and particularly his concept of the "definition of the situation."[57] Thomas's attention to the reciprocal interdependence between individual and social organization is rooted in the pragmatic perspective, even though Thomas claims not to have been influenced by Mead (W. Thomas 1973).[58] In order to avoid viewing adjustment to social organization and social change as a mechanistic process, Volkart argues, Thomas examined the subjective experience, first in terms of attitudes, then as the "four wishes," and finally in terms of "definitions of situations" (Volkart 1951, pp. 5ff.). Faris emphasized Thomas's conception of "social attitudes" more than Volkart, and was actively involved in the important examination of attitudes by Chicago sociologists (see E. Faris 1928, 1931, 1945).[59] Research on attitudes involved an effort by Chicago social scientists, in the spirit of Dewey and Mead, to develop alternatives to what Faris called "the behaviorist mutiny," which limits analyses to the overt and visible. The work of Angell, Dewey, Mead, Thurstone, and others, Faris maintains, is an important alternative to the "behaviorist" perspective. "To neglect the study of attitudes will be to fail to understand personality," Faris (1928) insists. The "attempt to discard all consideration of the subjective experiences neglects the . . . mediating part of the act, which is equally important with the objective and observable."

Thomas describes an attitude as "a state of mind toward a value," which indicates and determines the direction in which actions will be tending (Park 1931, pp. 30–31). Thomas and Znaniecki's attention to attitudes in *The Polish Peasant* was the starting point for an important research tradition; it sparked considerable debate and played a role in the development of survey research now so popular in the social sciences. Faris (1948) argues that Thomas's development of the concept influenced the work of Thurstone, Stouffer, and their co-workers despite the fact that Thomas "had no mathematics and was allergic to statistics" (cf. Lundberg 1960). By the time Kimball Young edited a volume on *Social Attitudes* in 1931, there were already, according to Faris, hundreds of articles and books published on the subject.[60] One early critique of Thomas and Znaniecki's approach to the study of attitudes was Bain's (1928) contention that they are too subjectivistic and confuse attitudes with opinions. Furthermore, he exclaims, statistical treatments of indirect evidences of overt behavior provide a superior approach for the studies of attitudes. Faris responded with an opposing article in 1928, and Markey reviewed the critiques in his 1929 "Trends in Social Psychology." The Social Science Research Council sponsored a conference a decade later to consider Thomas and Znaniecki's approach, beginning with a paper by Herbert Blumer (1939b; Bain et al. 1939). Responses to Blumer's critique were made by Bain, Gordon Allport, F. W. Coker, Max Lerner, George P. Murdock, Roy F. Nichols, E. G. Nourse, A. T. Poffenberger, Stouffer, Thomas, Warren S. Thompson, Willard W. Waller, Malcolm M. Wiley, Wirth, and Donald Young. Much of the discussion centered around the problem of how to verify or validate theoretical propositions formulated to explain social phenomena.[61] Although Thomas initiated the debate and did much to shape the tradition, it was clear that Thomas's own interests were not in the direction of much of the later developments in attitude research.[62] Thomas turned instead to his concept of the "four wishes" as a way of linking subjective experience with institutions—new experience, security, response, and recognition (see Janowitz 1966, pp. xxxvii–xxxix). Hinkle (1952) and Znaniecki (1948) have noted the relationship between Thomas's four wishes and Freud's psychoanalytic theories. Young argues that Thomas was one of the first Americans to recognize the importance of Freud, "with whom he had come in contact during his research on the Polish peasant in Europe" (Young 1924). Janowitz claims, nonetheless, that Thomas was "fiercely anti-Freudian" (1966, pp. xxii, xxxix–xl). The "four wishes" were not ultimately central to the substantive thrust of Thomas's work and Thomas later discarded both his emphasis on "attitudes" and the "four wishes." He retained, however,"the underlying principle that the study of social life demands concepts which will meet two criteria: they must mirror social reality in both its objective and subjective aspects and at the same time they must hold out a promise of discovering scientific (i.e., verifiable) regularities of adjustive behavior" (Volkart 1951, p. 5). The most persistent of Thomas's specific contributions is his emphasis on interaction and situations in the study of the subjective side of social life. His concept of the "definition of the situation" has become one of those concepts so widely used in sociological analysis that it is often not explicitly attributed to Thomas. His situational analysis is a result of the influence of pragmatism, and much of his later work can be encapsulated in his phrase "If men define situations as real, they are real in their consequences" (Janowitz 1966, p. xl). Much has been made of the formulation, called the "Thomas theorem" by Merton (1968, pp. 475ff.), including efforts to link it with dramaturgical and ethnomethodological perspectives (Perinbanayagam 1974, 1975).

Finally, an examination of Thomas's impact on social psychology must take into account his empirical approach to the study of human behavior. As I have already pointed out, Thomas was the person most responsible for the development of the characteristic interest in developing sociological theories out of the research process. It is somewhat arbitrary to speak of Thomas's "social psychology," because his interest in the subjective aspects of human behavior was integrated with his other concerns, in a broad research program. Although he made substantial contributions to social psychology as a separate field of inquiry, that was a secondary interest.

Pragmatic influences. The thrust of pragmatic influences on Chicago social psychology involves two major issues—the social aspects of the self and the question of Mead's relative influence during his lifetime. A recent revival of interest in symbolic interactionism has resulted in a renaissance of Meadian studies[63] and renewed charges that Mead's influence at Chicago in the 1920s and 1930s has been exaggerated. It is clear that there was no unified school of social psychology organized around Mead. Although Lewis and Smith (1980) go to great lengths to demonstrate that fact, it was acknowledged earlier by others including Blumer. Thomas insisted that he did not understand Mead, and Park claimed not to have read much of his work, although both held him in high regard.[64]

Lewis and Smith (1980) attempt to prove that Mead's influence was minimal; as Rochberg-Halton (1982) points out, however, it is difficult to know how many sociology students taking Mead's courses would be necessary to constitute a substantial percentage. The fact that much of his work was incorporated into their sociological thinking may be a stronger statement than explicit citation or enrollment. Many others disagree, claiming that Mead did have considerable influence (see Johnson and Shifflett 1981, p. 147; Mullins 1973, p. 76; Cottrell 1980). Furthermore, Lewis and Smith fail to note the small size and interdisciplinary nature of the Chicago faculty at the time in question.

It is clear that both Dewey and Mead played an important role in the formation of social psychology at Chicago. Dewey's 1896 article "The Reflex Arc Concept in Psychology" was a seminal contribution to those early efforts. Mead's student David Miller considers Dewey's "Reflex Arc" article to be both a turning point and a foundation for the pragmatic movement at Chicago (cf. Coughlan 1976).[65] In it he develops a critique of strict behaviorism which neglects the importance of "consciousness" in human behavior by demonstrating that the sharp division between the sensory and the motor was untenable (Faris 1945, pp. 425ff.;). The "reflex arc" article, as Faris indicates, was a stimulus to much of the subsequent research in social psychology.

Dewey was the more dynamic of the two and dominated the scene at the time they were together at Chicago. Increased interest in Mead's work in the late 1950s, however, shifted attention from Dewey to Mead a full twenty-five years after Mead's death.[66] Reck (1964) lamented that Mead had not been fully appreciated because he was overshadowed by Dewey (cf. Swanson 1968). By the late 1960s, however, some commentators (especially Petras 1968b) argued, to the contrary, that it was *Dewey* whose influence had been neglected, reminding his readers that Dewey had been the peer of Mead in the early stages of the development of symbolic interactionism. In the 1970s, the issue of the relative influence of Dewey and Mead was translated into the broader theoretical issues of nominalism and realism. Mead's work has been of particular interest, with a number of scholars denying Blumer's standard interpretations of it (Lewis 1972, 1976, 1979; Lewis and Smith 1980; McPhail and Rexroat 1979, 1980; Blumer 1977, 1980; Johnson and Shifflett 1981). Although Dewey himself (1931) and others (e.g., Jane Dewey 1939; Miller 1973) have claimed that Mead had a constitutive impact on Dewey's own thought, Dewey undoubtedly enjoyed greater stature in the university and in the larger academic community.

Interestingly, Mead is not mentioned in Dewey's most important treatise on social psychology, *Experience and Nature*, despite the similarities of their views (Geiger 1958, pp. 143ff.). Petras (1968c, 1970b) argues that the approach developed by E. Faris, Mead, Thomas, and Cooley differed from the earlier individualistic theories of motivation chosen by Small, Vincent, Lester Ward, and Giddings. Antecedents to the Chicago pragmatic approach to social psychology can be traced to intellectual experiences Dewey had at Johns Hopkins, with influences from Peirce, G. Stanley Hall, and George S. Morris, and their subsequent development at Michigan, where Dewey, Mead, and Angell interacted (Raphelson 1973). Of particular importance was Dewey's emphasis on the condition of the social group and the importance of social interaction, rather than the "unique individual" concept (Petras 1968; Coser 1977, 346).

Much that has been written about Chicago sociology concerns the symbolic interactionist perspective and the sociological implications of Mead's social philosophy.

Symbolic Interactionism

> [Mead's] influence was along the line of giving to students a clearer picture of the nature of social interaction between human beings, an understanding that the environment or social world of human beings consisted of meaningful objects, a recognition that human beings constructed their action through processes of self-interaction, and an appreciation that group life took the form of fitting together diverse lines of conduct. These features of Mead's social psychological thought exercised great influence on the research and scholarly perspectives in the so-called Chicago school. (Blumer 1979, p. 22)
>
> Mead's work was used relatively *little* within the Chicago tradition of doing sociology and the uses to which it was put were quite *diverse*.
>
> The most conspicuous use was not directly related to doing sociology at all: Mead was used as an intellectual resource for the

> teaching of social psychology, but social psychology was primarily a teaching rather than a research subject. (Fisher and Strauss 1979b, p. 10)

Until quite recently, much of Mead's work was utilized and adapted by "symbolic interactionists," and interpreted in large part by Blumer, who coined the term (Blumer 1969, p. 1). Blumer's work (especially Blumer 1966, 1969) remains the major statement on Mead's work, but a number of scholars have challenged his "naturalistic" perspective and interpretations of Mead, substituting instead a "behavioristic" or "objectivistic" interpretation and approach. A number of distinctions have been developed within the complex interactionist tradition: the "Chicago" versus the "Iowa" schools of thought (Meltzer and Petras 1970); a dual Chicago tradition, one coming primarily from Blumer and the other from Park, Thomas, and Hughes (Fisher and Strauss 1978); and the more recent "objectivist" approach of the "Illinois school" versus the "naturalistic" approach represented primarily by Blumer. The many differences, however, are not as important as the convergences.

A diverse interactionist tradition. Two questions are inextricably intertwined: first, what sort of interactionist theory and research methodologies are most appropriate for sociologists to develop and use in their research? Second, how are we to interpret Mead's contributions to interactionist social psychology? Frequently the answer to the former question implies an answer to the latter. Those who are convinced that a sociological social psychology should be developed within the context of a rigorous objectivistic methodology (i.e., the Iowa and Illinois schools) tend to find Mead's work supporting their approach. Those who believe that such an approach oversimplifies the reality of social life and human motivation find a different social psychology in Mead's work. Some recent commentators (Johnson and Shifflett 1981; Stewart 1981; Douglas 1970) argue that elements of both are present in Mead's work. What Kuhn noted in 1964 about debates over the interpretation of Mead is probably true today as well: much of the disagreement stems from ambiguities and contradictions in Mead's work itself, particularly a contradiction between *determinacy* and *indeterminacy* in Mead's overall point of view, as represented by his concept of the "I" and the "Me." It is likely that such ambiguities were a deliberate aspect of Mead's dialectical approach.

The problem of interpreting Mead is precipitated by the complexity of the approach, and the fact that Mead published little on his general approach, focusing instead on concrete social problems such as crime, philanthropy, and education in his published articles. For a number of years, interactionists relied on an oral tradition for interpretations of Mead.[67] Consequently, what we have of Mead's thought comes primarily from stenographic notes of Mead's lectures (Morris 1934; Faris 1937; cf. Deegan and Burger 1978) and from the diffusion of ideas through his students.

Faris suggests that Mead "wrote very little, partly because he did not find writing easy, but chiefly, I think, because he realized the difficult nature of the problems, whose solution were so confidently announced by men of lesser gifts" (1937, p. 392).[68] According to Faris, Mead maintained a close relation to sociology throughout his career. Faris earned a degree in psychology with a minor in philosophy, writing a thesis under Mead's direction. When he joined the sociology department faculty after Thomas's departure in 1919, Faris was asked by Mead to teach an introductory social psychology course that was then taken by students before taking Mead's course. After Mead's death (in 1931) the social psychology course was continued by Blumer, and the early sociological interpretations of Mead consequently came primarily through Faris and Blumer.[69] Some early discussions of Mead were written by Dewey after Mead's death (Dewey 1931a, 1932, 1936), although they were largely tributes to Mead, including Dewey's (1932) widely quoted assessment of Mead as having a "seminal mind of the very first order."

A biographical sketch of Mead was prepared by his son, Henry C. A. Mead (1931), but substantial treatments of his thought were not forthcoming until the first publication of his lectures by his students and the introductions by Morris (1934) and Moore (1936). Faris (1937) offered the first major sociological treatment of Mead's work (cf. Blumer 1938, pp. 180–84). Morris (1938) discussed the similarities in the writings of Peirce and Mead, noting the shift in pragmatism from the metaphysical idealism of Peirce through the radical empiricism of James to the empirical naturalism of Dewey and Mead. Morris, Brewster, Dunham, and Miller (1938, p. lxii) argued that "in contrast to a purely mechanistic interpretation of the order of events, Mead acknowledges the oncoming event as a determinant in action and thereby converts sheer action into a process with past, present, and future in it." Another of Mead's students, Murphy, published an article in 1939 on Mead's philosophy of the act, but debates about how to interpret Mead did not emerge in print until the following decade, and then primarily among philosophers.

In 1943 Miller (1943a, 1943b) outlined Mead's conceptions of the past and the present, and in the mid-1940s further discussion of Mead was precipitated by Kolb (1944) and Lee (1945). Lee argued that Mead had demonstrated that philosophy should be modeled on research science, which was the evolutionary process grown self-conscious, a thesis echoed by Moore (1936). De Laguna (1946) wrote a critical analysis of central concepts in Mead's thought which Miller (1947) argued was a misinterpretation of Mead's work. According to Miller, Mead never intended to suggest that the self can or should identify itself with society; cooperation and communication can exist even when actors have different purposes.

Although the 1950s signaled an increased interest in Mead among sociologists (Sprietzer and Reynolds 1973), the major discussions of his work were still carried out by philosophers (see Fen 1951; Natanson 1953, 1956; Kallen 1956; and Murphy 1959). One of the first sociologists to undertake an extensive treatment of Mead's work was Meltzer (1959).

Thirty years after Mead's death, sociologists became more explicit about the way in which Mead's work was being interpreted, a discussion initiated, in part, by Strauss's (1964) introduction to a collection of Mead's papers in the Heritage of Sociology series. Although Mead's concepts "became common property among sociologists" and "he remains an oft-quoted elder statesman" in sociology and social psychology, Strauss wrote, Mead's ideas "have been interpreted from viewpoints other than his own. Mead's position is radically different from that of most social psychologists and sociologists who have quoted him or incorporated his thinking into their own systems of thought" (Strauss 1964, pp. vii–viii).

Some of the difficulty, according to Strauss, stemmed from excessive reliance upon Mead's *Mind, Self, and Society*, a theme echoed throughout much of the subsequent debate on Mead's thought. Mead's ideas about socialization and his concepts of "generalized other" and socialized "self" appealed to sociologists in the twenties and thirties. They helped them to refute biological explanations, and were later helpful for countering Freudianism and individualistic psychologies as well as providing a way to think about socialization of group members. Although there is much to be said, Strauss postulates, about what functionalist theorists such as Parsons, Davis, and Merton, select from Mead,

> Mead's treatment of the self as a process was transformed into something much more static, in accordance with the sociological view of internalized social control. The "generalized other" became just another way of talking about reference group affiliation, and Mead's notion of role tended to be reinterpreted to fit with the structural concept of status and its associated role-playing. It is even possible to maintain that sociologists who tend principally to be social determinists, read Mead as if he too were a social determinist, although his reiteration of the potential influence of individuals upon society should have warned against any such interpretation. . . . Whether the main drift of Mead's thought was reinterpreted is perhaps debatable, but the selective attention given it is not. (1964, pp. xii–xiii)

Of particular concern for Strauss is the neglect by many interpreters of Mead of his emphasis on *process*. "Like Dewey, Mead is saying that the Darwinian revolution has forever unfettered us from static conceptions of social organization" (ibid., p. xix).

Kuhn (1964) reviews the progress of interactionist theory in the preceding twenty-five years, the "age of inquiry" in symbolic interaction. Kuhn addresses the determinacy-indeterminacy debate by focusing on ambiguities in Mead's concepts of the "I" and the "Me," noting the range of alternative solutions proposed. He reviews efforts to develop both determinist and indeterminist interactionist theories and research. Among the determinists he includes the development of role theory and reference group theory, and the work undertaken at Iowa. Among the indeterminists, he includes the dramaturgical school of Burke, Goffman, and possibly Foote and Stone. The major problem with the latter, he suggests, is their inability to derive the testable conclusions that characterize the the Iowa school of symbolic interactionism.[70]

Chicago school versus Iowa school. It was not until 1966 that Blumer provided a systematic statement of his interpretation of Mead's work. Blumer (1966) contends that "Mead saw the self as a process and not as a structure. Here Mead clearly parts company with the great bulk of students who seek to bring a self into the human being by identifying it with some kind of organization or structure." Consequently, Mead's "picture of society stands in significant contrast to the dominant views of society in the social and psychological sciences—even to those that pretend to view society as action. . . .The chief difference is that the dominant views in sociology and psychology fail alike to see human beings as organisms having selves. Instead, they regard human beings" as merely responding organisms and, accordingly, treat action as mere response to factors playing on human beings" (Blumer 1966).

A heated debated followed with Robert Bales (1966), who took exception to Blumer's distinction between the self as a structure and as process, arguing that one can choose one side of the dilemma only if one remains abstract rather than operationalizing the issue. As with the issue of free will and determinism, "if he tries to become operational, he discovers that he cannot decide the issue. His errors of measurement and lack of information about the will are so great that he cannot tell whether the will is free or whether he is simply ignorant of the determinants." Bales argues that for Mead "the process of social interaction was central—not Mind, not Self, not Society." Blumer "seems to start with the self, and in this sense he is not a social behaviorist, as was Mead." On the other hand, when Blumer discusses "joint action" (or "social action"), Bales concedes, he gives a good account of social behaviorism. "I like much of what Blumer likes," Bales concluded,

> but I get nervous when he seems to cut all ties with the empirical means by which one gains knowledge and urges me to fly straight to the mind of God without even a pair of was wings.
>
> In this he seems to me not be a follower of Mead. Mead was not a philosophical idealist, as Blumer seems to be; he was a pragmatist and a social behaviorist. (1966, p. 547)

Blumer argues that Bales's "discussion shows him to be ill-informed and misinformed on the nature of Mead's thought."

"Mead must shudder in his grave," Blumer exclaims, "at such butchering of his thought."[71] The issues debated between Bales and Blumer are essentially those reflected in the Chicago and Iowa schools of symbolic interactionism.

Meltzer and Petras (1970) suggest that the most fundamental difference is in methodology. Whereas Kuhn, the major proponent of the

Iowa school, argues for a commonality of method in all scientific disciplines, Blumer tends to argue for a distinctive methodology for the study of human behavior. Blumer's *verstehend* approach requires sympathetic introspection—"feeling one's way inside the experience of the actor," whereas Kuhn argues for the need to operationalize the key ideas of symbolic interactionism. Both believe themselves to be working within the spirit of Mead's social psychology, despite their different approaches.

A second difference between the two schools concerns the question of determinism. Again, with each school allegedly taking its cue from Mead, Blumer assumes that behavior is to be perceived in terms of the interplay between spontaneous and socially determined aspects of the self, seeing the self "not as a combination of the 'I' and the 'Me' but as *interaction* between them" (Blumer 1966, p. 547). Proponents of the Iowa school, on the other hand, "reject both indeterminism in human conduct and the explanation of social innovation based on the emergent, creative element in human action" (Meltzer and Petras 1970). Hence, whereas the Chicagoans perceive self and society in processual terms, the Iowans have stressed the structural aspects of those phenomena.

Although proponents of both the Chicago and Iowa variants agree that the self is a social self, there is a difference of opinion concerning the extent to which the self is determined by society. The "Iowa versus Chicago" distinction made by Meltzer and Petras assumes that Chicago sociologists viewed the self as less determined than the behaviorists. Debates emerging in the seventies continued to ask if the less deterministic position was appropriate in interpreting Mead, and finally, if the social psychology developed at Chicago was truly "Meadian." The debate was cast first in terms of whether or not Mead was a "behaviorist" and later in terms of the distinction between nominalism and realism.

Mead as "behaviorist." Robert Faris (1967, pp. 93ff.) emphasizes that "a particular feature of the Chicago development was the destructive attack on the instinct theory" (cf. Bernard 1942). Social behavior was perceived as consisting of "the interaction, not merely of physiological organisms but of conscious selves, constructed in imagination through a social process in the manner outlined by Cooley and Mead." (pp. 92–93). Consequently, developments "at Chicago constituted a major break from the physiological psychology that had earlier seemed to be so promising." That break was to be found in Dewey's and Mead's emphasis on ways in which the human *significant symbol* differs from dog gestures, for example, as indicated by Dewey in his discussion of the reflex arc and the function of consciousness (R. Faris 1967, p. 96).[72] Cook (1972) notes that Mead's earliest published treatments of the nature of human consciousness involve extensive references to Dewey's 1896 "reflex arc" article. In it, Dewey strongly criticizes the "stimulus-response model" of action, and Mead later developed a neo-Hegelian attempt to discuss the "dialectic within the act." "Mead's thought was indeed always concerned with conduct or 'behavior,' but never in quite the sense now suggested by the term 'behaviorism.'"[73] Douglas (1970) argues that Mead's thought does contain a fundamental conflict between social behaviorism on the one side, and more phenomenologically oriented ideas on the other (cf. Bolton 1981). Douglas maintains that Blumer and Becker's version of interactionism, for example, is generally phenomenological. Other scholars have pursued Mead's thought toward nonbehaviorist positions. Hinkle (1972) compares the generalizing concepts of Mead to the phenomenological and ethnomethodological implications in Schutz. She concludes that, despite similarities in content, their methodological positions diverge sharply, with Mead emphasizing processes of convergence and change, whereas Schutz seeks to understand human action in terms of typicalities.[74] A perceptive article by Weigert (1975) outlines the possibilities in Mead's thought when combined with the phenomenological perspective, noting especially Mead's emphasis on concomitant awareness and reflexivity.[75] Bolton (1981, p. 274) postulates that Mead "was blocked from a fuller development of the implications of his social psychology" because of his "commitment to a strict social behaviorism." The clear implication of his work, however, is a philosophy of emergence which could be fruitfully explored. Fletcher (1971) concludes that Mead was a social behaviorist, but avoided determinism (such as that found in Durkheim) because of his concern with the "teleological" qualities and capacities of the human mind and "self" discussed by Mill, Ward, Hobhouse, and Weber. Gillin (1975), however, in a comparison of the works of Mead and Buber, insists that Mead does not account for human freedom.

With recent critiques of Blumer by what Johnson and Shifflett call the Illinois school, the earlier debates have been revived and recast. One helpful consequence of the debate is that, in responding to the various charges, Blumer has developed a more explicit public position on a number of methodological, theoretical, and interpretive issues.[76] Once again, the issues revolve around (1) the methodologies appropriate for symbolic interactionism; (2) The degree to which human behavior is determined by the environment; and (3) the Mead's relationship to the social psychology developed at Chicago.

Huber (1973b) initiated the debates with a broad attack on the methodology of pragmatism and symbolic interactionism, insisting that it precipitates biases in research. Because theory emerges from the research process, participants contribute to it, resulting in a bias which reflects the social perspective of the researcher and the distribution of power in the interactive setting. The article precipitated considerable debate and may have sparked some of the later efforts by Lewis and Smith, McPhail and Rexroat, and others, to interpret Mead in what they considered a more methodologically sound light (cf. Cottrell 1980). Schmitt (1974), who studied under Kuhn, argues that Huber provides an inadequate treatment of symbolic interactionism, contending that interactionism should not be equated with participant observation. "Even the Chicago School adherents," Schmitt writes, "are quite willing to use any strategy that will provide a valid image."[77] Stone, Maines, Farberman, Stone, and Denzin (1974) respond to a number of issues raised by Huber, placing her work within a context of the debate over positivism and suggesting that she fails to understand the dialectical method and the insistence among interactionists on using a variety of investigative techniques.

The next round of debate appears in critiques developed by Lewis and Smith and by McPhail and Rexroat. Lewis and Smith's *American Sociology and Pragmatism* (1980) contains detailed arguments along the lines developed in Lewis's earlier articles (1972, 1976). Their general thesis is that Blumer's subjectivism, or nominalism, is a misinterpretation of Mead's fundamental objectivism, or realism. Lewis and Smith attempt to represent Mead's social theory as social and philosophical realism, claiming that "Chicago sociology was more dependent upon Dewey's nominalism than Mead's realism." Johnson and Shifflett (1981) offer three criticisms of Lewis and Smith's interpretation of Mead. First, they insist that Mead's philosophy is dialectical rather than dualistic as represented by Lewis and Smith. "For Mead the organism and the environment are functionally related: each determines the other" (p. 145; cf. Batiuk and Sacks 1981). A similar position on the issue is taken by Wiley (1979), who asserts that James and Mead translated Kant's insight into the Hegelian dialectic, presented by Mead in the "I-Me problem" (cf. Goff 1980). Subsequent discussions of Mead, however (citing Kolb 1944 and Lewis 1976), buried the issue as a false one and Blumer replaced the formulation with looser notions of "communication with oneself."

A second criticism of Lewis and Smith concerns Mead's image of society. Whereas Lewis and Smith say that Mead conceives of society as an a priori human reality, existing prior to and determining individual minds and selves, Johnson and Shifflett contend, as does Miller (1973), that Mead assumes society "at the biological level, not the human level." Mead, therefore, "begins his theory of the self not with social facts, but with a conversation of gestures between not yet human organisms. Mead's 'society' is not the 'society' of Durkheim or Parsons" (Johnson and Shifflett 1981, p. 146).

A third issue involves the reality status of universals. Lewis and Smith claim that Mead affirmed an independent reality of universals, in keeping with his realism, an interpretation which contradicts Blumer (1980) who writes that Mead holds to both realist and subjectivist tenets in his metaphysics. Johnson and Shifflett conclude that although Lewis (1979) presents a research program inspired by Mead that is neglected by Blumer, his reconstruction "does not constitute an obvious advance over the tactics of either Blumer or Kuhn. All three present a consistent reading of Mead's texts by emphasizing one dimension of the 'I' over another. A convincing interpretation of the 'I' would require an explanation of Mead's ambiguity. Lewis's (1979:266) explanation, which implies a conspiracy to misinterpret Mead among his editors, is merely an unconvincing claim." If Lewis and Smith's arguments were accepted, furthermore, "it would mean that nearly all of Mead's students, readers and critics would have completely misunderstood his thought. It is possible that Herbert Blumer, Ellsworth Faris, Everett Hughes, John Dewey, Alfred Schutz and a number of others were wrong. It is more likely however, that the Illinois school has overstated their case" (Johnson and Shifflett 1981, p. 149).

A second revisionist interpretation of Mead is in a series of polemics against Blumer written by McPhail and Rexroat (1979, 1980; cf. Mc-

Phail 1979). They challenge the assumption (attributed to Huber 1973, Stone et al 1974) that Blumer's symbolic interactionism is the legitimate extension of symbolic interactionist theory and methodology. McPhail (1979) writes that there is a convergence between experimental research and symbolic interaction, drawing upon quotations from Mead which state that "it is a mistake to emphasize the artificiality of the experimental apparatus and the technique of the psychological laboratory." Furthermore, McPhail points out that students of Mead other than Blumer have attempted to translate Mead's insights into sociological research, but in a quite different manner.[78] McPhail and Rexroat (1979, p. 449) contend that Blumer's "naturalistic inquiry neither complements nor extends Mead's methodological perspective, nor is Blumer's framework suited to the investigation and development of Mead's theoretical ideas." Whereas Blumer (1969, pp. 1–2) claims that Mead never developed an explicit methodology for social research, McPhail and Rexroat (1979, p. 450) argue that "Mead's position is far more detailed and explicit than Blumer suggests" and is quite different from the position developed by Blumer.

Blumer (1980) responds by questioning McPhail and Rexroat's charges of ontological and methodological differences between himself and Mead. According to Blumer, Mead's position includes elements of both realism and idealism. Although there is a real world "out there," the "real world does not have a basic intrinsic, fixed makeup but may change as human beings reconstruct their perception of it" (Blumer 1980, p. 410). Consequently, McPhail and Rexroat's interpretations imply a methodology quite different from Blumer's "naturalistic" studies and provide, in Blumer's opinion, an effort "to justify and promote a special mode of scientific inquiry that relies on controlled experiments or on observations closely akin to those made in controlled experiments." Such a position, Blumer argues, results from a grievous and narrow misrepresentation of Mead's ideas on scientific method, and "fail[s] overwhelmingly to catch what Mead had in mind in his conception of human social behavior" (Blumer 1980, pp. 416, 419).

Johnson and Shifflett (1981, pp. 149–51), in reviewing the debate between Blumer and McPhail and Rexroat, maintain that Blumer neglects the most important flaw in McPhail and Rexroat—the claim that Mead is a methodologist. "This error comprises the majority of their argument." Furthermore, Johnson and Shifflett argue, "the Illinois school denies the American character of Mead's philosophy. Mead, like James and Dewey, attempts to resolve the realism versus idealism controversy in human practice." Mead, they argue, stood midway between idealism and realism and constructed a compromise between the two. "Contemporary Meadian social psychology, then," Johnson and Shifflett argue, "is divided between the two sides which entered into Mead's compromise" (1981, p. 153), with Blumer losing some of the objectivity of Mead's method while maintaining the metatheoretical foundation and the Illinois school recovering the objectivity but losing the foundation.

A third major critique of the way in which Mead has been interpreted is that developed by Fisher and Strauss. Some of what they argue in their recent articles (1978, 1979a, 1979b) was outlined by Strauss earlier (1964). In short, they claim that "Mead's thought had only a partial and indirect impact on how Chicago sociology was actually done. Neither Mead's theory of society nor his theory of social psychology were incorporated, in his own terms, into the mainstream of Chicago research" (1979a, p. 9). Although Mead was a close contemporary of Thomas and Park, he had no direct successors in the sociology department, and "Mead's ideas were slotted in where they seemed to be helpful for doing sociology."

Consequently, they argue, the ways in which Mead's work have been used have been quite diverse, largely providing a philosophical justification for the general antideterminist thrust of Chicago sociology, which fought the behaviorism of the 1920s and 1930s, Freudianism and neo-Freudianism, biological determinism, and Marxism. The antideterminist posture, according to Fisher and Strauss, comes largely from the Thomas-Park tradition of doing sociology, rather than directly from Mead. In part, that is because the sociologists failed to address Mead in the context of his theory of social change.

All that can be clearly concluded about the debates concerning the construction of social-psychological theories at Chicago is that the debates are far from over. There are not only many issues of interpretation which remain unresolved, but, perhaps more importantly, there are aspects of the original corpus not yet fully explored.[79] It is relatively easy to isolate a number of distinctive developments in social-psychological theory and research that have emerged from the University of Chicago.[80] It is not, however, a simple task to identify exactly how those traditions developed, nor how true they are to the original work of

Thomas, Mead, Dewey, Faris, Park, Hughes, Blumer, et al. In the final analysis, the social-psychological theories that were developed by Chicago *sociologists* must be seen within the context of their overarching concern for social organization, and the relation of the individual to that organization. The issues they raised were not simply the issues of Chicago sociology. With the passage of time they become institutionalized in society as a whole.

IV. Sociological Theory Construction: Social Organization

The core concepts of Thomas's sociology—social control and processes of social change—concern phenomena resulting from the "reciprocal dependence between social organization and individual life organization." Chicago sociologists attempted to define the nature and processes of social organization, or the "socially systematized schemes of behavior imposed as rules upon individuals" (Thomas and Znaniecki, quoted in Janowitz 1966, p. xxxi; cf. Locke 1948; Floro 1976). The study of social organization at Chicago involved an emphasis on the relationship between individuals and social institutions, systems of social stratification, and the study of occupations. The Chicago sociologists had a dynamic conception of social organization rooted in their pragmatic philosophical assumptions (cf. Bowers 1944).

Institutional Analysis

Under the general rubric of the study of social organization, sociologists at Chicago studied a variety of institutions, taking their cue from *The Polish Peasant*. Their analysis moved from basic units of primary group to community and finally to a "selected series of large-scale organizations, which included such elements as the educational system, the press, and co-operative and voluntary associations," in an effort to identify formal properties of each institution (Janowitz 1966, p. xxxv). Using an ethnographic approach, Thomas examined linkages among the family, the residential community, and occupational communities.

The analysis is related to their social psychology, as in "the aphorism of John Dewey, that the instincts do not produce the institutions, but rather the institutions produce the instincts" (R. Faris 1967, p. 111). The character of institutions, according to Hughes, is more than a sum or average of the character of individuals involved in its processes, a position contrary to Allport's claim in the 1920s that an organization is no more than the sum of individuals (R. Faris 1967, pp. 112–13).

Many of the microsociological and macrosociological interests of the Chicago sociologists are combined in their institutional analysis.[81] Short (1971, p. xxvi) contends that it is in Hughes's work "that the study of social organization, as such, received its most sophisticated treatment and made the greatest impact on the discipline" (cf. Stein 1960, p. 324). Wirth's study of institutions in *The Ghetto* encompasses sociopsychological aspects of social organization, race and ethnic studies, and institutional analysis (Vergati 1976).

One institution of central concern to the Chicago sociologists was the family.

Studies of the family. The earliest Chicago sociologists were interested in the family, especially in terms of changes precipitated by urbanization and immigration (see O'Neill 1966). It was not until the 1920s that family research began to gain momentum, building on two theoretical orientations: first, an interactional approach developed by Cooley, Mead, and Thomas, and articulated by Burgess. A second approach was based on a concern with social change, leading to an analysis of family trends by Burgess and others, with attention to such topics as birth control, divorce trends, the effect of prosperity on the family, consequences of the depression, etc. (Nimkoff 1948).

Burgess was most responsible for the development of research on the family (Cottrell 1967), following Henderson's interest in the area. Burgess collaborated with Cottrell, whose 1933 doctoral dissertation utilized statistical analysis for the prediction of happiness in marriage, and later on a textbook with Locke (Burgess and Locke 1945) which examined broad changes in family styles. Other doctoral theses at Chicago studied changing functions of the family, variations of children by birth order, and racial variations in family form, notably Frazier's *The Negro Family in Chicago* (Frazier 1932; cf. R. Faris 1967, p. 104). Lasch (1978) indicates that Burgess and others associated with him were central in defining family studies in the 1920s and 1930s, with particular emphasis on the effects of urbanization on the family.

Organizations and occupations. The study of formal organizations was inherent in the study of urban institutions, and was developed by

Hughes and the Human Relations in Industry Group. The ecological perspective exerted a significant impact on contemporary organization research (Burns 1980); the two current reigning paradigms in organization theory explain organizational change in terms of "environmental selection" and "adaptation," both of which were anticipated in Chicago sociology. The Chicago faculty, especially Park, "examined the impact of technological advances and spatial distributions on professionalization, bureaucratization, and marketing and ultimately on custom, politics, and patterns of association" (Burns 1980, p. 342). Both Hughes and Shideler, writing dissertations under Park, explained the growth of economic institutions in ecological terms and described the effects of growth in cultural terms. Burns observes that there are some indirect links to contemporary organizational research through the community theorists at Chicago who maintained aspects of the ecological perspective. The reformulation of human ecology under the influence of McKenzie, and his student Hawley at Michigan and North Carolina, inspired the current research agenda in organization-environment analysis (Burns 1980, pp. 354, 356).

Faught (1980) points out that Hughes represents a link between Park's original formulations and later work which Hughes inspired. His attention to the study of institutional development in a dissertation on the Chicago Real Estate Board was elaborated into the study of roles, careers, professions, and occupational types. His examinations of the relationships between individuals and organizations precipitated a series of studies combining the social-psychological and social-organizational aspects examined by Thomas and Park. The criticism that interactionism fails to treat larger forms of social organization ignores the long line of research on the sociology of work and organizational settings stimulated by Hughes (Denzin 1970).

The Committee on Human Relations in Industry, organized in 1943, was an interdisciplinary group including Hughes, Warner, Whyte, George Brown, Allison Davis, Burleigh Gardner, Frederick Harbison, Robert Havighurst, and Neil Jacoby (Gardner and Whyte 1946). They describe the processes of interaction of members of a working group, "paying particular attention to factors outside the immediate group situation which affect the degree of integration of the group" (Shils 1948, p. 44). Although not methodologically innovative, their studies did provide some important applications of well-recognized methods to what was then a relatively new field of study (Gardner and Whyte 1946).

Warner's work on factory social systems and Hughes's work on ethnic groups in industry describe the processes of interaction of members of a working group, analyzing factors outside the immediate group situation more systematically than Elton Mayo's research group. Shils argues, however, that in those Chicago studies there was "an occasional disposition to believe that the scientific problems can be solved by the use of complicated diagrams of the intra-group relations. These diagrams actually overemphasize the importance of spatial aspects of the relationship, or obscure the situation by characterizing it in spatial metaphors" (Shils 1948, p. 44).

Other perspectives on organizations and occupations were developed outside of the sociology department, but affected sociological research in the area. Watson (1949) indicates that the formulations by Dewey on the formation of social norms forecast later trends such as the findings of the Hawthorne experiments. Merton (1940) maintains that "the transition to a study of the negative aspects of bureaucracy is afforded by the application of Veblen's concept of 'trained incapacity' and Dewey's notion of 'occupational psychosis.'" One of the most important developments in institutional research is Veblen's institutional analysis of economics.

Veblen's institutional analysis. Veblen took institutions—their origins, nature, function, and interrelationships—as the prime focus of the social scientist (Dowd 1966). His work is heavily indebted to Chicago pragmatism. Despite some differences, "Peirce's and James's pragmatism, Dewey's instrumentalism, Beard's economic determinism, Holmes's legal realism, and Veblen's institutionalism showed a striking philosophical kinship" (Coser 1977, p. 290).[82]

Veblen's *Theory of the Leisure Class* (1899) attracted the attention of radical scholars and activists (Dorfman 1945, p. 196). Ward (1900, p. 829) defended it against its critics, claiming that "The trouble with this book is that it contains too much truth." The book became the major statement of a general institutional approach to economic and social theory (Hacker 1957; White 1957), with some scholars comparing Veblen to Marx (Graham 1944; Mills 1960) and Freud (Schneider 1948).

Davis (1943) argues that Veblen's institutional analysis is part of a broad trend toward a more adequate theory than that offered by nineteenth-century positivists and classical economists. Although Veblen studied other institutions, his primary interest was in the analysis of economic institutions.

Veblen had a strong following among the institutional economists at Johns Hopkins and Wisconsin, who influenced both scholars and New Deal officials in the thirties (Diggins 1978, p. 213). Veblen's institutional analysis was a broad examination of human social evolution as "essentially a pattern of institutional change rooted in the development of the industrial arts" (Coser 1977, p. 265). In his analysis of that pattern, Veblen provides a strong critique of classical economic theory with its individualistic bases (Homan 1927; Naber 1958), which may help to explain Veblen's appeal to many sociologists.

Johnson (1934) argues that Veblen had little influence on economics, but did have an impact upon philosophy, sociology, and history. Not all economists agree, however, including Galbraith, who has drawn upon some of Veblen's ideas calling him "a genius, the most penetrating, original, and uninhibited—indeed the greatest—source of social thought of [his] time" (Galbraith 1973; Diggins 1978). The process of individual valuation, in contradiction to classical economic theory, was for Veblen a cultural phenomenon (Nabers 1958, p. 95). Like Marx, Veblen developed a sociological approach to economic phenomena and chose as his central problem the analysis of capitalism and institutional change (Hill 1958, p. 146).

Behind much of Veblen's institutional analysis is his concern about inequality. According to Mills (1960), the master clue to Veblen's work as a whole is the distinction between pecuniary and industrial employment, a distinction which parallels and extends Marx's distinction between the bourgeoisie and the proletariat (cf. Nabers 1958, p. 101). Veblen is concerned about what he sees as a long-term trend toward inequality in the United States (Qualey 1968). He emphasizes the non-economic functions of wealth, and the "conspicuous consumption" in American society,[83] with a conception of the class structure that differs significantly from the tradition of orthodox economics.

Although the Chicago sociologists per se usually approached the issue of stratification in a somewhat different, and certainly less polemical, fashion than did Veblen, it was an important aspect of their examination of social organization.

Social Stratification

With the exception of Warner, the development of an explicit, systematic theory of social stratification was not a significant part of the sociological enterprise at Chicago. Park, for example, was well aware of class stratification, but chose not to focus on it.[84] "The importance which he attributed to the impersonal market mechanism on the one hand and the binding force of tradition and custom on the other, as well as his great interest in racial relations, prevented him from attributing to class relations the central significance which some of his contemporary sociologists in Germany, and later sociologists in America, have done" (Shils 1948, pp. 15–16). Stratification is an implicit issue, however, in virtually everything produced by the Chicago school (Janowitz 1975). The most explicit work in stratification by Chicago sociologists was in the field of race and ethnic relations, Warner's theories of stratification, and Park's concept of the "marginal man." Those interests can be attributed, in part, to their interest in the problems of urban life, immigrant groups, and Simmel's sociological theories.

Warner's theory of stratification. Warner held a joint appointment in the sociology and anthropology departments at Chicago and developed an empirical approach to the study of social stratification in his community studies. In an effort to identify social classes and cliques, Warner elicited judgments from interviewees concerning the social rank of people in the Newburyport community. He was thus able to identify and evaluate variables involved in the hierarchy of a community power structure, and subsequently developed a methodology for the study of the class structure of American communities. His procedures for determining class structures of communities and the class levels of individuals were later outlined in Warner, Meeker, and Eels's *Social Class in America* (1949), precipitating considerable debate on both methodological and substantive grounds (see Shils 1948, p. 19; Hall 1951). Kornhauser (1953) has summarized Warner's major research findings and conceptual apparatus, as well as the controversies surrounding his work. She notes problems with his definition of class, his emphasis on prestige and its relevance for general American stratification studies, the accuracy of his portrayal of the status structure, methodological implications of his work, and his alleged value orientations (cf. Kimball 1979; Landis 1939). Cox (1942) develops a critique of the "caste school" of race relations, of which Warner is the leader, suggesting that their approach is neither original or accurate but that it has "none of the anti-color complexes of the instinct school."

Just as fruitful as Warner's study of stratification, and perhaps more central to the Chicago school, was the concept of marginality introduced by Park.

The "marginal man." Park's first treatment of the concept of marginality appears in his essay "Human Migration and the Marginal Man" (1928b) with its inspiration coming from Simmel's notion of the stranger.[85]

Park's notion of marginality has proven valuable in the study of a number of phenomena, particularly the status of immigrants. Levine, Carter, and Gorman (1976, p. 830) note, however,

> that in the borrowing Park altered the shape of the concept: his "marginal man" represents a configuration notably different from Simmel's "stranger." Thinking of the experience of ethnic minorities in zones of culture contact in American cities, Park conceived the marginal man as a racial or cultural hybrid—"one who lives in two worlds, in both of which he is more or less of a stranger." . . . Whereas Park's excluded marginal man was depicted as suffering from spiritual instability, intensified self-consciousness, restlessness, and malaise, Simmel's stranger, occupying a determinate position in relation to the group, was depicted as a successful trader, a judge, a confidant, and a personally attractive human being.

Stonequist (1937) extends Park's concept, acknowledging the difference between Park's marginal man and Simmel's stranger. Simmel's "conception of the stranger pictures him as one who is not intimately and personally concerned with the social life about him. His relative detachment frees him from the self-consciousness, the concern for status, and the divided loyalties of the marginal man" (Stonequist 1937, p. 178; cf. Levine, Carter, and Gorman 1976, p. 830). Hughes (1941) elaborates the concept further, noting its origins in Simmel and Gilbert

Murray's *Rise of the Greek Epic*.[86] A number of authors have followed suit, suggesting modifications or criticisms of the concept. Whereas many argue that the notion could be applied fruitfully to the study of minority groups (e.g., Frazier 1950), others claim that such an application dilutes the concept. Goldberg (1941) suggests a modification with reference to marginal culture groups (e.g., Jews), and Green (1947) insists that although it has been "taken over uncritically into the literature," it has an indifferent status as a scientific formulation and has not lent itself to statistical or case-study analysis.

Golovensky (1952) suggests that the theory has its rightful place, but only in a restricted sense when referring to "rootless drifters." Kerckhoff and McCormick (1955) address Green's (1947) criticism, attempting to reformulate it more adequately (cf. Dickie-Clark 1966). McLemore (1970) offers a broad critique of the literature on Simmel's concept of the stranger, including a discussion of Park, Stonequist, Rose, and others. He observes that the marginality literature confuses, albeit productively, two aspects of research on the stranger: social distance issues and the impact of "newcomers" on social organization.

In the final analysis, although Park, Hughes, and others have created some confusion in translating Simmel's notion of the stranger into the examination of marginality in social organization, they have provided a powerful concept that sensitizes students of immigrant groups and ethnic minorities to the ambivalence of marginal status (cf. Surie 1970). The marginality of those who are near and remote at the same time produces both alienation and exclusion, on the one hand, and a freedom from the constraints of the social order on the other. As with much of Simmel's sociology, loose interpretations or outright misinterpretations by the Chicago sociologists nonetheless resulted in productive investigations.

Social Disorganization

A final aspect of Chicago social organization studies is the concept of social disorganization. Efforts to examine the social organization of Chicago in the 1920s and 1930s led inevitably to the concept of disorganization. The concept was never explicitly defined, but neither was "social organization" (Carey 1975, pp. 106, 120). The Chicagoans had an insightful understanding of what they meant by social organization, but it remained for subsequent generations to spell it out in more detail (cf.

Short 1971, p. xxvi). The notion of social disorganization was central to Thomas's understanding of social change.[87] Park and Burgess (1921, p. 924–25) spoke of social disorganization and collective behavior within the context of ongoing social change, i.e., "the processes by which societies are disintegrated into their constituent elements and the processes by which these elements are brought together to form new societies."

In Burgess's course on "social pathology," students were sent out into the city to gather data for map-making activities, which revealed a distinctive urban structure. As they mapped out the locations of juvenile delinquency, dance halls, rooming houses, business and industrial structures, etc., they discerned patterns that enabled them to counter the claims of the eugenics approach to disorders. Chicago sociologists concluded that "the characteristic extremes of poverty, disease, and behavior troubles found everywhere in slum populations are products of social disorganization, rather than of low genetic quality in the populations" (R. Faris 1967, p. 57). They discovered "that juvenile delinquents were concentrated in certain areas of the city and that they tended to thin out in other areas. That was quite surprising, strange to say, to the personnel of the juvenile court, because they knew they had cases in all parts of the city. . . . Delinquents were concentrated in what we call the areas of deterioration and transition; they thinned out and almost disappeared in the better residential neighborhoods. There were, of course, juvenile delinquents in almost every area, but their distribution followed the zonal pattern" (Burgess and Bogue 1967, p. 7).

Park places organization and disorganization within his cycles of competition, conflict, accommodation, and assimilation. He is more willing "than Thomas and Znaniecki to identify economic factors as the fundamental causes of social change. Hence the beginning of the cycle of disruption and organization is initiated by the struggle for existence" (Carey 1975, p. 104). One of the earliest social disorganization studies published at Chicago is Anderson's classic study *The Hobo* (1923).[88] As in many of the Chicago studies, Anderson finds not only *disorganization*, but alternative forms of social organization as well.

The Chicago interest in social disorganization precipitated a broad series of studies and proved theoretically useful in interpreting much of what they found in the city. Mowrer draws a connection between family types and the ecology of the city, noting the intense social disorganization of family life in certain urban areas (see Faris 1967, pp. 67ff.).[89] A similar effort by Frazier in *The Negro Family in Chicago* (1932) suggests a relationship between marriage rates among blacks and ecological zones, suggesting that problems within the black population were a consequence of something other than racial mental capacities (Faris 1967, pp. 68–69).

Thrasher's *The Gang* (1927) and studies by Shaw and McKay resulted in the further development of the social organization perspective.[90] It was elaborated within the context of "social pathology" by Queen and Mann (1925), Sutherland (1945), and others.

The perspective precipitated debate as well as research in the genre. Mills's (1943) scathing "Professional Ideology of Social Pathologists" postulates that the backgrounds and careers of such social-disorganization theorists as Thomas, Ogburn, Ellwood, and Cooley affected their definitions of problems and the results of their research. Whyte's (1943) *Street Corner Society* (1943) anticipated later Chicago research by calling aspects of the disorganization perspective into question. In his participant observation study of an Italian working-class district, Whyte discovered not so much disorganization as forms of organization not previously recognized by students of the ghetto (Schwendinger and Schwendinger 1974, pp. 550–51). Robert Faris's *Social Disorganization* (1948) is criticized by Reiss (1949, p. 561) for being "replete with value statements" while eschewing value orientations (cf. Mowrer 1941).

Carey (1975, pp. 106–7) argues that the Chicago school's discussion of social disorganization implies a theory of human nature, an assumption of value consensus, and an assumption that social organization is "variable in the kind and degree of integration it entails and in its capacity to support or embody cultures." To say that institutions are "weak" means "simply that they are not able to prevent high rates of unemployment, infant mortality, and delinquency from arising and persisting. . . . Economic segregation is the ultimate causal variable" (Carey 1975, p. 107).

Both social organization and social disorganization were seen, by most Chicago sociologists, as aspects of what Park considered the central problem of sociology, that of social control.

V. Sociological Theory Construction: Conflict and Social Control

> All social problems turn out to be problems of social control (Park and Burgess 1921, p. 785).

Thomas, Park, and Burgess consider the concept of social control to be a basis for their empirical studies of social organization. Although the concept was not developed by Chicago sociologists[91] as much as by Ross and others, the Chicago group was instrumental in introducing the concept and in using it in empirical research as "a device for integrating diverse elements of sociological analysis" (Janowitz 1975, p. 92). Ross's classic formulation of the concept[92] was first published by Small as a series of articles in the *AJS*, and Thomas placed considerable emphasis on it in *The Polish Peasant* (see Janowitz 1975, pp. 89–91). Current understandings of the notion of social control are quite different from its early formulation as a broad sociological frame of reference (Janowitz 1975). Rather than implying a "social psychology of conformity," the concept originally "referred to the capacity of a society to regulate itself according to desired principles and values."[93]

> Social control has served and continues to serve as a shorthand notation for a complex set of views and viewpoints. It has been a "sensitizing concept," in the terminology of Herbert Blumer, or a "theoretical orientation," in that of Robert K. Merton. Moreover, social control has been directly linked to the study of total societies. It has stood for a comprehensive focus on the nation-state and a concern which has come to be called "macrosociology." (Janowitz 1975, p. 83)

Consequently, the opposite of social control is *coercive* control, "that is, the social organization of a society which rests predominantly and essentially on force—the threat and the use of force." Social control, therefore "has not been necessarily the expression of a conservative political outlook" (Janowitz 1975, p. 84).

Park writes in slightly different ways about social control in the abstract and in the examination of concrete problems. In his conceptualization, social control is related to ecological processes of competition and conflict, to which he added those aspects of social communication which govern the social order, which in turn interact dynamically with the ecological order (Turner 1967). "The 'natural' state of society is not one of peace derived from unanimity, but a working adjustment to differences." Hence, "conflict remains latent although antagonisms are regulated" (Turner 1967, p. xxxii), and conflict is perceived as a central component of ongoing social processes.[94] Because Park and Burgess emphasize both natural processes and the importance of competition and conflict, the Schwendingers (1974, pp. 388ff.) contend that they have one foot in traditional laissez-faire liberal doctrines, but they also develop a critique of pure competition. "Pure competition had existed only among plants. Every human society exerts some control over competitive processes: competition among humans operates within 'the limits the cultural process creates and custom, law and institutions impose'" (Park and Burgess 1921, p. 507; Schwendinger and Schwendinger 1974, p. 390; cf. Farberman 1979, p. 12).

Park and Burgess's conceptualization is perceived by some as inherently conservative. The claim is not totally accurate, however, because of their emphasis on conflict (see Kennedy 1951). Park and Burgess's pragmatic view of social orders as ongoing processes with inherent conflict, competition, and accommodation has attracted some attention in recent decades as an alternative to functionalist theorizing (Kuklick 1973). Park does, nonetheless, endorse Thomas's "ordering-forbidding" as an approach to social reform, and explicitly defers the practical contribution until the problem area has been studied in breadth and depth (Turner 1967, p. xvi).

The concept of social control was used as a pragmatic perspective to integrate theory and research about social change with attention to ecological processes, social-psychological phenomena, and aspects of social organization. In doing so, Chicago sociologists made significant advances in the study of a number of fields.

4

SUBSTANTIVE AREAS OF RESEARCH

In order to understand the contributions of the Chicago sociologists, it is helpful to examine in more detail their studies of urban and community life, race and ethnic studies, public opinion and communication, crime and deviance, and political phenomena.

I. Urban and Community Studies

The study of urban life provided a focal point for sociology at Chicago throughout the entire 1892–1950 period. The general outlines of urban research in sociology were first developed by Park and Burgess and their students (Reiss 1956). Their research monographs, methods of study, and research agenda resulted in the posing of questions which still dominate the discipline (Janowitz 1967a). The early notion of Chicago as a laboratory for investigation of social life led to the development of the human ecology perspective, debates over the nature of "urbanism as a way of life," and demographic studies of urban areas.

Chicago as a Research Laboratory

Although the notion of Chicago as a laboratory for social research is usually associated with Park and Burgess (e.g., R. Faris 1967, p. 52; cf. Park 1929), it was part of the program much earlier. A 1902 description of the graduate program in sociology at Chicago, for example, claims that

> the city of Chicago is one of the most complete social laboratories in the world. While the elements of sociology may be studied in smaller communities, and while it may be an advantage to begin-

> ners in the method of positive sociology to deal at first with more simple combinations, the most serious problems of modern society are presented by the great cities, and must be studied as they are encountered in concrete form in large populations. No city in the world presents a wider variety of typical social problems than Chicago. (Tolman 1902, p. 116.)

That keen attention to the social problems of the city was largely responsible, Hunter (1980) argues, for the emergence of the urban social sciences in Chicago. Chicago "presented a raw reality of the moment at the high point of industrial urbanization," offering an opportunity to study urban problems in a systematic, empirical fashion. The Chicago sociologists felt that "one of the goals of the research was to develop policies that would help ameliorate existing social problems" (Hunter 1980, p. 215; cf. Carey 1975).

Urban research at Chicago is related to the human ecology perspective and is consequently subjected to the same criticisms, i.e., that it is ethnocentric, deterministic, and conservative. The debates sparked by the department's research program are too numerous to discuss in any detail in this brief analysis. Some of the most important treatments of urban research at Chicago include Park (1929, 1939, 1973); Burgess (1924b, 1964); Burgess and Bogue (1964); Smith and White (1929); Shils (1948); Hollingshead (1948); Hughes (1956a, 1979a); Reiss (1956); Janowitz (1967); R. Faris (1967); Short (1971); Fischer (1972); Diner (1975); Matthews (1977); Castells (1977); Schwendinger and Schwendinger (1974); Bulmer (1980).[95]

Small recognized the importance of using the city as a laboratory for social research (see Hughes 1956a; Dibble 1975), and Thomas helped to stimulate interest in the study of immigrant communities in Chicago. The social scientists at Chicago were quite outspoken for tolerance and understanding of immigrant groups, and much of their work involved a "social work" orientation until the early 1920s (Burgess 1964).[96] The urban research accomplished by Chicago sociologists, and the debates it engendered, reveal the interdisciplinary nature of the enterprise. Although self-consciously sociological, the Chicago sociologists were operating within a context of interdisciplinary cooperation, particularly through the Local Community Research Committee (LCRC).[97]

The Local Community Research Committee

A proposal from the political science, sociology, anthropology, and political economics departments for the formation of the LCRC was approved in 1923. The committee, initiated by Charles Merriam (Shils 1970), supported the series of research projects that has become so closely identified with the Chicago school of urban research, such as the mapping of local community areas, patterns of urban growth, juvenile delinquency, family disorganization, and studies of homeless men and immigrant groups.

One component of their success which is often underestimated is the funding provided by various sources, particularly the Laura Spellman Rockefeller Memorial.[98] The LCRC had a number of connections to the Rockefellers in addition to the original tie between the university and John D. Rockefeller, who donated about $34 million for the creation of the university. Vincent, who obtained his Ph.D. from the sociology department and taught there until 1911, was president of the Rockefeller Foundation from 1917 until 1929. Beardsley Ruml, who earned his doctorate in psychology from Chicago, became director of the Laura Spellman Rockefeller Memorial (Bulmer 1980, p. 70). The Memorial gave the LCRC an initial grant of $21,000 shortly after its creation, and over the next decade allocated a total of $631,509, of which $180,509 was matched by other sources (Bulmer 1980, p. 77).

One focus of the committee's work was the study of natural areas in terms of spatial patterns and cultural life (Burgess 1964). There was a considerable esprit de corps among persons working on LCRC projects. As Hughes recalls it, graduate student morale was high, and LCRC fellows "quickly became a sort of club. They were young and most were unattached; they spent several hours together in seminars each week; they studied German with one of their number as tutor" (Hughes 1979a, p. 189). The committee also supported later work by Thurstone, Ogburn, Wirth, and others. It was replaced in 1930 by the Social Science Research Committee, with a more inclusive membership, including representation from philosophy, sociology, history, economics, political science, social service administration, commerce and administration, anthropology, home economics, psychology, medicine, law, and education. The LCRC remained, however, the model for the organization of interdisciplinary research at Chicago and "was a prototype for the organisation of university-based social science research, not only in America, but throughout the world" (Bulmer 1980, p. 109).

In addition to the LCRC, the institutionalization of research on the city was aided by the formation of the Chicago Area Project (see below;

Kobrin 1959; Burgess 1964) and the founding of the Society for Social Research (SSR) by Park in 1921 (Park 1939; Kurtz 1982). Unlike the LCRC, the SSR was almost exclusively an organization of sociologists, although their meetings included presentations by scholars from a wide variety of disciplines as well as representatives from various service organizations. Much of the debate about that research came to a head with the publication of Wirth's "Urbanism as a Way of Life" article in 1938.

The "Urbanism as a Way of Life" Debate

No other single paper has precipitated so much discussion, debate, and research in urban sociology as Wirth's (1938) article, "Urbanism as a Way of Life." In it, "Wirth spelled out the seminal theoretical concepts which were to occupy urban sociology for the next quarter-century" (Wilson and Schulz 1978). The article, which has often been interpreted as a summary statement of the Chicago school of urban sociology (e.g., Castells 1977), provided much of the impetus for the "mass society" debates. Wirth seems to depict urban life as "consisting of the substitution of secondary for primary contacts, the weakening of bonds of kinship, and the declining social significance of the family, the disappearance of the neighborhood, and the undermining of the traditional basis of social solidarity" (1938, p. 80).[99] While it is true that Wirth draws upon the urban studies of Chicago sociologists of the 1920s and '30s, as well as upon Durkheim[100] and Simmel,[101] it is somewhat misleading to characterize Wirth's picture of the city as representative of Chicago sociology (see, e.g., Wilensky and Lebeaux 1965, pp. 115ff.). Indeed, some important criticisms of Wirth have come from Chicago sociologists.

Early Chicago studies do sometimes emphasize the breakdown of community in the modern city, particularly in their studies of social disorganization, but they also affirm the existence of communities in the city, particularly what Janowitz calls the "community of limited liability."[102] The community press, for example, is seen as an indicator of symbolic dimensions of the city; it "acts as a mechanism which seeks to maintain local consensus through the emphasis on common values" (Janowitz 1967 [1952], p. 11).[103] Both Thomas and Park maintain an ambivalence toward the city, as does Park's mentor Simmel. Thomas "did not conform to the pattern of the rural-born sociologists—moralizers who abhorred the culture of the city; he was too urbane and sophisticated to long for the values of primitive and rural society" (Janowitz

1966, p. xxx–xxxi). Although Park was, as most sociologists of his time, greatly interested in "the loosening and disruption of communal bonds and the increase in personal freedom" as the main facts of modern society (Shils 1948, p. 10), he also recognized the establishment of new forms of community in the city's neighborhoods.

Stein argues that a central problem in Park's urban sociology is the effort to identify "control mechanisms through which a community composed of several quite different subcommunities can arrange its affairs so that each of them maintains its own distinctive way of life without endangering the life of the whole" (Stein 1960, p. 17). Although Park sees the breakdown of community as characteristic of the city, he also recognizes that "the processes of segregation establish moral distances which make the city a mosaic of little worlds which touch but do not penetrate" (Park 1967 [1915], p. 40), i.e., natural areas which often have some form of community.[104] The larger city itself, furthermore, has its own unity; it is a living entity with "a moral as well as a physical organization" (Park 1967 [1915], p. 4). Similarly, Burgess (1930b) observes that, rather than disappearing, local communities are becoming more and more interwoven with the entire structure of the city and are playing a new but significant role.

The most systematic attempt to interpret Wirth's article and to assess its critics is Fischer (1972; cf. Morris 1968). Although the brief discussion here cannot review all of the literature which addresses Wirth's article, it is helpful to look at a number of his critics. I will do so in terms of the four kinds of critiques suggested by Fischer: (1) those who argue for the substitution of social for ecological factors;[105] (2) the "urban subculture" theorists; (3) the range of scholars who specify the particular conditions under which Wirth's model holds true; and (4) those who advocate the study of urbanization as a societal-level phenomenon, rather than a local phenomenon.

Social factors and subcultures. Perhaps the most challenging of Wirth's critics are those who argue either that the variables identified by Wirth as most characteristic of urban life—size, density and heterogeneity—are not the most significant, or that the *gesellschaftlich* characteristics of the city are additions to, rather than substitutes for, aspects of nonurban social organization. Such critiques are often either the consequence of the study of other cities, or the discovery of *gemeinschaftlich* characteristics in urban communities including Chicago. The former criticism is similar to the charge of determinism leveled at the human ecology perspective, whereas the latter is associated with the alleged ethnocentrism of the Chicago ecologists.

Some critics argue that the critical variables to examine, rather than size, density, and heterogeneity, are such factors as class, ethnicity, stage in the life cycle, and values (Fischer 1972, pp. 216–17; cf. Sjoberg 1965; Lewis 1965; Gans 1962; Kolb 1954; Reiss 1955; Morris 1968). Richard Dewey (1960), for example, argues that the urban-rural continuum used by Wirth and Redfield was real, but relatively unimportant, and that the influences of density and size of the population must be distinguished from influences of culture (cf. Miner 1952; Mintz 1953). Hughes (1956a, p. 264) claims that the distinction is quite important in some cases, as in Africa, where "the studies of cities all point to an extreme lack of cultural links between the most urban and the most rural people."

Stefania (1976) claims that Wirth attempts to overcome the determinism of the ecological approach. In a sense, Wirth's own study, *The Ghetto*, ironically suggests a critique of his community breakdown thesis by showing the existence of a community within an urban area. The example is not an isolated one; an examination of the classic urban monographs produced by Chicago sociologists shows the same ambiguity. Chudacoff (1976), for example, suggests that in Zorbaugh's *Gold Coast and the Slum* his rich description of life in those areas reveal important forms of social organization that imply alternative types of community life, some of which Zorbaugh did not recognize as such because of his concern with social disorganization.[106] A number of studies, notably up-close ethnographic examination of urban life, call into question Wirth's images of urban life as anomic and isolating (see Gans 1962; Whyte 1955; Young and Willmott 1957; Suttles 1968; Abu-Lughod 1961; Bell and Boat 1957; Seeman et al. 1971; Mizruchi 1969). Guterman (1969), however, in reviewing a number of Wirth's critics, defends his hypotheses. Guterman maintains that the evidence on which the criticisms rely contains several inadequacies and presents data which show a negative correlation between the size of a locality and the intimacy of friendships.

Attention to cross-cultural research has resulted in the modification of a number of conclusions reached by Chicago sociologists (Short 1971, p. xxiv). Sjoberg's (1960) study, *The Pre-Industrial City* argues that

Wirth's and Redfield's overemphasis on secularization and disorganization have led to a neglect of much of the organization of the city (cf. Morris 1968). Furthermore, their folk-urban comparison blurs the distinction between folk societies and peasant communities.[107] Similarly, Hauser (1965) postulates that the characteristics of the city outlined by Wirth are not to be found in Asian cities, a conclusion echoed by Aldous's (1962) study of West African cities.[108] A French scholar, Ledrut (1968) even warns against the excessive integration of some urban neighborhoods.

In an insightful article entitled "The Chicago School: Continuities in Urban Research," Farberman (1979) observes that an important piece of the Wirth puzzle is the distinction between public and private spheres discussed by Park and Simmel. As the "post-Chicago School" (1940–60) "set out to demonstrate the existence of primary relationships in the urban milieu" (Farberman 1979, p. 16), they found them not in the public, but in the private sphere. "Of paramount interest," Farberman writes,

> is the plain fact that the very evidence which indeed humbles Wirth's proposition comes from research sites located in the private sphere of life. For, without exception, these sites form a web of relationships and institutions which lie within the bounds of the residential community and which people enter into as a spin-off from their nuclear families. Thus, factual evidence notwithstanding, implicit concern with the private sphere lifts into relief, once more, the essential paradigmatic continuity between the pre-Chicago, Chicago, and post-Chicago Schools. All schools presuppose in their meta-theoretical imagery an underlying split between the public sphere of necessity, which is coterminous with an overextended division of labor, and the private sphere of freedom, which is coterminous with an overextended kinship system. (1979, p. 17)

Urbanization as a societal phenomenon. Several critics of Wirth's picture of the city argue that "the nation, rather than the city, is the meaningful unit for analysis of urbanization" (Reissman 1964, p. 196). Urbanization is a phenomenon, they argue, which occurs in varying degrees throughout a nation—cities are "quantitatively but not qualitatively distinct from nonurban sectors of the nation" (Fischer 1972, p. 217; cf. Morris 1968; Stein 1964; Pahl 1970; Reissman 1964). Greer

(1956) argues that, rather than seeing urbanism as an atomistic mass society, as Wirth does, one should see it as part of a continuum of alternative lifestyles at the same economic level, which are concentrated in different urban subareas. Kin relations, Greer suggests, may in fact grow in importance in high-urban areas because of diminished reliance placed upon neighborhood and local community.

Chicago urban sociology, Greer notes, focused on social disorganization in the city coincidentally with the great depression, resulting in a bias against the city at a time when the nation was becoming rapidly urbanized. The consequent "massified" image of the city "was probably related to the general *weltschmerz* of the deep depression: poverty, unemployment, deficit financing at home; dictatorship, purges, and above all, the imminence of war abroad" (Greer 1962, p. 16). In a similar vein, Matza argues that "the Chicagoans conceived disorganization [but] they described diversity" (Matza 1969, p. 48; Short 1971, p. xxviii).

Specifying conditions. A final criticism is the "large range of theories which accept the Wirth model in whole or in part, but which specify the particular conditions under which it holds true" (Fischer 1972, p. 218). Some scholars suggest that some kinds of cities resemble his model, whereas others do not (Ledrut 1968; Lopez 1963; Redfield and Singer 1954; Abu-Lughod 1968; Cahnman 1966). The difference may be accounted for on the basis of characteristics of Western culture (Kolb 1954; Hauser 1965) or as a consequence of the industrialization process (Handlin 1963; Powell 1962; Redfield 1947; Lefebvre 1968).

Two conclusions can be drawn about Wirth's essay on urban life and the debates it engendered. First, it is clear that there are many problems with the model developed in Wirth's "Urbanism as a Way of Life" article, although those problems are not to be found in all aspects of the urban sociology developed at Chicago. Second, despite its many problems, Wirth's article serves a crucial function by formulating a picture of urban life and social organization which stimulated further research and provided an agenda for urban studies for decades to come.

Population and Demographic Studies

Demographic studies constitute another major development evolving out of Chicago urban studies (Duncan 1959a; Lundberg 1960; cf. McKenzie 1934). Burgess and Bogue note that "The starting point for urban analysis traditionally has been with demographic and ecological study. Knowledge about the population—its size, composition, and growth trends—is the foundation upon which other research may be based" (1967, p. 15).[109] Demographic studies were not abstracted from other aspects of sociology at Chicago, but were an integral part of the entire research program. As Short suggests, "ecological and demographic perspectives tend to merge with institutional and organizational analysis and with social-psychological concern" (1971, p. xxiv). As already noted, in laying the groundwork for ecological studies of the city, Park and Burgess initiated a mapping of populations and "natural areas" (Burgess 1964). They were influenced by surveys in England,[110] and the neighborhood studies carried out by Addams, Breckenridge, Edith and Grace Abbott and others (Addams 1895).

Chicago sociologists cooperated with the geographers and economists at the university as well as with the U.S. Census. Information from the data-gathering activities was combined with census information and published in the *Local Community Fact Book of Chicago*. A new edition was created after every census and provided a factual basis for many of the Chicago studies.

In 1946 Wirth and Burgess established the Chicago Community Inventory, which carried on the older urban studies, focusing primarily on demographic and ecological aspects of the metropolitan area (Burgess 1964, p. 13).

II. Public Opinion and Communications

Another persistent interest of Chicago sociologists was public opinion and communications. That interest reflected larger concerns with social control, racial conflict, urban communities, and democratic institutions, as well as social change. Ogburn argues that mass communication and transportation "constitute the second phase of the industrial revolution" (1935, p.). To some extent it even reflected a fundamental aspect of the pragmatic philosophical understanding of the nature of human beings as communicators of shared symbols attempting to find common ground for consensus. Clearly, Dewey and Mead saw the importance of communication, although there has been some debate about how to interpret their positions (see Shott 1976; Anderson 1979; De Laguna 1946; Miller 1947). Miller (1947), however, argued that De Laguna misinterpreted Mead. According to Miller, Mead thought that cooperation and communication could exist even when actors have different purposes.

In addition to the broader concern with communication as symbolic interaction, Chicago sociologists were also interested on a more practical level with particular forms of communication as an aspect of social control. Both Thomas and Park gave substantial attention to the newspaper (Janowitz 1952), and Blumer examined forms of mass communication such as the movie industry (Freidson 1953). Thomas and Znaniecki indicated that the mass media could function as symbolic devices for societal integration (Janowitz 1966, p. xxxvii).

In an effort to compare the experience of Polish immigrants with other groups, Thomas examined a collection of letters from immigrants in the *New York Jewish Daily Forward*, a Yiddish socialist newspaper (Bressler 1952; cf. Janowitz 1966, p. xxviii).[111] Park's interest in the press came quite naturally from his own career as a journalist, during which he recognized both the importance and limitations of the medium (Park 1950, 1973; Raushenbush 1979; Waterman 1926). Following Thomas, Park (1929b) studied the immigrant press as a mechanism for assimilating immigrants into American society.[112] The publishers' ties with local foreign-language communities, however, prevented them from being completely successful in that role. "Their ties to ethnic values acted as a barrier to the development of a completely commercial and instrumental outlook" (Janowitz 1967b, p. 21).

Park's influence, furthermore, can be seen in work by his student Louis Wirth, whose 1947 presidential address to the American Sociological Society was entitled "Consensus and Mass Communication." In it, he spoke of the role of the mass media in achieving a new consensus in urban society (see Kolb 1956; Reiss 1964).

A third aspect of the area of communications is the study of public opinion, which is related to an interest in social control, social problems, and the study of attitudes. Bogardus (1929), for example, points out that a series of race relations studies initiated by Park in 1924 were case studies of public opinion intended to examine the effect on race relations of public opinion concerning Japanese immigrants.

III. Race and Ethnic Studies

Investigations of racial and ethnic phenomena began with the examination of the heterogeneous population of Chicago by Thomas, Znaniecki, and Park, followed by studies by Johnson, Frazier, Wirth (Lyman 1972, pp. 15, 22, 51, 58–60; cf. Etzioni 1959), and others.[113] Just as Park and Burgess's human ecology studies and Wirth's "Urbanism as a Way of Life" article provided a major impetus for the study of urban phenomena, so the study of race relations by Park and his students set the stage for that area of research for decades.

Early Studies

The most important early studies in the area were, of course, initiated by Thomas (Lyman 1972, pp. 15, 19–20, 22). Although Ellwood wrote about current racial stereotypes of "racial temperament," his influence in the area was fortunately minimal.[114] Thomas anticipated a shift in sociological studies of race relations which occurred following World War I (Frazier 1947). The earliest American sociologists, according to Frazier, assumed that blacks were inferior. Following the lead of Thomas and Park, later Chicago scholars based their studies on the assumption that race was a sociological concept. Stocking (1968) discusses work in the field by Thomas and Dewey, noting the development of Thomas's thought and his later lack of emphasis on innate differences in racial temperament.[115] Chicago quickly became a center for training black sociologists (Blackwell and Janowitz 1974). Park was one of the first sociologists to send students out to study the institutions in which interracial contacts take place (Banton 1974). Park's interest in race relations came, in part, from his work with Washington, and Park in turn inspired a number of students to study in the field.[116] One of the earliest empirical studies in the area was *The Negro in Chicago: A Study of Race Relations and a Race Riot*,[117] which Park (1924) claimed was the most painstaking and complete study of a racial group in the United States. It was an analysis of the 1919 race riots in Chicago and was sponsored by the Chicago Commission on Race Relations, of which Johnson was associate executive secretary.[118] Another important black sociologist who studied under Park was Frazier, whose classic *The Negro Family in the United States* provided an inclusive study of the family culture of an ethnic group (Pearl 1949; Hughes 1956b). Frazier was also concerned with the role of the black middle class as a catalyst for social change (Hughes 1956b; Landry 1978).

Robert Park on Race Relations

Park's work in the field of race and ethnic studies was unquestionably path-breaking. As R. Faris puts it, "While Ross at Wisconsin was still thundering about the yellow peril of Asia, Park was helping Negro students to investigate discrimination, prejudice, and even interracial violence with clinical objectivity" (1967, p. 131). Bracey, Meier, and Rudwick (1970) suggest that although Park's moderation in the area of racial equality has led to criticisms of his work, he was instrumental in facilitating a "transition of mainstream sociology's stance from racism to an attempt at objectivity in racial studies."[119] Park's fundamental hypothesis, according to Lipset (1950), is that race prejudice "is created when groups or individuals try to resist a change in social organization; changes in status produce conflicts of interest and race hostility." There have been three major criticisms of Park's approach: first, that it is "naturalistic" and implies the difficulty or impossibility of deliberate social change; second, that he is insufficiently structural in his approach; and finally, that he is an "assimilationist" who fails to recognize the value of ethnic pluralism.

The most controversial aspect of Park's theories of race relations is his suggestion that there are inevitable cycles of relations which occur naturally within the human community.[120] Myrdal (1944) criticizes Park's naturalistic approach to racial problems as fatalistic, leading to resistance to social change. Myrdal's critique, perhaps the most significant early comment, extended to Thomas and Ogburn as well (see Myrdal 1944, pp. 1049–57).[121] Wacker (1976) defends Park against Myrdal's charges, however, by arguing that Park is less optimistic than Myrdal about the possibility of rapid change in the area of race relations in the United States. Park believes that racism in the United States is deeply rooted in the history and customs of American society, and in its frontier heritage (Wacker 1976). Richards (1976), however, agrees with Myrdal, arguing that Park's sociology, especially his emphasis on ecological processes and structure, contains an implicit ideology. According to Richards, Park's theories assume that inequities such as race discrimination must be seen as intrinsic to the social order and will be eliminated only through gradual evolutionary processes.

Myrdal's criticisms are echoed by Cox (1965), who attacks the influence of Faris, Ogburn, and Park on Frazier and his followers (see also Chrisman 1970). Despite their praiseworthy attitudes toward blacks, Cox argues, they are opposed to blacks' taking initiatives that would increase the pace of progress toward racial equality.[122] Lyman (1968) claims that Park's notion of the race-relations cycle is one of the most important contributions to sociological thought, but that Park's work establishes the framework for subsequent studies of American race relations within a narrow Aristotelian perspective that focuses on orderly, continuous, cyclical processes. Banton (1974) disagrees with Lyman, suggesting that he underrates the extent to which Park sought an alternative to Social Darwinist thought.

Masuoka and Yokley (1954) discuss Park's emphasis on race conflict and race consciousness. They applaud much of his work, but argue for a redefinition of the field that would emphasize structural rather than psychological elements, drawing upon the work of Blumer, Hughes, and others (cf. Frazier 1947, 1950).

Finally, Metzger (1971) objects to Park's "assimilationist" theories, claiming that he overlooks the functions that ethnic pluralism may perform in a democratic society. Higham (1974), however, maintains that Park takes a position somewhere in between an integrationist and a pluralist position, suggesting that he sees the two as alternating phases in a long history of widening human contacts. Carey (1975, p. 169) argues that both Thomas and Park were pluralists who supported the preservation of diverse cultural and linguistic traditions.[123] It is clear, furthermore, that Park's position, although sometimes easy to criticize in light of recent developments, was considerably advanced in his own time. Hughes (1964) recalls that Park once remarked that there was no "Negro" problem in the United States, because the problem is with *whites* rather than blacks; he asked, moreover, why there should be racial peace before there was racial justice (cf. Mogey 1969; Rose 1950).

IV. Crime and Deviance

Chicago sociologists made four major contributions in the field of crime and deviance: Thrasher's early social disorganization theories; Shaw and McKay's social control and subcultural theories; and Sutherland's interactionist notions of "differential association" and "white collar crime."[124] A fourth contribution, "labeling theory," was developed by Frank Tannenbaum, Edwin Lemert, Kai Erikson, Howard S. Becker, and others. Because it was developed after the 1892–1950 period discussed in this treatment of Chicago sociology, however, I will only discuss the first two contributions. Except for the strain models of deviance,[125] delinquency theory originated at the University of Chicago (Kornhauser 1978).

It was no accident that in the city of such infamous residents as Al Capone, sociologists turned to the study of crime. As R. Faris (1967, p. 72) suggests, "perhaps the most conspicuous aspect of the reputation of the city of Chicago in the 1920's was the magnitude of its crime. Beer wars, bombings, racketeering, holdups, and gang murders made the newspaper copy all over the world."

Early Social Disorganization Theories

Both Shaw and McKay's work and Sutherland's approach are rooted in pragmatism, human ecology, and the sociology of W. I. Thomas (W. I. Thomas 1923; cf. Tudor-Silovic 1973). Of particular interest is the phenomenon of social disorganization. Disorganization theories assume that deviance "is caused not by commitment to different norms, but indifference to, or weakness of, shared norms" (Kornhauser 1978, p. 30; cf. Hirschi 1969, p. 29). Thus, it is not the *content* of values and norms that is important, as in subcultural theories that developed later, but rather the strength of commitment to social norms and values.

One of the most important early works in the area is Thrasher's *The Gang* (1927).[126] The basic factor resulting in the formation of gangs, according to Thrasher, is weak social controls, i.e., "the failure of the normally directing and controlling institutions to function efficiently" (1927, p. 22; Kornhauser 1978, p. 52). The study represents an early attempt to relate the emerging human ecology approach to the study of deviant behavior (K. Young 1931).

The Schwendingers argue that Thrasher has an "atomistic concept of individual adolescents" and that his explanations of gang behavior grow out of Park and Burgess's key concepts of competition and conflict. Consequently, Thrasher proposes that ceremonies and institutions be established for community *reorganization* which would provide ways to control delinquency (Schwendinger and Schwendinger 1974, pp. 479–81). Although Thrasher suggests that gangs provide a substitute for conventional social groups (cf. Cohen 1955; Cloward and Ohlin 1960), a number of investigators claim that "relations among delinquents may be characterized more by brittleness and threat than by solidarity and warmth" (Empey 1978, p. 236; Yablonsky 1963, p. 196; Hirschi 1969, pp. 145–52; Matza 1964, pp. 53–55; Short and Strodtbeck 1965, pp. 221–34; Klein and Crawford 1967). Other studies, however, lend support to Thrasher's view (Empey and Lubeck 1968; Hindelang 1973, p. 479; cf. Bordua 1961). Kornhauser, moreover, maintains that studies which question the warmth and intimacy of the gang as a primary group may be based on a misunderstanding of primary groups. Psychoanalytic theory, for example, suggests that "primary emotions include envy and hatred as well as cooperation and love, and that primary relations entail distortion and concealment as well as openness and trust" (1978, p. 54). The social disorganization perspective as a theory of crime and deviance was not fully developed with Thrasher, but took a dramatic step forward with Shaw and McKay.

Shaw and McKay and the Chicago Area Project

The work of Shaw and McKay marked the beginning of effort in the United States to construct theories of the sociology of delinquency on a foundation of empirical research. Their approach to the problem was guided by ecological and social psychological theory, the former derived from the writings of Robert E. Park, the latter from those of W. I. Thomas (Kobrin 1971). Few scholars would dispute the centrality of Shaw and McKay, not only in the study of delinquency, but also in the general development of theories of crime and deviance. Shaw and McKay and their associates, working with the Institute for Juvenile Research and the Chicago Area Project, explored the implications of ecological studies by Park and Burgess and their students, developing them into a larger perspective for the study of delinquency (see Shaw et al. 1929; Shaw and McKay 1942; Burgess 1942; Sorrentino 1959).

The Chicago Area Project was founded by Shaw in an effort to combine research with a practical program for social change (Kobrin 1959). The project was, according to Janowitz, "the first large-scale attempt to throw off in the inner city what was later to be called welfare colonialism" and became a source of stimulation for later federal "community action" programs (Janowitz 1966, p. lvii).[127] A number of efforts have been made to analyze Shaw and McKay's theoretical model, notably Kobrin (1971) and Kornhauser (1978, pp. 62ff.), who suggests that it is a mixture of "control theory" with a "cultural deviance" model. Shaw and McKay observe that certain community characteristics associated with social disorganization are correlated with delinquency rates. Kornhauser indicates that they posit three classes of correlates—economic status (the most important factor), population mobility, and heterogeneity (measured by the percentage of foreign-born and black individuals in the community). Poverty, high mobility, and heterogeneity, they argue, "result in ineffective community cultures and structures, which in turn lead to the weak controls that account for delinquency" (Kornhauser 1978, pp. 65–66; see her summary chart of Shaw and McKay's model, p. 73).

A number of scholars have tested their theories, especially their contention that economic status is the most important determinant of delinquency rates. Whereas Shaw and McKay rely on zero-order correlations, later studies use partial correlations, multiple regressions, factor analysis and subclassifications. Lander (1954), Polk (1957–58), Bordua (1958–59), and Quinney (1964) conclude that economic levels of an area are less important than noneconomic factors, or that some specified conditional relation is nil (Kornhauser 1978, p. 84).

Perhaps the most significant challenge to Shaw and McKay comes from Lander's (1954) study of Baltimore. He rejects their conclusions about economic indicators, arguing that they are not actually related to delinquency rates; delinquency is related, he argues, to anomie and community stability rather than to the socioeconomic conditions of an area. Kornhauser (1978, p. 84) insists that Lander's own conclusions actually support Shaw and McKay's identification of social disorganization as the crucial intervening factor (cf. Hirschi and Selvin 1967, p. 151; and Gordon 1967). Despite similar results in Lander (1954) and Bordua (1958–1959), Chilton (1964) argues, it is not clear that Lander (1954)'s emphasis on anomie is accurate. A discussion of the methodological problems in Lander, Bordua, and Chilton by Gordon (1967) affirms the correlation between socioeconomic status and delinquency rates, although the extremely low end of the socioeconomic status range is most relevant.

Although the expected relationship between delinquency and individual economic status has been called into question, Kornhauser argues that "a uniformly high relation between individual SES and delinquency is neither predicted nor required in Shaw and McKay's theory. The conditional nature of the socioeconomic status-delinquency relation in part reflects the influence of community contexts. A high ecological correlation and a moderate individual correlation, apparent only under specified conditions, is all the theory demands" (Kornhauser 1978, p. 106).

Another consequence of the effort to test Shaw and McKay's ecological correlations is a debate concerning methodological techniques and ecological correlations. In addition to some of the studies already discussed, questions were raised by Robinson (1950), who argues that ecological correlations cannot be validly used as substitutes for individual correlations. Rosen and Turner (1967) suggest that widely used statistical methods are inappropriate for the task that Lander and others have undertaken.

Testing the importance of *mobility* in determining delinquency rates, however, is more problematic. Some studies (Stuart 1936; Robins, Jones, and Murphy 1966; cf. Savitz 1970) suggest that area mobility rates are important. Similarly, Reiss (1951), Robins, Jones, and Murphy (1966), Nye (1958), and Savitz (1970) all find some relationship between individual mobility and delinquency. Other studies yielded more inconsistent results, however (Stuart 1936; Simpson and Van Arsdol 1967).

Finally, there have been mixed results in testing Shaw and McKay's heterogeneity hypothesis. One early critique of Shaw and McKay (Jonassen 1949, p. 145) suggests that Shaw and McKay are on questionable ground in entertaining the "possibility that all nativity, racial, and nationality groups are not equal in their ability to resist the 'disorganization' of juvenile delinquency." In examining Shaw and McKay's data, Jonassen finds internal contradictions in their theories and suggests that their conclusions be used cautiously.

Kornhauser (1978, p. 113ff.) reviews a number of studies, concluding that the effect of heterogeneity on delinquency rates is conditioned by the socioeconomic condition of the community, and is an important factor only in middle- and low-status neighborhoods (see Bordua 1958–59, pp. 231–33; Chilton 1964, p. 78; Willie and Gershenovitz 1964, pp. 740–44). Shaw and McKay's suggestion that subcultures develop in low-income areas which precipitate delinquency is criticized by Lerman (1967), who postulates that their assumptions hinder theoretical and empirical understanding of deviant youth cultures.

Kornhauser (1978, p. 138) concludes that efforts to test the importance of the relationship between neighborhood economic status and delinquency, which was most important to Shaw and McKay, remain unchallenged. There is some support for their positions concerning mobility and heterogeneity, although it is more equivocal.

Edwin Sutherland

Sutherland, who received his degree from Chicago in 1913, is, according to Vold (1951), "America's best known and singularly consistent sociological criminologist" who always viewed crime from the standpoint of social processes and the impact of social organization and cultural heritage.[128] His impact was felt, not only through his own work on "differential association" (McKay 1960; Short 1960) and "white collar crime" (Cressey 1961), but also through the work of his students, such as Albert J. Cohen, Fred L. Strodtbeck, and his collaborator, Donald R. Cressey.

Cohen (1968) argues that Sutherland did more than any other individual to shape the substantive theory and methodological orientation of contemporary criminology. At Chicago, Sutherland was influenced by Henderson, Thomas, Park, Burgess, McKay, and others (Sutherland 1973). His view of crime as a consequence of differential association is a direct reflection of the work of Mead and Cooley, and an effort to counter biological and psychodynamic control theories (Empey 1978, p. 317).[129]

Some critics (e.g., Short 1960) suggest that Sutherland's theory of differential association does not lend itself to rigorous scientific testing. Furthermore, Glueck and Glueck (1950, pp. 163–64; cf. Glueck 1956) and Hirschi (1969, pp. 135–38) argue that delinquents become members of delinquent groups *after* having becoming delinquent, rather than before (Empey 1978, p. 329). Other critics have argued that his theory of differential association is too deterministic (Matza 1964; Sykes and Matza 1957) or that lower-class gangs may well provide support for conventional, as well as deviant values (Short and Strodtbeck 1965).

In addition to the concept of differential association, Sutherland's concept of "white collar crime" inspired a number of works in the field[130] and has received considerable attention. Hartung (1953), for example, remarks that Sutherland's *White Collar Crime* "freed criminology from its long empirical dependence upon *Uniform Crime Reports* through the simple means of bringing all known criminals within the purview of the discipline, not just those caught by the police."

There are a number of critics, including Burgess, who maintain that a criminal should be defined as "a person who regards himself as a criminal and is so regarded by society" (Aubert 1952). Tappan (1947) goes even further, insisting that it is confusing to define crime as Sutherland does, and that it is better for sociologists to study crime as legally defined (cf. Caldwell 1958; Hall 1960). Someone is not a criminal, according to Tappan, until he or she is *punished* for having committed a crime, a position with which Cressey takes issue (1964, pp. v ff.).

Kornhauser observes that there is a strong element of populism in

Sutherland's theories, with a tendency to excuse the behavior of slum boys who become delinquents and to accuse the rich of abominations. These sentiments, she argues, "are a luxury affordable only by professors who, in the safety of their studies, are immune to the consequences of grimy-collar crime" (1978, p. 203). The lasting merit of Sutherland's *White Collar Crime*, argues Cressey (1964, p. xii), "is its demonstration that a pattern of crime can be found to exist outside both the focus of popular preoccupation with crime and the focus of scientific investigations of crime and criminality." Despite criticisms of the concept, it has entered into the vocabulary of social scientists and society as a whole, and continues to be a significant aspect of the sociological study of crime.

V. Political Sociology

A final substantive area to which the Chicago sociologists made major contributions is that of political sociology. Much of the work of Chicago sociologists "neglects the political process *per se* as if it were a derivative aspect of society" (Janowitz 1966, p. xxxviii),[131] so that their contribution in this area is somewhat indirect, and sometimes emerged as part of the interdisciplinary context within which they worked. They did, nonetheless, have some impact on the study of political institutions, citizenship and voting, and public policy and social problems.

From the earliest days of the University of Chicago, the sociology faculty were quite involved in, and attentive to, public affairs, especially through the Local Community Research Committee. As the examination of the substantive issues of the Chicago school so clearly shows, it is impossible to perceive of the sociology that developed at Chicago without the concern for social problems and public affairs that was manifest throughout the 1892–1950 period (See Carey 1975; Tolman 1902; Bulmer 1980).

Political Institutions

Perhaps because social problems were perceived as rooted in larger social forces, sociologists at Chicago did not devote a great deal of attention to the study of political institutions per se. That negligence is somewhat surprising, given their active involvement in civic affairs and their focus on institutional analysis and social control.[132] Chicago sociologists were more likely to cooperate with, and in some cases attempt to affect, political institutions than to perceive of them as subject matter for their research.[133] The study of crime, for example, tended to focus on criminals (see e.g. Sutherland 1937; Landesco 1929) and delinquents (Shaw and McKay 1942), rather than on institutions of justice, or the lawmaking process.

There was some attention to political institutions by graduate students in their doctoral dissertations (R. Faris 1967). One of the first two graduates of the department, Raymond, for example, wrote his dissertation on American municipal government (1895). Maclean's master's thesis in 1897 was entitled "Factory Legislation for Women in the United States" (Deegan 1978, p. 19). Bernard's interest in political processes is reflected in his dissertation "The Transition to an Objective Standard of Control" (1910) and his later work *War and its Causes* (1944; Odum 1951, pp. 162–63).[134] Dewey was vitally interested in political processes (see Hook 1950), and Veblen wrote on the relationship between foreign and domestic policy (W. Williams 1957). Perhaps the most important attention to political processes grew out of work on local communities and cooperation with community agencies (see Street 1930). The LCRC had strong ties to civic and political institutions such as the Children's Bureau, the City of Chicago, and the Smithsonian Institution, all of which funded research projects sponsored by the Committee (White 1929), as well as with the U. S. Census (Burgess and Bogue 1967). Chicago sociologists maintained close ties to political scientists Merriam (See Karl 1974, 1968) and Lasswell, who had an impact on later Chicago sociologists such as Shils and Janowitz (Marvick 1977).

One political institution which received considerable attention from Chicago sociologists was the military. Janowitz and Shils produced studies of primary groups in the military (see Madge 1962, pp. 232–26; Merton and Lazarsfeld 1950, pp. 16–39); and Stouffer was the senior author of the classic study, *The American Soldier* (see Hauser 1961; Merton and Lazarsfeld 1950; Lazarsfeld 1962).[135] M. Smith (1968) suggests that *The American Soldier* is a model of mass production in research, with an emphasis on quantitative evidence, an avoidance of theoretical speculation except in close contact with the data, and a close connection with applied problems.

Chicago sociologists were also concerned with questions of citizenship and voting. A volume of essays, *American Society in Wartime* (Ogburn 1943), for example, includes discussions by Warner on the American town and Faris on the role of the citizen. More importantly, perhaps, were the implications of the notion of social control for the concept of citizenship. Because Chicago scholars like Mead, Vincent, Park, and others thought of social control as "the capacity of a society to regulate itself according to desired principles and values" (Janowitz 1975, p. 28), the notion of citizenship became an important issue, even if not always examined directly. Most of the political sociology developed by Chicago sociologists focused not so much on political institutions as on policy studies.

Social Policy and Social Problems

Sociology at the University of Chicago and the social problems of the city of Chicago were inextricably intertwined from the founding of the department in 1892.[136] The strong ties of Chicago social scientists to reform groups, which influenced so much of their early work, is well documented (see e.g. Tolman 1902; Bulmer 1980; Short 1971; Diner 1975; Faris 1967; Friedrichs 1970; Farberman 1979; Hunter 1980; Coser 1978; Hughes 1964, 1979; Deegan and Burger 1981). Small set the stage from the beginning by combining his concern for social reform, rooted in the Social Gospel, with an interest in the possibilities of sociological research. House (1954) contended that "what stands out more than anything else in [Small's work] is his lifelong concern with the practical and ethical guidance for individuals and societies that might be drawn from sociological inquiry" (cf. Hayes 1927). Small was influenced by the Verein fur Sozialpolitik and believed that sociological research could aid governmental and voluntary agencies in the improvement of society (Diner 1975, p. 523). Similarly, Ellwood (see Jensen 1947) and Henderson (see Queen 1951) were not only involved in research on social problems, but were engaged in social reform activities themselves (Diner 1975).

A number of University of Chicago faculty and administrators were active in the progressive movement in Chicago from the university's earliest days, including William Rainey Harper, who chaired the education committee of the Civic Federation, was a member of the Chicago Board of Education, and headed a commission to study the Chicago public schools. His successor, Harry Pratt Judson, avoided spending too much time on extrauniversity affairs but lent his name to many progressive causes (Diner 1975, p. 522). Similarly, Thomas "never segregated his intellectual interests from his social concerns" (Janowitz 1966, p. xxiv), and the work directed by Park and Burgess was continually oriented toward insight into social problems (see, e.g., Burgess 1961, Hughes 1944, 1955; Steiner 1930).

Of particular importance was the tie between the university and the settlement movement (Addams 1910; Taylor 1930; McDowell 1901). Dewey's work was much influenced by his relation to Addams and Hull House (Mills 1966, pp. 307–24; Daniel Levine 1971), and he was actively involved in Hull House affairs during his time in Chicago (Addams 1929; Brickman 1970; Dykuizen 1973; Frankel 1968; McCaul 1959).[137] Although not as actively involved in Hull House activities as Dewey, Mead maintained a relationship with that group[138] as well as other reform groups such as the City Club (Leavitt 1912; cf. Deegan and Burger 1981; Chasin 1964; Tufts 1931; Petras 1968a; Schwendinger and Schwendinger 1974; Campbell 1981; Batiuk and Sacks 1981).

Burgess lived at Hull House for a period (Hughes 1979a, p. 182), as did Zueblin (Deegan 1981, p. 18). Small published a number of Addams's papers in the *AJS*, and in 1913 asked if she would be interested in a half-time appointment in sociology (Diner 1975, p. 536). In addition to her activism, for which she received a Nobel Peace Prize in 1931, she was a social theorist of considerable talent.[139] As already mentioned above, the work by Addams, Abbott, and Breckenridge was extremely influential in the formation of urban research and the human ecology perspective, although many of the details of the connection have yet to be investigated (see Addams 1895; Deegan 1978b, 1981). There was a strong network linking the Chicago sociologists, the Hull House group, and the university's School of Civics and Philanthropy , which in 1920 became the School of Social Service Administration (Bernard 1964). As Deegan (1978b) has demonstrated, there was a network of outstanding women who tied the three institutional entities together.[140]

Maclean received her Ph.D. from the Sociology Department in 1900 and had various jobs within the department off and on from 1900 to 1937, including a position as "Extension Assistant Professor of Sociology" from 1900 until the School of Social Service Administration was founded (see Maclean 1923). McDowell was head of the University of Chicago Settlement House (1903–33), which was an integral part of the graduate program at Chicago (see Tolman 1902).[141] Edith Abbott taught sociology at the University from 1914 to 1920, although she was never promoted to assistant professor and remained a "lecturer in Methods of Social Investigation." Eventually she became dean of the School of Social Service Administration, but maintained her ties with some of the Chicago sociologists, especially through the Local Community Research Committee. Both Abbott and Sophonisba Breckenridge lived at Hull House from 1908 to 1920, and Abbott returned to live there from 1949 to 1953.[142] Breckenridge was influential in introducing the case method to students in the School of Social Service Administration (see Wright 1948, p. 448). Finally, Marion Talbot taught "Sanitary Science" in the early sociology department, although it was later placed in a separate department of household administration (Talbot 1936, pp. 2–5; Diner 1975, p. 538). She had a doctorate in law and was interested in sanitation as an aspect of social progress. In addition to McDowell, Abbott, MacLean, Breckenridge, and Talbot, the Chicago sociologists had other links to the profession of social work. Taylor, who taught in the department as a part-time instructor from 1902 to 1906 (Wade 1964; Taylor 1930, 1936), founded the Chicago Commons as an institution for the training of social workers (Taylor 1936).

Henderson was the only sociologist who was president of the National Conference of Social Workers (Odum 1951a, p. 71; cf. Henderson 1971). A number of social workers found the Chicago community studies valuable, and Burgess and others maintained active ties with the developing profession (see Bowman 1930; Burgess 1930b; Street 1930; Breckenridge and White 1929).

Chicago sociologists, however, tended to be quite critical of what they thought were temporary reforms (Janowitz 1967a), and an increased emphasis on objectivity in research during the twenties moved them away from more practical solutions and from the social workers. According to R. Faris, "Park was probably the only one who directly attacked the humanitarian attitude when it appeared among sociologists. More than once he drove students to anger or tears by growling such reproofs as, 'You're another one of those damn do-gooders'" (Faris 1967, p. 35). Park's criticism of reformers is probably a consequence both of his aversion to simple-minded reform and a defensive reaction against tendencies to associate sociology with social work and degrade its status as a science.

Chicago sociologists maintained their interest in social problems, however, and in political solutions to them. Wirth participated actively in the examination of policy issues and worked with governmental agencies (see Braude 1970; Burgess 1952; Hauser 1956). Ogburn and Merriam participated in Hoover's President's Committee on Social Trends (Chambers 1963, pp. 243–45), and William C. Bradbury, who taught at Chicago from 1941 until 1958, did research for governmental agencies (Hauser 1959a).

A major reason for the participation of a number of Chicago sociologists, especially Ogburn and Hauser, in research for governmental agencies was their use of research techniques which those agencies found useful. Research techniques developed or refined at Chicago are the topic of the next chapter.

5

METHODS OF RESEARCH

The thread that runs through virtually all Chicago sociology after Thomas is empirical investigation, much of it marked by large-scale research combined with intense involvement with the subject matter (Shils 1948). "To the extent that there existed a Chicago school," Janowitz writes, "its identifying feature was an empirical approach to the study of the totality of society" (1966, p. viii).

From the mapping of neighborhoods (Burgess and Bogue 1964; Jonassen 1949; Wright 1954; Deegan 1978b), to ethnographic field studies (Park 1937; Palmer 1928; P. Young 1944), to the development of quantitative research methods (Bulmer 1980; Lundberg 1960; Lazarsfeld 1962b), the methods used by Chicago sociologists were grounded in the pragmatic principle of the application of science to solve problems. Although Chicago methods were rooted in early efforts by Small and Henderson to develop a program of empirical research (see Lazarsfeld 1962), it was Thomas and Znaniecki's classic study *The Polish Peasant* that established the general style of research at Chicago.

I. *The Polish Peasant*

Thomas and Znaniecki's *Polish Peasant* (1918–19) marks an epoch in the development of sociological thought and research in the U.S., signaling a shift from a speculative to a research base (House 1934, pp. 283–90; cf. Burgess 1956b; Redfield 1945, 1948; K. Young 1948; cf. Bulmer 1982a). The massive 2,244-page work contains an elaborate store of detailed information on peasant life and social organization in Europe and the United States, innumerable theoretical insights, and a significant "Methodological Note" (W. Thomas 1966, pp. 257–88).

The Polish Peasant became the model for sociological research at Chicago, particularly in terms of its intimate connection between theory and the large-scale collection of data. According to Janowitz, Thomas was reluctant to write the Methodological Note, which was initiated by Znaniecki who wanted to include an explicit statement of their methodology.

The Social Science Research Council, judging it to be the most important contribution to American sociology, commissioned Blumer to develop an extensive critique of *The Polish Peasant*. In his comments on the work, Blumer (1939b) argues that it is unsuccessful in providing general propositions that could be established by the particular facts adduced. Instead, it should be viewed not as a monograph on Polish peasant society, but as a basis for scientific social research and theory based on four considerations: (1) the desire to construct an approach adapted to the character of life in a complex civilized society; (2) the need for an approach that fits the unique character of change or interaction in human social life; (3) the need to devise means of discerning the "subjective factor" and to study it in interaction with objective factors; and (4) the need for a theoretical framework in order to study social life.[143]

In addition to a discussion of the importance of empirical investigations which use large masses of data, there is considerable examination of problems in verifying or validating theoretical propositions formulated to explain social phenomena. Of particular interest is a critique by Stouffer (Bain et al. 1939, pp. 167–70), who discusses the advantage of broader nonpsychological approaches. Janowitz claims that the discussion "seemed to approach *The Polish Peasant* in narrow epistemological terms with little regard for its substantive issues," although "few sociological volumes . . . could bear the weight of such repeated critiques" (1966, p. xlvii).

Much of the earlier discussion has subsided, but there are occasional revivals of interest in *The Polish Peasant*. John Thomas (1950), for example, criticizes Thomas and Znaniecki's predictions of marital instability among American Poles. Evan Thomas (1978) discusses Blumer's critique and the panel discussion that followed, noting that at the time most sociologists were skeptical of the value of personal document research, whereas in recent years there has been renewed interest in that method as an approach to the study of the subjective meaning of concrete social life. The examination of personal documents and life histories was a major methodology used by Chicago sociologists. Those examinations were combined with participant observation techniques and case studies to provide the empirical base for many of the early Chicago studies.

II. Life Histories, Personal Documents, Case Studies, and Participant Observation

Burgess (1948) recalls that most courses in the Chicago department used to some degree the personal documents approach developed by Thomas. For Thomas, "personal life-records, as complete as possible, constitute the *perfect* type of sociological material" (Thomas and Znaniecki 1918–19, p. 12). Thomas and Znaniecki made extensive use of personal documents in *The Polish Peasant*, and Thomas included extended quotations from them in much of his writing.[144] Case studies, life histories, and personal documents were employed by Shaw (Becker 1966; Rice 1931), Thrasher (Burgess 1930a), and many other authors of the Chicago monographs. Between 1920 and 1940, personal documents were examined in significant studies by Frazier, Johnson, Burgess, Cavan, Pauline Young, Zorbaugh, Sutherland, Mowrer, and others (Angell 1945), often in conjunction with participant observation (Lohman 1937).

As one might expect, methodological debates were often quite heated. As statistical techniques were developed, questions were raised about the use of personal documents (Redfield 1945; Gottschalk, Kluckhohn, and Angel 1945). R. Faris (1967, pp. 114ff.) reports that there was considerable debate in the late 1920s concerning the relative merits of statistical and case study methods. Whereas Burgess and Blumer defended the case study method, Ogburn, his student Thomas C. McCormick, and Stouffer argued in favor of the superiority of statistical methods. In 1934, House examined techniques developed by Chapin, Bogardus, Thurstone and Rice, suggesting that it is doubtful whether their efforts to obtain knowledge through quantitative techniques (especially in the study of attitudes) can be fruitful except under certain favorable conditions. Chapin (1935) responded that whereas, in sociology, word symbols are used as means of description, in physics, numerical symbols are more widely used. Concepts such as attitudes, social distance, and social status, he argued, are not intrinsically more complex concepts than such physical concepts as the molecule, atom, or electron, and numerical symbols of description would allow the sociologist to be more precise. Bain (1935) also took issue with House, forecasting a gradual development from case studies to the use of statistical methods, as a large number of cases were studied.

Something of a compromise was accomplished, however, at least temporarily within the department, and both quantitative and qualitative techniques often went hand in hand. In 1928, for example, Burgess attended Ogburn's statistics courses and began to use statistical methods in his work (R. Faris 1967, p. 114). Stouffer's dissertation (1930) called into question arguments about the relative merits of statistical and case study methods by having a large sample of students both write life histories and fill out an attitudinal survey. There was considerable agreement between the conclusions drawn in each study, suggesting, as R. Faris (1967, p. 115) put it, that "as far as the scale score was concerned, nothing was gained by the far more lengthy and a laborious process of writing and judging a life history." Ogburn spoke favorably of the importance of case studies in providing hypotheses for further research and testing by other means. Faris suggested that within the Chicago department "the two approaches became complementary rather than rival" (p. 115). The debate was far from over, despite the efforts to see them as complementary. W. I. Thomas (1939) insisted that the case study methods continued to be valid. In responding to critiques of *The Polish Peasant*, he argued that his and Znaniecki's lack of statistical methods and controls was a defect of their method and materials, and yet "it is evident that statistical studies of the behavior of populations will have a limited meaning so long as the statistical data are not supplemented by individual case histories" (cf. K. Young 1924).

The development of quantitative methods at Chicago was quite significant, however, despite the current tendency to identify the Chicago school with so-called "qualitative methods."[145]

III. Quantitative Research Methods

Martin Bulmer (1981b) argues that the generalized image of the Chicago department does not reflect the richness and range of methods in Chicago sociology. Especially neglected are the developments of quantitative techniques of research initiated by Burgess, Ogburn, Thurstone, Stouffer, Merriam, Gosnell, Wooddy, White, Field, Palmer, and others.

In addition to the Hull House neighborhood studies of the 1890s, one of the earliest social surveys conducted in the United States was conducted by the Chicago Commission on Race Relations (see above). Johnson and other Chicago graduate students and their assistants combined interviews of 274 black families with census data, responses from questionnaires sent to 850 employees in the city, and other data (Bulmer 1981a; Waskow 1967; Philpott 1978).

Quantitative techniques were later developed along interdisciplinary lines, primarily under the auspices of the Local Community Research Committee (Bulmer 1981b; Gosnell 1929). There were, in fact, some jurisdictional disputes over the teaching of statistical methods within the university.[146] Ogburn taught the first statistics courses in the sociology department and inspired a number of students, including Stouffer (R. Faris 1967, p. 114; cf. H. Hughes 1959; Hauser 1959; Lundberg 1960; Nimkoff 1959; Rice 1951).

Thurstone, with his work on attitude scales, represented the most important influence from outside the sociology department (Fleming 1967). Thurstone, who was influenced by Mead as a graduate student (Thurstone 1952),[147] had a considerable impact on sociologists at Chicago. Although his work was certainly not without its critics,[148] he influenced a number of sociologists, including Burgess, who generally sided with the qualitative school in debates about methodology (Bogue 1974, p. xix; cf. Rice 1951). Leonard Cottrell recounts studying multiple factor analysis under Thurstone and explaining it to Burgess, leading to Cottrell and Burgess's application of the method to sociological data in their study of the family.[149] Another force in the development of quantitative techniques of research was Stouffer, who was a graduate student in the department (Bulmer 1981b; cf. Hauser 1961; Smith 1968). After taking all of the statistics available to him at Chicago, Stouffer went to study with R. A. Fisher and Karl Pearson for a year in England, and later returned to teach in the Chicago department (R. Faris 1967, p. 114).[150] Stouffer went on to become the director of the Harvard Laboratory of Social Relations, and made a number of significant contributions, the most notable of which was *The American Soldier* (Stouffer et al. 1949a, 1949b).[151] The development of an eclectic set of research techniques was an important part of the overall effort at Chicago to institutionalize sociology as a field of inquiry.

6

SOCIAL CHANGE AND COLLECTIVE BEHAVIOR

> Thomas' and Park's respective approaches to the problems of society were rooted in their theories of social change. These, in turn, were themselves deeply intertwined with contemporary affairs and how these men responded to them: to the patterns of massive immigration, the increasing conflict of labor-capital, the rapid urbanization, and the widening scope of war. (Fisher and Strauss 1978b, p. 6)

Because the study of social problems and social reform was such a major agenda item for Chicago sociology, processes of social change became important topics for investigation at the University of Chicago. For W. I. Thomas, "the task of social theory was to account for social change in developmental terms" (Janowitz 1966, pp. xxi–xxii, xxxii).[152] In addition to the basic direction of social theories laid down by Thomas and Park, it is also important to examine Park's work on collective behavior, and Ogburn's theory of "cultural lag."

I. Thomas and Park on Social Change

The most comprehensive discussion of social change within the Chicago tradition is that of Fisher and Strauss (1978a, 1978b).[153] They divide their discussion into four topics: the *prospect* of social reform; the role of *science* in social reform; the *agents* of change; and the *mode* of social change (1978a, 1978b, p. 6). A general theory of progress underlies all of Thomas's work, they argue,[154] in a world in which disorganization, reorganization, and integration of shifting groups poses the major problem. The progress of less advanced groups, while based on force, could result from such factors as economic emancipation and education (p. 7).

Park switches "back and forth between images of inevitable collision and images of cohesion and liberty" (p. 10). His notion of progress contains three elements: an evolutionary outlook stressing competition and conflict,[155] a concern for communication and the possibility of understanding and consensus derived from Dewey; and an element from James that acknowledges an emancipation made possible by sheer awareness, which overcomes what James calls "a certain blindness" in human beings (pp. 8–9). Park's position on the possibility "of social reform reflects a highly muted and qualified optimism" (p. 9).

Both Thomas and Park emphasize "the development of knowledgeable, rational control over social behavior" (p. 10), with which sociology could be useful, although Fisher and Strauss argue that Park's image of sociology is less utopian than Thomas's (p. 11). Neither of them, however, hold a simple concept of sociology's usefulness (p. 12). Because change requires transformations of values, institutions, and attitudes, Thomas identifies an educated elite as the primary agent of social change. Park, too, affirms the importance of leadership, but is more skeptical about the role of social movements in bringing about reform. For Thomas, social change occurs as a consequence of two mechanisms—education and institution-building. Park, on the other hand, emphasizes the historical appropriateness for different mechanisms of social change. Because of differences of emphasis in their theories of social change, Fisher and Strauss argue (pp. 17ff.), Thomas and Park precipitated two relatively different strands of the Chicago tradition, in terms of theories of social change, despite a complex interweaving of their careers and ideas. Burgess and Janowitz, they suggest, are successors to Thomas's general approach, whereas Blumer and Hughes are more oriented toward Park's work. Becker, on the other hand, has combined aspects of both strands of the Chicago tradition.

Another significant aspect of Park's contribution to the social change literature is his theory of collective behavior (see Hughes 1955).

II. Park on Collective Behavior and Social Change

Robert Park's interest in collective behavior as an aspect of social change can be seen in his doctoral dissertation "The Crowd and the Public" (1904; cf. Levine 1972).

The general character of the work "was inspired by Simmel's conception of sociology as the science of social forms" (Levine 1952, p. xxvii). As Turner (1967, p. xli) indicates, "Park named the field and identified the major forms and process of collective behavior in much the fashion that prevails today." [156] Park was the first scholar to establish a distinctively sociological approach to analyzing social movements; the central concern of students of collective behavior, he argues, should be the way in which such phenomena function as an integral part of the normal operation of society (Turner 1967). Park, and the Chicago sociologists inspired by him, reject commonsense assumptions that collective behavior is something aberrant or atypical, i.e., that is different from normal social processes. Collective behavior, nonetheless, does modify existing institutional arrangements. The crowd and the public, for example, are two fundamental categories of change-inducing behavior, and that idea of collective behavior has remained central to the concept as it is currently conceived (Elsner 1972, p. xi).

The study of collective behavior is closely linked to the study of social movements, as the crowd and the public are forms of association which "bring individuals out of their existing bonds and into new ones" (Levine 1972, p. xxx). The sect, the mass movement, and revolution are all mentioned in passing in "The Crowd and the Public", with Park observing that "all great mass movements tend to display, to a greater or less extent, the characteristics that Le Bon attributes to crowds" (1904, p. 871; Elsner 1972, p. xii). Shils (1981, p. 188) recalls that Park included considerable discussion of social movements in his course on collective behavior at Chicago. "The Crowd and the Public" presents two contrasting aspects of collective behavior, and two differing explanations of the phenomenon. On the one hand is the crowd, which is spontaneous, short-lived, and ephemeral; it is a group "without tradition." The public, on the other hand, although also without a past, "is the polar opposite in its recognition of individual differences in value and interest, in its engaging in rational discussion and debate, and in arriving at a consensus which does not impose unanimity on its members" (Elsner 1972, p. xiv). Thus, although Park's explanation of the crowd focuses on internal factors such as suggestibility and imitation,[157] the public is a consequence of external factors, or social forces. Thus, "Park's inclusion of the public within the category of change-inducing groups radically altered the thrust of their tradition, for an irrational mechanism of change is now balanced by a mechanism that is rational and reasonable" (Elsner 1972, p. xv). His theory of social change therefore combines "the individualistic approach of political economy with the collectivistic approach of group psychology" (Levine 1972, p. xxviii).

The major purpose of the study of collective behavior, for Park, is to identify processes of disorganization and reorganization. Social unrest "represents at once a breaking up of the established routine and a preparation for new collective action" (Park and Burgess 1924, p. 866; Turner 1967, p. xlii). "In identifying collective behavior as a normal operation of society," Turner (1967, p. xli) argues, "Park was in tune with trends which developed much later." A number of Park's students carried out work on collective behavior, incorporating his insights (R. Faris 1967, p. 106), including Blumer (1939a), Turner and Killian (1957) and Lang and Lang (1953).

III. Ogburn's "Cultural Lag" Concept

Ogburn's notion of "cultural lag" is firmly established in the current sociological vocabulary.[158] Ogburn argued, in *Social Change: With Respect to Culture and Original Nature*, (1922; cf. R. Faris 1967, p. 115ff), that material aspects of culture tend to change more swiftly and with less stress than nonmaterial culture. Those differential rates of change precipitate social problems. The concept and its application by Ogburn (see especially Ogburn 1933) has received considerable attention from critics and admirers alike.[159] It has been used by a number of scholars to explain aspects of social disorganization, although not without some controversy.[160] Even those who appreciate Ogburn's theory sometimes caution against ignorance of the subjective aspects of its application, especially with reference to changes one wishes to occur (cf. Woodard 1934, 1936).

Others find the concept fruitful, however, such as Choukas (1936), who attempts to formulate an explicit, systematic outline of the concept and its relationship to fundamental sociological principles. Herman (1937) answers the concept's critics, and Huff (1973) examines Ogburn's work in terms of its usefulness for studying scientific advances through conceptual innovation.

7

THE INSTITUTIONALIZATION OF SOCIOLOGY

The history of sociology in America, according to Coser, from the First World War to the mid-1930s, can be written largely as the history of the Chicago department (1978, pp. 311–12). Although not the first sociology department, the Chicago department represents the first major effort to institutionalize the discipline (cf. Shils 1970, p. 770). A number of reasons have been given for the success of the Chicago department in that effort. The resources of the university were essential, including the grants from the Rockefellers, the general intellectual climate, and interdisciplinary fertilization of the university.[161] It was more than that, however, because the sociologists at Chicago were more productive than other departments at the university during the 1920s and 1930s (Reeves et al. 1933). Those resources were combined with a set of creative individuals, notably Small, Thomas, and Park, who were able to take advantage of the unusual opportunities available to them.

Clearly, Albion Small's leadership was crucial.[162] R. Faris argues that

> probably the most important factor in the growth at Chicago was the intelligent perception by Small, accepted enthusiastically by his colleagues and successors, of the inhibiting consequences of doctrines, schools of thought, and authoritative leaders. Unlike Small's leading rivals who were confident that they had the right basic principles for a sociology and who sought to convert disciples in order to perpetuate through them competition with conflicting doctrines, the Chicago faculty renounced the principle of authority and encouraged open, modest searching in the spirit of an inductive science. (1967, p. 128)

Small's administrative skill was coupled with the intellectual skill of Thomas (Park 1939) and Park (Shils 1970, pp. 771ff.; Hughes 1979a). Oberschall (1972) emphasizes Park's ability to motivate others and to help them with their work, organizing research around an integrated series of research projects on the same topics—urban sociology, ecology, and the contemporary Chicago scene. Certainly the location of the department in Chicago at a time of rapid social change was of critical importance—the subject matter immediately available was of dramatic inherent interest. Madge (1962) attributes the fame of the Chicago school to its characteristic approach and a highly developed interest in the real world. Certainly the world of ethnic immigrant neighborhoods, taxi dance halls, hoboes, gangs, high finance, and the infamous Chicago underworld provided plenty of motivation for anyone with a sense of sociological imagination.

The Chicago department was founded after the department at Brown and only a year before the one at Columbia. Yet the rigorous research program developed by Chicago sociologists, combined with a graduate teaching program that emphasized empirical investigation, shaped the direction of the discipline (cf. Burgess 1956b; Shils 1970).

I. The Graduate Program

With the department's early lead in the field established, the graduate program became the training ground for much of the country's sociological leadership. For many years, the sociology at nearly every important state university in the Midwest and Far West was Chicago sociology (Shils 1970, p. 792). Chicago students played key roles in various departments and in the discipline as a whole. More than half of the presidents of the American Sociological Association from its founding until 1971 were faculty or students at Chicago:

1913 Small	1933 Reuter	1952 D. S. Thomas
1914 Small	1934 Burgess	1953 Stouffer
1916 Vincent	1935 Chapin	1954 Znaniecki
1921 Hayes	1937 E. Faris	1955 D. Young
1924 Ellwood	1939 Sutherland	1956 Blumer
1925 Park	1941 Queen	1960 Becker
1927 Thomas	1942 Sanderson	1961 R. Faris
1928 Gillette	1945 K. Young	1963 E. C. Hughes

1929 Ogburn	1947 Wirth	1968 Hauser
1931 Bogardus	1948 Frazier	1970 Turner
1932 Bernard	1950 Cottrell	1971 Bendix

A number of Chicago students played an important role in other universities, including Blumer at Berkeley; Reuter at Iowa (Hart 1946); H. P. Becker at Wisconsin (Hartung 1960; Barnes 1960); Watson at Southern Methodist University (King and Pringle 1969); Vincent at Minnesota; Rosenquist (King and Pringle 1969) and Gettys at Texas; Steiner at North Carolina and Washington (Schmid 1963; Brooks 1963); Bernard at Washington University (Barnes 1968c; Odum 1951c); Johnson at Fisk (Burgess 1956a; Robbins 1974; C. U. Smith 1972; Valien 1958, 1968); Frazier at Howard (Edwards 1962, 1968); McKenzie at Washington (Hawley 1968b; R. Faris 1967); and Ellwood at Missouri and Duke (Cramblitt 1964; Barnes 1968b). R. Faris (1967, p. 124) also mentions Krueger at Vanderbilt, Reckless at Ohio, Sutherland at Indiana, Cottrell at Cornell, Dawson at McGill, and Lind at Hawaii. Ralph Turner, at the University of California at Los Angeles, has been a key figure in the development of symbolic interactionism.

Thomas's collaborator, Znaniecki, was influential in the development of Polish sociology, founding the Sociological Institute at the university in Poznan (Chalasinski 1968); and Nock (1974) claims that Chicago sociology had considerable impact on the development of Canadian sociology. Teaching was considered an important factor of the Chicago program, not only in the classroom, but also as part of the research process. Students and faculty felt themselves to be engaged in a common enterprise (Park 1941).

Park and Burgess's *Introduction to the Science of Sociology* quickly became a standard text for the teaching of sociology courses throughout the country. Often referred to as the "Green Bible," the text helped to establish the contours of the discipline. A far cry from today's simplistic introductory texts, Park and Burgess's work included meaty selections from Simmel, Durkheim, Hobhouse, Bacon, Rousseau, Adam Smith, Spencer, Comte, Bergson and others.[163] Janowitz (1969) observes that they fused sociology into the classical problems of social philosophy, focusing on a set of process categories—competition, conflict, and accommodation—all of which are elements of social control. Braude (1971) suggests that the text defined sociology as an interactionist, spatial discipline, concerned with both order and change, and directed to the testing of propositions about human social life, as distinct from developing all-embracing explanatory schemes. Park and Burgess suggest in their preface that "the first thing that students in sociology need to learn is to observe and record their own observations" (1924, p. v).

II. The American Journal of Sociology

The most successful students in the Chicago department were rewarded with publication in the *AJS* or with a book in the Chicago Sociology Series (Shils 1948). The founding of the *AJS* in 1895 was a major coup for the Chicago department.[164] Not only was it the first journal of sociology created anywhere,[165] it was the official organ of the American Sociological Society (now the American Sociological Association).

The *Journal* provided a forum for the dissemination of work being carried out at Chicago, making their work visible throughout the country. It also gave the Chicago faculty a prominent position in forging the shape of American sociology (Friedrichs 1970; E. C. Hughes 1979b; H. M. Hughes 1973; Schwendinger and Schwendinger 1974; Shanas 1945; Wirth 1947 and in establishing the boundaries and subject matter of the discipline (see Kuklick 1980).

III. The End of the Chicago Dominance

Coser (1976) dates the end of the Chicago dominance with the "American Sociological Society rebellion" of 1935. The Chicago department maintained considerable continuity, however, until about 1950. As Faris (1967, p. 123) points out, the faculty who succeeded Small, Henderson, Vincent, and Thomas remained intact until about the time of Park's retirement in 1934. Faris retired in 1939 and Burgess and Ogburn in 1951; Wirth died in 1952.

The rapid spread of sociology departments throughout the country meant that by the mid-thirties Chicago no longer had a substantial edge in terms of sheer numbers. More importantly, there was growing resentment in many quarters of the department's hegemony in the discipline. Much of the discontent was symbolized by objections to having the American Sociological Society's official journal (the *AJS*) based in, and largely controlled by, Chicago. Lengermann (1979) provides a detailed account of the rebellion, arguing that it was precipitated by the interaction of five factors: various long-standing personal animosities, professional expansion, changes within the Chicago department, criticisms of the increasing use of quantitative research techniques, and the unsettling consequences of the Great Depression.[166] A major consequence of the rebellion was the formation of the *American Sociological Review* as the official journal of the society. Although some changes ensued, it is questionable as to how much impact was made on the role of Chicago sociologists. Chicago sociologists continued to be very active in the society,[167] and in the *ASR*.[168] Ironically, despite the initial reasons for the rebellion, the *ASR* developed a stronger emphasis than the *AJS* on the positivistic side of sociological research.

Chicago influences on sociology remain ubiquitous, especially in such fields as social psychology, urban and community studies, race and ethnic studies, crime and deviance, public opinion and communication, and political sociology. The *AJS* remains one of the two major journals in the field, and the ideas of Thomas, Mead, Park, and Burgess continue to make their mark. Intellectual advances are made not only as a consequence of positive contributions, but also *via negativa*. Chicago sociologists advanced the field of sociology not only by means of their contributions, which are remarkable in themselves, but also through the debates and controversies they engendered.

The Chicago school reminds us of a rich sociological tradition that contrasts sharply, in many ways, with present-day sociology. Although many of its ideas and methods are better left on the historical shelf, there is still much to be learned from the Chicago sociologists. Of particular value is their affirmation of the dialectical relations between individual and society, thought and action, theory and empirical research, large-scale data analysis and "on-the-hoof" examinations of everyday human life. The contributions of Chicago sociology have yet to be exhausted, and the sociological traditions initiated by Thomas and Small, Park and Burgess, Dewey, Mead, and Veblen, Blumer and Hughes, and Ogburn and Stouffer are served as much by continuing debate as by praise.

NOTES

[1]I use the term "Chicago school" throughout this volume with some hesitation. Although it is a convenient, frequently employed term, the reader should not assume that it indicates a monolithic, homogeneous tradition. Like all "schools" of thought, the Chicago school evaporates under close inspection.

[2]Much of the history and critical analyses of Chicago sociology are to be found in introductions to various volumes of the Heritage of Sociology Series of the University of Chicago Press, edited by Morris Janowitz. Even the broadest effort to develop a history of the department, Robert E. L. Faris's *Chicago Sociology* (1967), focuses on a short period of the department's history, 1920–1932.

[3]In the following year, the department suffered a series of major personnel losses (cf. Janowitz 1967, p. x). Burgess retired in 1951 and Wirth died in 1952, the same year that Blumer moved to Berkeley. Thus, 1950 is the end point for this study although some research falls into other time periods.

[4]The most comprehensive treatment of the early history of the department is Diner (1975). Howerth, Raymond, Zueblin, Bedford, and Rainwater were not central figures in the department and had relatively short tenures.

[5]For further information on Small consult biographies by Christakes (1978), Dibble (1975), House's (1926) bibliography of his writings, and Becker (1971), and Wirth (1934).

[6]See J. Bernard (1929) and Burgess (1948). The most thorough discussions of Thomas's contributions are contained in Volkart (1951) and Janowitz (1966); as well as a concise treatment by Coser (1977). Janowitz's discussion is particularly helpful in that he provides a succinct summary of Thomas's intellectual development and impact as well as an outline of his work.

[7]For a bibliography of Thomas's writings, see Hare (1951); and Janowitz (1966).

[8]Although the charges were eventually thrown out of court, Thomas was arrested by the Federal Bureau of Investigation for an alleged violation of the Mann act. Although the circumstances remain unclear, some have suggested that the arrest was an effort to discredit Thomas's wife, who was involved in Henry Ford's peace movement (See Janowitz 1966, p. xiv; Volkart 1951, p. 323).

[9]Two recent biographies provide helpful overviews of Park's life and work, Matthews (1977) and Raushenbush (1979); cf. Hughes (1979a, 1979b).

[10]Courses by Dewey, Mead, and Veblen were listed in a description of Sociology Department course offerings (Tolman 1902).

[11]Park studied under Dewey as an undergraduate at Michigan. So much has been written about both Dewey and Mead that it is difficult to know where to begin. For Dewey, perhaps the best source on his Chicago period is Coughlan (1976). Also consult the comprehensive reference works by Boydston with Andersen (1969) and Boydston and Poulos (1974). Blumer's classic, but controversial, article "Sociological Implications of the Thought of George Herbert Mead" (1966) is an important statement of the Chicago school of symbolic interactionism, but should now be read alongside the numerous critiques of his interpretation, such as Lewis and Smith (1980). A lucid treatment of his work from a more philosophical point of view is Miller (1973), which can be supplemented with Corti's edited volume (1973), which contains an extensive bibliography, including reviews of Mead's work (Broyer 1973). Other valuable sources include H. C. Mead's biographical sketch (1931), and introductions to volumes of Mead's work by Strauss (1964), Moore (1936), and C. Morris (1934, 1938).

[12]See also Morton White (1947), who argues that Dewey, Veblen, and Holmes were united in a common revolt against formalism in American social thought.

[13]One indicator of Veblen's broad influence is an anthology edited by Malcom Cowley, *Books That Changed Our Mind* (1938). Cowley and the *New Republic* editors asked several leading American intellectuals to cite non-fiction authors and books that had produced the greatest "jolt" in their own thinking and writing. Veblen came in first, with 16 mentions, followed by Charles Beard (11), John Dewey (10), Sigmund Freud (9), Oswald Spengler and Alfred North Whitehead (7 each), and V. I. Lenin and I. A. Richards (6 each) (Diggins 1978, p. 216). For discussion of Veblen's relatively negative reception among sociologists, such as Parsons and Bell, see Diggins (1978, pp. 220ff.).

[14]Actually, Burgess's estimate was too late—the Hull House Papers (1889) contained results of similar research done much earlier.

[15]Cf. Mead (1917); Ratner (1951); Russell (1945); and Shils (1963). There is some debate about Hegel's influence, especially on Dewey, who was trying to escape Hegelianism, as was James. Thayer (1968), Bowers (1944), and others have argued that Hegel was important, however. Miller (1973, p. xxi) has argued that "we should not be led to believe that Mead (and Dewey for that matter) was not affected by Hegel," especially because of the importance of the dialectical process in their work. That is not to say, however, that Mead was Hegelian. He later noted that "the supreme test of any present-day philosophy of history must be found in its interpretation of experimental science, the great tool of human progress, and here Hegel's philosophy was an almost ridiculous failure" (Mead 1938, p. 505); quoted in Miller 1973b, p. xxi). Hook (1939) suggests that Mead "never made up his mind about the value of the Hegelian logic."

[16]Mead claims that pragmatism has two great figures: James and Dewey. "Back of the work of both lies the common assumption of the testing of the truth of an idea, of a hypothesis, by its actual working" (Mead 1936, p. 344).

[17]Feibleman (1945), for example, claims that Dewey was much influenced by James. M. White (1957, pp. 142–46), however, indicates a number of differences between James and Dewey.

[18]See, e.g., Miller (1973); Murphy (1939); Scheffler (1974); Van Wesep (1960); Pfeutze

(1954); Stevens (1967); Tremmel (1957); Troyer (1946); and Victoroff (1952, 1953). The social aspect of pragmatism also appealed to Durkheim, who undertook a serious study of Dewey's thought (see Deledalle 1959); Stone and Farberman (1967) argue that Durkheim was moving toward a symbolic interactionist perspective before his death (cf. Choy 1926).

[19] Santayana (1953), for example, has suggested that Dewey "genuinely represents the mind of the vast mass of native, sanguine, enterprising Americans."

[20] See, e.g., Blumer 1939; Bain et al. 1939; Burgess 1956b; Park 1931, 1939; Kolb 1957; Volkart 1968; House 1936.

[21] "The major vice of American sociology," Shils wrote in 1948, "turns out, thus, to take the obverse side of its chief and distinguishing virtue; its hitherto predominant indifference to the formation of a general theory is closely conncected with its eagerness for precision in first-hand observation" (1948, p. 56).

[22] Although Odum (1951a) and Hinkle and Hinkle (1954) both claimed that Ellwood was a clergyman, Jensen (1957a) claims that Ellwood had no professional experience or employment as a clergyman. Graham Taylor, who taught part-time in the department from 1902 to 1906 and was active in civic affairs and a colleague of Jane Addams, was a professor at the Chicago Theological Seminary (Taylor 1930; Wade 1964).

[23] "It only seemed so," Hughes wrote, "to people who were used to drinking their theory in straight philosophical draughts, unmixed with the empirical juices of life" (Hughes 1956, p. 255).

[24] See, e.g., Small's article on "The Sociology of Profit" (*AJS* 30:439–61); cf. D. Smith 1965).

[25] See Small's articles in the *AJS* such as his 1895 "Private Business is a Public Trust" (pp. 276–89). According to Janowitz, Small, "coming from a religious background, preached against the sins of capitalism in a polysyllabic langauge" (1966, p. liii). Cf. Barnes (1948); Carey (1975, p. 57); Farberman (1979, p. 5); Page (1940).

[26] See *AJS* (1895). The same issue of the *Journal*, as the editorial pointed out, carried an article by Bemis, who had been fired from the university allegedly for being anticapitalist, a controversy mentioned by the outraged letter-writer. (Cf. Schwendinger and Schwendinger 1974)

[27] The discussion on Simmel that follows relies heavily upon Levine, Carter, and Gorman (1976). As Morris Janowitz has suggested, Simmel's writings "articulated with the orientation of American sociologists of the pragmatic persuasion" (1975, p. 91). The pragmatic philosophers recognized Simmel's contributions and Santayana wrote to James about Simmel in the late 1880s.

[28] "To call the sociologists 'back to Simmel,' as Drs. Park and Spykman do, means to call them back to a pure speculation, metaphysics, and a lack of scientific method" (Sorokin 1928, p. 502); cf. Levine, Carter and Gorman (1976, p. 817).

[29] An organization of sociology students and faculty founded by Park in 1921; see Park (1939).

[30] The Park and Burgess text included, in addition to the selections from Simmel already mentioned, selections from Durkheim, Espinas, Hobhouse, Bacon, Rousseau, Sombart, Gumplowicz, Darwin, Mueller, Buecher, Adam Smith, Spencer, Sorel, Le Bon, Comte, Bergson, and others.

[31] The pragmatists were also interested in Hegelian dialectics.

[32] Shils, on the other hand, argues that Lasswell was the first person to bring psychoanalysis into American social research (Shils 1948, p. 59).

[33] Cf. Levitt's (1960) comparison of Freud and Dewey, and Schneider's (1948) study of Freud and Veblen.

[34] Znaniecki's work, Coser argues, contains "a storehouse of suggestive leads and concepts" for a sociology of knowledge and of intellectuals (Coser 1968).

[35] Reiss (1956) notes that the major outlines of the entire field were laid down by Park and Burgess and that during the 1946–56 period efforts in urban studies focused on the study of ecological organization.

[36] As Burgess put it, "the processes of competition, invasion, succession, and segregation described in elaborate detail for plant and animal communities seem to be strikingly similar to the operation of these same processes in the human community" (Burgess 1924b).

[37] See also Yale Levin and Alfred Lindesmith, "English Ecology and Criminology of the Past Century" and Terence Morris, "Some Ecological Studies of the 19th Century," both reprinted in Voss and Petersen (1971), pp. 47–64 and 65–76 respectively.

[38] For example, C. M. Child, "Biological Foundation of Social Integration," *Proceedings and Papers of the American Sociological Society* 22 (June 1928), and *The Physiological Foundations of Behavior* (New York: Holt, 1924); and F. E. Clements, *Plant Succession: An Analysis of the Development of Vegetation* (Washington: Carnegie Institution, 1916), and *Research Methods in Ecology* (Lincoln: University of Nebraska Press, 1905); cf. Gettys (1944).

[39] Notably distribution economics and the studies of land values, especially in work by Richard M. Hurd.

[40] Especially in writings of Vidal de la Blache, Ratzel, Gras, and Brunhes.

[41] Including the works of Le Play, Buckle, Huntington, and Semple, and the social survey movement.

[42] Such as those of Galpin and Kolb.

[43] Greer (1962, pp. 7–8). Alihan (1938, pp. 95ff.) maintains that there are similarities between Hobbes' "natural man" and the ecological "natural individual."

[44] See, for example, Duncan and Schnore (1959), who attempt to outline the theoretical aspects implicit in the ecological perspective, arguing that the early exponents of the approach did not recognize its possibilities and implications, observing that Park denied attempting to construct a theory.

[45] Park and Burgess's purpose, however, was in part to point out the sharp differences between animal and human societies: "Human society," they wrote, "unlike animal society, is mainly a social heritage, created in and transmitted by communication" (1921, p. 163). See their selections from William M. Wheeler, *Ants, Their Structure, Development, Behavior* (New York: Columbia University Press, 1910), on pp. 169–72, 182–84; and Eurenius Warming, *Oecology of Plants* (Oxford University Press, 1909) on pp. 175–82.

[46] See also Sophonisba P. Breckenridge and Edith Abbott, *The Delinquent Child and the Home*. New York: Russell Sage Foundation, 1912, which represents another example of the genre which was a precursor to the sociological studies later done at the University.

[47] Burgess argued that urban areas evolved naturally into five concentric circular zones:

(1) the Central Business District; (2) the Zone in Transition: (3) the Zone of Workingmen's Homes; (4) the Zone of Better Residences; and (5) the Commuters' Zone.

[48] Two surveys of those studies are particularly helpful, and have been drawn upon in the section that follows: an early survey by Quinn (1940a) and a recent Marxist evaluation by Castells (1977).

[49] Their findings, Burgess says, were often refuted by visitors from other cities, who said, "That may be what happens in Chicago; but in our city, juvenile delinquents are evenly scattered all over the area."

[50] Presumably Farberman means here within mainstream academic circles. Within that context, he is probably accurate—even the critiques of the ecological approach provide no fundamentally-different alternatives, but usually offer, instead, suggested modifications.

[51] Furthermore, if one looks at the biological model from which the perspective was initially taken, one finds that change often occurs only through violence and conflict. In a forest dominated by beech trees, for example, the maple trees on the forest floor are allowed to grow only when a violent storm creates an opening in the canopy of the forest, allowing light to reach the stunted maples.

[52] See the program description published in the *AJS* in 1902, which lists three courses by Dewey (Sociology of Ethics, The Psychology of Ethics, and The Evolution of Morality) and one by Mead (Contemporary Social Psychology) (Tolman 1902, p. 121). Under the listing of Small's course, The Ethics of Sociology, the description read, "It is recommended that Professor Dewey's courses, the logic, the psychology, and the sociology of ethics, be taken either before or with" Small's course (Tolman 1902, p. 120).

[53] Kluckhohn and Murray (1948, p. xiii) note that Thomas was the first to map systematically the research territory for the field of personality and culture.

[54] One curious fact is that Faris, in his 1945 discussion of the development of social psychology as a discipline fails to mention Thomas except to cite his notion of the "four wishes" as an example of social psychological concepts that were "proposed, advocated, and abandoned or neglected" (1945, p. 425). In other places, however (E. Faris 1948a, 1948b, 1951), he suggests a more central role for Thomas.

[55] As Hinkle (1952) does in claiming that all of Thomas's thought is encompassed within an internal, dialectic theory of change.

[56] For a very different interpretation of Thomas, see Schwendinger and Schwendinger's (1974, pp. 371ff.) scathing critique of Thomas's theories, comparing them to Freud's and arguing that they were basically psychological and individualistic. His concept of the "definition of the situation," for example, "was a refinement of the liberal concept of reason" (p. 376).

[57] House (1929, p. 191) points out that Park used the term "attitude," (and "sentiment-attitude") in a privately published pamphlet, *Principles of Human Behavior*, in 1915. Because of his close relationship with Thomas at the time, however, one might suppose that his focus on attitudes were influenced by Thomas (or vice versa).

[58] Thurstone, on the other hand, who was important in the later development of statistical studies of attitudes, claimed that he was very much influenced by Mead as a graduate student at Chicago (Thurstone 1952).

[59] House (1929, p. 198) also points out that Leopold von Wiese was influenced by

Thomas's work on attitudes and wishes, and cites him approvingly in his *Allgemeine Soziologie, Teil I. Beziehungslehre* (Munich and Leipzig, 1924).

[60] See especially Bain (1928) and E. Faris (1928, 1945). Note also some of the applications of the approach, such as L. L. Bernard, "A Theory of Rural Attitudes," *AJS* 22 (1917): 630–49; E. S. Bogardus, "Personality and Occupational Attitudes," *Sociology and Social Research* 12 (1927): 73–79, and "Sex Differences in Racial Attitudes" *Sociology and Social Research* 12 (1928): 279–85; E. Faris, "Racial Attitudes and Sentiments," *Southwestern Political and Social Science Quarterly* 9 (1929): 479–90; B. Glueck, "The Significance of Parental Attitudes for the Destiny of the Individual," *Mental Hygiene* 12 (1928): 722–41; Bruno Lasker, *Race Attitudes in Children* (New York, 1929): W. E. McLennan, "Wrong Attitude to Law as Cause of Crime," *Survey 26* (1911): 442–45; W. C. Smith, "The Rural Mind: A Study in Occupational Attitude," *AJS 32* (1927): 771–86; W. I. Thomas and D. S. Thomas, *The Child in America* (New York, 1928); L. L. Thurstone, "An Experimental Study of Nationality Preference," *Journal of General Psychology* 1 (1928): 405–25; and E. K. Wickman, *Children's Behavior and Teacher's Attitudes* (New York, 1928).

[61] For a later critique of *The Polish Peasant*, see J. Thomas (1950), who argues that the problem lies in their lack of statistical verification of the representativeness of their data and their simplification of reality. See also Znaniecki's response following the article.

[62] For further treatment of the development of attitude research, see Fleming's thorough article, "Attitude: The History of a Concept" (1967), in which he discusses influences from Darwin on Thomas. Fleming traces Elton Mayo's indirect debt to Thomas through Park and Shaw, and notes Thomas's influence on Thurstone's efforts to measure attitudes quantitatively and Stouffer's research with Guttman and Lazarsfeld.

[63] One important aspect of that renaissance was the founding of the Society for the Study of Symbolic Interaction and especially the publication of its official journal, *Symbolic Interaction*, beginning in the fall of 1977. Mead's influence is ubiquitous in its articles, culminating in the Fall 1981 issue, which is entirely devoted to interpretations of Mead and discussions of the impact and possibilities of his work.

[64] See Coser 1977, pp. 345ff., who cites a conversation with Blumer, 9 April 1969, and Strauss 1964, p. xi.

[65] Miller notes that at the time Dewey wrote the article, he and Mead were discussing philosophy with each other almost every day, suggesting that the article "was a result of their discussions" (Miller 1973, p. xxvi).

[66] Sprietzer and Reynolds (1973) documented the "Meadian renaissance" by analyzing references to Mead in the *AJS*, the *American Sociological Review*, and in sociology textbooks, finding that references to Mead were most frequent in journal articles during the 1956–60 period, although the frequency has remained almost constant since then.

[67] Kuhn (1964) has pointed out that Mead was not the only interactionist who failed to publish clear theoretical formulations of their social psychology, noting similar patterns with Thomas, Dewey, Blumer, and Faris.

[68] A similar conclusion was reached by Strauss (1964, p. x), who emphasized Mead's humility, belated recognition of his own genius, his slight interest in fame, and his "continuous—and possibly laborious—refining and extending of his ideas;" cf. Jane Dewey (1939).

[69] Faris's *The Nature of Human Nature* (New York: McGraw-Hill, 1937) incorporated

much of Mead's thought into a series of essays on social psychology. Although the book is dedicated to Mead, there are only four explicit references to Mead recorded in the index.

[70]In addition to Kuhn's own Twenty Statements Tests, another early effort to test Mead's basic assumptions can be found in Miyamoto and Dornbusch (1956).

[71]The debate continued in the subsequent volume, with a comment by Joseph Woelfel, who suggested that from a Meadian standpoint Bales's interpretation has some legitimacy because he has found in Mead what is useful for what Bales is doing, i.e., empirical research.

[72]Faris also points to Ellsworth Faris's critique of instinct theory in *The Nature of Human Nature* (1937) and earlier in Bernard's *Instinct: A study in Social Psychology* (1924).

[73]Cook (1977) makes a similar argument in his discussion of Mead's early commitment to an organic conception of conduct underlying the psychological functionalism of the Chicago school. Cook points to fundamental differences between Mead and the behaviorist tradition in American psychology.

[74]McAulay (1977), in fact, developed a critique of Mead's treatment of language and meaning in *Mind, Self and Society*, on the basis of difficult inherent in his work that are raised by the ethnomethodological perspective. Perinbanayagam also developed a comparison of the work of Mead, Schutz and Cooley (1975) and of Mead and Wittgenstein and Schutz (1974).

[75]Weigert notes, however, that Mead unduly restricted his notion of reflexivity to a sequential reflexivity, contrary to models of time found elsewhere in his writings.

[76]See the review of the current debates in Johnson and Shifflet (1981), to which I am indebted in this section. Even those who disagree with their conclusions, I believe, will find the summary of the debates valuable.

[77]It is interesting to note that the differences between the Chicago and Iowa schools noted above seem to shade into insignificance in light of a more general attack on interactionism such as Huber's. On the diversity of research strategies developed by the Chicago sociologists, cf. Janowitz (1966, p. vii) and Diner (1975, p. 553).

[78]Cottrell, for example, developed an experimental investigation of covert physiological processes accompanying overt behaviors in interpersonal interactions (see Cottrell 1971, 1980). McPhail traces a lineage of the Chicago and Iowa schools (1979, p. 91), noting that Kuhn studied with Kimball Young, another of Mead's students. McPhail himself studied under one of Kuhn's students, Robert L. Stewart, at Iowa. Richard Smith studied with Meltzer (a student of Blumer's) and Stewart at Central Michigan University and later with Stewart at South Carolina. Smith also studied with McPhail at Illinois. Cf. Stewart (1981), who argues that Mead's work itself accounts for both convergences and divergences in interpretations.

[79]See, e.g., Batiuk and Sacks's (1981) call for a Meadian reading of Marx to extend Mead beyond the microsociological realm.

[80]Note the important work in social psychology by Ralph Turner, a Chicago graduate influenced by the tradition.

[81]A characteristic example of the way in which all of the issues were combined in the study of institutions at Chicago is related in a story told by Burgess. Anderson complained to Burgess of a boring landlady in the roominghouse district where he was studying homeless men. "Why, this is valuable, you must get it down on paper," Burgess told him. Bur-

gess kept the resulting document which, he claims gives one "more insight into how life moves in the roominghouse area . . . than you do from a mountain of statistics that might be gathered" (Burgess 1964, p. 9).

[82] White (1957, p. 6) argues that they were all suspicious of approaches which were "excessively formal; they all protest[ed] their anxiety to come to grips with reality, their attachment to the moving and vital in social life."

[83] Davis (1943) argues that Veblen's concept of conspicuous consumption is the opposite of the asceticism of the Protestant Ethic discussed by Weber; cf. Diggins (1978, p. 104).

[84] As Turner (1967, p. xvii) points out, Park failed to develop a theory of stratification. That may be, in part, because his major concern was exposing the broad setting of social organization, rather than specific mechanisms for reform. "The problems he examined are not those that would have preoccupied an investigator convinced that reduction of inequalities was the most urgent agendum."

[85] In "Der Raum und die Räumlichen Ordnungen der Gesellschaft," chapter 9 of *Sociologie* (Leipzig: Duncker & Humblot, 1908). See Levine, Carter, and Gorman (1976, pp. 829ff.) for an excellent discussion of the ways in which Simmel's work was interpreted and misinterpreted by Chicago sociologists and others. I am indebted in this section to their article.

[86] Levine, Carter, and Gorman (1976, p. 831) point out that Hughes uncritically repeats Park's error in identifying marginality with Simmel's concept of the stranger.

[87] See his essay, "Social Disorganization and Reorganization," reprinted in Thomas (1966); cf. Janowitz (1966, p. xxxii).

[88] See Anderson's account of his research in which he discusses his own personal history and the place of the hobo as an "in-between worker" and "one of the heroic figures of the frontier" (Anderson 1975).

[89] See Sutherland (1945) on the relationship between the social disorganization and ecological perspectives.

[90] See Burgess's (1942) discussion of the relationship between Shaw and McKay's work and his own concentric zone theories; cf. Kornhauser 1978, pp. 51–59, 61–138; Bordua 1961.

[91] Consequently, much of the literature that analyzes the concept and its development does not dwell explicitly in great detail on its use by Chicago sociologists. The most important sources on Chicago developments of the concept are Janowitz (1966, 1975, 1978) and Turner (1967).

[92] E. A. Ross, *Social Control: A Survey of the Foundations of Order* (New York: Macmillan, 1901). See Schwendinger and Schwendinger (1974, pp. 389–400), who insist that the concept of social control turned an ideological rationale into a theoretical category.

[93] Janowitz quotes Mead as representing a widespread orientation when he said that "social control depends . . . upon the degree to which individuals in society are able to assume attitudes of others who are involved with them in common endeavors (1975, p. 82)."

[94] The influence of Simmel can be seen here (see Levine, Carter, and Gorman 1976, p. 1121). Small, too, placed more emphasis on conflict than did contemporaries such as Sumner and Giddings (Fuhrman 1980; page 1940).

[95] See also Steiner's (1929) early appraisal, as well as Oberschall (1972); Stein (1960); Waterman (1926); Hauser (1956a); Hawley (1968a); and Hinkle and Hinkle (1954).

[96] Henderson, for example, was extremely influential in social service reform, serving as president of a variety of civic agencies on a local and national level (Diner 1975, p. 524).

[97] The most detailed account of the LCRC is in Bulmer (1980); cf. Smith and White (1929); Breckenridge and White (1929); Burgess (1929a, 1929b, 1929c, 1964); Merriam (1929); Mitchell (1930); L. White (1929a, 1929b, 1930); and Wirth (1940).

[98] For details on the funding of the LCRC, see White (1929), who includes a table listing funding sources from 1924 to 1929, and Bulmer (1980).

[99] Wirth hedges his bets somewhat by saying that that description is how "the distinctive features of the urban mode of life have often been described sociologically" (p. 80), rather than simply representing it as his own opinion.

[100] Especially *De la division du travail social* (Paris, 1893). Translated by Richard Simpson as *The Division of Labor in Society* (New York: Free Press, 1933).

[101] Georg Simmel, "Die Grossstadt und das Geistesleben," pp. 187–206 in *Die Grossstadt*, edited by Theodor Petermann (Dresden, 1903). Translated by Edward Shils and reprinted in *Georg Simmel on Individuality and Social Forms*, edited by Donald Levine (Chicago: University of Chicago Press, 1971).

[102] See Shils's important critique of the mass society perspective in *Center and Periphery: Essays in Macrosociology* (Chicago: University of Chicago Press, 1975, pp. 91ff. That approach can be seen especially in later work by such Chicago sociologists as Janowitz, Suttles, and Gans.

[103] Greer (1967) discusses how Janowitz's work treats mechanisms which "allow individuals to participate meaningfully in a small unit of larger structure," hence avoiding "crude dichotomies" such as *Gemeinschaft* and *Gesellschaft*.

[104] Stein (1960, pp. 3334) argues that Park's approach to "natural areas" involves the following dimensions: disorganization patterns, distribution (e.g., of populations), subcommunity social structures, urbanization, and reorganization.

[105] Called the "nonmaterialist school" by Sjoberg (1965).

[106] Similar examples could be cited, such as Thrasher on the gang (1927). Although youthful gangs appear to be an example of social disorganization, they are in fact a form of alternative social organization which provide a community for their participants in the midst of the city.

[107] Sjoberg does argue, however, that despite his criticisms, the city can be seen as a factor in "determining" selected types of social phenomena.

[108] See Epstein's (1967) review of African studies, and Hanna and Hanna (1971).

[109] R. Faris (1967, p. 115), on the other hand, implies that the relationship between population and urban studies developed at a later period, following some disagreements within the department concerning research methods, particularly between Ogburn and Stouffer, on the one hand, and Burgess and Blumer on the other.

[110] Charles Booth's *Life and Labour of the People of London* was required reading for Park's students (Hughes 1954, p. 47). The British surveys, according to Hughes, "were a sort of scientific counterpart of the novels of Dickens and Zola, sprinkled with tables on wages, household expenditures, housing, health, drinking, and crime" (Hughes 1954, p. 47).

[111] Although the study was unfinished at the time of Thomas's death in 1947, some of the letters were excerpted in *Old World Traits Transplanted* and *The Unadjusted Girl*.

[112] See Janowitz (1952, pp. 20–23). Park claimed, however, that the press reflects rather than makes public opinion, according to Sorokin (1928, p. 708).

[113] Shils (1948, p. 26) suggests that the most notable contributions by Park's students were Wirth's *The Ghetto* (1928); Frazier's *The Negro Family in Chicago* (1922); Johnson's *The Negro in Chicago* (1938); Lind's *An Island Community: Ecological Succession in Hawaii* (1937); Doyle's *The Etiquette of Race Relations in the South* (1937); and P. Young's *The Pilgrims of Russian Town* (1932); cf. also Reuter (1934), which contains a collection of essays written primarily by Park's students.

[114] Ellwood "credited the advancement that the Negro had attained to the infiltration of white blood" (Odum 1951a, p. 331).

[115] Stocking also examines influences from Boas on Thomas's thought (1968, pp. 260–63); cf. a different perspective by Schwendinger and Schwendinger 1974, pp. 198ff., 371).

[116] See Burgess (1961), who notes especially Johnson, Reuter, Wirth, Frazier, Lohman, Stouffer, E. C. Hughes, H. M. Hughes, Hugh Cayton, Lewis, Copeland, Bingham Dai, John Dollard, Frederick Detweiler, Guy B. Johnson, William H. Jones, Forest La Violette, Lind, Charles Parrish, Donald Pierson, Redfield, Stonequist, Robert Sutherland, Edgar T. Thompson, Doyle, and others.

[117] The research for the commission was essentially the work of Charles Johnson—see Bulmer's (1981a) detailed study of the report and Johnson's career; cf. Burgess (1956a, 1964); G. Johnson (1925, 1957); Bracey, Meier, and Rudwick (1973); Robbins (1974); Diner (1980); and Shils (1970).

[118] Graham Romeyn Taylor, Graham Taylor's son, was executive secretary; see G. Johnson (1957); C. Smith (1972); Valien (1958). Johnson also undertook some important studies of blacks in Chicago for the Chicago Urban League, of which Park was president (Bulmer 1980, pp. 295ff.).

[119] Similarly, C. Johnson (1944b) claims that "Dr. Park became without doubt the wisest scholar in the strangely difficult sphere of human relations as influenced by the factor of race."

[120] Park argues that those cycles involve contact, competition, accommodation, and assimilation.

[121] It is interesting to note that Stouffer assisted Myrdal on the project (D. Young 1961).

[122] Cox (1942) makes a similar criticism of Warner and the "caste school" of race relations, suggesting that Warner's approach is neither original nor accurate, although admitting that it has "none of the anti-color complexes of the instinct school."

[123] Carey (1975, p. 169) refers to their arguments for pluralism in *Old World Traits Transplanted* and *The Immigrant Press and Its Control*. He also quotes from a personal interview with Cottrell, who argued that Park's belief in assimilation did not mean an elimination of cultural pluralism (pp. 169–70); cf. Etzioni (1959) on Wirth and Park.

[124] Perhaps the most comprehensive treatment of all three perspectives is in Kornhauser (1978), and I have relied upon it considerably in this section. Cf. also Voss and Petersen (1971) for a collection of articles relating to Shaw and McKay; and Empey (1978) which treats the three approaches somewhat differently than Kornhauser.

[125] Developed out of Merton's work, especially by Albert Cohen, Richard A. Cloward and Lloyd E. Ohlin. Cohen, however, was a student of Sutherland, who was trained at Chicago, and was influenced by the Chicago traditions (Voss and Petersen 1971).

[126]It should be noted, as Kornhauser (1978, p. 51) does, that Thrasher's theory of delinquency is only rudimentary, and that "the word 'gang' in Thrasher is *not* coterminous with 'delinquent gang.'"

[127]For more information, see Burgess, Lohman, and Shaw (1937); Short (1969); and Sorrentino (1959). Janowitz (1966, p. lvii) notes that Cottrell and Ohlin were influenced by the project and later urged the development of the programs. He also observes that Saul K. Alinsky studied sociology at Chicago during that period, and that some of his community action and organizing programs are "strikingly parallel to those developed in this project." Alinsky, however, denied any influence from the University of Chicago, and was very critical of the sociology department (Sanders 1970, p. 14).

[128]Kornhauser remarks that he is "probably the most influential figure in American criminology" (1978, p. 189); Lindesmith (1951); and Schuessler (1973).

[129]Sutherland was an indefatigable opponent of psychological theories and maintained a strong emphasis on social factors in this theory construction; see Wood's (1951) critique of Cressey and Sutherland, in which he argues that one cannot make universal generalizations concerning individual behavior because individuals are unique; cf. Kornhauser (1978, p. 189).

[130]See Cressey (1964, p. iii), who lists Clinard (1952, 1956) and Hartung (1949, 1950) as particularly significant.

[131]Although speaking primarily of Thomas, Janowitz argues that the same could be said of much of the Chicago school.

[132]Thomas, despite his attention to institutions, provides "little analysis of the over-all structure of politics in Poland and none for the United States" (Janowitz 1966, p. xxxvii).

[133] Satariano (1979) discusses ways in which Chicago social scientists provided the most important opposition to restrictive immigration laws in the 1920s and 1930s, when popular journals and magazines were supporting restrictions.

[134]Other dissertations on political institutions and processes include those written by Charles J. Bushnell, "A Study of the Stock Yards Community at Chicago, as A Typical Example of the Bearing of Modern Industry upon Democracy, with Constructive Suggestions" (1901); Mollie R. Carroll, "The Attitude of the American Federation of Labor toward Legislation and Politics" (1920); Samuel Ratcliffe, "Pauper Law and Institutions in Illinois" (1921); George Roussouw, "Nationalism and Language" (1910); Harmon DeGraff, "A Study of the Juvenile Court of Iowa with special Reference to Des Moines" (1926); and Hughes, "A Study of a Secular Institution: The Chicago Real Estate Board" (1928).

[135]See also Zentner (1951) who compares Blumer's discussion of the concept of "morale" to data on morale in *The American Soldier*, arguing that those data suggest that Blumer's conceptualization is "grossly inadequate."

[136]For a fairly complete discussion of kinds of social problems and the reform movements in which the Chicago sociologists were involved see Carey (1975).

[137]Dewey was also influenced, as Eastman (1941) suggests, by his "reform-minded" wife.

[138]Mead also served as treasurer of the Settlement House movement for several years; see Miller (1973); Barry (1968).

[139]See Farrell (1967); Levine (1971). See Linn 1935, p. 160, on efforts at the University of Chicago to give her an honorary degree.

[140] See her helpful summary chart, p. 21. The discussion that follows relies considerably on Deegan's discussion, pp. 19ff.

[141] For more information about McDowell, see McDowell (1901); Wilson (1929); Drier (1950); and Linn (1935).

[142] For more on Abbott and Breckenridge see Wright (1954).

[143] Cf. Park's (1931b) similar conclusions, arguing that *The Polish Peasant* represented a new approach to social problems and a system of concepts, rather than a body of fact.

[144] See also his use of letters to the editor as a form of personal document, in *Old World Traits Transplanted* and *The Unadjusted Girl* (Bressler 1952).

[145] Schmitt (1974) argues that even symbolic interactionism should not be equated with participant observation, despite the fact that it often is.

[146] See, e.g., Bornemann (1940) on disputes between Small and J. Laurence Laughlin, head of the political economy department at Chicago.

[147] Thurstone was also influenced by Thomas's concept of social attitudes, as was Stouffer (Fleming 1967; E. Faris 1948b).

[148] See, e.g., Furfey and Daly (1937), who claimed that factors are mere figments of the imagination, interesting to the mathematician, but not to social scientists.

[149] Cottrell (1967); Bogue (1974, p. xix) noted that Burgess and his colleagues were the first sociologists to apply multiple factor analysis to sociological data, and that he was the first sociology professor at Chicago to use electronic computers.

[150] Lazarsfeld (1962a) reviews Stouffer's career and includes a bibliography of his writings.

[151] Demerath (1949) compares the work to *The Polish Peasant*, arguing that not since Thomas and Znaniecki's classic had there been a sociopsychological work of such scope, imaginativeness, technical rigor, and important results. See also D. Young (1961), who discusses Stouffer et al., *The American Soldier*, and Myrdal, *An American Dilemma*.

[152] Cf. Hinkle (1952) and Volkart's (1952) somewhat different interpretation.

[153] See also articles by Deegan and Burger (1978, 1981) on Mead and Thomas respectively.

[154] Janowitz argues, however, that although Thomas perceives of social change as a continuous process (1966, p. xxxii), he rejected theories of unilinear evolution and a "simple-minded theory of *Gemeinschaft* and *Gesellschaft* (p. xxxvi); cf. Fisher and Strauss (1978, p. 7).

[155] With influences from William Graham Sumner's emphasis on ceaseless change precipitated by group conflict;

[156] I am indebted to Steve Lyng for a discussion on this issue.

[157] Concepts which are taken for the most part from LeBon.

[158] Although the concept is usually attributed to Ogburn, who developed it, it was apparently used earlier by Veblen; see Watson (1958); Davis (1957c).

[159] See, e.g., Schneider's (1944) discussion of the concept's importance; cf. Hauser (1959); Hinkle and Hinkle (1954); and Allport (1924). Duncan (1964) argues that it is erroneous to characterize Ogburn's theory of social change as "the cultural-lag theory," because it is much broader than that.

[160] See Martindale (1957, pp. 349–54); Schwendinger and Schwendinger 1974, p. 460; House (1929, pp. 154–55); and Sutherland (1945).

[161] See Small (1916); Faris (1967, pp. 127ff.); Carey (1957, pp. 64–65); Diner (1975); Lasswell (1971); Storr (1966); Veblen (1969); Weeks (1956); see also Bogardus (1962), who notes that university curricula at Chicago and other midwestern universities were less rigid, leaving more room for the development of sociology than in established northeastern universities. Note also the role of the Chautauqua society (Gould 1961; Martindale 1976; T. Morrison 1974).

[162] On Small's role, see Barnes (1926, 1948a); Becker (1971); Hughes (1979b); Dibble (1975); Furner (1975); Goodspeed (1926); Hayes (1926, 1927); Wirth (1934, 1953); Herbst (1959); Maclean (1926); Smith (1965); Stern (1933); and Sutherland (1929).

[163] Cf. Burgess (1939c) on the use of Freud in the text, and R. Faris (1967) on Thomas's influence; cf. Shils (1981), and Wirth (1953).

[164] See Small (1895), in which he outlines the "platform" of the *Journal*, and Small (1916), in which he recounts Harper's suggestion that it be created.

[165] Durkheim's journal, *Année sociologique*, was founded the following year.

[166] Lengermann's interpretation, based on extensive reviews of archival data, calls into question previous explanations for the rebellion offered by Kuklick (1973), Martindale (1960), and R. Faris (1967).

[167] Nine of the American Sociological society presidents from 1935 to 1950, for example, were Chicago graduates or faculty members.

[168] A perusal of the first volumes of the journal shows a large number of articles by Chicago sociologists.

Addendum to the Bibliography

Barnes, Harry Elmer, ed. 1948. *An Introduction to the History of Sociology*. Chicago: University of Chicago Press. A collaborative work on the growth of sociological thought from its origins to the Second World War, containing forty-seven essays and emphasizing the period from Compte to Sorokin. See individual essays by Barnes on Small, Hayes, and Thomas.

BIBLIOGRAPHY

Aaron, Daniel. 1951. *Men of Good Hope*. New York: Oxford University Press. Includes a chapter entitled "Thorstein Veblen: Moralist and Rhetorician" which treats Veblen's social criticism and analysis of economic institutions.

Abbott, Walter F. 1974. "Moscow in 1897 as a Preindustrial City: A Test of the Inverse Burgess Zonal Hypothesis." *ASR* 39 (August): 542–50. Assesses Burgess's zonal hypothesis, using a study of Moscow to demonstrate Sjoberg's "inverse Burgess zonal hypothesis," which suggests that preindustrial cities tend to have the inverse of the American pattern posited by Burgess.

Abel, Theodore. 1958. "Florian Znaniecki, 1882–1958." *ASR* 23 (August): 429–30. Brief memorial comments review his career first as a poet and later as a sociologist, his collaboration with Thomas and his work in the sociology of knowledge and culture.

Abu-Lughod, Janet. 1961. "Migrant Adjustment to City Life: The Egyptian Case." *AJS* 67 (July): 22–32.

———. 1968. "The City is Dead—Long Live the City: Some Thoughts on Urbanity." Pp. 154–65 in *Urbanism in World Perspective: A Reader* edited by Sylvia F. Fava. New York: Crowell. Outlines a series of problems with the ecology of the "early Chicago school"—Wirth, Burgess, and Park—and recent developments which provide a fuller and more complicated understanding of the relationship between environmental factors and social life.

Addams, Jane. 1910. *Twenty Years at Hull-House*. New York: Macmillan. Addams's own account of her settlement house in Chicago, 1889–1909, including references to the University of Chicago and the University of Chicago Settlement House. See Commager (1961).

———. 1929. "Toast to John Dewey." *Survey* 63 (November): 203–204. Indicates Dewey's impact on social welfare problems, as a member of the first board of Hull House trustees and an active participant in public affairs on an international level. Suggests that such involvement was "part of his life-long effort to embody truth in conduct." Reprinted in *John Dewey: The Man and His Philosophy* (1930, pp. 140–52), and in Lasch (1965, pp. 177–83); cf. Levine (1971).

———. 1930. *Second Twenty Years at Hull House*. New York: Macmillan. A wide-ranging account of Addams's activities from 1909 to 1929, noting work on immigrants (pp. 302–303) and delinquency (pp. 207, 364–65) by Chicago sociologists. Contains a discussion of pioneering work on urban areas antedating the first sociological work by three years (pp. 404ff.).

Addams, Jane, ed. 1895. *Hull House Maps and Papers*. New York: Crowell. Written by the residents at Hull House, this collection of papers established the areas of major study for subsequent Chicago sociologists. In addition, their mapping of sociological and demographic characteristics in the districts surrounding Hull House were the first efforts in this direction. A seminal book illustrating the major concerns of Chicago sociology for decades.

Adkins, Dorothy. 1968. "L. L. Thurstone." Pp. 22–25 in Sills (1968), vol. 16. Recalls Thurstone's development of statistical techniques, especially multiple-factor analysis and attitudinal scales.

Adler, Mortimer Jerome. 1941. "The Chicago School." *Harper's Magazine* 183 (September): 377–88. Assesses the sense in which a Chicago school of philosophy existed and comments on James, Dewey, Mead, Angell, and others. Recalls a basic homogeneity of the entire university until the arrival of Hutchins, suggesting that its faculty was united in a common enterprise and, with a few exceptions, "consisted of men who saw eye to eye on fundamentals, whether they were professors of geology or economics, of physiology or religion, of education or sociology."

Adler, Solomon. 1957. "Imperial Germany and the Industrial Revolution." *Monthly Review* 9 (July-August): 76–82. Discussion of Veblen's book, *Imperial Germany*, as part of a memorial tribute to Veblen. See Huberman and Sweezy (1957).

Adorno, T. W. 1941. "Veblen's Attack on Culture: Remarks Occasioned by the Theory of the Leisure Class." *Studies in Philosophy and Social Science* 9 (3): 389–413. Examines Veblen's attack on "barbarian culture," maintaining that Veblen "stands for the bad conscience of leisure" (p. 399). Criticizes his Darwinian orientation, noting the differences between pragmatism and Marxist dialectics (p. 409).

Aldous, Joan. 1962. "Urbanization, the Extended Family, and Kinship Ties in West Africa." *SF* 41 (October): 6–12. Objects to Wirth's contention that the city is a social organization that substitutes secondary for primary group relationships; reviews other critics; and analyzes cities in West Africa in which kinship ties persist contrary to Wirth's expectations.

Aldrich, Howard. 1975. "Ecological Succession in Racially Changing Neighborhoods: A Review of the Literature." *Urban Affairs Quarterly* 10 (March): 327–48. Outlines Park's concept of ecological succession and emphasizes the extent to which findings from research on racial succession fit Park's description of an orderly sequence of changes.

Alihan, Milla Aissa. 1938. *Social Ecology: A Critical Analysis*. New York: Cooper Square Publishers. A thorough critique of the human ecology perspective, its sources, basic assumptions, and methodologies. Declares that the human ecologists have encountered difficulties which invariably arise from an application of natural science approaches to human phenomena, e.g. in the lack of attention to social, technological, and especially volitional factors and an excessive emphasis on the determination of social processes by the iron laws of nature.

Allport, Floyd H. 1924. "Social Change: An Analysis of Professor Ogburn's Culture Theory." *SF* 2 (September): 671–76. Criticizes aspects of Ogburn's theory, especially his treatment of organic factors, while nonetheless assessing it as a "brilliant achievement."

Allport, Gordon W. 1939. "Dewey's Individual and Social Psychology." Pp. 263–90 in Schilpp (1939). Outlines Dewey's contributions to and impact on psychology, with his emphasis on the reciprocal interpenetration of impulse, habit, thought and the environment.

American Journal of Sociology. 1895. "Free Investigation." *AJS* 1 (September): 210–14. An editorial (presumably written by Small) which prints a letter from a critic who claimed to expect "no lasting good from a work that is conducted by an educational institution founded by the arch-robber of America," citing Bemis's dismissal as a case in point. The editorial responds by pointing out that an article by Bemis appears in the issue and contends that the "*Journal* will not be equivocal in exposing the usurpations of capitalism, or in explaining principles to which the people must learn to hold corporations accountable."

———. 1954. "In Memoriam: Ellsworth Faris, 1874–1953." *AJS* 59 (March): 470–71. An unsigned memorial reviewing Faris's studies in Africa and at Chicago, noting that he succeeded Small as chair of the department and as editor of the *AJS*.

Ames, Edward S. 1931. "George Herbert Mead." Pp. 3–9 in Ames et al. (1931). Memorial comments about Mead's life and work, noting that "his class room lectures were vigorous pulsations of outreaching, exploring thought." Describes his social psychology course and his emphasis on how one becomes aware of oneself and others in mutual relations of social interaction. Recalls that Mead knew much of Milton, Shelley and Shakespeare by heart.

———. 1944. "Robert E. Park." Pp. 3–6 in Ames et al. (1944). Personal comments about Park's life and work, his interest in the Hebrew prophets, race relations, and his 'search for facts." Notes Park's sense of humor and includes one of Park's favorite poems, a tribute to Abraham Lincoln written by Walt Whitman.

Ames, Edward S., Everett C. Hughes, John U. Nef, Louis Wirth, and Charles S. Johnson. 1944. *Robert Ezra Park, 1864–1944*. Chicago: Privately published. A collection of "appreciations" read by friends, colleagues, and students at a memorial service held in Bond Chapel at the University of Chicago, 9 February 1944. (A copy is available in the Joseph Regenstein Library, University of Chicago; see separate entries under each author.).

Ames, Edward S., John Dewey, James H. Tufts, and Henry C. A. Mead. 1931. *George Herbert Mead*. Chicago: Privately published. Contains remarks from a memorial service held for Mead at Bond Chapel, University of Chicago, 13 April 1931, with a biographical statement by his son. See separate entries for each author. (A copy is available in the Regenstein Library, University of Chicago.).

Ames, Van Meter. 1931. "George Herbert Mead: An Appreciation." *University of Chicago Magazine* 23 (19 June): 370–73. A memorial tribute to Mead.

———. 1955. "Mead and Husserl on the Self." *Philosophy and Phenomenological Research* 15 (March): 320–31. Evaluates similarities and differences in Mead's and Husserl's theories of the self; to Mead the self is social; to Husserl the self is essentially outside of society. Reprinted in Corti (1973), pp. 193–224.

———. 1956. "Mead and Sartre on Man." *Journal of Philosophy* 53 (March): 205–19. Analyzes similarities and differences in the thought of Mead and Sartre, on process, science and magic, the act, time, human freedom, dualism, evolution, and other topics.

———. 1959–1960. "Zen to Mead." *Proceedings and Addresses of the American Philosophical Association* 33 (Annual): 27–42.

———. 1973. "No Separate Self." Pp. 43–58 in Corti (1973). Reviews Mead's theory of the self, indicating that for Mead, both self and mind grow out of the social process.

Anderson, Karl L. 1933. "The Unity of Veblen's Theoretical System." *Quarterly Journal of Economics* 47 (August): 598–626. Reconstructs Veblen's theoretical system with particular attention to his institutional approach as opposed to "orthodox" economics. Maintains that whereas the latter has been amply elaborated, Veblen's integrated system of economic theory has been neglected.

Anderson, Nels. 1923. *The Hobo: The Sociology of the Homeless Man*. Chicago: University of Chicago Press. One of the early classic ethnographic monographs and a forerunner of the human ecology studies (cf. Anderson 1975).

———. 1975. "Introduction to the Phoenix Edition." Pp. v–xxi in *The Hobo: The Sociology of the Homeless Man.* by Nels Anderson. Chicago: University of Chicago Press. A fascinating retrospective account of Anderson's research on the hobo, noting that his father was a hobo and that his family lived for a time in Chicago's "Hobohemia." Anderson sold newspapers "in the very streets, alleys, saloons and other places I was later to study." Discusses his going to Chicago to study sociology and his work with Park and Burgess.

———. 1983. "A Stranger at the Gate: Reflections on the Chicago School of Sociology." *Urban Life* 11 (January): 396–406. Personal reflections on his study at Chicago, especially with Park, Burgess, and E. Faris, with discussion of Anderson's *The Hobo* (1923).

Anderson, Nels, Read Bain, and George Lundberg, eds. 1929. *Trends in American Sociology*. New York: Harper. See discussions of Chicago sociology in separate entries under J. Bernard and J. Markey.

Anderson, Quentin. 1979. "John Dewey's American Democrat." *Daedalus* 108 (Summer): 145–59. Extols American individualism and claims that Dewey's positions are fantastic and spread illusions, reducing people to interchangeable communicators and cancelling their personal histories.

Anderson, Theodore R. 1955. "Intermetropolitan Migration: A Comparison of the Hypotheses of Zipf and Stouffer." *ASR* 20 (June): 287–91. Uses a study of migration to draw conclusions about Stouffer's and Zipf's hypotheses, suggesting modifications. See a comment by F. Ikle in the *ASR* 20 (December, 1955):713–14, and a reply from Anderson (pp. 714–15).

Anderson, Theodore R., and Janice A. Egeland. 1961. "Spatial Aspects of Social Area Analysis." *ASR* 26 (June): 392–98. Reports a test of Burgess's concentric zone and Hoyt's sector hypothesis, finding support for Burgess's hypothesis with respect to urbanization but not with respect to social rank, and vice versa for Hoyt's work.

Andersson, Sten. 1972. *En fenomenologisk lasning av George H. Mead. Eller varfor verkligheten ar verklig och inte ett skadespel*. Gothenburg, Sweden: Sociologiska institutionen. Examines phenomenological aspects of Mead's philosophy.

Angell, Robert C. 1940. "Roderick Duncan McKenzie: 1885–1940." *AJS* 46 (July): 78. A brief memorial statement noting McKenzie's graduate career and summer teaching at Chicago and his role in developing the human ecology approach.

———. 1945. "A Critical Review of the Development of the Personal Document Method in Sociology 1920–1940." Pp. 175–232 in Gottschalk, Kluckhohn, and Angell (1945). An extensive review of sociologists' use of personal documents in research, including much discussion of Thomas and Znaniecki's *The Polish Peasant* (1918–19) and Blumer's (1939) analysis. Mentions other efforts by Chicago sociologists to use personal documents, including Thomas's *The*

Unadjusted Girl (1923) and work by Shaw, Frazier, Johnson, Burgess, Cavan, Park, Miller, P. Young, Zorbaugh, Thrasher, Sutherland, Mowrer, Cottrell, and others.

Ansbro, James. 1978. "Albion Woodbury Small and Education." Ph.D. thesis, Loyola University of Chicago. Insists that although Small has been largely forgotten, to do so is a mistake. Ranks him as a "first-rank educator" who made considerable contributions as a teacher, administrator, and writer; comments on his founding of the *AJS*.

Antonovsky, Aaron 1956. "Toward a Refinement of the 'Marginal Man' Concept." *SF* 35 (October): 57–62. An effort to redefine Park's and Stonequist's concept of marginality, looking at different types of Jewish orientations. Objects to speaking of *the* American Jewish definition of marginality, because there are varying definitions.

Arnaud, Pierre, and Julien Freund. 1969. "Review of Park and Burgess, *Introduction to the Science of Sociology*." *Année sociologique* 20 (Annual): 90–92. Evaluates Park and Burgess's famous "Bible verte" of American sociological texts and discusses its role in American sociology.

Aubert, Vilhelm. 1952. "White-Collar Crime and Social Structure." *AJS* 58 (November): 263–71. Objects to looking at white-collar crime as simultaneously crime and not crime. Recounts Sutherland's formulation of the concept and a discussion between Hartung and Burgess in 1950 in which Burgess took a position opposite to that of Sutherland's.

Axelrod, Morris. 1956. "Urban Structure and Social Participation." *ASR* 21 (February): 13–18. Takes issue with the Chicago school of sociology and "the classic expression of this view," Wirth's "Urbanism as a Way of Life" (1938) article, noting a more recent view that recognizes the importance of informal contacts, including Whyte's *Street Corner Society* (1943) and Janowitz's *The Community Press in an Urban Setting* (1952). Data from the Detroit Area Study found that informal group association was nearly universal and that formal and informal group participation were found to vary positively.

Ayres, C. E. 1958. "Veblen's Theory of Instincts Reconsidered." Pp. 25–38 in Dowd (1958). Contends that Veblen "was a social theorist of the first rank, and by far his most important contribution was his theory of instincts," despite the fact that the notion of instincts "is now scientifically obsolete."

Bain, Read. 1928. "An Attitude on Attitude Research." *AJS* 33 (May): 940–57. Criticizes attitude research, particularly in *The Polish Peasant* (1918–19), claiming that Thomas and Znaniecki are too subjectivistic and confuse attitudes with opinions. Insists that statistical treatments provide the best approach for studies of attitudes (cf. Faris 1928, and Markey 1929).

———. 1935. "Measurement in Sociology." *AJS* 40 (January): 481–88. Takes issue with House (1934) in his criticism of quantitative methodologies, arguing that communication makes it possible for subjective experience to become objective knowledge. Objects to House's interpretation of Dewey, admitting that case studies are acceptable, but arguing that if researchers study enough cases, they "will be forced to use statistical methods and by this declension, may eventually arrive at some dependable scientific knowledge." Cf. Chapin (1935).

———. 1951. "L. L. Bernard: Sociological Theorist (1881–1951)." *ASR* 16 (June): 285–97. Relatively extensive review of Bernard's life and work, including discussion of his graduate school career at Chicago where he was most influenced by Thomas and Vincent. Includes a bibliography of Bernard's work.

Bain, Read, Gordon W. Allport, Herbert Blumer, F. W. Coker, Max Lerner, George P. Murdock, Roy F. Nichols, E. G. Nourse, A. T. Poffenberger, Samuel A. Stouffer, W. I. Thomas, Warren S. Thompson, Willard W. Waller, Malcolm M. Willey, Louis Wirth, and Donald Young. 1939. "Part Two: Proceedings of the Conference on Blumer's Analysis." Pp. 99–102 in Blumer (1939b). Transcript of a discussion by all of the above of Blumer's appraisal of *The Polish Peasant* (Thomas and Znaniecki 1918–19), with summary statements by Allport, Murdock, and Wiley, and with a summary and analysis of the conference by Bain. Much of the discussion centered around the contribution of Thomas and Znaniecki in turning sociologists toward empirical investigations which employ large masses of data, and toward the problem of how to verify or validate theoretical propositions formulated to explain social phenomena (e.g., an important critique by Stouffer, pp. 167–70, who discusses the advantage of broader nonpsychological approaches).

Baker, Paul J. 1973. "Introduction: The Life Histories of W. I. Thomas and Robert E. Park." *AJS* 79 (September): 243–60. Introduces autobiographical sketches prepared by Thomas and Park for Bernard in the 1920s, indicating that both Thomas and Park came to sociology with little or no interest in many of the issues prevalent in the sociological thought of their time and that their work marks a transition from philosophical disputes and reformist activities to less grandiose theory and empirical observation. See Thomas (1973) and Park (1973).

Baldensperger, Fernard. 1923. "Notes sur les universelles étrangères." *Revue des sciences politiques* 43 (April): 197ff. Refers to Veblen as the principal and most vehement critic of the American system of higher education.

Bales, Robert F. 1966. "Comment on Herbert Blumer's Paper." *AJS* 71 (March): 545–47. Insists that Blumer's account of the sociological implications of Mead's thought in Blumer (1966) misinterprets Mead, who was not a philosophical idealist, but a pragmatist and a social behaviorist. See the reply by Blumer (pp. 547–48); cf. McPhail and Rexroat (1979, 1980).

Banks, J. A. 1979. "Thorstein Veblen." Pp. 147–55 in *The Founding Fathers of Social Science* edited by Timothy Raison; revised edition by Paul Barker. London: Scolar Press. Outlines the career of Veblen as a sociologist whose words are often quoted but whose works are little read.

Banton, Michael. 1974. "Race in the American Sociological Tradition: From Park to Parsons." *Jewish Journal of Sociology* 16 (June): 85–93. A review article on Lyman (1972) asserting that Lyman underrates the extent to which Park sought an alternative to Social Darwinist thought. Notes that Park was one of the first sociologists to send students out to study the institutions in which interracial contacts take place.

Baran, Paul A. 1957. "The Theory of the Leisure Class." *Monthly Review* 9 (July-August): 83–91. Appraises Veblen's first and most popular work, observing that it provides the central scaffolding of Veblen's thought; comments on his concepts of pecuniary emulation, conspicuous leisure, and conspicuous consumption. See Huberman and Sweezy (1957).

Barber, Bernard. 1970. "Introduction." Pp. 1–53 in *L. J. Henderson on the Social System* edited by Bernard Barber. Chicago: University of Chicago Press.

Barnes, Harry Elmer. 1924. "Review of Albion Small, *Origins of Sociology*." *SF* 3 (November): 157–60. Review of Small's volume on the history of sociology (Chicago: University of Chicago Press, 1924) which also discusses some of Small's other works. Suggests that Small views sociology as "a collection of techniques for discovering the group factor in human experience," which differs from Giddings's perception of sociology as a rather distinct and well defined subject. Notes Small's role in the institutionalization of sociology.

———. 1926. "The Place of Albion Woodbury Small in Modern Sociology." *AJS* 32 (July): 15–48. Outlines Small as an intermediary between "systematizers," e.g. Comte, Spencer, Ward, Giddings, and a subsequent generation of sociological specialists.

———. 1948a. "Albion Woodbury Small: Promoter of American Sociology and Expositor of Social Interests." Pp. 766–92 in Barnes (1948).* Reviews Small's contributions, suggesting that he provided a transition between the "systematizers" and the subsequent generation of specialists. Discusses his founding of the department and the *AJS*, noting that he was the most voluminous American sociological writer of his generation, who interpreted the development of Germanic social science for American readers. Concludes that in advancing the subject matter of sociology Small was second only to Ward and Giddings in his generation, "while in promoting the professional and academic position of sociology, he was without any close rival."

———. 1948b. "The Sociological Theories of Edward Cary Hayes." Pp. 869–83 in Barnes (1948). Treats the career and work of one of Small's better-

*For Barnes (1948), see p. 112.

known disciples, with a section on the influence of Chicago sociology on his thought.

———. 1948c. "William Isaac Thomas: The Fusion of Psychological and Cultural Sociology." Pp. 793–804 in Barnes (1948). Summarizes Thomas's major ideas and his "psychocultural" analysis of the social situation as well as the personal and professional background of his sociological concepts. Indicates that he is "regarded by many . . . as the most erudite and creative of American social psychologists," and that Thomas developed the idea "that more could be gleaned from *inspecting* both literature and social situations than from encyclopedic reading of formal sociological materials." Reviews his relations with Znaniecki and influences from Dewey, Mead, and Cooley.

———. 1960. "Howard Paul Becker, 1899–1960." *AJS* 66 (November): 289. Memorial statement for one of Park's students who made major contributions to sociological theory.

———. 1968a. "Albion W. Small." Pp. 320–22 in Sills (1968), Vol. 14. Contends that Small did more than any other American sociologist to establish recognition of sociology as an academic discipline; discusses his founding of the *AJS* and his contributions to theory and methodology, although they are overshadowed by his administrative and teaching roles.

———. 1968b. "Charles A. Ellwood." Pp. 31–33 in Sills (1968), Vol. 5. Charts Ellwood's career and contributions, mentioning influences from E. A. Ross Thomas, Mead, Dewey, Small, Hobhouse, and Cooley. Notes Ellwood's contributions in the field of "psychological sociology" and as a teacher of Reuter, L. Bernard, Blumer, and others.

———. 1968c. "Luther Lee Bernard." Pp. 64–65 in Sills (1968), Vol. 2. Recounts Bernard's work, his graduate study at Chicago, and his relationship to Ellwood.

Barnes, Harry Elmer, and Howard Becker. 1938. *Social Thought from Lore to Science. Vol. II: Sociological Trends throughout the World.* Boston: D.C. Heath. Includes a brief, but fairly comprehensive, discussion of the Chicago sociology department (pp. 979–83), its major figures and their contributions to the field.

Barry, Robert M. 1968. "A Man and a City: George Herbert Mead in Chicago." Pp. 173–92 in *American Philosophy and the Future: Essays for a New Generation* edited by Michael Novak. New York: Scribner's Sons. Outlines Mead's work and the milieu in which it was developed; analyzes Mead's involvement with Chicago reform groups and Addams's settlement movement.

Batiuk, Mary Ellen. 1982. "Misreading Mead: Then and Now." *Contemporary Sociology* 11 (March): 138–40. This review of Lewis and Smith (1980) contends that although they are correct in claiming that a fresh reading of Mead is necessary, their interpretation of Mead's work is as problematic as the one they critique. Insists that any reinterpretation should begin with Mead's own efforts to overcome the difficulties encountered in restricting oneself to either subjectivistic or objectivistic interpretations of social experiences.

Batiuk, Mary Ellen, and Howard L. Sacks. 1981. "George Herbert Mead and Karl Marx: Exploring Conciousness and Community." *Symbolic Interaction* 4 (Fall): 207–23. Suggests that current efforts to return to Mead's original insights and extend Meadian thought beyond the micro realm as well as to link his ideas to constructive social action are complementary to Marxist efforts to provide a systematic social psychology. Argues that a Meadian reading of Marx, unlike the Marx-Freud synthesis, is consistent with sociological assumptions.

Baumann, Bedrich. 1967. "George H. Mead and Luigi Pirandello: Some Parallels between the Theoretical and Artistic Presentation of the Social Role Concept." *Social Research* 34 (Autumn): 563–607. A Czechoslovakian scholar agrees with Berger (1966) that Mead has made the most important theoretical contribution to the social sciences in America. Compares Mead's work with that of the Italian dramatist Pirandello, noting remarkable similarities in their conceptions of the social role, despite different backgrounds and modes of expression.

Becker, Ernest. 1971. *The Lost Science of Man*. New York: Braziller. Examines the tension in Small's career between an effort to develop ethical solutions to the "social problem" and an effort to create an objective science of society (pp. 3–70). Argues that Small's most profound intellectual and methodological contributions were made to the fields of economics and political science, rather than sociology (pp. 63ff.).

Becker, Howard P. 1932. "Space Apportioned Forty-Eight Topics in the *AJS*, 1895–1930." *AJS* 38 (July): 71–78. A comprehensive analysis of *AJS* articles indicates a wider spread of sociological interests among the various subtopics designated.

Becker, Howard, and Alvin Boskoff, eds. 1957. *Modern Sociological Theory in Continuity and Change*. New York: Holt, Rinehart and Winston. A broad edited volume with considerable treatment of Chicago sociology throughout; see separate entries under Jensen, Kolb, and Martindale.

Becker, Howard S. 1966. "Introduction." Pp. v–xviii in *The Jack-Roller: A Delinquent Boy's Own Story* by Clifford R. Shaw. Reissue, Chicago: University of Chicago Press. Comments on Shaw's work as part of the life-history genre of research done at Chicago after the arrival of Park in 1916, observing that it is "theoretically grounded in Mead's social psychology, its practicality in research attested by *The Polish Peasant* (Thomas and Znaniecki 1918–19), and its use persuasively urged by Ernest W. Burgess."

Becker, Howard S., and Irving Louis Horowitz. 1972. "Radical Politics and Sociological Research: Observations on Methodology and Ideology." *AJS* 78 (July): 48–66.

Bell, Daniel. 1969. "Introduction." Pp. 2–35 in *The Engineers and the Price System* by Thorstein Veblen. New York: Harcourt, Brace and World.

Bell, Wendell. 1957. "Anomie, Social Isolation, and Class Structure." *Sociometry* 20 (June): 105–16.

Bell, Wendell, and Marion D. Boat. 1957. "Urban Neighborhoods and Informal Social Relations." *AJS* 62 (January): 391–98. Questions Wirth's "Urbanism as a way of Life" article, claiming that impersonal, anonymous and secondary social relations were not found in the authors' study of San Francisco neighborhoods.

Bendix, Reinhard. 1954. "Social Theory and Social Action in the Sociology of Louis Wirth." *AJS* 59 (May): 523–29. Indicates that Wirth developed social theories as an aspect of social research, not a separate body of knowledge, viewing social science and social action as inextricably linked.

Bennett, James O. 1980. "Dewey on Causality and Novelty." *Transactions of the Charles S. Peirce Society* 16 (Summer): 225–41. Considers Dewey's theory of causality and his position with regard to the "fallacy of misplaced concreteness" or of "selective emphasis"; declares that Dewey explains novelty through the interaction of processes, hence avoiding excessive determinism.

Bennett, James. 1981. *Oral History and Delinquency*. Chicago: University of Chicago Press. Explores the use of oral histories for the study of delinquency, including considerable discussion of Chicago sociologists, notably Shaw and McKay.

Bernard, Jessie. 1929. "The History and Prospects of Sociology in the United States." Pp. 1–71 in *Trends in American Sociology* edited by George A. Lundberg, Read Bain, and Nels Anderson. New York: Harper. Includes considerable discussion of Chicago sociology (especially pp. 49–54 on Chicago and Columbia as early dominant departments). Asserts that Thomas was, perhaps more than any other single individual, responsible for the so-called Chicago school of sociology (pp. 25–26).

———. 1964. *Academic Women*. University Park, Penn.: Pennsylvania State University Press. Includes a passage on Breckinridge, E. Abbott, and Talbot, with comments on Abbott's reorganization of the School of Social Service Administration and the hiring of women faculty members.

Bernard, Luther L. 1909. "The Teaching of Sociology in the United States." *AJS* 15 (September): 164–213. Although not specifically about the University of Chicago, this survey of sociology programs and courses in the U.S. provides some interesting data; e.g., of 732 graduate students in 1909, 391 were at Chicago (p. 187). Small and Vincent's *Introduction to the Study of Society* was the most frequently used text.

———. 1910. "The Transition to an Objective Standard of Control." Ph.D. thesis, University of Chicago.

———. 1924. "Recent Trends in Social Psychology." *SF* 2 (September): 737–43. This extensive review of works in social psychology includes discussions of Bogardus, Ellwood, and others, noting particularly controversies surrounding the place of instincts and the concept of social control.

———. 1936. "The Great Controversy: Or, Both Heterodoxy and Orthodoxy in Sociology Unmasked." *SF* 14 (October): 64–72. Critiques Ellwood's *Methods in Sociology: A Critical Study* (Durham, N.C.: Duke University Press, 1933), claiming that his work represents a general confusion in the field between two different aspects of scientific method: investigation and generalization. Claims that the two are supplementary despite conflicts between investigators and generalizers (or "reformers"). Followed by a rejoinder by Ellwood (p. 72).

———. 1942. "Some Recent Discussions in Social Psychology." *AJS* 48 (July): 13–28. Traces the development of interactionist social psychology as an alternative to behaviorist psychology, and takes issue with Reuter's (1940) claim that the former has outlived its usefulness. Discusses Thomas, Dewey, Mead, Faris, Cooley, Baldwin, Adam Smith, Blumer, and others. Indicates that both the social interactionist approach and that which emphasizes quantitative measurement have contributed toward the growth of an autonomous science of social psychology.

———. 1944. *War and its Causes*. New York: H. Holt & Co.

———. 1945. "The Teaching of Sociology in the United States in the Last Fifty Years." *AJS* 50 (May): 534–48. An update of Bernard (1909).

Bernstein, Richard J. 1960. "Introduction." Pp. ix–xlvii in Dewey (1960). Reviews Dewey's intellectual development and responds to his critics; considers Dewey's career at Chicago (pp. xxiv ff.) and implications of his thought.

Bierstedt, Robert. 1968. "Florian Znaniecki." Pp. 599–602 in Sills (1968), Vol. 16. Znaniecki's studies of the Polish peasant and the social role of the "man of knowledge" are considered, as are his efforts to develop the cultural sciences and a systematic method of sociology and his relationship with Thomas.

———. 1969. "Introduction." Pp. 1–34 in Znaniecki (1969). Sketches Znaniecki's career and life, from his emigration from Poland to his collaboration with Thomas on *The Polish Peasant* (1918–19); briefly examines his early philosophical writings, his work on sociological method, his typology of social action, his lectures on the social role of the "man of knowledge" (Znaniecki 1940), and his work on the cultural sciences.

Billingsley, Andrew. 1970. "Horace R. Cayton, 1903–1970." *American Sociologist* 5 (November): 380–81. A brief statement about Cayton's career; he began his Ph.D. work at Chicago but found his formal training interrupted by his involvement in the black struggle in Chicago. Notes his authorship with St. Clair Drake of *The Black Metropolis* and other contributions.

Bittner, C. J. 1931. "G. H. Mead's Social Concept of the Self." *Sociology and Social Research* 16 (September): 6–22. On the occasion of Mead's death, Bittner reviews Mead's thought, especially his concepts of the "generalized other," and the "social self," and his distinction between the "I" and the "Me."

Blackwell, James E., and Morris Janowitz, eds. 1974. *Black Sociologists: Historical and Contemporary Perspectives*. Chicago: University of Chicago Press. A collection of papers growing out of a National Conference on Black Sociologists, held at Chicago, 5–6 May 1972; includes discussion of C. Johnson and Frazier, influences of Park and Thomas on black sociologists, and the role of the Chicago department in training black sociologists.

Blumer, Herbert. 1938. "Social Psychology." Pp. 144–98 in *Man and Society: A Substantive Introduction to the Social Sciences* edited by Emerson P. Schmidt. New York: Prentice-Hall. Traces developments in social psychology at Chicago, including Thomas (on the "definition of the situation," "attitudes," and "wishes," pp. 165, 180, 185–86), Mead (esp. pp. 180–84), and Thurstone (p. 190).

———. 1939a. "Collective Behavior." Pp. 221–80 in *An Outline of the Principles of Sociology* edited by Robert E. Park. New York: Barnes and Noble.

———. 1939b. *Critiques of Research in the Social Sciences, I: An Appraisal of Thomas and Znaniecki's "The Polish Peasant in Europe and America."*. New York: Social Science Research Council, Bulletin 44. Argues that *The Polish Peasant* (1918–19) was unsuccessful in providing general propositions that could be established by the particular facts adduced. Instead, it should be viewed not as a monograph on Polish peasant society, but as a basis for scientific social research and theory construction. See Thomas (1939), Znaniecki (1939), and Bain et al. (1939).

———. 1952. "In Memoriam: Louis Wirth, 1897–1952." *AJS* 58 (July): 69. Memorial statement reviews Wirth's study at Chicago and his teaching there from 1926 until his death on 3 May 1952. Comments that he "was equally at home in the realm of theory and in the field of minute empirical fact."

———. 1956. "Foreword." Pp. v–x in *Community Life and Social Policy: Selected Papers by Louis Wirth* edited by Elizabeth Wirth Marvick and Albert J. Reiss, Jr. Chicago: University of Chicago Press. A brief review of Wirth's talents and contributions—his impact as a teacher, a consultant on urban and social problems, and a sociological researcher. Contends that there are three noteworthy features of Wirth's writings: the unity of his thought, his concern with the analysis and understanding of the basis of a human society, and his realistic study of group life in its natural character.

———. 1957. *Collective Behavior*. Englewood Cliffs, N.J.: Prentice-Hall.

———. 1966. "Sociological Implications of the Thought of George Herbert Mead." *AJS* 71 (March): 535–44. Traces sociological ideas in Mead's philosophy with its emphasis on human group life as the essential condition for the emergence of consciousness, reversing traditional philosophical assumptions that humans possess minds and consciousness as original "givens." Explores Mead's notions of the self, the act, social interaction, objects, and joint action. Comment by Robert Bales (see Bales 1966), and reply by Blumer. Comments by Joseph Woelfel in *AJS* 72 (January, 1967): 409, and Gregory P. Stone and Harvey A. Farberman, *ibid.* (pp. 409–10), with a reply by Blumer, *ibid.* (pp. 411–12). Reprinted in Blumer (1969): 61–77.

———. 1967. "Ernest Watson Burgess, 1886–1966." *American Sociologist* 2 (May): 103–104. Recalls Burgess as a central figure at Chicago during the "zenith period of its eminence," commenting on his association with Park, Shaw, McKay, Merriam, Millis, and others. Notes that Burgess shared in the tradition of Thomas and Park: "to catch and respect human group life as it is being lived. . . ."

———. 1968. "Joseph D. Lohman, 1910–1968." *American Sociologist* 3 (August): 255–56. Remarks on the career of a Chicago-trained criminologist who studied primarily under Park and Burgess and was active in "social engineering." Notes similarities with Park, who also had "a restless imaginative mind, marked by incessant brooding over underlying social problems."

———. 1969. *Symbolic Interactionism: Perspective and Method.* Englewood Cliffs, N.J.: Prentice-Hall. An exposition of the symbolic interactionist approach (a term coined by Blumer; see p. 1), and the influences and implications of the work of Mead, and of Thomas and Znaniecki. Includes reprints of Blumer (1939a, 1966).

———. 1973. "A Note on Symbolic Interactionism." *ASR* 38 (December): 797–98. In responding to Huber (1973), Blumer contends that the real issue raised by Huber's charge "is not that the symbolic interactionist approach lacks theory but, instead, how the scientific problem is to get its theoretical shape. My impression is that she believes that this shaping must precede empirical observation." Although Huber is in line with dominant methodological positions in the discipline, Blumer prefers that theories grow out of ongoing examinations of the empirical field.

———. 1977. "Comment on Lewis' 'The Classic American Pragmatists as Forerunners to Symbolic Interactionism.'" *Sociological Quarterly* 18: 285–89. Contends that Lewis was inaccurate in arguing that Blumer was more influenced by Dewey than by Mead. Argues that symbolic interactionism does not represent a deviation from Mead's "social realism."

———. 1979. "Comments on 'George Herbert Mead and the Chicago Tradition of Sociology.'" *Symbolic Interaction* 2 (Fall): 21–22. Takes exception to

Fisher and Strauss's (1979b) contention that "Mead's work was used relatively *little* within the Chicago tradition."

———. 1980. "Mead and Blumer: The Convergent Methodological Perspective of Social Behaviorism and Symbolic Interactionism." *ASR* 45 (June): 409–19. Insists that McPhail and Rexroat (1979) have given an erroneous picture of (a) Blumer's view of social reality, (b) Blumer's view of naturalistic study, (c) Mead's view of scientific methods, and (d) Mead's view of social behavior. Contends further that they have reduced Mead's thought to a narrow scheme of how human behavior should be studied.

———. 1981. "Review of David Miller, *George Herbert Mead: Self, Language, and the World.*" *AJS* 86 (January): 902–904. Suggests that the notion of the "significant symbol" is the key element in Mead's thought and that Mead's scheme calls for a significantly different form of study and analysis of human society than most social science, although it is far from being complete.

Bogardus, Emory S. 1929. "Public Opinion as a Social Force: Race Relations." *SF* 8 (September): 102–105. Reviews race relations studies inaugurated in 1924 under the direction of Park as case studies of public opinion, noting the effect of public opinion concerning Japanese immigrants.

———. 1940. *The Development of Social Thought*. New York: David McKay. Surveys major figures in social thought, with substantial chapters on Thomas (Chapter 35), Park (Chapter 36) and Ellwood (Chapter 37).

———. 1949. "The Sociology of William I. Thomas." *Sociology and Social Research* 34 (September-October): 34–48. One of Thomas's students comments on Thomas's teaching methods, his interest in the study of ethnic groups, and his concepts of the four wishes, control, attitudes and values, the social situation, leaders, social institutions, and social disorganization.

———. 1950. "The Sociology of Charles A. Ellwood." *Sociology and Social Research* 34 (May-June, July-August): 365–73, 451–59. A two-part discussion of Ellwood's social thought, reporting that his study of human relations, "guided by humanized science," paid more attention to the intangible and imponderable factors in the human mind than to the factors which are measurable and observable.

———. 1959. "William I. Thomas and Social Origins." *Sociology and Social Research* 43 (May-June): 365–69. Recalls Thomas's course "Social Origins" in 1909–10; describes his socioevolutionary approach and comparative methods, and summarizes Thomas's lectures on the origins of intelligence, invention, language, emotions, races, personal control, and social control.

———. 1962. "Some Pioneer American Sociologists." *Sociology and Social Research* 47 (October): 25–33. Discusses six sociologists under whom Bogardus studied including Small, Thomas, Mead, and Park; postulates that the large universities in the Middle West had a favorable climate for the rise of sociology because of their less rigid curricula (compared to Eastern universities).

Bogue, Donald J. 1974. "Introduction." Pp. ix–xxv in Burgess (1974). Perhaps the most comprehensive account of Burgess's life and career, recounting his graduate work with Vincent, Thomas, Henderson, and Small and his collaboration with Park and others. Discusses his efforts in encouraging students (e.g., Hughes, Tibbits, McKay, Landesco, Anderson, Zorbaugh, Wirth, and Frazier) to do empirical research. Outlines his work in urban studies, the family, and gerontology and comments on his research methods (he was the first Chicago faculty member to use an electronic computer). Claims that Burgess was a social psychologist, a functionalist, and a positivist who believed interpersonal interaction to be the central mechanism for explaining social behavior, and social values to be the social phenomenon most worthy of study.

Bokszanski, Zbigniew. 1968. "Florian Znaniecki's Concept of Social Actions and the Theory of Action in Sociology." *Polish Sociological Bulletin* 1 (17): 18–29. Outlines Znaniecki's theory of action and compares his work to that of Weber, Simmel, Parsons, and others, arguing that Znaniecki's action theory involved extreme "sociologistic" attempts to eliminate psychological factors.

Bolton, Charles D. 1981. "Some Consequences of the Meadian Self." *Symbolic Interaction* 4 (Fall): 245–59. Analyzes Mead's conception of the self as an internal interaction process, looking at his distinction between the "I" and the "Me" from a phenomenological perspective. Notes problems created by influences from Darwin and his commitment to a strict behaviorism.

Bordua, David J. 1958–1959. "Juvenile Delinquency and Anomie." *Social Problems* 6 (Winter): 230–38. Discusses Lander's critique of Shaw and McKay and presents data from the Detroit Area Study that essentially confirm his findings, but suggest that Lander's concept of anomie serves to obscure the analysis. Reprinted in Voss and Petersen (1971, pp. 175–87).

———. 1961. "Delinquent Subcultures: Sociological Interpretations of Gang Delinquency." *The Annals of the American Academy of Political and Social Science* 338 (November): 120–36. Claims that the best book on gangs and delinquency is Thrasher's *The Gang* (1927), which he defends against criticisms from Cloward and Ohlin. Reprinted in Wolfgang et al. (1962, pp. 289–301).

Bornemann, Alfred. 1940. *J. Laurence Laughlin: Chapters in the Career of an Economist*. Washington, D.C.: American Council on Public Affairs. Study of the career of the head of the political economy department at the University of Chicago, who brought Veblen to Chicago and had several jurisdictional disputes with Small, particularly over the teaching of statistical methods.

Bougle, C., R. Marjolin, and R. Aron. 1936. "Revues Critiques, Analyses et

Bibliographie: I. Methodologie." *Annales sociologiques* Series A. (fasc. 2). Includes reviews of work by Znaniecki, Rice, Thomas, Ellwood, Chapin, and Ogburn.

Bowdery, Barbara Klose. 1951. "The Sociology of Robert E. Park." Ph.D. thesis, Columbia University. Treats Park's sociological career, and his contributions, commenting that his "zeal for social reform" and his efforts toward improvement of the situation of blacks led him into sociology. Suggests that Park's insights were not as fruitful as might have been expected, because of his failure to ask significant questions and to form hypotheses.

Bowen, Louise de Koven. 1946. *Open Windows: Stories of People and Places*. Chicago: R. F. Seymour and Company. This autobiography by a Chicago activist includes considerable discussion of Addams and the Hull House.

Bowers, David Frederick. 1944. "Hegel, Darwin and the American Tradition." Pp. 146–71 in *Foreign Influences in American Life* edited by David F. Bowers. Princeton: Princeton University Press. Discusses influences of Hegel and Darwin on American sociology and psychology, including the work of Veblen (p. 163) and especially that of Dewey (pp. 163–71). Suggests that Dewey's instrumentalism, in large part attributable to influences from Hegel and Darwin, provided a major break with American social thought, reinterpreting it in monistic, relativistic, and institutional terms.

Bowers, Raymond V. 1939. "The Ecological Patterning of Rochester, New York." *ASR* (April): 180–89. Provides some support for Burgess's zonal hypothesis in a study of Rochester.

Bowman, LeRoy E. 1927. "Review of Robert E. Park, Ernest W. Burgess, Roderick D. McKenzie, *The City*, and Ernest W. Burgess, ed., *The Urban Community*." *SF* 5 (June): 668–69. Remarks that these papers provide "a preliminary charting of aspects of a study of the city, regarding the city as the behavior of humans in a situation brought about by increased mobility and better means of communication," indicating that they are both suggestive of methods and promising of further developments. Discusses Wirth's comprehensive bibliography.

———. 1930. "Local Community Studies and Community Programs." *SF* 8 (June): 493–95. Argues that "the possible value of the studies made at the University of Chicago to social workers is great and fundamental," noting that of most importance is the hypothesis of the city as in some respects an organism and the city-making process a growth. Comments on the importance of work by Burgess and "that genius George Meade" (sic).

Boydston, Jo Ann, ed. 1970. *Guide to the Works of John Dewey*. Carbondale: Southern Illinois University Press. A collection of reviews of various aspects of Dewey's work; note especially Herbert W. Schneider,"Dewey's Psychology" (pp. 1–14); Wayne A. R. Leys, "Dewey's Social, Political, and Legal

Philosophy" (pp. 131–52); and William W. Brickman, "Dewey's Social and Political Commentary" (pp. 218–56).

Boydston, Jo Ann, with Robert L. Andersen, editor, compiler. 1969. *John Dewey: A Checklist of Translations, 1900–1967*. Carbondale, Ill.: Southern Illinois University Press. Lists all printings of translations of Dewey's works, including a comprehensive chronological table, demonstrating the breadth of Dewey's world-wide impact.

Boydston, Jo Ann, and Kathleen Poulos. 1974. *Checklist of Writings About John Dewey, 1887–1973*. Carbondale, Ill.: University of Southern Illinois Press. A detailed and comprehensive bibliography of Dewey's work and scholarly analyses of it; an indispensible aid to the analysis of Dewey's influence on sociology and American thought.

Bracey, John H., August Meier, and Elliott Rudwick, eds. 1970. *The Black Sociologists: The First Half Century*. Belmont, Cal.: Wadsworth. A collection that includes an introduction discussing the role of Chicago, particularly Park, in training black sociologists C. Johnson, Frazier, Doyle, Drake, and Cayton, whose works are featured in the selections of the volume. Indicates that although Park's moderation in the area of racial equality has evoked criticism, he was instrumental in facilitating a "transition of mainstream sociology's stance from racism to an attempt at objectivity in racial studies."

Bramson, Leon. 1961. *The Political Context of Sociology*. Princeton: Princeton University Press. Finds a tension between European sociological concepts and the liberalism which appears dramatically in the works of such men as "Park and other members of the German-influenced Chicago school of sociology" (p. 17). See especially chapters 3 (on collective behavior) and 4 (esp. pp. 86–93) in which he comments on Park, Veblen, Thomas, Wirth, Burgess, McKenzie, Ogburn, Mead, and Faris.

Brandt, Gunther. 1974. "The Origins of American Sociology: A Study in the Ideology of Social Science, 1865–1895." Ph.D. thesis, Princeton University. A study of the emergence of American sociology, with an emphasis on the values, assumptions, and ideologies of some of the discipline's key progenitors, including Small, Ward, and Giddings.

Braude, Lee. 1970a. "Louis Wirth and the Locus of Sociological Commitment." *American Sociologist* 5 (August): 233–39. Suggests that contemporary debates over the relevance of sociology to social problems could be improved by reviewing Wirth's effort to use sociology as a method for confronting social problems. Argues that when Wirth came to the Chicago department he was captivated by "its largely pro-Russian political climate; under the influence of Albion Small he saw in sociology the possibility of bringing to fruition a Marxist-Leninist version of social equality." Notes efforts by Breckenridge (arrested for leading an immigrants' protest) and Thomas.

———. 1970b. " 'Park and Burgess': An Appreciation." *AJS* 76 (July): 1–10. Assesses the influence of Park and Burgess's *Introduction* (1921) on those sociologists who studied at Chicago and subsequently helped to define the discipline.

Breckenridge, Sophonisba P., and Leonard D. White. 1929. "Urban Growth and Problems of Social Control." Pp. 194–219 in Smith and White (1929). Reviews research conducted under the auspices of the LCRC to determine the boundaries and social organization of local communities in Chicago, including work by E. Abbott, Merriam, Burgess, Beyle, White, Gosnell, Leland, Jeter, Ogburn, and others. Notes cooperation with the Union League Club, the International City Managers' Association, the Rosenwald Fund, the Marshall Field Estate, the School of Social Service the Helen Crittenden Memorial Fund, and other institutions.

Bressler, Marvin. 1952. "Selected Family Patterns in W. I. Thomas' Unfinished Study of the Bintl Brief." *ASR* 17 (October): 563–71. Comments on Thomas's unfinished study of letters to the editor of the Yiddish socialist newspaper, *The New York Jewish Daily Forward*. Thomas found the letters to be an excellent resource for the study of patterns of interaction and adaptation, and definitions of the situation developed by immigrant Eastern European Jews. The study was unfinished at the time of Thomas's death in 1947, although some of the letters were excerpted in *Old World Traits Transplanted* (1921) and *The Unadjusted Girl* (1923).

Brickman, William W. 1970. "Dewey's Social and Political Commentary." Pp. 218–57 in Boydston (1970). Summarizes Dewey's social thought, including influences provided by his association with Addams and her Hull House in Chicago (pp. 221–23).

Brodsky, G. M. 1969. "Absolute Idealism and John Dewey's Instrumentalism." *Transactions of the Charles S. Peirce Society* 5 (Winter): 44–62. Observes the importance of Dewey's interest in classical problems of nineteenth century idealism and his solution based on the relation between inquiry and the world of experience, and between meaning and practice.

Brooks, Lee M. 1938. "Review of Edith Abbott, *The Tenements of Chicago, 1908–1935* and Edward M. Bassett, *Zoning*." *SF* 16 (March): 432–34. Comments on Abbott's volume (Chicago: University of Chicago Press, 1936), indicating that she and her group had been studying and re-studying Chicago's tenements for over twenty-five years.

———. 1963. "Jesse Frederick Steiner (1880–1962)." *SF* 41 (May): 403–404. Memorial tribute noting Steiner's study under Park at Chicago, his civic and social services, his involvement with the early volumes of *Social Forces* and his teaching at North Carolina, Tulane, and Washington, as well as visiting at Chicago.

Brotherston, B. W. 1943. "Genius of Pragmatic Empiricism." *Journal of Philosophy* 40 (7, 21 January): 41–21, 29–39. Applauds insights in the approaches developed by Dewey and Mead, but contends that a spurious metaphysical realism in Mead hides the genius of pragmatic empiricism.

Broyer, John A. 1973. "Bibliography of Writings of George Herbert Mead." Pp. 243–60 in Corti (1973). A valuable source book which indicates contents and cites reviews of each of Mead's published works.

Bulmer, Martin. 1980. "The Early Institutional Establishment of Social Science Research: The Local Community Research Committee at the University of Chicago, 1923–1930." *Minerva* 18 (Spring): 51–110. Discusses the organization of the LCRC and sketches the purposes of the committee and its history, noting the importance of funding from the Laura Spellman Rockefeller fund and other foundations. Outlines the diverse approaches and interests of the Committee, including work by Park and Burgess and their students, especially Thrasher, Zorbaugh, E. and R. Mowrer, Anderson, Hayner, Cressey, Wirth, Stephan, Brown, Lind, Tibbitts, E. Hughes, Palmer, and others. Notes the role of Small in founding the Committee and others, e.g., Merriam, Burgess, Ogburn, Thurstone, and E. Abbott.

———. 1981a. "Charles S. Johnson, Robert E. Park, and the Research Methods of the Chicago Commission on Race Relations, 1919–1922: An Early Experiment in Applied Social Research." *Ethnic and Racial Studies* 4 (July): 289–306. A detailed analysis of the methods and conclusions of studies by Johnson and the Chicago Commissions on Race Relations, of blacks in Chicago. Includes a biographical sketch of Johnson and information about the Commission and the Chicago Urban League, of which Park was president.

———. 1981b. "Quantification and the Chicago Social Sciences in the 1920s: A Neglected Tradition." *JHBS* 17 (July): 312–31. Summarizes quantitative research developed at Chicago, noting that the richness and range of methods in Chicago sociology is not reflected in the generalized image of the department. Outlines methodological developments initiated by Burgess, Park, Ogburn, Thurstone, Stouffer, Merriam, Gosnell, Woody, White, Field, Palmer, and others, and comments on the importance of the LCRC.

———. 1982a. "*The Polish Peasant in Europe and America*: A Neglected Minor Classic." *New Community* 11 (Winter). Discusses the methodological and substantive importance of Thomas and Znaniecki's *The Polish Peasant* and its significance for the study of minority group and race relations at Chicago.

———. 1982b. "Support for Sociology in the 1920's." *American Sociologist* 17: 185–92. Examines the history of the principle source of funding for social science research at Chicago in the 1920's and discusses the extent to which foundations influenced academic developments.

———. 1983a. "The Society for Social Research: An Institutional Underpinning to the Chicago School of Sociology in the 1920's." *Urban Life* 11 (January): 421–39. The history of the Society in the 1920's, when it served as a means of promoting research in the sociology department, with an active seminar program, Summer Institute, and a *Bulletin* to members. The latter two were very important elements in maintaining the network of Chicago alumni and the influence of Chicago sociology up to 1935.

———. 1983b. "The Methodology of *The Taxi-Dance Hall*: An Early Account of Field Research by Paul G. Cressey." *Urban Life* 12 (April). An unpublished account from the late 1920's of his field-work methods by Paul G. Cressey is preceded by an introduction which discusses the evolution of field research during the decade.

———. 1983c. "The Methodology of Early Social Indicator Research: William Fielding Ogburn and *Recent Social Trends* 1933." *Social Indicators Research* 13 (August): 109–30. An unpublished "note on method," written in 1932 by Ogburn for the President's Research Committee on Recent Social Trends, is published with an introduction discussing the work of the committee and Ogburn's conception of scientific method.

———. 1984. *The Chicago School of Sociology: Institutionalization, Diversity, and the Rise of Sociological Research*. Chicago: University of Chicago Press. Focuses on the conditions fostering the Chicago school of sociology in the period 1915 to 1930, concentrating on two themes: the institutionalization of social science research and the contribution of Chicago to social research methodology. The history of the department, the key importance of Thomas and Park, and the organizing abilities of Burgess, are set in the context of the development in the 1920's of the Local Community Research Committee and the Society for Social Research. The growth of both qualitative and quantitative methods of research is considered, with particular emphasis on the latter, which have been underemphasized. Other figures discussed include Ogburn, Thurstone, Merriam, Gosnell, White, Shaw and McKay, Stouffer, Stephan, and Charles S. Johnson.

Bulmer, Martin, and Joan Bulmer. 1981. "Philanthropy and Social Science in the 1920's: The Case of Beardsley Ruml and the Laura Spelman Rockefeller Memorial, 1922–29." *Minerva* 19 (Autumn): 347–407. Traces the way in which philanthropic beneficence helped to transform the condition of the social sciences in America in the 1920's, before the advent of significant federal government support for research. An amplification of Bulmer (1980), which includes a discussion of grant aid to the University of Chicago.

Burger, John S., and Mary Jo Deegan. 1981. "George Herbert Mead on Internationalism, Democracy and War." *Wisconsin Sociologist* 18 (Spring-Summer): 72–83. Examines Mead's conception of the relation between the self and the world community. Methods for containing armed conflict include the exercise of democracy and reflection.

Burgess, Ernest W. 1924a. "Can Neighborhood Work Have a Scientific Basis?" *Proceedings of the National Conference of Social Work* 51 (Annual): 406–11. Discusses research in urban neighborhoods and its implications for social workers, noting the examination of urban zones, cultural and political forces, and the use of the city and settlement houses as laboratories for social research.

———. 1924b. "The Growth of the City: An Introduction to a Research Project." *Publications of the American Sociological Society* 18 (Annual): 85–97. Presents "the point of view and methods of investigation which the [Chicago] department of sociology is employing in its studies in the growth of the city, namely, to describe urban expansion in terms of extension, success, and concentration; to determine how expansion disturbs metabolism when disorganization is in excess of organization; and finally, to define mobility and to propose it as a measure both of expansion and metabolism." Discusses work by Park, Anderson, Mowrer, Reckless, Shideler, Thrasher, Zorbaugh, and others, and outlines his zonal hypothesis. Reprinted, pp. 47–62 in Park, Burgess, and McKenzie (1925).

———. 1929a. "Basic Social Data." Pp. 47–66 in Smith and White (1929). Discusses the LCRC's research and summarizes the compilation of data from the Illinois Health Insurance Commission, the Cook County Jail Survey, news clippings of the Chicago Citizens' Association, files of the Committee of Fifteen, data from the Illinois Crime Survey made by the Illinois Association for Criminal Justice, and materials from the U.S. Census Bureau. Reviews mapping activities and efforts to determine boundaries of local communities (under under Palmer's supervision) and other activities of the Committee.

———. 1929b. "Studies of Institutions." Pp. 139–76 in Smith and White (1929). Discusses efforts of the LCRC to study social institutions in Chicago, notably projects undertaken by E. Abbott and Breckinridge, Burgess, Thomas, E. and H. Mowrer, Shaw, Frazier, Anderson, Zorbaugh, Kincheloe, Holt, Marshall, Magee, Stone, Hughes, Tibbitts, Cressey, Thrasher, Landesco, Sapir, and others.

———. 1929c. "Urban Areas." Pp. 113–38 in Smith and White (1929). Outlines the zonal theory of urban formation and studies of Chicago by Shideler, Anderson, Zorbaugh, Breckinridge, Edith Abbott, Tibbitts, Wirth, Reckless, Glick, Gosnell, Shaw, and others.

———. 1930a. "Discussion." Pp. 184–97 in Shaw (1930). Talks about the autobiography and Shaw's presentation of it, with comments on the life-history approach to investigation and treatment of delinquency. notes the work's relation to the study of delinquency by Shaw, Thrasher, and other Chicago studies.

———. 1930b. "The Value of Sociological Community Studies for the Work of Social Agencies." *SF* 8 (June): 481–91. Summarizes policy implications of studies developing out of Chicago studies in community life, noting work by Anderson, Thrasher, Mowrer, Palmer, Shaw, Wirth, Zorbaugh, Smith, White, and others. Observes that rather than disappearing, local communities are becoming more and more interwoven with the entire structure of the city and are playing a new but significant role.

———. 1932. "Introduction." Pp. xi–xvi in Cressey (1932). A brief, but informative, treatment of the purposes of Cressey's study of taxi-dance halls and its role in the sociological examination of urban institutions and social life.

———. 1939a. "Discussion." Pp. 235–54 in Shaw (1939). Outlines the advantages of the life-history approach to research and comments on the case of Sidney reported in the volume.

———. 1939b. "Editor's Preface." Pp. ix–xvii in Frazier (1939). Assesses Frazier's work on the black family, contending that it is the most valuable contribution to the literature on the family since *The Polish Peasant* (Thomas and Znaniecki 1918–19) and that it establishes the background for further research. Emphasizes that blacks in America constitute "a cultural and only secondarily a biological group."

———. 1939c. "The Influence of Sigmund Freud upon Sociology in the United States." *AJS* 45 (November): 356–74. Assesses the influence of psychoanalysis on sociology in terms of both personal orientation of sociologists and sociological theory; considers Freud's influence on Chicago sociologists and indicates that Park and Burgess's *Introduction* was the first textbook in sociology to introduce psychoanalytical concepts and findings.

———. 1942. "Introduction." Pp. ix–xiii in Shaw and McKay (1942). Concludes that the work is a *magnum opus* in criminology, and traces the development of Shaw and McKay's research into the relationship between the distribution of juvenile delinquents and the physical structure and social organization of the American city, relating it to Burgess's own concentric zones theory.

———. 1944. "Robert E. Park, 1864–1944." *AJS* 49 (March): 478. Briefly traces Park's career and major scholarly contributions; contends that he combined in rare degree the capacity for research upon concrete problems and the drive to work out an integrated system of sociology.

———. 1945. "Sociological Research Methods." *AJS* 50 (May): 474–82. Examines past fifty years of the *AJS* to discern research trends in sociology (1895–1945), from the formulation of ideology in the early period, to the development of concepts and fashioning of methods of research; includes discussion of Chicago sociologists and issues of general methodology in 1945.

———. 1948. "William I. Thomas as a Teacher." *Sociology and Social Research* 32 (March-April): 760–64. Comments on courses he took from Thomas, as well as those offered by Small, Henderson, and Vincent, discussing Thomas's methods of teaching and subject matter covered in his courses. Concludes that the great majority of courses in the Chicago department use the conceptual system and personal documents developed by Thomas. Summarizes Thomas's attempts to develop a scientific social psychology and his concern with using data to demonstrate the equality of blacks and women.

———. 1952. "Louis Wirth, 1897–1952." *ASR* 17 (August): 499. A brief memorial statement reviewing Wirth's career and interests, noting his strong belief in the value of research findings for the shaping of social policy and programs.

———. 1953. "Review of Robert Park, *Human Communities: The City and Human Ecology*." *AJS* 58 (January): 439–40. Review of the volume by Park (Glencoe, Ill.: Free Press, 1952), discussing Park's love of the city, both as a journalist and as a sociologist. Notes his encounters with James, Dewey, Mead, Royce, Santayana, Ford, Windelband, and most importantly, Simmel. Notes that when Park developed a systematic sociological system he was in close association with Thomas and that they kept their theoretical formulations in close relationship with the concrete reality of social life. Discusses Park's development of the human ecology approach.

———. 1956a. "Charles S. Johnson: Social Scientist and Race Relations." *Phylon* 17 (Fourth Quarter): 317–21. Summarizes Johnson's work on race relations and the influence of Park, Thomas, Faris, and Mead on his approach.

———. 1956b. "Seven Significant Changes in Sociology." *Sociology and Social Research* 40 (July-August): 385–86. A very brief discussion including a distinction among three generations of sociologists: (1) the founders (including Small and others), who surveyed the field and constructed conceptual systems; (2) the movement for research exemplified by and *The Polish Peasant* (Thomas and Znaniecki 1918–19); and (3) the development of rigorous methods, conceptualization of the problem, project design, and methods of proof, exemplified by Stouffer et al., *The American Soldier* (1949a, 1949b).

———. 1957. "Charles Spurgeon Johnson, 1893–1956." *ASR* 22 (April): 226–27. A brief memorial outlining Johnson's career and his study under Park, Small, Thomas, and Faris at Chicago, his research on racial problems, and other accomplishments.

———. 1961. "Social Planning and Race Relations." Pp. 13–25 in Masuoka and Valien (1961). Examines Park's interest in race relations, his work with Washington and his training of sociologists for research in the field, especially C. Johnson, Reuter, Wirth, Frazier, Lohman, Stouffer, E. C. Hughes, H. M. Hughes, Cayton, Copeland, Dai, Dollard, Detweiler, G. Johnson, Jones, La Violette, Lind, Parrish, Pierson, Redfield, Stonequist, R. Sutherland, Thompson, Doyle, and others.

———. 1967. "A Short History of Urban Research at the University of Chicago before 1946." Pp. 2–12 in Burgess and Bogue (1967c). A revision of an informative talk given by Burgess before a seminar dealing with "New Directions for Urban Research." Reviews developments at Chicago in urban sociology, including the work of Thomas, Park, E. Abbott, Breckenridge, Taylor, Johnson, Ruml, Shaw, Faris, Dunham, Anderson, Wirth and others, as well as the founding of the LCRC.

———. 1974. *The Basic Writings of Ernest W. Burgess*. edited by Donald J. Bogue. Chicago: Community Family Study Center, University of Chicago.

Burgess, Ernest W., and Donald J. Bogue. 1967a. "The Delinquency Research of Clifford R. Shaw and Henry D. McKay and Associates." Pp. 293–317 in in Burgess and Bogue (1967c). Discussion and abstracts of the research on juvenile delinquency carried out by Shaw, McKay, and others, noting that "empirical American sociology was perhaps popularized and transmitted to all corners of the world by the Shaw monographs more than any other examples of this brand of social research."

———. 1967b. "Research in Urban Society: A Long View." Pp. 1–14 in Burgess and Bogue (1967c). Traces development of sociological studies of urban areas, particularly at the University of Chicago; includes Burgess (1967).

———, eds. 1967c. *Urban Sociology*. An abridged edition of *Contributions to Urban Sociology*, edited by Ernest W. Burgess and Donald J. Bogue (Chicago: University of Chicago Press, 1964), containing a collection of essays by Chicago urban sociologists. See Burgess and Bogue (1967a, 1967b) and Burgess (1967).

Burgess, Ernest W., and Harvey J. Locke 1945. *The Family: From Institution to Companionship*. New York: American Book Co.

Burgess, Ernest W., Joseph Lohman, and Clifford R. Shaw. 1937. "The Chicago Area Project." Pp. 8–28 in *Yearbook of the National Probation and Parole Association*. New York. Details the history, nature, and purpose of the Chicago Area Project, which was established to study delinquency in Chicago in order to determine to what extent constructive changes could be affected in the social environment to reduce delinquency. Discusses Shaw, McKay, and Dewey. Reprinted in Bogue (1974).

Burgess, Robert L. and Ronald L. Akers. 1966. "A Differential Association-Reinforcement Theory of Criminal Behavior." *Social Problems* 14 (Fall): 128–47. Applies principles of modern behavior theory to reformulate Sutherland's differential association theory, commenting on the lack of major theoretical revisions despite the growth in experimental findings of the processes of learning.

Burke, Kenneth. 1938–39. "George Herbert Mead." *New Republic* 97 (11 January): 292–93. A review of the three volumes of Mead's lectures.

Burke, Richard J., Jr. 1960. "George Herbert Mead and Harry Stack Sullivan." Ph.D. thesis, University of Chicago.

Burnet, Jean. 1964. "Robert E. Park and the Chicago School of Sociology: A Centennial Tribute." *Canadian Review of Sociology and Anthropology* 1 (August): 156–64. Insists that the notion that Park transmitted only a few field work techniques and a limited doctrine to his students is false. Reports Park's social theory and concerns with social problems, his influence on colleagues and students (e.g., Redfield), and Simmel's influence on Park.

Burns, Lawton R. 1980. "The Chicago School and the Study of Organization-Environment Relations." *JHBS* 16 (October): 342–58. Observes that reigning paradigms in contemporary organization research have an ecological perspective with its roots in Chicago sociology, especially the works of Park and his students Shideler, Hughes, McKenzie, and Hawley. Notions of "environmental selection" and "adaptation" are anticipated in earlier Chicago models of ecological, economic, and cultural organization, continued in the writings of community theorists.

Bursik, Robert J., Jr., and Jim Webb. 1982. "Community Change and Patterns of Delinquency." *AJS* 88 (July): 24–42. Reexamines Shaw and McKay's contention that the distributional pattern of delinquency in Chicago remained relatively stable over time despite processes of ethnic and racial invasion and succession; finds their proposal to be true only between 1940–50.

Cahnman, Werner J. 1966. "The Historical Sociology of Cities: A Critical Review." *SF* 45 (December): 155–61. Refers primarily to Sjoberg and Reissman, but includes a discussion of Wirth, observing that most discussions of his characteristics of the city include size, density, and heterogeneity, but omit a fourth—individuation (p. 157).

———. 1977. "Toennies in America." *History and Theory* 16 (No. 2): 147–67. Includes discussion of Park's relation to Toennies.

———. 1978. "Robert Park at Fisk." *JHBS* 14 (October): 328–36. Cahnman's personal reminiscences of Park during the time Cahnman was teaching with Park at Fisk; discusses Park's concern about racial issues and Park's relation to Redfield, James, Dewey, Washington, Frazier, and others.

Caldwell, Robert G. 1958. "A Reexamination of the Concept of White Collar Crime." *Federal Probation* 22 (March): 30–36. Critiques Sutherland's notion of "white collar crime," insisting that no one should be called a criminal if he or she has not been convicted in a criminal court.

Campbell, James. 1981. "George Herbert Mead on Intelligent Social Reconstruction." *Symbolic Interaction* 4 (Fall): 191–205. Examines Mead's theory of social change, claiming that the traditional focus on his social psychology, especially in Mead (1934), has blinded readers to its importance. Notes the relationship between his approach to social change and pragmatic philosophy, particularly Mead's analysis of collective action which stresses the "possibility of intelligent action to address, to mitigate, and at times to solve, our collective ills.

Cantril, Hadley. 1935. "A Psychological Reason for the Lag of "Non-Material" Culture Traits." *SF* 13 (March): 376–79. Complains that Ogburn is too vague in his discussion of cultural lag and discusses psychological factors affecting attitudes and non-material traits.

Carey, James T. 1975. *Sociology and Public Affairs: The Chicago School.* Beverly Hills: Sage. Considers the Chicago department focusing on the period from the end of World War I until the early 1930s. Contends that the vigor and creativity of the Chicago School cannot be understood without consideration of a number of factors: their reaction to social and technological trends; the intellectual power of their explanatory scheme; the academic setting which encouraged teaching, research, and public service; and the unusual and supportive relations Chicago sociologists developed with other professional groups.

Castells, Manuel. 1968. "Y a-t-il une sociologie urbaine?" *Sociologie du Travail* 1 (January-March): 72–90. Outlines various aspects of Chicago urban sociology, particularly the social disorganization and urban subcultures examined by Park, Burgess, and others, as well as Wirth's "urbanism as a way of life" perspective. Discusses their critics and the context in which they worked.

———. 1977. *The Urban Question: A Marxist Approach.* Translated by Alan Sheridan. Cambridge: MIT Press. Develops a Marxist critique of Wirth, Park, Redfield, and the Chicago School (pp. 75–80), objecting particularly to their urban-rural dichotomy. Suggests that Wirth, as Park's most brilliant disciple, developed what was probably the most serious theoretical attempt within sociology to establish a theoretical object and domain of research specific to urban sociology. Criticizes Burgess's concentric zone theory and human ecology as ethnocentric (pp. 116ff.).

Cavan, Ruth Shonle 1928. *Suicide.* Chicago: University of Chicago Press.

———. 1983. "The Chicago School of Sociology, 1918–1933." *Urban Life* 11 (January): 407–20. Personal recollections of the department focusing on developments 1918–33 (she was a graduate student 1922–26), a period of "transition between the founding period and the establishment of objective research," with discussions of Small, Park, Burgess, Faris, and others.

Chalasinski, Jozef. 1968. "Florian Znaniecki: Tenth Anniversary of the Death of Florian Znaniecki." *Polish Sociological Bulletin* 2 (18): 7–8. Discusses Znaniecki's career and influence and his association with Thomas, as well as his Sociological Institute at the University in Poznan.

Chambers, Clarke A. 1963. *Seedtime of Reform: American Social Service and Social Action, 1918–1933*. Minneapolis: University of Minnesota Press. Although not directly concerned with Chicago sociology, this work provides background information on social reform movements, settlement houses, and the New Deal. Includes discussion of the ideas and activities of Addams, Grace and Edith Abbott, Breckenridge, Dewey, Zueblin, and others. Discusses Hoover's President's Research Committee on Social Trends (pp. 243–45) which included Ogburn, Merriam, and Odum.

Chapin, F. Stuart. 1934. "The Present State of the Profession." *AJS* 39 (January): 506–508. Comparing the number of graduate students in sociology in 1933 with the number of academic positions in the discipline in the United States, Chapin contends that there is a dangerous over-production of sociology Ph.D.'s, especially at Chicago and Columbia.

———. 1935. "Measurement in Sociology." *AJS* 40 (January): 476–80. Defends Chapin's quantitative techniques (esp. the "living-room scale") criticized by House (1934), suggesting that in sociology qualitative word symbols are used as means of description, that in physics the numerical symbol is more widely used. Argues that attitudes, social distance, and social status are not intrinsically more complex concepts than such physical concepts as the molecule, atom, or electron, and that numerical symbols of description would allow the sociologist to be more precise. See also Bain (1935).

Charon, Joel M. 1979. *Symbolic Interactionism: An Introduction, an Interpretation, an Integration*. Englewood Cliffs, N.J.: Prentice-Hall. An exposition of interactionist theory contains lengthy treatments of the work of Mead and Blumer, with additional comments on Thomas, Dewey, and others. Notes the role of Mead, Blumer, pragmatism, Darwin, and behaviorism in the development of symbolic interactionism.

Chasin, Gerald. 1964. "George Herbert Mead: Social Psychologist of the Moral Society." *Berkeley Journal of Sociology* 9: 95–117. Articulates Mead's conception of the ideal society to show how Mead's social psychology was intended to help make that society possible. In a comment (pp. 118–22), Blumer claims that Chasin's presentation is a caricature of Mead's thought, advising students not to go to Chasin's article in order to understand Mead's views; Chasin responds (pp. 123–26).

Chilton, Roland J. 1964. "Continuity in Delinquency Area Research: A Comparison of Studies for Baltimore, Detroit, and Indianapolis." *ASR* 29 (February): 71–83. Evaluates Shaw and McKay's work and their critics, comparing data from a study of Indianapolis with studies of Baltimore (Lander 1954) and Detroit (Bordua 1958–1959), noting a similarity of results in all three studies, but raising questions about Lander's emphasis on anomie. Reprinted in Voss and Petersen (1971), pp. 189–208.

Chombard de Lauwe, P. H. 1950, 1952. *Paris et l'agglomération parisienne.* Paris: Presses Universitaires de France. Includes some evidence of support for an application of the ecological approach to Paris.

Choukas, Michael. 1936. "The Concept of Cultural Lag Re-examined." *ASR* 1 (October): 752–60. Attempts to present an explicit, systematic outline of Ogburn's concept of "cultural lag" and its relation to fundamental sociological principles.

Choy, Jyan. 1926. *Etude comparative sur les doctrines pedagogiques de Durkheim et de Dewey.* Lyon: Bosc Fières & Riou. Compares the work of Durkheim and Dewey, with particular attention to implications of their philosophies of education.

Chrisman, Robert. 1970. "Ecology is a Racist Shuck." *Scanlan's Monthly* 1 (August): 46–49. A scathing critique of racist implications of the ecological perspective.

Christakes, George. 1978. *Albion W. Small.* Boston: Twayne. A biography and intellectual portrait of Small as a transitional figure between the dedicated preacademic type of sociologist (e.g., Ward) and the professional academic sociologist (e.g., Ross); emphasizes ideas about society and social change that Small developed, adopted, borrowed, and imported (especially from German social thought).

Chudacoff, Howard P. 1976. "Introduction, 1976." Pp. vii–xv in *The Gold Coast and the Slum: A Sociological Study of Chicago's Near North Side* by Harvey Zorbaugh. Chicago: University of Chicago Press. Discusses Zorbaugh as one of the first to recognize that patterns of neighborhood life resulted from historical processes in the growth of the city. Claims that his richly detailed descriptions reveal important forms of social organization that imply alternative types of community life, some of which Zorbaugh himself did not recognize.

Ciacci, Margherita. 1972. "Gli Insegmamenti di Chicago: G. H. Mead l'Interazionismo Simbolico." *Rassegna italiana di Sociologia* 13 (April-June): 263–95. Examines the basic concepts of Mead's perspective on the relationship between the individual and society, with an assessment of the influence of this perspective on later sociologists, notably in the Chicago School.

Clark, Caroll D. 1954. "The Contribution of William Fielding Ogburn." *Midwest Sociologist* 16 (Spring): 3–7. Reviews Ogburn's work in "helping to forge sound methods of sociological research" and increase our tested knowledge, noting his role in Chicago sociology.

———. 1962. "Sociology and the Midwest in the Perspective of Twenty-Five Years." *Sociological Quarterly* 3 (October): 267–77. Includes some review of the Chicago department's influence on sociology in the midwest and mentions the authors work with Park on collective behavior.

Clausen, John A., and Melvin L. Kohn. 1954. "The Ecological Approach in Social Psychiatry." *AJS* 60 (September): 140–48. Takes stock of various efforts to explain the frequency of mental illness on the basis of ecological variables, notably Faris and Dunham's (1939) *Mental Disorder in Urban Areas*. Followed with a comment by Dunham (pp. 149–51) and a rejoinder.

Clayton, A. S. 1943. *Emergent Mind and Education: A Study of George H. Mead's Bio-Social Behaviorism from an Educational Point of View*. New York: Columbia University, Bureau of Publications, Teachers College. Details Mead's theories of the self and mind and their implications for educational policy and practice.

Clinard, Marshall B. 1951. "Sociologists and American Criminology." *Journal of Criminal Law and Criminology* 41 (January-February): 549–77. Reviews the history of sociological American criminology, noting Thomas and Znaniecki's *Polish Peasant* (1918–19) and the development of urban sociological studies by Park and Burgess as the chief stimuli in its development. Comments on work by Henderson, Burgess, Thrasher, Shaw, McKay, Sutherland, Reckless, Blumer, Hauser, Cavan, and others.

Cloward, Richard A., and Lloyd E. Ohlin. 1960. *Delinquency and Opportunity: A Theory of Delinquent Gangs*. New York: Free Press. Includes an examination of two closely related theoretical perspectives from the "Chicago tradition": Shaw and McKay's "cultural transmission" theory and Sutherland's "differential association" concept (see esp. pp. 35–36, 154ff.). Portion reprinted in Wolfgang et al. (1962, pp. 255–58).

Cochran, Thomas C. 1968. "Business in Veblen's America." Pp. 47–71 in Qualey (1968). Comments on Veblen as a pioneer in the study of business administration and business history, noting his belief that American business could be better run by engineers and experts than by profit-seeking business people.

Cohen, Albert K. 1968. "Edwin H. Sutherland." Pp. 438–39 in Sills (1968), Vol. 15. A brief review of Sutherland's work, especially his theory of differential association, by one of Sutherland's students. Argues that Sutherland did more than any other individual to shape the substantive theory and methodological orientation of contemporary criminology.

Cohen, Albert J. 1955. *Delinquent Boys: The Culture of the Gang*. New York: Free Press. Contains numerous brief references to and discussions of Shaw, McKay, and Thrasher throughout.

Cole, Fay-Cooper. 1943. "In Memoriam: Franz Boas." *AJS* 48 (March): 603. A brief review of Boas's career by one of his Chicago students, who claims that Boas, more than any other person, had dominated and influenced American anthropology in the previous half-century.

Cole, Fay-Cooper, and Fred Eggan. 1959. "Robert Redfield: 1897–1958." *American Anthropologist* New Series 61 (August): 652–62. A memorial account of Redfield's life and work, especially his interest in the comparative study of civilization, with a bibliography of his published writings.

Commager, Henry Steele. 1961. "Foreword." Pp. vii–xvi in *Twenty Years at Hull-House* by Jane Addams. New York: New American Library (Signet Books). A brief discussion of Addams's life and work, her Hull House activities and her interest in issues of racial prejudice and poverty, as part of this reissue of Addams (1910).

Conway, Jill. 1964. "Jane Addams: An American Heroine." *Daedalus* 93 (Spring): 761–80. Comments on the social context of Addams's work, her relations with the Abbotts, and her reform activities, noting that Hull House became an intellectual center in Chicago, and commenting on influences from Darwin and Spencer.

Cook, Gary A. 1972. "The Development of G. H. Mead's Social Psychology." *Transactions of the Charles S. Peirce Society* 8 (Summer): 167–862. Analyzes Mead's published articles from 1900 to 1913 in order to avoid being restricted to *Mind, Self and Society* (1934; cf. Strauss 1964), suggesting that by the publication of "The Social Self" in 1913, Mead's inquiries had led him "to almost all of the major ideas of his mature social psychology." Later works "involve no significant departure from the genetic and social functionalism" developed in the earlier essays.

———. 1977. "G. H. Mead's Alleged Behaviorism." *JHBS* 13 (October): 307–16. Treats Mead's early commitment to the organic conception of conduct underlying the psychological functionalism of the Chicago School and points to fundamental differences between Mead and the behaviorist tradition in American psychology.

———. 1979. "Whitehead's Influence on the Thought of G. H. Mead." *Transactions of the Charles S. Peirce Society* 15 (Spring): 107–31. Examines evidence of Whitehead's influence on Mead following 1921, arguing that although he was neither a disciple nor a systematic critic of Whitehead, Mead found a source of inspiration in Whitehead's work.

Cooper, Edna. 1945. "Bibliography of Robert E. Park." *Phylon* 6 (Fourth Quarter): 372–83. An extensive bibliography of Park's publications, including books, articles,and book reviews.

Corey, Lewis. 1937. "Veblen and Marxism." *Marxist Quarterly* 1 (January-March): 162–68. This review essay of Mitchell (1936) examines the relationship between Veblen and Marxism, claiming that Veblen "more than any other American thinker offers material and ideas of utmost significance to Marxism, despite the fact that Veblen was not an "American Marx." Examines Veblen's critique of Marxism and refutes his Darwinism.

Corti, Walter Robert, ed. 1973. *The Philosophy of George Herbert Mead.* Wintherthur, Switzerland: Amriswiler. A varied collection which includes a thorough bibliography of the writings of Mead which indicates contents and reviews of each work. See separate entries under Ames, Broyer, E. Eames, S. Eames, Geyer, Jamali, List, and Miller.

Coser, Lewis A. 1968. "Introduction." in Znaniecki (1940). Assesses Znaniecki's role as a "founding father" in both American and Polish sociology, his work with Thomas on *The Polish Peasant* (1918–19), and his founding of the Polish Sociological Institute and the *Polish Sociological Review*. Remarks that the most important contribution of *The Social Role of the Man of Knowledge* (1940) is that "it provides a storehouse of suggestive leads and concepts for a future well-rounded sociology" of people of knowledge.

———. 1976. "Sociological Theory from the Chicago Dominance to 1965." *Annual Review of Sociology* 2 (Annual): 145–60. Includes a brief discussion of the period during which the Chicago department dominated general sociology and sociological theory, dating the end of that dominance in 1935 with the founding of the *ASR*.

———. 1977. *Masters of Sociological Thought*. Second Edition. New York: Harcourt, Brace, Jovanovich. A standard text on sociological thought with significant sections on Mead (pp. 332–55), Park (pp. 356–84), Thomas and Znaniecki (pp. 510–59), and Veblen (pp. 262–302).

———. 1978. "American Trends." Pp. 287–320 in *A History of Sociological Analysis* edited by T. Bottomore and R. Nisbet. New York: Basic Books. Comments on Small as a representative of the distinctive character of early American sociology, with influences of Christian moralism (especially the Social Gospel movement) and Progressive reform, and the impact of Veblen's critical sociology which attempted to undermine the assumptions of traditional economics. Reviews the work of Mead and Cooley and their "pragmatic sociology" (pp. 309–11) and has a section on "Thomas and Park: Chicago Sociology as Exemplar and Pathsetter" (pp. 311–17).

Cottrell, Leonard S, Jr. 1967. "Ernest Watson Burgess, 1886–1966: Contributions in the Field of Marriage and the Family." *American Sociologist* 2 (August): 145–48. Personal remembrances of Cottrell's study under Burgess and his contributions as a researcher and teacher. Recounts studying multiple factor analysis under Thurstone and explaining it to Burgess, leading to Cottrell and Burgess's application of the method to sociological data. Reprinted in *Journal of Marriage and the Family* 30 (February, 1968): 6-11.

———. 1971. "Covert Behavior in Interpersonal Interaction." *Proceedings of the American Philosophical Society* 115 (December): 462–69. Reports an experimental test of an aspect of Mead's concept of role-taking and some of the basic assumptions of Mead's social behaviorism.

———. 1978. "George Herbert Mead and Harry Stack Sullivan: An Unfinished Synthesis." *Psychiatry* 41 (May): 151–61. Contends that both psychiatric theory and practice and social psychological theory and research could benefit from a synthesis of the theories of Mead and Sullivan.

———. 1980. "George Herbert Mead: The Legacy of Social Behaviorism." Pp. 45–65 in *Sociological Traditions from Generation to Generation: Glimpses of the American Experience* edited by R. K. Merton and M. W. Riley. Norwood, N.J.: Ablex. Recalls Mead's teaching style, and the content of his courses, claiming that there has been considerable misinterpretation of Mead among sociologists and that Blumer's interpretations "seem to me to be somewhat ambiguous mixtures of Mead's social behaviorism and a nonbehavioral subjectivism that is more akin to European phenomenology" (p. 59).

Coughlan, Neil. 1976. *Young John Dewey: An Essay in American Intellectual History*. New York: Free Press. Details Dewey's career and influences up to the time he left the University of Chicago (1904), with chapters on Mead (pp. 113–33), the development of Dewey's pragmatism (pp. 134–48), and his influence on social thought and philosophy (pp. 149–62). Reviewed by Janowitz (1978).

Cox, Oliver C. 1942. "The Modern Caste School of Race Relations." *SF* 21 (December): 218–26. Takes issue with the "caste school" of race relations, of which Warner is the leader, suggesting that their approach is not original, nor is it accurate, although it has "none of the anti-color complexes of the instinct school."

———. 1965. "Introduction." Pp. 15–31 in *The Black Anglo-Saxons* edited by Nathan Hare. New York: Marzani and Munsell. Places Hare's work in the context of a school of thought initiated by Frazier, with critical remarks concerning the influence of Faris, Ogburn and Park on Frazier and his followers. Insists that despite praiseworthy attitudes toward blacks, they were opposed to blacks taking initiatives that would increase the pace of progress toward racial equality.

Cramblitt, Mary V. 1964. *A Bibliography of the Writings of Charles Abram Ellwood*. Durham, NC: Duke University Library. An annotated bibliography of Ellwood's work, with a brief introduction and discussion of his graduate work at Chicago and his teaching at Missouri (1910–30) and Duke (1930–44).

Cravens, Hamilton. 1971. "The Abandonment of Evolutionary Social Theory in America: The Impact of Academic Professionalization upon American Sociological Theory, 1890–1920." *American Studies* 12 (Fall): 5–20.

Cressey, Donald R. 1955. "Changing Criminals: The Application of the Theory of Differential Association." *AJS* 61 (September): 116–20. Examines the implications of Sutherland's theory of differential association for the diagnosis and treatment of criminals, advocating the development of a "clinical sociology" as suggested by Wirth and Alinsky.

———. 1960a. "The Theory of Differential Association: An Introduction." *Social Problems* 8 (Summer): 2–6. Reviews Sutherland's theory, its development and impact in social theories of crime, observing that it received more attention in the previous five years (1955–60) than in its first fifteen years.

———. 1960b. "Epidemiology and Individual Conduct: A Case from Criminology." *Pacific Sociological Review* 3 (Fall): 47–54. Reviews theories of differential association and differential social organization and their critics. Reprinted in Wolfgang et al. (1962, pp. 81–90).

———. 1961. "Foreword." Pp. iii–xii in *White Collar Crime* by Edwin H. Sutherland. New York: Holt, Rinehart and Winston. Reviews Sutherland's impact on criminology including controversies and studies inspired by him. Indicates that the lasting merit of the book is "its demonstration that a pattern of crime can be found to exist outside both the focus of popular preoccupation with crime and the focus of scientific investigations of crime and criminality."

———. 1964. *Delinquency, Crime and Differential Association*. The Hague, Netherlands: Martinus Nijhoff. Introduces Sutherland's theory of differential association, with a discussion of its history and Sutherland's work on criminology. Comments on influences from Thomas, Park, Burgess and others, and reviews both reviews criticisms of the theory and efforts to apply it in sociological research and clinical practice (e.g., Synanon).

———. 1968. "Culture Conflict, Differential Association, and Normative Conflict." Pp. 43–54 in *Crime and Culture: Essays in Honor of Thorsten Sellin* edited by Marvin E. Wolfgang. New York: Wiley. Discusses Sellin's work with Sutherland as part of a Social Science Research Council project on delinquency, and the relationship between Sellin's concept of "culture conflict" and Sutherland's notion of "differential association."

Cressey, Paul G. 1932. *The Taxi-Dance Hall: A Sociological Study in Commercialized Recreation and City Life*. Chicago: University of Chicago Press. One of the classic urban ethnographic monographs which examines social organization and disorganization.

Cronk, George Francis. 1973. "Symbolic Interactionism: A 'Left-Meadian' Interpretation." *Social Theory and Social Practice* 2 (Spring): 313–33. Defends Mead's dialectical theory of self and society against "unfair and misdirected criticisms" by radical writers and develops Meadian theory "in a direction consistent with theories of radical social change."

Crosser, Paul K. 1955. *The Nihilism of John Dewey*. New York: Philosophical

Library. See especially Chapter Two, "The Disassembling of the Subject-Matter of Social Science," which contends that Dewey's extreme relativism leads to cognitive indeterminableness, sophism, and defeatism.

Daugert, Stanley M. 1950. *The Philosophy of Thorstein Veblen*. New York: King's Crown Press. Traces the philosophical assumptions of Veblen's thought and influences from Kant, Spencer, Peirce, James, Dewey and others, observing that he applied to economic phenomena a variant of the philosophy and psychology of James and Dewey.

Davie, Maurice R. 1937. "The Pattern of Urban Growth." Pp. 133–61 in *Studies in the Science of Society* edited by George Peter Murdock. New Haven. Argues that New Haven exhibits great irregularities with no clearcut zones in an early effort to test the Burgess zonal hypothesis (cf. Quinn 1940a).

Davis, Allen. 1973. *American Heroine: The Life and Legend of Jane Addams*. London: Oxford University Press. This biography of Addams includes brief discussions of Dewey (pp. 96–97, 102, 109, 131, 243), Mead (pp. 97, 148), Small (p. 97), Henderson (p. 334), and Zueblin (p. 97). Explores the important relationship between Addams and several University of Chicago faculty and her place in social thought and history. Observes that Addams, who is sanctified and villified, is a major American scholar interpreted primarily by the popular press rather than by academic analysis.

Davis, Arthur K. 1943. "Veblen on the Decline of the Protestant Ethic." *SF* 22 (December): 282–86. Outlines Veblen's *Theory of the Leisure Class* (1899) and its importance for sociology, noting its insights into the non-economic functions of wealth. Recommends that it be viewed in light of Weber's study of the Protestant ethic, noting that Veblen's "conspicuous consumption" is the opposite of the early asceticism stressed by Weber.

———. 1945. "Sociological Elements in Veblen's Economic Theory." *Journal of Political Economy* 53 (June): 132–49. Assesses Veblen's criticism of orthodox economic theory, the sociological elements in his social theory, and ethical elements in his thought.

———. 1957a. "The Postwar Essays." *Monthly Review* 9 (July-August): 91–98. Scrutinizes three volumes of Veblen's essays, concluding that he was the most original and prophetic figure in American academic circles.

———. 1957b. "Thorstein Veblen and the Culture of Capitalism." Pp. 279–93 in *American Radicals: Some Problems and Personalities* edited by Harvey Goldberg. New York: Monthly Review Press. Observes that the core of Veblen's social theory is largely Marxian, but that it also includes a utopian anarchism and agrarian populism, Darwinian evolution, and skepticism. Argues that Veblen's *Theory of the Leisure Class* (1899), written at Chicago, was his only really famous work and that "his ideas provided to be too iconoclastic for the conservative spirit prevailing in American academic life."

———. 1957c. "Thorstein Veblen Reconsidered." *Science and Society* 21

(Winter): 52–85. Argues that Veblen's stature as analyst, critic, and prophet will loom even larger with the passage of time; reviews Veblen's career and theories of social evolution, instincts, habits, culture lag and social crises; discusses Veblen's relationship to socialism.

———. 1968. "Thorstein Veblen." Pp. 303–306 in Sills (1968), Vol. 16. Traces career of Veblen as sociologist and social critic, including fourteen years on the faculty at Chicago; claims that although he founded no school, Veblen's influence was pervasive, perhaps more among economists than sociologists.

Davis, Arthur P. 1962. "E. Franklin Frazier 1894–1962: A Profile." *Journal of Negro Education.* 31 (Fall): 429–35. A memorial tribute to Frazier which reviews his work at Chicago, Fisk, and Howard.

Davis, Kingsley. 1944. *Human Society*. New York: Macmillan. See the discussion and reformulation of Wirth's "urbanism as a way of life" perspective, pp. 328ff.

Dawson, Carl A., and Warner E. Gettys. 1935. *An Introduction to Sociology*. Revised edition. New York: Ronald Press. Includes a report on the mapping of Montreal, in which the zones take the form of irregular ovals and crescents, requiring some modifications of Burgess's concentric zone theory.

Deegan, Mary Jo. 1978. "Women and Sociology: 1890–1930." *Journal of the History of Sociology* 1 (Fall): 11–32. Examines the milieu of early sociologists and their attitudes toward women's higher education, particularly at the University of Chicago. The "Chicago network" of women is documented, including the five women who held positions in the department. Postulates that the reasons for their exclusion from sociological accounts of the Chicago School include both sexism and political bias against their ideas and work.

———. 1981. "Early Women Sociologists and the American Sociological Society: The Patterns of Exclusion and Participation." *American Sociologist* 16 (February): 14–24. A treatment of the exclusion of women in the American Sociological Society which includes considerable discussion of Small, who had a "separate but equal policy" in hiring women but for work in "their specialized areas": household administration, sanitary science, social settlements, and statistics. Discusses Addams's significant influence on Chicago sociologists and a network of women sociologists including Emily Green Balch (Nobel Peace Prize winner who studied with Small and Simmel), Julia Lathrop, Grace and Edith Abbott, Susan Kingsbury, Ethel Sturgess Dummer (who aided Thomas and was the founder of the ASA section on the family).

Deegan, Mary Jo, and John S. Burger. 1978. "George Herbert Mead and Social Reform: His Work and Writings." *JHBS* 14 (October): 362–73. Contends that Mead's work and publications in the area of social reform challenge prevailing assumptions that Mead published little during his lifetime and that his major preoccupation was with the genesis of the self and the nature of the mind. Indicates several sources of the misunderstanding of Mead's work, including a move away from an interest in social reform among sociologists and the influence of notes from just one of Mead's courses, published as *Mind, Self and Society* (1934).

———. 1981. "W. I. Thomas and Social Reform: His Work and Writings." *JHBS* 17 (January): 114–25. Examines a neglected aspect of Thomas's work, his commitment to social reform, which is crucial for the interpretation and assessment of his writings. Treats his relation with Park, Hull House, and other reform groups.

Deegan, Mary Jo, and Valerie Malhotra. 1977. "Symbols in the Thought of Alfred Schutz and George Herbert Mead." *International Journal of Symbology* 8 (March): 34–45. Compares the writings of Mead and Schutz on the concept of the "symbol," concluding that they are basically compatible. Schutz's work is more comprehensive and precise than Mead's, however, and his analysis expands the categorical treatment of Mead.

Defleur, Melvin L., and Frank R. Westie. 1963. "Attitude as a Scientific Concept." *SF* 42 (October): 17–31. An analytical and historical examination of the concept of "attitude," including discussion of Thomas and Znaniecki, who were the first to use it in an extensive and systematic way, and developments by Thurstone, Bogardus, and others. See comment by C. Norman Alexander, Jr. (*SF* 45 [December, 1966]: 278–81).

DeFleur, Melvin, and Richard Quinney. 1966. "A Reformulation of Sutherland's Differential Association Theory and a Strategy for Empirical Verification." *Journal of Research in Crime and Delinquency* 3 (January): 1–11. Reviews and translates Sutherland's formulation into set theory statements and develops a set of underlying postulates for which the nine major propositions of the theory can be formally derived, concluding with a strategy for its empirical verification.

De Laguna, Grace A. 1946. "Communication, the Act, and the Object with Reference to Mead." *Journal of Philosophy.* 43 (April): 225–38. Provides a critical analysis of central concepts in Mead's thought; he asserts that the acts of thinking human beings are fragments of social acts embracing other acting individuals, even though he fails to make adequate application of this conception.

Deledalle, Gerard. 1959. "Durkheim et Dewey, un double centenaire." *Etudes philosophiques* 14 (October-December): 493–98. Compares and contrasts the work of Durkheim and Dewey, noting that both were influenced by Darwin and theories of evolution. Although Dewey apparently did not read Durkheim, the latter undertook a serious study of Dewey's thought.

Demerath, N. J. 1949. "Review of *The American Soldier*." *SF* 28 (October):

87–90. Review of Stouffer et al. (1949a, 1949b); remarks that not since Thomas and Znaniecki's *The Polish Peasant* (1918–19) has there been a socio-psychological work of such scope, imaginativeness, technical rigor, and important results.

Denzin, Norman K. 1970. "Symbolic Interactionism and Ethnomethodology." Pp. 261–86 in *Understanding Everyday Life* edited by Jack Douglas. Chicago: Aldine. Evaluates the theoretical and methodological assumptions of symbolic interactionism, the work of Mead, Dewey, Blumer, Hughes, and others, and synthesizes their approach with that of ethnomethodology. Declares that the criticism of interactionism that it fails to treat larger forms of social organization ignores the long line of research on the sociology of work and organizational settings stimulated by Hughes and perspectives on the problems of mass society developed by interactionists such as Blumer.

Desmonde, William H. 1957. "G. H. Mead and Freud: American Social Psychology and Psychoanalysis." Pp. 31–50 in *Psychoanalysis and the Future* edited by Benjamin Nelson. New York: National Psychological Association for Psychoanalysis. Discusses Mead's place among the founders of social psychology, the important influences of Darwin's thought on Mead's work, and the distinction between the "I" and the "Me." Argues that Mead has exerted more influence on psychologists and sociologists than philosophers. Portion reprinted as "The Position of George Herbert Mead," Pp. 55–62 in *Social Psychology Through Symbolic Interactionism*, edited by Gregory P. Stone and Harvey A. Farberman. Waltham, Mass.: Xerox College Publishing, 1970.

Dewey, Jane M. 1939. "Biography of John Dewey." Pp. 1–45 in Schilpp (1939). A biographical sketch that includes discussion of influences on Dewey's thought, including Mead (pp. 25ff.), Jane Addams (pp. 29–30) and others; claims that Mead's influence on Dewey was as important as James's.

Dewey, John. 1910. *The Influence of Darwin on Philosophy*. New York: Henry Holt & Co.

———. 1922. *Human Nature and Conduct: An Introduction to Social Psychology*. New York: Henry Holt & Co.

———. 1925. *Experience and Nature*. Chicago: Open Court Publishing Co.

———. 1931a. "George Herbert Mead." Pp. 10–23 in Ames et al. (1931). Dewey's remarks at Mead's funeral in which he characterizes Mead's style and ideas, suggesting that it was his social psychology and social interpretation that would have the widest influence and had "worked a revolution in my own thinking." Claims that Mead was "the most original mind in philosophy in American of the last generation." Reprinted in the *Journal of Philosophy 28* (4 June 1931):309–14.

———. 1931b. "The Pragmatism of Peirce." Pp. 301–308 in *Chance, Love, and Logic* by Charles S. Peirce. New York: Harcourt, Brace and Co. A summary and assessment of Peirce's thought and definition of pragmatism, and similarities and differences between his work and that of James, who was more of a nominalist.

———. 1932. "Prefatory Remarks." Pp. xxxvi–xl in Mead (1932). Insists that Mead was "a seminal mind of the very first order," who was an original thinker who had no sense of being original. Argues that practically all of Mead's inquiries and problems developed out of his original question—that of the nature of consciousness as personal and private as well as social.

———. 1936. "The Work of George Mead." *New Republic* 87 (22 July): 329–30. A general review of Mead's work following the publication of his lectures; contends that despite his lack of systematic publication, Mead's "intellectual influence upon associates and students in his classes was so profound as to be revolutionary." Asserts that Mead's "mind, in contrast to his published writings, was of the unifying and systematizing type to an unusual degree."

Dewey, Richard. 1960. "The Rural-Urban Continuum: Real But Relatively Unimportant." *AJS* 66 (July): 60–66. Analyses the rural-urban continuum, particularly as defined by Wirth's "Urbanism as a Way of Life" article, comparing it with Redfield and others, suggesting that, although Wirth's task is still important, the influences of density and size of population must be distinguished from influences of culture.

Dibble, Vernon K. 1975. *The Legacy of Albion Small*. Chicago: University of Chicago Press. Reviews Small's contributions to sociology, notably his vision of sociology as a science, his teaching, his appointments of others to the Chicago department, and his administrative work in the Chicago department, the American Sociological Society and the *AJS*; includes several appendixes, including letters concerning the founding of a sociology department at Chicago and the founding of a sociology journal, as well as an autobiographical letter (pp. 201–204).

Dicken, Georges. 1971. "John Dewey: Instrumentalism in Social Action." *Transactions of the Charles S. Peirce Society* 7 (Fall): 221–32. Suggests that Dewey's reliance on a biological model causes him to blur the difference between conflicting needs of a single organism and problems generated by intergroup conflict. That accounts, in part, for Dewey's tendency to suggest that social ills can be remedied if only people will adopt "the method of intelligence." Notes also Dewey's commitment to values associated with the democratic way of life.

Dickie-Clark, H. F. 1966. "The Marginal Situation: A Contribution to Marginality Theory." *SF* 44 (March): 363–70. Reviews Park's and Stonequist's marginality theory and attempts to clarify the nature of marginal situations by combining a hierarchical approach with the notion of inconsistency in rankings.

Diggins, John P. 1978. *The Bard of Savagery: Thorstein Veblen and Modern Social Theory*. New York: Seabury Press. A comprehensive treatment of Veblen's place in modern social theory which compares his work with that of the classical economists (pp. 45–60), Marx (pp. 61–84), Weber (pp. 113–38) and others. Describes his 14-year career at Chicago (pp. 36ff.) and his critique of the university as well as influences on his thought from Mead, Dewey, Peirce, Boas, and others (see especially pp. 36–37, 55–56, 98ff.). Notes that he refused to grant capitalism its historical legitimacy and yet shunned political activism.

Diner, Steven J. 1975. "Department and Discipline: The Department of Sociology at the University of Chicago, 1892–1920." *Minerva* 13 (Winter): 514–53. Outlines the first years of the department's history, attributing success to three primary factors: (1) administrative independence; (2) Small's flexibility and efforts to diversify; and (3) resources and problems of Chicago. Examines the issues of social reform, organization of the faculty, and relationships with other parts of the university. Comments on Small (esp. pp. 517–19, 522–23), Harper (pp. 514–20), Henderson (pp. 519–21), Starr (pp. 518–19), Talbot (pp. 520–21, 538), Addams (p. 522, 536), Zueblin (pp. 525–26), Vincent (p. 526), Thomas (pp. 526–28), Park (p. 529), Raymond (pp. 529–30), Bedford (p. 531), Rainwater (p. 531), E. Abbott (pp. 531–32), Burgess (p. 534), Mathews (pp. 528, 540–41), Dewey, and Mead (p. 544).

———. 1978. "George Herbert Mead's Ideas on Women and Careers: A Letter to His Daughter-in-Law, 1920." *Signs* 4 (Winter): 407–10. A brief introduction and manuscript letter in which Mead argues that women ought to combine family and career.

———. 1980. *A City and Its Universities: Public Policy in Chicago, 1892–1919*. Chapel Hill: University of North Carolina Press. Analyzes relationship between the University of Chicago and various reform movements in Chicago, notably in areas of education, criminal justice, social welfare, and municipal administration.

Dittberner, Job L. 1979. *The End of Ideology and American Social Thought: 1930–1960*. Ann Arbor: UMI Research Press. Examines the contributions of Small, Becker, and especially Wirth and Shils in the sociology of knowledge (pp. 25–31; 36–39). Discusses efforts by Arthur Child and C. Wright Mills (1939) to adapt Mead's thought to the sociology of knowledge (pp. 51–55).

Doan, Frank M. 1958. "Remarks on G. H. Mead's Conception of Simultaneity." *Journal of Philosophy* 55 (27 February): 203–209. Suggests that Mead's analysis of simultaneity has implications for relativity theory in physics; notes that relativity theory began as a reform movement in physics which rejected subjectivism.

Dobriansky, Lev E. 1957. *Veblenism: A New Critique*. Washington, D.C.: Public Affairs Press. Provides a systematic view of Veblen's work and the philosophical foundations of his thought; comments on Veblen's career at Chicago (pp. 13ff.) and his relations to Dewey (esp. pp. 99–101), Mead (pp. 101, 249), Small (p. 101), and Thomas (pp. 15, 366).

Dorfman, Joseph. 1933. "An Unpublished Project of Thorstein Veblen for an Ethnological Inquiry." *AJS* 39 (September): 237–41. Provides a very brief introduction to a proposal prepared by Veblen in 1910 when he was without employment.

———. 1945. *Thorstein Veblen and His America*. New York: Viking Press. An intellectual biography of Veblen, including remarks on his stormy career at Chicago. Explores Veblen's relationship to Small (pp. 92–93 and elsewhere), Thomas (pp. 125–26), Veblen's articles in the *AJS* (pp. 165ff., 175ff., 260), and the controversy surrounding Veblen's social criticism and teaching of socialism (e.g., pp. 125ff.). Examines visits by Ward to Chicago (pp. 141, 194) and a comment by Ward that Small "is under instructions from the capitalist censorship that controls the University of Chicago" (p. 210). Cf. Landsman (1957).

———. 1958. "The Source and Impact of Veblen's Thought." Pp. 1–12 in Dowd (1958). Suggests that Veblen was an artist as well as an economist, and that he played a dual role of theorist and catalyst of reform. Sketches influences from the German historical school, reform movements of his time, and his focus on central economic institutions, the corporation, and the technological process.

———. 1968. "Background of Veblen's Thought." Pp. 106–30 in Qualey (1968). Recapitulates influences on Veblen's thought, including Laughlin, Loeb, Darwin, Ward, Morgan, John Clark, Boas, Morgan, Ely, Peirce, Dewey, Wells, and Spencer, noting Lyndon Johnson's ironic use of Veblen's terminology and concepts in his messages to Congress in 1965.

———. 1973. "New Light on Veblen." *Thorstein Veblen: Essays, Reviews and Reports: Previously Uncollected Writings* edited by Joseph Dorfman. Clifton, N.J.: A. M. Kelley. Comments on changes in interpretations and appraisals of Veblen for a period of years, making remarks on further promising areas to pursue in Veblen's works.

Douglas, Jack D., ed. 1970. *Understanding Everyday Life: Toward the Reconstruction of Sociological Knowledge*. Chicago: Aldine. Contains considerable reference to Mead (esp. pp. 16–19, 264–66), as well as briefer treatments of other Chicago sociologists. Points out a fundamental conflict in

Mead's thought between social behaviorism and more phenomenologically oriented ideas, observing that the behavioral symbolic interactionists "mistakenly see themselves as descended from Mead." Suggests that Blumer and Becker have generally done phenomenological interactionism. See also Denzin (1970).

Dowd, Douglas F. 1964. "Thorstein Veblen and C. Wright Mills: Social Science and Social Criticism." Pp. 54–65 in *The New Sociology: Essays in Social Science and Social Theory in Honor of C. Wright Mills* edited by I. L. Horowitz. New York: Oxford University Press. Compares and contrasts the work of Veblen and Mills, commenting on the similarities in their social criticism.

———. 1966. *Thorstein Veblen*. New York: Washington Square Press. A broad examination of Veblen's work, arguing that he remains America's most noted economist, despite the obscurity into which his work has fallen. Attempts to systematize his eclectic writings, arguing that Veblen took institutions—their origins, nature, function and interrelationships—as the prime focus of the social scientist.

Dowd, Douglas F., ed. 1958. *Thorstein Veblen: A Critical Reappraisal. Lectures and Essays Commemorating the Hundredth Anniversary of Veblen's Birth*. Ithaca: Cornell University Press. An eclectic collection of essays on Veblen's work. Contends that "Veblen was and remains the most eminent and seminal thinker in the area of social analysis yet to emerge in America." Paradoxically, however, his writings are studied by a small and shrinking number of students. Postulates that the cause of the paradox is Veblen's unorthodox views and his lack of a system of thought. See separate entries under Dorfman, Hamilton, Ayres, Kaplan, Nabers, Hill, Sweezy, Morrison, and Watkins.

Doyle, Bertram W. 1937. *The Etiquette of Race Relations in the South*. Chicago: University of Chicago Press.

Dubin, Steven C. 1983. "The Moral Continuum of Deviancy Research: Chicago Sociologists and the Dance Hall." *Urban Life* 12 (April): 75–94. Explores research on dance halls of the 1920s in terms of the diversity of attitudes concerning the morality of the halls; notes especially studies by Roe, Alinsky, P. G. Cressey, and Gold.

Duffus, Robert L. 1944. *The Innocents at Cedro: A Memoir of Thorstein Veblen and Others*. New York: Macmillan. A chatty autobiographical piece by one of the students who lived at Veblen's house near Stanford, with a few insights into his work, style of life and approach to scholarship.

Duncan, Otis Dudley. 1959a. "Human Ecology and Population Studies." Pp. 678–716 in *The Study of Population: An Inventory and Appraisal* edited by Philip M. Hauser and Otis Dudley Duncan. Chicago: University of Chicago Press. Although containing little explicit reference to the Chicago School, Duncan discusses the relation between the ecological perspective and demographic studies, including the work of Burgess, Park, Ogburn, Wirth, Hawley, McKenzie, Hauser, and others.

———. 1959b. "Personal Notes: An Appreciation of William Fielding Ogburn." *Technology and Culture* 1 (Winter): 277–81. A biographical sketch and discussion of Ogburn's interest in the study of cultural evolution, cultural lag, the social effects of inventions, standards of living, and the measurement of social trends. Observes that although Ogburn made a sharp distinction between the roles of scientist and citizen, the kind of science he advocated "has great significance for the intelligent exercise of the citizen's duties."

———. 1964. "Introduction." Pp. vii–xxil in Ogburn (1964). Summarizes Ogburn's interests in social change, social problems, and research methodologies; objects to characterizing Ogburn's theory of social change as "the cultural-lag theory."

Duncan, Otis Dudley, and Leo F. Schnore. 1959. "Cultural, Behavioral, and Ecological Perspectives in the Study of Social Organization." *AJS* 65 (September): 132–45. This examination of three perspectives in sociological theory—cultural, behavioral, and ecological—contains considerable discussion of Chicago sociology. Concludes that the ecological perspective is the most useful, despite the fact that the early exponents of the approach did not recognize its possibilities and implications. Znaniecki's cultural sociology is examined as is that of Hawley, Wirth, Ogburn, and others.

Durant, William James. 1926. *The Story of Philosophy: The Lives and Opinions of the Greater Philosophers*. New York: Simon and Schuster. Includes discussions of Santayana (pp. 530–53), James (pp. 553–65) and Dewey (pp. 565–75). Claims that Dewey thought that the work of philosophy should lie in the application of human knowledge to our social antagonisms.

Durkheim, Emile. 1964 [1913–1914]. "Pragmatism and Sociology." Pp. 386–436 in *Essays on Sociology and Philosophy by Emile Durkheim, et al.* edited by Kurt H. Wolff. New York: Harper and Row. A translation by Charles Blend of Durkheim's series of lectures on pragmatism, especially the work of Peirce, James, and Dewey, given at the Sorbonne in 1913 and 1914. On the implications of the lectures, see Stone and Farberman (1967).

Dykhuizen, George. 1973. *The Life and Mind of John Dewey*. Carbondale: Southern Illinois University Press. An intellectual portrait of Dewey tracing influences on his thought and his impact on American social thought. Outlines his efforts to build a philosophy department at Chicago (pp. 76–115); his relationship to "the group of liberal thinkers" on the Chicago faculty, including Small, Thomas, Veblen and Mead (pp. 103ff.), and his relations with Addams and the Hull House (pp. 104–105).

Eames, Elizabeth Ramsden. 1973. "Mead's Concept of Time." Pp. 59–81 in Corti (1973). Comments on Mead's concept of time in the context of recent scientific trends in evolution, psychology, mathematical innovations, and relativity.

Eames, S. Morris. 1973. "Mead and the Pragmatic Conception of Truth." Pp. 135–51 in Corti (1973). Describes Mead's conception of truth as a philosophical statement of what takes place in the procedures of science, observing that the pragmatists tend to defend truth as "success in inquiry."

———. 1977. *Pragmatic Naturalism: An Introduction.* Carbondale: Southern Illinois University Press. A general survey of pragmatism, with substantial sections on Mead and Dewey as well as James and Peirce, and a chapter on Darwinian influences.

Eastman, Max. 1941. "John Dewey." *Atlantic Monthly* 168 (December): 671–85. A biographical sketch which describes of his reform-minded wife, his period at Chicago (pp. 675–80), his relationships with James (p. 677) and Mead (p. 681), and his championship of a fair trial for Trotsky (p. 684).

Edgar, Patricia M. 1975. "Directions in Mass Communication Research." *Australian and New Zealand Journal of Sociology* 11 (June): 21–27.

"Edith Abbott Memorial Issue." 1957. *Social Service Administration Newsletter* 1. A memorial to Abbott, who provided a link between sociology and social work.

Edwards, G. Franklin. 1962. "Edward Franklin Frazier: 1894–1962." *ASR* 27 (December): 890–92. A memorial to Frazier's life and work, noting influences by Burgess and Park and Frazier's work on the black family and the black bourgeoisie.

———. 1968. "E. Franklin Frazier." Pp. 553–54 in Sills (1968), Vol. 5. Emphasizes Frazier's work in the fields of race and culture contacts and family behavior, remarking that his sociological conceptions were shaped mainly by his graduate training at Chicago, where he studied with Faris, Park, Ogburn, and Burgess and worked with Wirth, Hughes, and Blumer in Park's urban research program.

———. 1974. "E. Franklin Frazier." Pp. 85–117 in Blackwell and Janowitz (1974). Summarizes Frazier's career and work, and describes influences from Chicago sociologists Park, Burgess and Thomas, Faris, and Ogburn on his analysis of the black experience in the United States.

Eisenstadt, S. N., with M. Curelaru. 1976. *The Form of Sociology: Paradigms and Crises.* New York: Wiley. Includes discussion of the role of the Chicago department in the broader development of the discipline (see especially pp. 130ff.).

Elsner, Henry Jr. 1972. "Introduction." Pp. vii–xxv in *The Crowd and the Public and Other Essays* by Robert E. Park; edited by Henry Elsner, Jr., and translated by Charlotte Elsner. Chicago: University of Chicago Press. Analyzes Park's doctoral dissertation, its place in the sociology of collective behavior and Park's later work.

Empey, LaMar T., and Steven G. Lubeck. 1968. "Conformity and Deviance in the Situation of Company." *ASR* 33 (October): 761–74. Tests Sutherland's notion of differential association, attempting to ascertain the nature of delinquent subcultures in rural and urban areas; delinquents share values with non-delinquents and vice versa.

Engel-Frisch, Gladys. 1943. "Some Neglected Temporal Aspects of Human Ecology." *SF* 22 (October): 43–47. Recommends that in addition to the utilization of space, temporal factors need to be taken into account in human ecology.

Epstein, A. L. 1967. "Urbanization and Social Change in Africa." *Current Anthropology* 8 (October): 275–96. Reports that many of Wirth's hypothesized characteristics of the city are present in African cities, except that there are also complex networks of social relationships including some tribal connections.

Etzioni, Amitai. 1959. "The Ghetto—a Re-Evaluation." *SF* 37 (March): 255–62. A reassessment of Wirth's *The Ghetto* on the occasion of the re-issue of the book by the University of Chicago Press. Maintains that Wirth's study presents a theory—Park's model of a natural history of race relations—and data which disproves the theory. Claims that Wirth's findings support a pluralist rather than an assimilationist perspective. Cf. Lyman's different perspective on Wirth's theories (1968:21).

Farberman, Harvey. 1970. "Mannheim, Cooley and Mead: Toward a Social Theory of Mentality." *Sociological Quarterly* 11 (Winter): 3–13. Postulates that Mead's theory of mind and self as symbolic interaction makes social factors intrinsic to mentality, providing the basis for a convergence between social psychology and the sociology of knowledge foreseen by Wirth.

———. 1979. "The Chicago School: Continuities in Urban Sociology." Pp. 3–20 in *Studies in Symbolic Interaction: A Research Annual* edited by Norman K. Denzin. Vol. 2. Greenwich, Conn.: JAI Press. Reviews Gouldner's (1970) charge that the Chicago School consisted of academic status seekers who declined to point the finger at vested interests and offers an alternative metatheoretical analysis outlining the underlying paradigmatic continuity of the pre-Chicago, Chicago, and post-Chicago tradition of urban sociology. Discusses the Chicago sociologists' attitudes toward social reform and their view of the urban community from Small, Park, and Burgess to Wirth and Mead, relating their approaches to European social theory, particularly Durkheim, Toennies, Weber, Simmel, and Marx.

Faris, Ellsworth. 1928. "Attitudes and Behavior." *AJS* 34 (September): 271–81. Takes issue with the "behaviorist mutiny," which limits analyses to the overt and visible. Describes the work of Angell, Dewey, Mead, Thurstone, and others, and concludes that "to neglect the study of attitudes will be to fail to understand personality" and that the "attempt to discard all consideration of the subjective experiences neglects the . . . mediating part of the act, which is equally important with the objective and observable."

———. 1931. "The Concept of Social Attitudes." Pp. 3–16 in *Social Attitudes* edited by Kimball Young. New York: Holt. Reviews the development of the concept of social attitudes, noting Thomas and Znaniecki's role in introducing it and the subsequent developments in the area. Delineates issues surrounding the study of attitudes and argues that despite some limitations they are important to an understanding of the personality.

———. 1936. "Review of G. H. Mead's *Mind, Self, and Society*." *AJS* 41 (May): 809–13. Faris's review of Mead (1934) suggesting that "mind, self and society" is the reverse order of the way in which Mead structured his thought. Faris notes the significance of Mead's influence on sociology at Chicago.

———. 1937a. *The Nature of Human Nature*. New York: McGraw-Hill. A treatise on social psychology which incorporates much of Mead's social theory.

———. 1937b. "The Social Psychology of George Mead." *AJS* 43 (November): 391–403. Introduces fundamental aspects of Mead's social psychology and discusses his relation to sociology. Recalls his study under Mead and teaching a preliminary course in social psychology to prepare students for Mead's. Remarks that Blumer took over Mead's course and that the sociologists carried on Mead's tradition after his death. Comments on Mead's teaching methods and contends that his relation to sociology was very close throughout his career.

———. 1944. "Robert E. Park." *ASR* 9 (June): 322–35. Traces Park's career, focusing on his years at Chicago, his style of teaching, and his approach to sociology.

———. 1945. "The Beginnings of Social Psychology." *AJS* 50 (May): 422–28. Reviews 50 years of history of social psychology, noting contributions of Wundt, Durkheim, Sumner, James, Dewey, Mead, Cooley, Ross, and others; discusses Dewey's concept of the reflex-arc and Mead's position that even the inner musings of the solitary hermit are necessarily social.

———. 1948a. "In Memoriam: William Isaac Thomas, 1863–1947." *AJS* 53 (March): 387. Brief memorial discussing Thomas's major accomplishments and his influence on the field.

———. 1948b. "William I. Thomas, 1863–1947." *Sociology and Social Research* 32 (March-April): 755–59. Brief sketch of Thomas's contributions to sociology, especially *The Polish Peasant* (1918–19) and the concept of social attitudes. Observes that Thomas's development of that concept influenced the work of Thurstone, Stouffer, and their co-workers, despite the fact that Thomas "had no mathematics and was allergic to statistics."

———. 1951. "Review of *Social Behavior and Personality: Contributions of W. I. Thomas to Theory and Social Research*, edited by Edmund H. Volkart." *ASR* 16 (December): 875–77. Outlines Thomas's accomplishments in the course of reviewing Volkart's edited volume on the topic, with notes on courses Faris took from Thomas. Suggests that Volkart paid less attention to Thomas's concept of "social attitudes" than he might have. Notes the importance of *The Polish Peasant* (1918–19) and names a number of important graduate students inspired by Thomas's work.

Faris, Robert E. L. 1945. "American Sociology." Pp. 538–61 in *Twentieth Century Sociology* edited by Georges Gurvitch and W. E. Moore. New York: Philosophical Library. Contains discussions of work at Chicago, including that of Small (pp. 542–43), Thomas and Znaniecki (pp. 545–46, 551, 553), Park and Burgess (pp. 547, 553), Ogburn (pp. 551, 557–58), and Dewey, Mead, and Faris (pp. 554–55).

———. 1948. *Social Disorganization*. New York: Ronald Press. A textbook on the social disorganization perspective which draws upon and discusses ideas by Thomas, Park, Burgess, and others, incorporating Parsons's functionalism into the perspective.

———. 1951. "Review of James A. Quinn, *Human Ecology*." *AJS* 56 (January): 384–86. A review which talks more about the development of human ecology by Park and others at Chicago than about Quinn's work (see Quinn 1950), suggesting that the Chicago investigations "contain examples of some of the most successfully interconnected general theory and empirical research in sociology."

———. 1964. "The Discipline of Sociology." Pp. 1–35 in *Handbook of Modern Sociology* edited by R. E. L. Faris. Chicago: Rand, McNally and Co. Outlines areas included in the discipline of sociology and provides a brief history, including discussions of Ogburn (pp. 12–14) and the development of sociology at Chicago in "The Emergence of Modern Sociology in the United States" (pp. 23–28).

———. 1967. "Review of *W. I. Thomas on Social Organization and Social Personality*." *SF* 46 (September): 115. Review of the volume edited by Morris Janowitz (University of Chicago Press, 1966) with discussion of Thomas's career, noting that he came to sociology with a doctorate in literature. Assesses his relationships with Znaniecki and Park, noting that Park thanked Thomas "for the point of view and scheme of organization of materals which have been largely adopted in" his and Burgess's *Introduction to the Science of Society* (1921).

———. [1967] 1970. *Chicago Sociology: 1920–1932*. San Francisco: Chandler. A standard history of the Chicago department from 1920 to 1932. Emphasizes the broad range of Chicago sociology, its strengths in urban studies and social psychology. Appendices list doctoral and master's dissertations as well as pictures and brief biographical sketches of Small, Thomas, Mead, Park, Burgess, Faris, Ogburn, and Wirth. See Janowitz (1970b).

———. 1969. "Paul F. Cressey, 1899–1969." *American Sociologist* 4 (August):

259. Comments on Paul F. and the other two Cresseys at Chicago, Paul G., author of *The Taxi-Dance Hall*, and Donald R., collaborator with Sutherland of *Criminology*. Although the first two were cousins (they met in one of Ellsworth Faris's classes), the latter was not related. Paul F. Cressey wrote "one of the central investigations of the ecological distributions of population of the metropolis in that decade of productive urban investigations at Chicago."

Faris, Robert E. L., and H. Warren Dunham. 1939. *Mental Disorders in Urban Areas*. Chicago: University of Chicago Press.

Farrell, John C. 1967. *Beloved Lady: A History of Jane Addams' Ideas on Reform and Peace*. Baltimore, Md.: Johns Hopkins Press. An analysis of Addams's thought that is also noteworthy for its complex and thorough bibliography of her writings. Citing 514 publications, Farrell locates duplicate articles and publication reprints (see esp. pp. 220–41).

Faught, Jim. 1980. "Presuppositions of the Chicago School in the Work of Everett C. Hughes." *American Sociologist* 15 (May): 72–82. Identifies six presuppositions of the "Chicago School paradigm" in Park and Burgess's *Introduction to the Science of Sociology* (1921) and discusses how five of them are central to the work of Hughes, one of Park's students.

Feibleman, James Kern. 1945. "The Influence of Peirce on Dewey's Logic." *Education* 66 (September): 18–24. Contends that Peirce was a realist and that Dewey, although a realist by his predilections, came to hold an explicit nominalistic position because of his interest in the metaphysical importance of activity.

———. [1946] 1970. *An Introduction to the Philosophy of Charles S. Peirce*. Cambridge: MIT Press. An analysis of Peirce's philosophy, its sources and influences, with comments on Peirce's impact on James's pragmatism (pp. 467–73) and Dewey's logic of inquiry (pp. 474–83). Argues that Dewey sees correctly that James's doctrine of pragmatism implies nominalism while that of Peirce implies realism, but that Dewey (a nominalist) misunderstood aspects of Peirce's work.

Fen, Sing-Nan. 1951. "Present and Re-Presentation: A Discussion of Mead's Philosophy of the Present." *Philosophical Review* 60 (October): 545–50. Assesses Mead's notion of the interdependence of the present, past, future, and its application to history as a 'science."

Ferrarotti. 1974. *Il pensiero sociologico da Auguste Comte a Max Horkheimer*. Milan. Includes considerable discussion of Veblen with a critique of Riesman's psychological interpretation (pp. 139–44).

Feuer, Lewis S. 1953. "Thorstein Veblen: The Metaphysics of an Interned Immigrant." *American Quarterly* 5 (Summer): 99–112. Contends that Veblen "was the first American scientific thinker who, within all the restraints of

American academic circles, undertook to set forth a socialist critique of society and thought." Comments on Veblen's criticism of pragmatism, although noting that he directed them against James without mentioning Dewey.

———. 1960. "The Standpoints of Dewey and Freud: A Contrast and Analysis." *Journal of Individual Psychology* 16 (November): 121–36. Contrasts Dewey's work with that of Freud, noting the sociological situations to which each was responding.

Fine, William F. 1979. *Progressive Evolutionism and American Sociology, 1890–1920*. Ann Arbor: UMI Research Press. Argues that progressive evolutionism was the major framework in terms of which early sociologists addressed the problematics of social life and articulated their conceptions of sociology. Examines the work of Small, Thomas, Mead, Dewey, and interactionism (pp. 131–43 and passim), as well as sociologists from other departments.

Firey, Walter. 1945. "Sentiment and Symbolism as Ecological Variables." *ASR* 10 (April): 140–48. Suggests that the "economic ecology" developed by Hughes, McKenzie and others has had a certain explanatory adequacy, but needs alteration. Uses a case study of Boston to suggest that space should be viewed not only as having an impeditive quality but also serves as a *symbol* for cultural values, and "that locational activities are not only economizing agents but may also bear *sentiments*" which can influence the locational process.

———. 1947. *Land Use in Central Boston*. Cambridge: Harvard University Press. A major critique of human ecology theories accomplished by means of an empirical study of land use in Boston and the development of an alternative ecological theory that emphasizes the importance of the cultural component of land use patterns. In contradiction to the deterministic schemes formulated by Burgess, Hoyt, McKenzie, Park, Alfred Weber, and others, Firey suggests that land use patterns in Boston were too variable to warrant forcing them into simple concentric or sector schemes (see especially pp. 323ff.).

Fischer, Claude S. 1972. "*Urbanism as a Way of Life*: A Review and an Agenda." *Sociological Methods and Research* 1 (November): 187–242. Evaluates Wirth's (1938) classic article and its impact on urban studies, and develops an analytical model from the article in order to identify the myriad phenomena which Wirth described and to outline the basic mechanisms that he hypothesized produced those phenomena. Reviews studies examining Wirth's (1938) issues and concludes that the current data are often inadequate and contradictory.

———. 1975. "Toward a Subcultural Theory of Urbanism." *AJS* 80 (May): 1319–41. Criticizes both Wirth and his major critics, especially Gans (1962), in terms of the social effects of urbanism, developing a subcultural theory alternative. Examines Wirth's contention that urbanism results in social disorganization and individual alienation, and Gans's argument that no particularly significant social effects can be attributed to urbanism.

Fisher, Berenice, and Anselm Strauss. 1978a. "Interactionism." Pp. 457–98 in *History of Sociological Analysis* edited by T. Bottomore and R. Nisbet. New York: Basic Books. Outlines the history and issues of the "interactionist" perspective, noting its diverse character and its dual tradition, one coming primarily from Mead (especially Blumer), and the other stemming more from Park, Thomas, and Hughes. Develops a brief chronology from Small, Thomas, and Znaniecki through Dewey and Mead, Faris and Blumer, to their better-known students Lindesmith, Rose, Shibutani, H. S. Becker, Klapp, Freidson, Dalton, Davis, Gusfield, Turner, Bucher, Quarantelli, Marcson, Strauss, Killian, Goffman, Kurt and Gladys Lang, and Stone. Examines the approach's historical background, interactionist theories of social change and interest in reform, and its Meadian influences. Discusses limitations surrounding the problems of progress, process, consent, limitations, power and equity, and the intellectual's role.

———. 1978b. "The Chicago Tradition and Social Change: Thomas, Park, and Their Successors." *Symbolic Interaction* 1 (Spring): 5–23. Observes that Thomas and Park exemplified for Chicago sociologists how to "do" sociology, noting the centrality of their conceptions of social change, reform and progress; the role of sociology; the agents of social change; and the arenas and mechanisms of social change. Indicates differences between the two and the diversity of the intellectual heritage developed at Chicago, contending that Small and Mead played relatively indirect roles in its formation.

———. 1979a. "George Herbert Mead and the Chicago Tradition of Sociology (Part One)." *Symbolic Interaction* 2 (Spring): 9–26. Claiming that Mead had little influence on Chicago sociology during his time at the University, the authors advance the thesis that Mead's work was quite distinct from the Chicago tradition of sociology. Discusses his relations with Dewey, Thomas, and Park, and his interest in social progress and social change.

———. 1979b. "George Herbert Mead and the Chicago Tradition of Sociology (Part Two)." *Symbolic Interaction* 2 (Fall): 9–20. A continuation of Fisher and Strauss (1979a) which explores the relationship between Mead's thought and the ongoing work of the Chicago sociology department, noting that he had no direct successors in the sociology department because he was a philosopher. Identifies the ways in which Mead's ideas have been used, concluding that Mead's thought "was used relatively *little* within the Chicago tradition of doing sociology and the uses to which it was put were quite *diverse*."

Fleming, Donald. 1967. "Attitude: The History of a Concept." *Perspectives in American History* 1: 287–365. This lengthy article on the notion of "attitude" includes a substantial discussion of Thomas (especially pp. 322–31), commenting on influences from Darwin, Thomas's works *Sex and Society* (1907) and *The Polish Peasant* (1918–19). Notes Elton Mayo's indirect debt to Thomas through Park and Shaw (p. 334). Discusses Thurstone's efforts to measure attitudes quantitatively (pp. 340–43) and Stouffer's research with Guttman and Lazarsfeld (pp. 345–47).

Fletcher, Ronald. 1971. *The Making of Sociology: A Study of Sociological Theory*. 2 vols. London: Michael Joseph. Includes a chapter (volume 2, pp. 512–41) on Mead as a social behaviorist, arguing that he avoided determinism (such as that Fletcher finds in Durkheim) because of his concern with the "teleological" qualities and capacities of the human mind and "self" discussed by Mill, Ward, Hobhouse and Weber.

Floro, George K. 1976. "The Task of Updating Selected Themes in Thomas and Znaniecki's *Methodological Note*." *Wisconsin Sociologist* 13 (Spring-Summer): 99–104. In response to Coser's American Sociological Association presidential address, Floro calls for an updating of Thomas and Znaniecki's "Methodological Note"; sketches its themes and suggests that the sociological question it asks is "what kinds of institutions are appearing and are needed?"

Form, William H. 1954. "The Place of Social Structure in the Determination of Land Use." *SF* 32 (March): 317–23. Argues for the need to consider social structure in addition to ecological and cultural factors in the study of changes in land use, with references to Hughes, Whyte, Blumer, McKenzie, and others.

Frankel, Charles. 1960. "Introduction." Pp. 1–17 in *The Golden Age of American Philosophy* edited by Charles Frankel. New York: Braziller. Examines the philosophies of Peirce, James, Royce, Santayana , Dewey and others, suggesting that there are three sets of ideas to which their ideas respond: the theory of evolution, the deterministic ideals of nineteenth-century science, and the social outlook represented by Spencer (notably the first of the three).

———. 1968. "John Dewey." Pp. 155–59 in Sills (1968), Vol. 4. Sketches Dewey's career and central ideas, his work at Chicago and his involvement in Addams's Hull House, as well as his conception of the social sciences.

Frankel, Hyman H. 1958. "The Sociological Theory of Florian Znaniecki." Ph.D. thesis, University of Illinois. A critical analysis of Znaniecki's theoretical/methodological research agenda for the sociological enterprise.

Franks, David D., and Francis F. Seeburger. 1980. "The Person Behind the Word: Mead's Theory of Universals and A Shift of Focus in Symbolic Interactionism." *Symbolic Interaction* 3 (Spring): 41–58. Examines Mead's theory of univerals, noting that although he avoids any realistic hypostatization of separate universals, he eschews nominalistic and conventionalistic views of language. His principle of the objective reality of perspectives (in *The Philosophy of the Present*) allows him to grant objective reality to universal characteristics of concrete objects. Declares that Mead's theory of universals serves to counteract mistaken tendencies toward nominalism and extreme conventionalism within contemporary symbolic interaction.

Frazier, E. Franklin. 1932. *The Negro Family in Chicago*. Chicago: University of Chicago Press.

———. 1939. *The Negro Family in the United States*. Chicago: University of Chicago Press.

———. 1947. "Sociological Theory and Race Relations." *ASR* 12 (June): 265–71. Examines the history of sociological studies of race relations, arguing that the earliest American sociologists assumed that blacks were inferior. Argues that a shift occurred following World War I, with Park the chief figure in the formulation of studies based on the theory that race was a sociological concept, but still without significant attention to social structural factors; a new school of thought, although anticipated by Thomas, focused attention upon the concept of caste. Although progress has been made, Frazier calls for the need for an approach that discards rationalizations of race prejudice.

———. 1950. "Review of Robert E. Park, *Race and Culture*." *AJS* 55 (January): 413–15. Reviews Park (1950), remarking that the essence of Park's theories involve an interest in the ecological, economic, and political phases of race and culture contacts, with particular attention to that phase dealing with personality and culture, using such concepts as social distance, culture conflict, and the marginal man.

Freedman, Florence B. 1970. "A Sociologist Views a Poet: Robert Ezra Park on Walt Whitman." *Walt Whitman Review* 10 (December): 99–109. Comments on and includes the text of an unpublished lecture on Whitman in which a sixty-six-year-old Park contrasts his youthful enthusiastic response to ideas in "Leaves of Grass" with his later disillusion.

Freidson, Eliot. 1953. "Communications Research and the Concept of the Mass." *ASR* 18 (June): 313–17. Includes substantial discussion of Blumer's research on mass communications, especially motion pictures, and their implictions for the notion of the "mass."

Friday, Charles B. 1968. "Veblen on the Future of American Capitalism." Pp. 16–46 in Qualey (1968). Observes that Veblen's critique of orthodox economics focussed on its irrelevance to major problems of modern society and notes that Veblen, like Marx, thought capitalism to be a transitory phenomenon.

Friedrichs, Robert W. 1970. *A Sociology of Sociology*. New York: Free Press. This broad effort contains considerable treatment of sociology at Chicago; reports that after the rise of Parsons and functionalism, Chicago maintained a self-conscious distance from the new orthodoxy through its graduates and the

AJS. Surveys Mead's interactionism (esp. pp. 18, 111ff., 185, 209, 299); the "prophetic mode" of early Chicago sociologists, with their clergy influences (Henderson, Small, Thomas, Vincent, Hayes, and E. Faris, p. 73); Park and "muckraking prose" of Chicago monographs culminating in *The Polish Peasant* (Thomas and Znaniecki 1918–19).

Fuhrman, Ellsworth R. 1980. *The Sociology of Knowledge in America: 1883–1915*. Charlottesville: University Press of Virginia. Examines sociology of knowledge themes in early American sociology and contrasts Small's work (pp. 129–58, with a short biographical introduction) with that of Sumner, Ward, Giddings, Ross, and Cooley. Argues that Small placed more stress on the importance of conflict in social life than did the others, particularly Sumner and Giddings.

Furfey, Paul Hanley, and Joseph F. Daly. 1937. "A Criticism of Factor Analysis as a Technique of Social Research." *ASR* 2 (April): 178–82. Takes issue with Thurstone's techniques, arguing that factors are mere figments of the imagination, interesting to the mathematician, but not interesting to the social scientist. Anonymous critique and a rejoinder follow (pp. 182–86).

Furner, Mary O. 1975. *Advocacy and Objectivity: A Crisis in the Professionalization of American Social Science, 1865–1905*. Lexington: University of Kentucky Press. Surveys debates and controversies over the nature of the social sciences, including the controversy over progressive economist Edward Bemis at Chicago (pp. 163ff.), discussing Small's role in it (pp. 176ff.) and his ambiguous position concerning the role of sociology in social reform. Also discusses Small's role in the self-conscious effort to turn sociology into a profession (pp. 295ff.).

Galbraith, John Kenneth. 1973. "A New Theory of Thorstein Veblen." *American Heritage* 24 (April): 32–40. Suggests that Veblen is the nearest thing in the U.S. to an academic legend, equivalent to Scott Fitzerald in fiction, or the Barrymores in the theatre. Claims that although the legend exaggerates the truth, the substance behind it lies in the fact that one one has looked with such a cool and penetrating eye at the way the pursuit of pecuniary gain makes men and women behave. Also published in an introduction to the 1973 edition of *The Theory of the Leisure Class* (New York: Houghton Mifflin).

Gans, Herbert J. 1962. "Urbanism and Suburbanism as Ways of Life." Pp. 625–48 in *Human Behavior and Social Process* edited by Arnold Rose. Boston: Houghton Mifflin. Criticizes Wirth's theory of urbanization, suggesting that he failed to distinguish city life from other areas in mass society and that his chracterization of urban life applies primarily to select areas of the inner city, not the city as a whole. Gans also claims that Wirth ignores the different types of city dwellers, some of whom are protected from social consequences of size, density, and heterogeneity of the population.

Gardner, Burleigh B. 1970. "W. Lloyd Warner, 1898–1970." *American So-*

ciologist 5 (November): 384–85. Discusses Warner's work, including his teaching at Chicago from 1935, noting that "his research interests spanned all aspects of our society . . . from caste and class organization to religious beliefs, big business, education, and the personality of the executive." Discusses his Yankee City studies and his work with Allison Davis and Gardner, as well as his founding of Social Research, Inc.

Gardner, Burleigh B., and William Foote Whyte. 1946. "Methods for the Study of Human Relations in Industry." *ASR* 11 (October): 506–511. Reviews the creation and work of the Committee on Human Relations in Industry organized at the University of Chicago in 1943, an interdisciplinary group including George Brown, Allison Davis, Burleigh Gardner, Frederick Harbison, Robert Havighurst, E. Hughes, Neil Jacoby, Warner, and Whyte. Discusses problems and opportunities in such research, suggesting that the Committee has not suggested any fundamental methodological innovations, but are rather concerned with the application of well recognized methods to a relatively new field.

Geiger, George Raymond. 1939. "Dewey's Social and Political Philosophy." Pp. 335–68 in Schilpp (1939). Discusses Dewey's philosophical method as it relates to social and political questions, and his positions on the relationship between the individual and society, the state and democracy, and liberalism and collectivism.

———. 1958. *John Dewey in Perspective*. New York: Oxford University Press. Broad treatment of Dewey's philosophy, including relevant chapters on "Inquiry, Knowing, and Truth" (pp. 61–84), and "Thinking, Logic, and Scientific Method" (pp. 85–106), as well as a section on the relationship between Dewey's thought and that of Mead's. Geiger points out that, strangely enough, there is no mention of Mead in Dewey's "Experience and Nature," despite the similarity to Mead's position (see pp. 143ff.).

Geis, G. 1982. "The Appeal, the Person, and the Impact." Pp. 121–34 in Snodgrass (1982). Discusses Shaw (1930) and Snodgrass's (1982) follow-up study.

George, Pierre. 1961. *Précis de géographie urbaine*. Paris: Presses Universitaires de France.

Gerth, Hans H. 1960. "Howard Becker, 1899–1960." *ASR* 25 (October): 743–44. Recounts Becker's life and work, noting his graduate study at Chicago and his dedication to the kind of field work developed by the Chicago school during the 1920s.

Gettys, Warner E. 1940. "Human Ecology and Social Theory." *SF* 18 (May): 469–476. Develops a "socio-ecological theory" which reviews the development of human ecology suggesting it stems largely from the physiological writings of Child and from plant and animal ecologies, with Park, Burgess, and McKenzie being "chiefly instrumental in setting the pattern of human ecological study in the United States." Objects to the perspective's failure to account sufficiently for individual behavior, and comments on Alihan's (1938) critique.

Geyer, Hans F. 1973. "One Dimensional Man and Mind, Self and Society." Pp. 225–34 in Corti (1973). Contrasts Mead's perspective with that of Marcuse, noting their differences concerning social control and social change.

Gibbs, Jack P., and Walter T. Martin. 1959. "Toward a Theoretical System of Human Ecology." *Pacific Sociological Review* 2 (Spring): 29–36. Recommends a redevelopment of ecological theory around human organization for sustenance, claiming that Park and Hawley's borrowed concepts, such as "competition," have dominated theory without contributing to its advancement.

Gidijnski, Joseph C. 1958. "Florian Znaniecki: Original Thinker, Philosopher and Sociologist." *Polish Review* 3 (Autumn): 77–87.

Gillin, Charles Talbot. 1975. "Freedom and the Limits of Social Behaviorism: A Comparison of Selected Themes from the Works of G. H. Mead and Martin Buber." *Sociology* 9 (January): 29–47. Finds differences between works of Mead and those of Buber, arguing that Mead does not account for human freedom, concluding with a critique of positivistic sociology.

Gist, Noel P. 1957. "The Ecology of Bangalore, India: An East-West Comparison." *SF* 35 (May): 356–65. Calls aspects of Wirth's characterization of urban life into account on the basis of Bangalore, India.

Glaser, Daniel. 1960. "Differential Association and Criminological Prediction." *Social Problems* 8 (Summer): 6–14. Outlines criteria for an adequate criminological theory and uses them to evaluate Sutherland's differential association theory, briefly reviewing efforts to test it. Concludes that it is superior to alternative theories, except a "differential anticipation" theory.

Glueck, Sheldon. 1956. "Theory and Fact in Criminology." *British Journal of Criminology* 7 (October): 92–98. Critiques Sutherland's theory of differential association, claiming that it fails to organize and integrate the findings of significant research findings.

Glueck, Sheldon, and Eleanor Glueck. 1950. *Unraveling Juvenile Delinquency*. New York: Commonwealth. Refutes aspects of Sutherland's theory of differential association, claiming that delinquents join delinquent gangs after rather than before becoming delinquent.

Goddijn, H. P. M. 1972. "De Amerikaanse Klassieken: Cooley en Mead." *Tijdschrift voor Sociale Wetenschappen* 17 (No. 3): 263–77. Compares Mead and Cooley with other American sociologists noting the influence of European (esp. German) sociology on Cooley and Mead. Outlines the relation between Mead and Chicago sociologists, and his impact on symbolic interactionism.

Goff, Tom W. 1980. *Marx and Mead: Contributions to a Sociology of Knowledge*. London: Routledge & Kegan Paul. Surveys Mead's social behaviorism and sociology of knowledge, in an effort to develop a synthesis of Mead and Marx in advancing the sociology of knowledge by examining a central issue: that of the relativism implied by the insight that knowledge is fundamentally social in nature.

Goldberg, Milton M. 1941. "A Qualification of the Marginal Man Theory." *ASR* 6 (February): 52–58. Explores Park and Stonequist's theory of marginality, suggesting a modification concerning marginal culture groups (e.g., Jews).

Golovensky, David I. 1952. "The Marginal Man Concept: An Analysis and Critique." *SF* 30 (March): 333–39. Critiques Park's concept of the "marginal man" as popularized by Stonequist and evaluates the marginality literature. Admits that the theory has its rightful place, but only in a restricted sense when referring to "rootless drifters."

Goodspeed, Thomas W. 1916. *A History of the University of Chicago*. Chicago: University of Chicago Press. A history of the early years of the university with brief comments on the appointments of Small (pp. 206, 208) and Henderson (pp. 215, 451), and the founding of the *AJS* (p. 320).

———. 1926. "Albion Woodbury Small." *AJS* 32 (July): 1–14. A biographical sketch following Small's death, discussing Small's early influences, his efforts in founding the Chicago department and the *AJS*, and the interdisciplinary nature of his training and impact.

Gordon, Robert A. 1967. "Issues in the Ecological Study of Delinquency." *ASR* 32 (December): 927–44.

Gosnell, Harold F. 1929. "The Technique of Measurement." Pp. 78–89 in Smith and White (1929). Assesses efforts by the Local Community Research Committee to develop quantitative methods for the study of social phenomena in Chicago, notably the work of Falk, McMillen, Jeter, Monk, Burgess, Ogburn, Schultz, Douglas, White, Gosnell, Thurstone, and others.

Gottschalk, Louis, Clyde Kluckhohn, and Robert C. Angell. 1945. *The Use of Personal Documents in History, Anthropology and Sociology*. New York: Social Science Research Council, Bulletin 53. A volume prepared by the Social Science Research Council as part of an effort to examine the use of personal documents in research, beginning with Blumer's appraisal of Thomas and Znaniecki's *The Polish Peasant* (1918–19) (see Bain et al. 1939; Blumer 1939b; Redfield 1945; and Angell 1945).

Gould, Joseph E. 1961. *The Chautauqua Movement: An Episode in the Continuing American Revolution*. Albany: State University of New York Press. Indicates that Harper's acquaintance with leading social scientists and his interest in sociology were initiated by his involvement with Chautauqua (pp. 13–38).

Gouldner, Alvin W. 1970. *The Coming Crisis of Western Sociology*. New York:

Basic Books. This broad critique includes brief, but significant, discussions of Chicago sociology, arguing that American sociology after World War I was entrenched at Chicago (p. 21). Discusses influences of Romanticism on Mead and the Chicago School (p. 116), and differences from Eastern Seaboard sociology. Indicates that with the decline of Parsonsian functionalism, Goffman's (from Mead and Burke) dramaturgy (pp. 378–90) and Becker's theories of deviance constitute a new stage in the development of the "Chicago School," which may have more of an affinity with the neo-Marxists than with the neo-Functionalists.

Graham, Frank D. 1944. "Ethnic and National Factors in the American Economic Ethic." Pp. 67–83 in *Foreign Influences in American Life* edited by David F. Bowers. Princeton: Princeton University Press. Claims that Veblen was "the most original, and perhaps the most significant of American economists"; although in some respects a Marxist, Veblen had little of Marx's optimism. Traces the growth of institutional economics to Veblen, whose chief contribution lay in pointing out the continuing conflict between pecuniary and productive motivations, and between the development of the machine and predatory psychology and institutions associated with a regime of status.

Green, Arnold W. 1947. "A Re-Examination of the Marginal Man Concept." *SF* 26 (December): 167–71. Raises objections to the "marginal man" concept, arguing that although it has been "taken over uncritically into the literature," it has an indifferent status as a scientific formulation and has not lent itself to statistical or case-study analysis; suggests a number of qualifications of the concept.

Greer, Scott. 1956. "Urbanism Reconsidered: A Comparative Study of Local Areas in a Metropolis." *ASR* 21 (February): 19–25. Suggests that rather than seeing urbanism as atomistic mass society, as Wirth does, urbanism should be seen as part of a continuum of alternative life-styles at the same economic level, which are concentrated in different urban sub-areas. In high-urban areas, social participation is organized around organizational contexts, e.g., the corporation, politics, labor unions, or categories derived from the mass media, but kin relations may grow in importance because of diminished reliance placed upon neighborhood and local community.

———. 1962. *The Emerging City*. New York: Free Press. Reformulates urban social theory, with numerous critiques of Chicago sociology. Contends that the assumptions of laissez faire are built into the ecological image and that competition, conflict, accommodation and assimilation take place within a framework of rules similar to those advocated by Spencer (pp. 7–8). Criticizes the "social disorganization" perspective and the subsequent negative image of the "massified city" developed under the direction of Park and Wirth (esp. pp. 15–18).

———. 1967. "Postscript: Communication and Community." Pp. 245–70 in *The Community Press in an Urban Setting: The Social Elements of Urbanism* by Morris Janowitz. 2nd edition. Chicago: University of Chicago Press. Discusses Janowitz's "rediscovery of the community" within the metropolis through the study of communications.

Guest, Avery M. 1971. "Retesting the Burgess Zonal Hypothesis: The Location of White-Collar Workers." *AJS* 76 (May): 1094–1108. Tests Burgess's zonal hypothesis by analyzing 17 U.S. metropolitan areas, observing only a slight tendency for the decentralization of white-collar workers Burgess had hypothesized. The effect is mitigated, Guest indicates, by the spacial location of certain groups, e.g., blacks and couples with children, and of housing types.

Guglielmi, Saverio. 1964. *Individuo e societa in John Dewey*. Bologna: Zanichelli. Bologna Universita, Facolta di Lettere e Filosofia Studi e Ricerche. An Italian study of Dewey's social philosophy.

Guterman, Stanley S. 1969. "In Defense of Wirth's 'Urbanism as a Way of Life.'" *AJS* 74 (March): 492–99. Reviews criticisms of Wirth's (1938) "Urbanism as a Way of Life" essay and argues that the evidence on which the criticisms rely contains several inadequacies. Presents data which show a negative correlation between the size of a locality and the intimacy of friendships, suggesting the need for a fresh look at Wirth's (1938) theories with adequate measures and design.

Hacker, Louis M. 1957. "Introduction." Pp. v-ix in *The Higher Learning in America: A Memorandum on the Conduct of Universities by Business Men* by Thorstein Veblen. New York: Sagamore Press. Provides a brief introduction to Veblen's career and work, noting his "institutional" approach to economics and social theory.

Haggerty, L. J. 1972. "Another Look at the Burgess Hypothesis: Time as an Important Variable." *AJS* 76 (March): 1084–93. A longitudinal approach confirms a trend toward a relationship between socioeconomic status and distance from the city center as hypothesized by Burgess.

Halbwachs, Maurice. 1921. "Le facteur instinctif dans l'art industriel." *Revue philosophique* 91 (March-April): 214–33. Refers to Veblen as a well-known American sociologist who offers a penetrating analysis of the social forms of modern life; examines his *The Instinct of Workmanship* (1914) and the effect of technological change on the organization of life.

———. 1932. "Chicago, experience ethnique." *Annales de histoire économique et sociale* 13 (January): 11–49. An important summary of Chicago urban sociology with an emphasis on the study of ethnic groups in Chicago communities.

Hall, Jerome. 1950. "Edwin H. Sutherland, 1883–1950." *Journal of Criminal Law, Criminology, and Police Science*. 41 (November-December): 393–96.

A brief memorial review of Sutherland's work and his contribution to the field of criminology.

Hall, Oswald. 1951. "Review of W. Lloyd Warner, Marchia Meeker, and Kenneth Eells, *Social Class in America: A Manual of Procedure*." *AJS* 56 (January): 366–68. Review of Warner et al. (1949), outlining their procedures for determining class structures of communities and the class levels of individuals.

Hamilton, Walton. 1958. "Veblen—Then and Now." Pp. 13–23 in Dowd (1958). Reviews some areas in which Veblen was a maverick, contending that "in spite of the rhetoric employed, he was among the least dogmatic of scholars" (p. 21).

Handlin, Oscar. 1963. "The Modern City as a Historical Field of Study." Pp. 1–27 in *The Historian and the City* edited by O. Handlin and J. Burchard. Cambridge: MIT Press.

Handy, Rollo. 1973. "The Dewey-Bentley Transactional Procedures of Inquiry." *Psychological Record* 23 (Summer): 305–17. Argues that Dewey's (and A. F. Bentley's) theories of methods of scientific inquiry provide a critique of "interactional" approaches, which make inappropriate distinctions between an organism and its environment. Observes that Mead's work was seen by Dewey and Bentley as similar to their own holistic, "transactional" approach, although with some interactional elements.

Hanna, William J., and Judith L. Hanna. 1971. *Urban Dynamics in Black Africa*. Chicago: Aldine-Atherton.

Harder, Werner Paul. 1976. *The Emergence of a Profession: Social Work Education in Chicago, 1903–1920*. Chicago: University of Chicago School of Social Service Administration. A short history of the creation of a social work program at Chicago, particularly through the efforts of Taylor, Harper, Breckinridge, and Edith Abbott. Notes similar efforts by Taylor at his Chicago Commons, assisted by Addams, Henderson, Dewey, and others; comments on the role of Breckinridge and Lathrop.

Hare, A. Paul. 1951. "Bibliography of W. I. Thomas." Pp. 319–22 in *Social Behavior and Personality: Contributions of W. I. Thomas to Theory and Social Research* edited by Edmund H. Volkart. New York: Social Science Research Council. A complete bibliography of Thomas's writings, with information about reissued editions and republications.

Harris, Abram L. 1953. "Veblen as Social Philosopher—A Reappraisal." *Ethics* 63 (April): 1–32. Summarizes Veblen's views on industrial reform; social change and technology; business, the machine process, and the state; absentee ownership and the corporation; monopoly, erialism; his relationship to economic theory; and the ethical and methodological questions raised by his work.

Harris, Chauncy D., and Edward L. Ullman. 1945. "The Nature of Cities." *The Annals of the American Academy of Political and Social Sciences* 242 (November): 7–17.

Hart, Clyde W. 1946. "Edward Byron Reuter, 1880–1946." *AJS* 52 (September): 106–11. Memorial to Reuter, who studied under Small, Thomas, Park, and Mead and spent most of his career at the University of Iowa. Includes an extensive bibliography of Reuter's work, prepared by Donald G. Reuter (pp. 106–11).

Hartung, Frank E. 1960. "Howard Paul Becker, 1899–1960." *AJS* 66 (November): 289–90. Review of the career of a Chicago student who taught in the Wisconsin department from 1937 until his death in 1960.

Hauser, Philip M. 1956a. "Ecological Aspects of Urban Research." Pp. 229–54 in L. White (1956). Provides a historical sketch of the ecological approach, mentioning its major statements by Park, McKenzie, and Wirth (including a list of a "series of Urban Analysis Reports," pp. 238–39).

———. 1956b. "Introduction." Pp. 1–3 in Wirth (1956). A brief introduction to Wirth's thought by way of discussing his selected papers included in the volume. Emphasizes his interest in the sociology of knowledge and his perception of sociology as a discipline, his research on the city and minority groups, and his concern for social policy issues. Foreword by Blumer (1956).

———. 1959a. "William Chapman Bradbury, 1915–1958." *ASR* 24 (June): 406. Memorial comment on Bradbury, who taught at Chicago from 1941 until his death, noting that much of his work is unpublished because it is in classified government reports; observes that he was an unusually effective teacher.

———. 1959b. "William Fielding Ogburn: 1886–1959." *AJS* 65 (July): 74. Suggests that Ogburn will be remembered most for his efforts to make sociology a science through the development of empirical research. Despite his extensive use of quantitative methods, he made a lasting contribution to sociological theory.

———. 1961. "Samuel Andrew Stouffer, 1900–1960." *AJS* 66 (January): 364–65. Review of the career of Stouffer, who, along with Ogburn, was a pioneer in promoting quantitative methods. Discusses his work on *The American Soldier* (Stouffer et al. 1949a, 1949b), his presidency of the American Sociological Association, and other achievements.

———. 1965. "Observations on the Urban-Folk and Urban-Rural Dichotomies as Forms of Western Ethnocentrism." Pp. 503–17 in *The Study of Urbanization* edited by Philip M. Hauser and Leo F. Schnore. New York: Wiley & Sons. Objects to dichotomies developed by Wirth and Redfield, suggesting that expected characteristics of urban life outlined by Wirth are not found in Asian urban areas. Assesses critics of the approach (e.g., Lewis, Kolb), noting that Kolb misread Park (cf. E. Hughes 1954), but concedes that generalizations based on the study of Chicago need to be subjected to tests in other urban areas.

Hawley, Amos H. 1944. "Ecology and Human Ecology." *SF* 22 (May): 398–405. Reviews the concepts and impact of the human ecology approach, noting its sudden ascent to popularity and the confusion that surrounds it. Suggests that some of the chaos in the field is a consequence of the failure to maintain a close working relationship with general ecology or bioecology, an undue preoccupation with the concept of "competition" and the persistence of a misplaced emphasis on spatial relations.

———. 1950. *Human Ecology: A Theory of Community Structure*. New York: Ronald Press. Outlines the field of human ecology, with a historical sketch of its origins, noting the term's first use in Park and Burgess's *Introduction* (1921); contains numerous references to Park, Burgess, McKenzie, and others.

———. 1951. "The Approach of Human Ecology to Urban Areal Research." *Scientific Monthly* 73 (July): 48–49. Sketches developments in human ecology by Park and others; suggests that its theoretical development in terms of areal research seems to have ended with the work of Burgess and McKenzie, although the concepts of "zone" and "natural area" are still widely used.

———. 1968a. "Human Ecology." Pp. 328–37 in Sills (1968), Vol. 4. Outlines basic aspects of the human ecology perspective with a brief discussion of its origins and history (see p. 329 on Park, McKenzie and Duncan) and Burgess's hypothesis of city growth (p. 336).

———. 1968b. "Introduction." Pp. vii–xxii in McKenzie (1968). Traces McKenzie's career, particularly his association with Thomas, Park, and Burgess, and his elaboration of the human ecology approach.

Hayes, Edward Cary. 1926. "Masters of Social Science: Albion Woodbury Small." *SF* 4 (June): 669–77. Discusses Small's contributions to sociology, particularly his founding of the *AJS* and the Chicago department, and his efforts in bringing the results of European scholarship to the attention of American scholars.

———. 1927. "Albion Woodbury Small." Pp. 147–87 in *American Masters of Social Science* edited by Howard W. Odum. New York: Holt. Outlines Small's career and his efforts in founding the Chicago department and the *AJS*, suggesting that Small's sociological point of view involved the recognition of two facts—that social life has a unitary character and that it is pervaded by ethical realities.

Hayes, James R., and John W. Petras. 1974. "Images of Persons in Early American Sociology, Part III: The Social Group." *JHBS* 10 (October): 391–96. Remarks that although group determinism played an important role in European sociology, it was not significant in American sociology in which the prevailing orientation was toward individualistic explanations of motivation. Argues that the Chicago School of symbolic interactionism played a major role in the bringing about a recognition of the importance of the group—Dewey, Mead, Thomas, and Cooley viewed the individual and the group as a unity. See O'Kelly and Petras (1970) and Petras (1970b).

Heberle, Rudolf. 1956. "Review of Robert Park's *Society: Collective Behavior, News and Opinion, and Sociology and Modern Society.*" *AJS* 62 (July): 97–98. Reviews Park (1955), suggesting that the question of why Park, who was not an outstanding theorist or a sophisticated methodologist, made such an impact on the development of sociology, can be found in this third volume of Park's collected papers, edited by Hughes. They are full of ideas that have become cornerstones of contemporary sociological theory and show the affluence of Park's imagination.

Heilbroner, Robert. 1953. *The Worldly Philosophers: The Lives, Times and Ideas of the Great Economic Thinkers*. New York: Simon and Schuster. Includes a broad treatment of Veblen's life and work replete with biographical anecdotes (pp. 199–235: "The Savage World of Thorstein Veblen"). Concludes that despite numerous caveats "there is much to be learned from the polite bitterness of this skeptical mind" (p. 234).

"Henderson, Charles Richmond 1848–1915." 1971. Pp. 579–81 in *Encyclopedia of Social Work* Vol. 1, 16th issue. New York: National Association of Social Work. Brief biographical sketch noting his interest in social reform, "scientific charity," the causes and prevention of crime, and problems of workers.

Herbst, Jurgen. 1959. "From Moral Philosophy to Sociology: Albion Woodbury Small." *Harvard Educational Review* 29 (Summer): 227–44. Examines Small as representative of a group of American scholars whose careers started in "old-time" denominational colleges and ended in newly-formed departments of social sciences. Notes influences of the German historical relativists on Small's thought and suggests that Small "piloted the American college on its voyage from the age of religion into the age of relativity," substituting sociology for moral philosophy and empirical investigation for speculative idealism. "At the same time he held fast to religion and to the Hegelian belief in the unity of science."

———. 1965. *The German Historical School in American Scholarship*. Ithaca, NY: Cornell University Press. Traces influences of German historical scholarship on American scholarship, especially Small (pp. 154–58) and Dewey (pp. 157–59). Small's achievement, Herbst argues, "lay in his demonstration of a logical connection between the empiricism of the historical school and the reform activities of the *Verein für Sozialpolitik*" (p. 156).

Herman, Abbott P. 1937. "An Answer to Criticisms of the Lag Concept." *AJS* 63 (November): 440–51. Assesses Ogburn's concept of cultural lag and responds to its critics, including Woodard (1934) and Wallis (1935), noting its value for interpreting social disorganization. A response was made by Wallis in *AJS* 43 (March 1938, pp. 805–807), with a rejoinder by Herman (p. 807).

Herman, Thelma. 1944. "Pragmatism: A Study in Middle Class Ideology." *SF* 22 (May): 405–10. Looks at recent criticisms of positivism by Robert Hutchins, Archibald MacLeish and Reinhold Niebuhr and discusses the conditions which have led to acceptance and rejection of pragmatism. Examines the work of James, Cooley, Dewey, Mead and John R. Commons, noting a correspondence between pragmatic concepts and the experience of the American middle class.

Hewitt, John P. 1976. *Self and Society: A Symbolic Interactionist Social Psychology*. Boston: Allyn and Bacon.

Higham, John. 1974. "Integration vs. Pluralism: Another American Dilemma." *The Center Magazine* 7 (July-August): 67–73. Delineates Park's place in the debate between integration and pluralism, suggesting that he saw the two as alternating phases in a long history of widening human contacts (cf. Myrdal 1944).

Hill, Forest G. 1958. "Veblen and Marx." Pp. 129–49 in Dowd (1958). Observes that despite Veblen's criticisms of Marx, he felt that Marx had asked the right questions and revised Marxism for his own purpose, making it Darwinian rather than Hegelian.

Hindelang, Michael J. 1973. "Causes of Delinquency: A Partial Replication and Extension." *Social Problems* 20 (Spring): 471–87.

Hinkle, Gisela J. 1952. "The 'Four Wishes' in Thomas' Theory of Social Change." *Social Research* 19 (December): 464–84. Places Thomas's work within the context of his concern with social change and the effort to achieve a rational control of social evolution. Argues that basic problems pervaded his work, leading him to one explanatory theory, an internal, dialectic theory of change. Compares Thomas's "four wishes" to Freudian thought. See Volkart (1953).

———. 1953. "Rejoinder to Volkart." *Social Research* 20 (Winter): 473–77. Attempts to answer questions raised by Volkart (see separate entry, Volkart 1953) about Hinkle's article on Thomas (1952).

———. 1957. "Sociology and Psychoanalysis." Pp. 574–603 in Becker and Boskoff (1957). Traces relations between Freud and American sociology, noting Park's references to psychoanalysis in 1919, the similarities between Thomas's and Freud's work, and Park and Burgess's introducing Thomas's "four wishes" in a psychoanalytic context in their *Introduction* (1921). Comments on Ogburn's interest in psychoanalysis (pp. 582–83), use of Freud by Burgess and Locke, and critiques by Bernard, E. Faris, and Ogburn; observes a similarity between psychoanalytic and life-history methods acknowledged by Lasswell and Kreuger.

———. 1972. "*Forms* and *Types* in the Study of Human Behavior: An Examination of the Generalizing Concepts of Mead and Schutz." *Kansas Journal of Sociology* 8 (Fall): 91–110. Because of frequent linking of symbolic interactionism and ethnomethodology, Hinkle compares the generalizing concepts of Mead (symbolic interactionism) and Schutz (phenomenology and ethnomethodology). Concludes that despite similarities in content, their methodological positions diverge sharply, with Mead emphasizing processes of convergence and change, whereas Schutz seeks to understand human action in terms of typicalities.

Hinkle, Roscoe C. 1963. "Antecedents of the Action Orientation in American Sociology Before 1935." *ASR* 28 (October): 705–15. Discusses antecedents to the action frame of reference (as developed by Parsons, Znaniecki, and MacIver) in the sociology of Mead, Thomas, Faris, Small and others.

———. 1975a. "Basic Orientations of the Founding Fathers of American Sociology." *JHBS* 11 (April): 107–22. Places Small's work, along with that of Ward, Sumner, Giddings, and Ross, in a schema for instituting continuous, explicit, and systematic comparison of the intellectual orientations of sociologists.

———. 1975b. "Toward Periodization of the History of Sociological Theory in the U.S." *Journal of the History of Sociology* 1 (Spring): 68–89. Develops an analytical scheme and applies it to early American social theory. See Hinkle (1980).

———. 1980. *Founding Theory of American Sociology, 1883–1915*. London: Routledge & Kegan Paul. Characterizes early American sociological thought in terms of an analytical scheme, focusing on evolutionary naturalism; includes considerable discussion of Small, Thomas, and others (See Hinkle 1975b).

Hinkle, Roscoe C., Jr., and Gisela J. Hinkle. 1954. *The Development of Modern Sociology: Its Nature and Growth in the United States*. New York: Random House. Includes considerable discussion of Chicago sociology, particularly its impact on social psychology, especially Faris, Dewey, Mead, Thomas and others (pp. 28–33); sociology of the community (Park, pp. 33–37); social change (Ogburn, pp. 37–40); and action theory (Znaniecki, pp. 58–60, and Becker, pp. 62–64).

Hirschi, Travis. 1969. *Causes of Delinquency*. Berkeley: University of California Press. Includes a critique of disorganization theories.

Hirschi, Travis, and Hanan C. Selvin. 1967. *Delinquency Research*. New York: Free Press.

Hobson, John A. [1936] 1963. *Veblen*. New York: Kelley. Originally published by Chapman and Hall, 1936. Ranks Veblen as "one of the great sociologists of our time" and provides an introduction to his sociological contribution, which Hobson argues has been somewhat obscured by the dramatic prominence given to Veblen's earlier work on economic forces. See Moore (1938) for a review.

Hofstadter, Richard. 1944. *Social Darwinism in American Thought*. Boston: Beacon. Although making little direct reference to Chicago sociology, Hofstadter discusses the general intellectual climate in which it developed and suggests that there were major influences from Spencer and Social Darwinism on Small (pp. 33, 70, 84, 156–58), Dewey (esp. pp. 134–42, 159–60), Veblen (esp. pp. 143–45, 152–56, 159), Ellwood (p. 158), and Vincent (p. 158). Reissued by University of Pennsylvania Press, 1945.

Hollingshead, August B. 1939. "Human Ecology and the Social Sciences." Pp. 65–74 in *An Outline of the Principles of Sociology* edited by Robert E. Park. New York: Barnes and Noble. Discusses the history and general principles of the human ecology perspective, noting its development at Chicago by Park, Burgess, McKenzie, and others.

———. 1941. "The Concept of Social Control." *ASR* 6 (April): 217–24. Review of the notion of "social control" as introduced by Small and Vincent in 1894 and developed by Ross and Cooley.

———. 1948. "Community Research: Development and Present Condition." *ASR* 13 (April): 136–56. Includes discussion of Chicago contributions to the field at key points—first in turning from reform to analysis in 1900 (Bushnell and Gillette), a second turning point with the publication of Park's "The City" (1915); the development of the human ecology approach; and finally, topological approaches, such as Wirth and Redfield. Discussions follow by J. Quinn (pp. 146–48), H. Kaufman (pp. 148–59), G. Swanson (pp. 149–152), W. Firey (pp. 152–53), A. Hawley (pp. 153–56).

Homan, Paul T. 1927. "Thorstein Veblen." Pp. 231–70 in *American Masters of Social Science* edited by Howard W. Odum. New York: Holt. Differentiates Veblen's thought from classical economic theory with its individualistic bases. Remarks that Veblen's best work has consisted in an examination of business enterprise in the machine era under the modern forms of ownership, with collusive control of the industrial system by the "key industries" and the great banking enterprises.

———. 1928. *Contemporary Economic Thought*. New York: Harper. Includes a chapter on Veblen (pp. 105–92) in which he contends that no single mind has done more to develop "economic science" as a discipline committed to a realistic explanation of economic behavior with an emphasis on processes of the economic order.

———. 1933. *Essai sur la pensée économique contemporaine des Anglo-Americains*. Paris: Sirey. This survey of developments in economic thought includes substantial discussions of Veblen.

Hook, Sidney. 1935. "A Philosophic Pathfinder." *Nation* 140 (13 February):

195–96. A review of Mead's *Mind, Self, and Society* (1934) suggesting that it represents the ripe fruit of one of America's most original, but comparatively neglected, philosophers.

———. 1936. "New Trend in Philosophy." *Nation* 143 (22 August): 220–21. Reviews Mead's *Movements of Thought in the Nineteenth Century* (1936), commenting on the originality of Mead's treatment of the relationship between nineteenth-century philosophy and the Industrial Revolution, as well as the relation between Mead's thought and that of Dewey, Hegel, Marx, and Darwin.

———. 1939. *John Dewey: An Intellectual Portrait*. New York: John Day Company. A broad introduction to Dewey's thought, with brief discussions of the University of Chicago (pp. 8, 15–17) and of Thomas (p. 16) and Mead (pp. 16, 122).

———. 1950. "The Place of John Dewey in Modern Thought." Pp. 483–503 in *Philosophic Thought in France and the United States* edited by Marvin Farber. Buffalo: University of Buffalo. Suggests that Dewey's influence on professional philosophers has been negligible, but that no American philosopher has so vitally affected jurists, sociologists, psychologists, educators, and other investigators. Concludes that since 1929 Dewey's social philosophy has been of a democratically socialist character.

Hook, Sidney, ed. 1950. *John Dewey: Philosopher of Science and Freedom*. New York: Dial Press. A collection of articles on Dewey's thought, including Horace M. Kallen, "Instrumentalism and the History of Philosophy"; Lawrence K. Frank, "Culture and Personality"; Horace L. Friess, "Social Inquiry and Social Doctrine"; Felix Kaufmann, "John Dewey's Theory of Inquiry"; Pal D. Wienpahl, "Dewey's Theory of Language and Meaning"; Wilfrid Sellars, "Language, Rules and Behavior"; Jim Cork, "John Dewey and Karl Marx"; and others.

House, Floyd N. 1926. "A List of the More Important Published Writings of Albion Woodbury Small." *AJS* 32 (July): 49–58. A bibliography compiled from university reports, *AJS* indexes, and other sources compiled in part by Small.

———. 1928. "Development in the Theory of the Social Personality." *SF* 6 (March): 357–67. Comments on Thomas, Znaniecki, Faris, Dewey, Park and Burgess. Suggests that Park and Burgess have solved the problem of the unity and distinctiveness of the personality by demonstrating that the individual has a role in each of the groups in which he or she participates and that one's personality must correspond somehow to the social role one plays.

———. 1929. *The Range of Social Theory: A Survey of the Development, Literature, Tendencies and Fundamental Problems of the Social Sciences*. New York: Henry Holt. An extensive review of theories in the social sciences, with analyses of work by Abbott, Anderson, Bogardus, Burgess, Dewey, Ellwood, Faris, McKenzie, Mead, Mowrer, Ogburn, Park, Small, Sutherland, Thomas, Znaniecki, and others.

———. 1934. "Measurement in Sociology." *AJS* 40 (July): 1–11. Evaluates problems of quantitative methods in sociological research, noting Dewey's observation that the effect of the scientific method is to "substitute data for objects." Examines techniques developed by Chapin, Bogardus, Thurstone, and Rice, concluding that it is doubtful whether their efforts to obtain knowledge through quantitative techniques (esp. in the study of attitudes) can be fruitful except under certain favorable conditions; cf. Chapin (1935) and Bain (1935).

———. 1936. *The Development of Sociology*. New York: McGraw-Hill. Includes discussions of the Chicago department (pp. 245, 247–49, 283–84, and elsewhere), and a chapter on Thomas and Znaniecki's *The Polish Peasant* (1918–19) (pp. 283–90, 294). Also examines the development of social psychology by Thomas and Znaniecki, Small, Vincent, Ellwood, Dewey, Mead, and others (pp. 313–30); criminology (Park and Burgess, Shaw and McKay, pp. 335–37); urban and rural sociology (Henderson, pp. 338ff.); and the family (Burgess, Faris, pp. 355–66).

———. 1954. "A Centenary Appreciation of Albion W. Small." *AJS* 60 (July): 1–5. Concludes that what stands out most in Small's work is his lifelong concern with the practical and ethical guidance for individuals and societies that might be drawn from sociological inquiry."

———. 1957. "Review of *Community Life and Social Policy: Selected Papers by Louis Wirth*." *AJS* 62 (March): 524–25. Reviews a volume of collected papers by Wirth (see Marvick and Reiss 1956). Observes that Park's influence can be seen in Wirth's choice of subject matter, in the manner of conceptualization, and in the general style of his thought.

House, James S. 1977. "The Three Faces of Social Psychology." *Sociometry* 40 (June): 161–77. Describes symbolic interactionism as developed by Mead, Blumer, Thomas, Cooley, and others as a more "social" alternative to the experimental social psychology of F. Allport and others.

Hovland, Carl I., Arthur A. Lumadaine, and Frederick D. Sheffield. 1949. *Experiments on Mass Communication. Studies in Social Psychology in World War II, vol. 3*. Princeton: Princeton University Press.

Hoyt, H. 1964. "Recent Distortions of the Classic Models of Urban Structure." *Land Economics* 40 (May): 199–212. Reviews Burgess's concentric zone theory and his own modification of it, noting the ways in which urban growth since 1930 has changed some of the earlier patterns.

Huber, Joan. 1973a. "Reply to Blumer: But Who Will Scrutinize the Scrutinizers?" *ASR* 38 (December): 798–800. Replies to Blumer (1973), arguing that the "vigorous orienting actions" Blumer lists may be theoretical *actions* but they are not theory, that the pragmatic model lacks clear rules for deciding what is a "satisfactory" outcome, and that the people who write about symbolic interactionist research don't do it; the people who do it do not use the basic interactionist paradigm.

———. 1973b. "Symbolic Interaction as a Pragmatic Perspective: The Bias of Emergent Theory." *ASR* 38 (April): 274–84. Assesses the development of symbolic interactionism out of the work of Mead, Dewey and others, concluding that the methodology of pragmatism and symbolic interactionism precipitates biases in research. Because theory emerges from the research process, participants contribute to it, giving the research a bias which reflects the social perspective of the researcher and the distribution of power in the interactive setting. Blumer comments (see Blumer 1973) and Huber replies (Huber 1973a). Comments by Schmitt (1974) and Stone, Maines, Farberman, Stone, and Denzin (1974), are followed by a rejoinder by Huber (*ASR* 39 (June, 1974):463–67.

Huber (Rytina), Joan, and Charles Loomis. 1970. "Marxist Dialectic and Pragmatism: Power as Knowledge." *ASR* 35 (April): 308–18. Compares pragmatism (especially Dewey) and Marx's dialectic, claiming that both involve an activist criterion of truth and that both encourage a situation in which the production of knowledge may be influenced by mechanisms of social control.

Huberman, Leo, and Paul M. Sweezy. 1957. "Thorstein Bunde Veblen, 1857–1957." *Monthly Review* 9 (July-August): 65–75. Biographical sketch and tribute to Veblen by the editors of the socialist *Monthly Review* claiming that Veblen was an astute observer of American capitalism and one of the great intellectual figures of the twentieth century. (See separate entries under Adler, Baron, Davis, Morrison, Sweezy, Williams, and Wilson.).

Huff, Toby E. 1973. "Theoretical Innovations in Science: The Case of William F. Ogburn." *AJS* 79 (September): 261–77. Examines Ogburn's work in terms of his development of new conceptual categories to explain sociocultural process, emphasizing the importance of scientific advance through conceptual innovation, notably his concepts of "material culture," and "nonmaterial culture," as well as the distinction between nonmaterial "adaptive" and nonmaterial "nonadaptive" culture.

Hughes, Everett C. 1941. "Social Change and Status Protest: An Essay on the Marginal Man." *Phylon* 10 (First Quarter): 58–65. Summarizes and extends Park's concept of marginality, noting its origins in Simmel and in Gilbert Murray's *Rise of the Greek Epic*.

———. 1944. "Robert Park." Pp. 7–14 in Ames et al. (1944). A memorial statement that emphasizes Park's efforts as a reformer who looked upon the world as a laboratory. Discusses Park's style of research and teaching and includes an autobiographical statement later published in *Race and Culture* (Park 1950).

———. 1950. "Preface." Pp. xi–xiv in *Race and Culture* by Robert Park. Glencoe, Ill.: Free Press. Assesses Park's work on race relations, noting a dialectic in his life between "reform and action as against detached observation" and concluding that "Park probably contributed more ideas for analysis of race relations and cultural contacts than any other modern social scientist."

———. 1952. "Introduction." Pp. 5–7 in Park (1952). A very brief introduction to Park's development of the human ecology approach and his efforts to enlist his students in that work.

———. 1954. "Robert E. Park's Views on Urban Society: A Comment on William L. Kolb's Paper." *Economic Development and Cultural Change* 3 (October): 47–49. Claims that Kolb's (1954) reading of Park differs from his. Contend that Park's emphasis is on interaction of orders of things, not on time sequences, and that Kolb underestimates Park's interest in the moral aspects of society. Indicates that Park made a distinction of which Kolb seems unaware, between biotic competition and conscious competition of a highly organized market with rules and sanctions.

———. 1955. "Preface." Pp. 5–8 in Park (1955). Discusses Park's work, especially in the areas of collective behavior, news and opinion, and sociology and modern society; recalls that although Park was an enthusiast for the cause of sociology, he had little reverence for established departmental lines. Notes Park's interest in social change.

———. 1956a. "The Cultural Aspect of Urban Research." Pp. 255–68 in L. White (1956). Describes the context of urban research at Chicago, the influence of English surveys (p. 258), and Toennies's distinction between *Gemeinschaft* and *Gesellschaft* (pp. 256ff.), noting the work of Redfield, Wirth, and others, as well as reactions against their approach (pp. 260ff.). Insists that Park's work on cities was not atheoretical (p. 255; cf. Hauser 1956a and Shils 1948).

———. 1956b. "Review of Franklin Frazier, *Bourgeoisie noire*." *ASR* 21 (June): 383–84. Reviews Frazier's book on a black middle class (Paris: Librairie Plon, 1955) which accuses darker-skinned Americans of being vain, trivial, pompous parasites and accuses lighter-skinned Americans of having made them so.

———. 1959. "Robert Redfield, 1897–1958." *ASR* 24 (April): 256–57. This memorial comments on Redfield's career and contributions, his relationship to Chicago, his study under Park, Cole, Faris, Sapir and Mead, and his work in anthropology and sociology.

———. 1964. "Robert Park." *New Society* 31 (31 December): 18–19. Remarks that "sociology was a social movement before it was part of the academic establishment" and that Park played a key role in its development. Sketches Park's career, his combination of German philosophical training with a concern for the problems of American cities, and his efforts to make sociology deal with the news but also develop a theoretical scheme based on Simmel's abstract sociology. Includes some discussion of Small, Burgess, Thrasher, Shaw and Wirth.

———. 1970. "Teaching as Fieldwork." *American Sociologist* 5 (February): 13–18. Discusses insights gained from teaching at McGill and at Chicago from interactions with students and colleagues, including Dawson. Reports anecdotes of McGill and Chicago students, particularly what Hughes learned about occupations and professions, noting that teachers and students are professionals and clients. Discusses backgrounds of Thomas, MacIver, Burgess.

———. 1979a. "Epilogue: Park and the Department of Sociology." Pp. 178–92 in Raushenbush (1979). An important account of the Chicago department and Park's role in it which includes discussion of Small, Vincent, Faris, Ogburn, Mead, Breckenridge, Addams, E. Abbott, Taylor, Anderson, P. Young, B. Dai, C. Johnson, Frazier, the Hugheses, McKenzie, Wirth, Lind, Blumer, Ogburn, Redfield, Stouffer, and others. Reviews Park's relations with Thomas and Burgess, his teaching methods, and his organizational activities. Reviews the formation of the Local Community Research Committee and discusses Park's tenure as the American Sociological Society president. The meeting at which he presided was the acme of his career and the point at which human ecology came to the fore. Park invited Thomas to read a paper, his first appearance since his resignation from Chicago. Observes that Park's favorite topics were collective behavior, news, race relations, cities, and human ecology.

———. 1979b. "Foreword: Concerning the Raushenbush Biography of Robert Park." Pp. vii–viii in Raushenbush (1979). Introduces Raushenbush's biography of Park by placing his career in the context of the Chicago department as "the first big and lasting" department in the country. Reviews Small's organizational work with the Chicago department, the American Sociological Society and the *AJS*, and Park's association with Washington and Thomas.

———. 1979c. "Robert E. Park." Pp. 204–12 in *The Founding Fathers of Social Science* edited by Timothy Raison; revised edition by Paul Barker. London: Scolar Press. Reviews Park's career, emphasizing his role in "a great social movement for the investigation of human societies," and his combination of German philosophical training with a concern for problems of American cities.

Hughes, Helen MacGill. 1959. "William Fielding Ogburn." *SF* 38 (October): 1–2. Outlines Ogburn's interests in child labor laws, the minimum wage, the cost of living, technology and social change, cities, the family, and especially quantitative methods of social research. Comments on his personal qualities and interests, his role in founding the Chicago Institute of Psychoanalysis and his interest in art.

———. 1968. "Robert E. Park." Pp. 416–19 in Sills (1968), Vol. 11. Surveys Park's work, emphasizing influences from Dewey, James, Simmel and Washington; his work on defining the discipline and his textbook with Burgess; his interest in journalism, race and ethnicity and human ecology.

———. 1973. "Maid of All Work or Departmental Sister-in-Law? The Faculty Wife Employed on Campus." *AJS* 78 (January): 767–72. An autobiographical account of her 17 years of service on the *AJS* from editorial assistant to managing editor, with some mention of what was occurring in the department at the time. Comments on problems created by her being an assistant to the editors, of whom three had been fellow graduate students (Blumer, Wirth, and Hughes, to whom she was married) and a fourth, Burgess, one of her former teachers.

———. 1980. "Robert Ezra Park: The Philosopher-Newspaperman-Sociologist." Pp. 67–79 in *Sociological Traditions from Generation to Generation: Glimpses of the American Experience* edited by R. Merton and M. W. Riley. Norwood, N.J.: Ablex. Reminiscences of her encounters with Park, emphasizing his relationships with Dewey, Simmel, Washington, Thomas, Burgess, and others, his teaching style and field work.

———. 1980–1981. "On Becoming a Sociologist." *Journal of the History of Sociology* 3 (Fall-Winter): 27–39. Recalls that her interest in sociology was first aroused by Raushenbush, Park's research assistant, and later by Park himself, who persuaded her to attend the University of Chicago. Discusses her research with Park and the Local Community Research Committee, Park's first course on ecology (1926), and collaborations with Cavan, Tibbitts, Wirth, Burgess, E. C. Hughes, Lind, and others.

Hunter, Albert, with the assistance of Nancy Goldman, Leonard S. Cottrell, Jr., James F. Short, Jr., and Morris Janowitz. 1973. "Introductions." Passim in *Ernest W. Burgess on Community, Family, and Delinquency* edited by L. Cottrell, Jr., A. Hunter, and J. Short, Jr. Chicago: University of Chicago Press. Surveys Burgess's contributions in community, family, and delinquency studies.

Hunter, Albert. 1974. *Symbolic Communities: The Persistence and Change of Chicago's Local Communities*. Chicago: University of Chicago Press. A study of communities which includes considerable discussion of Chicago urban sociology.

Hunter, Albert. 1980. "Why Chicago? The Rise of the Chicago School of Urban Social Science." *American Behavioral Scientist* 24 (November/December): 215–27. Argues that the urban social sciences emerged in Chicago because

Chicago presented a raw immediate reality that was studied through inductive, empirical research at the high point of industrial urbanization. Furthermore, one of the goals of the research was to develop policies that would help to ameliorate existing social problems. Reviews the Chicago urban studies, particularly by Park, Thomas, Znaniecki, Wirth, Redfield, Hoyt, Burgess, McKenzie, Merriam, Anderson, Thrasher, and Zorbaugh, noting the importance of Addams's Hull House.

———. 1983. "The Gold Coast and the Slum Revisited: Paradoxes in Replication Research and the Study of Social Change." *Urban Life* (January): 461–76. Reports an examination of Chicago's Near North Side, subject of Zorbaugh's (1929) study, *The Gold Coast and the Slum*, finding a paradoxical combination of continuity and drastic change found in the earlier Chicago urban studies. Although the area had changed radically since Zorbaugh's study,the juxtaposition of neighborhoods with very different socioeconomic populations persisted.

Innis, Harold A. 1929. "The Work of Thorstein Veblen." *Southwestern Political and Social Science Quarterly* 10 (March): 56–68. Charges that Veblen's critics have neglected the significance of his main contribution which is in the more popular journals such as the *Dial* and the *Freeman*; includes a section on Veblen at Chicago (pp. 20–23). Reprinted in pp. 17–26 of *Essays in Canadian Economic History*, by Harold A. Innis, edited by Mary Q. Innis. Toronto: University of Toronto Press, 1956.

Jaffe, A. J. 1959. "William Fielding Ogburn, Social Scientist." *Science* 130 (August): 319–20. A memorial tribute written by a former student who concludes that Ogburn was "the last of the great social scientists who wished to know it all." Assesses his emphasis on obtaining verifiable scientific knowledge and his distinction between scholarship and science.

———. 1968. "William Fielding Ogburn." Pp. 277–81 in Sills (1968), Vol. 11. Sketches Ogburn's career and contributions, especially in quantitative methodology and theories of social and cultural change.

Jaffe, William. 1924. *Les théories économiques et sociales de Thorstein Veblen: Contribution à l'histoire des doctrines économiques aux Etats-Unis*. Paris: Marcel Giard. Systematizes Veblen's theories for a French audience, noting that his writings are fragmentary and dispersed. Treats his general conception of the political economy and his critique of traditional economy, his discussion of psychological factors and their evolution in a constantly-changing environment (noting influences from James), and his analysis of industry and corporations as well as forces and inherent contradictions which act to modify the economic system. Reviews Veblen's career at Chicago and his term as managing editor of the *Journal of Political Economy* (1895–1905).

Jakubczak, Franciszek. 1968. "Subjectivism and Objectivism in Sociology."

Polish Sociological Bulletin 2 (18): 8–21. Attempts to relate Znaniecki and Thomas's work, especially the "Methodological Note" and Znaniecki's "humanistic coefficient," to Marxist materialist dialectics. Discusses the popular movement of life-record writing in Poland initiated by Znaniecki.

Jamali, Mohammed Fahdel. 1973. "Some Comments on George Herbert Mead's Philosophy." Pp. 235–41 in Corti (1973). Affirms Mead's emphasis on the social nature of humans, but takes issue with some of his comments on Islam and suggests that Mead represents thc optimistic mood of the twenties in the United States.

Janowitz, Morris. 1952. *The Community Press in an Urban Setting*. Glencoe, Ill.: Free Press. Includes discussion of studies by Park and Thomas and Znaniecki on the immigrant press and its role in American urban life (esp. pp. 29–33; 223).

———. 1966. "Introduction." Pp. vii–lviii in *W. I. Thomas, On Social Organization and Social Personality* edited by Morris Janowitz. Chicago: University of Chicago Press. Provides the most comprehensive available examination of Thomas's role in the Chicago school and in sociology generally, noting particularly his concern with social organization, social control, social change, the subjective aspects of social reality, and his interests in comparative analysis, social policy, and personal documents. Outlines Thomas's intellectual development, his perceptions of the subject matter of sociology, his institutional analysis, and the concept of the "definition of the situation" as well as Thomas's perspective on the methods of sociology. Reviews his collaboration with Znaniecki and notes his rejection of Toennies's conception of social change.

———. 1967a. "Introduction." Pp. vii–x in *The City* by Robert E. Park, Ernest W. Burgess, and Roderick D. McKenzie. Chicago: University of Chicago Press. Evaluates the Chicago school of urban sociology from 1915 to 1940 and its diverse impact, noting particularly their research monographs with vivid descriptions of urban life, their initiating of the case-study tradition, and their posing of crucial question which still dominate the thinking of urban sociologists. Treats the role of Thomas, Park, Burgess, and McKenzie and their view of the city as an embodiment of human nature.

———. [1952] 1967b. "Preface to the Second Edition." Pp. ii–xx in *The Community Press in an Urban Setting* by Morris Janowitz. Second Edition. Chicago: University of Chicago Press. The author examines his study of the community press as a continuation of efforts by Park and Burgess to study the social space and social definitions of urban communities.

———. 1968. "Preface." Pp. vii–ix in *The Social Order of the Slum: Ethnicity and Territory in the Inner City* by Gerald D. Suttles. Chicago: University of Chicago Press. Describes Suttles's research on Chicago's Near West Side as a revitalization of Chicago urban sociology, but based on a more precise methodological base and a sounder theoretical frame of reference.

———. 1969. "Introduction." Pp. v–x in *Introduction to the Science of Sociology* by Robert E. Park and Ernest W. Burgess. Third Edition, Revised. Chicago: University of Chicago Press. Assesses the importance of Park and Burgess's textbook in the early development of American sociology and as representative of the Chicago school. Observes that they fused sociology into the classical problems of social philosophy, focusing on a set of process categories—competition, conflict, and accommodation—all elements of social control. Provides a refutation of the argument that the American sociological tradition avoided the analysis of conflict.

———. 1970a. "Foreword." Pp. vii–x in *Willard W. Waller On the Family, Education and War* edited by W. J. Goode, F. F. Furstenberg, Jr., and L. R. Mitchell. Chicago: University of Chicago Press. Suggests it was unfortunate that Waller did not succeed in establishing Chicago empirical sociology at Columbia, because it would have sped up the end of institutional parochialism in American sociology.

———. 1970b. "Foreword." Pp. vii–xii in *Chicago Sociology 1920–1932* by Robert E. L. Faris. Heritage of Sociology edition. Chicago: University of Chicago Press. Evaluates Faris's book and locates the contribution of the Chicago school in the general development of sociology. Accentuates the Chicago sociologists' emphasis on integrating empirical data into a theoretical framework and efforts to have all aspects of sociology actively represented. Comments on the interdisciplinary nature of sociology at Chicago and the central place of Thomas and Park.

———. 1970c. "Preface to the Student Edition; Introduction." Pp. v–x in *Introduction to the Science of Sociology* by Robert E. Park and Ernest W. Burgess. Student edition, abridged by Morris Janowitz. Chicago: University of Chicago Press. Discusses Park and Burgess's 1921 textbook and its efforts to stimulate empirical research that addresses classical issues of social philosophy and sociology.

———. 1972. "Professionalization of Sociology." *AJS* 78 (July): 105–35. Provides a "natural history" of efforts to create an applied sociology, including those in the Chicago department. Indicates difficulties encountered because of the nature of the theoretical and empirical content of the discipline.

———. 1975. "Sociological Theory and Social Control." *AJS* 81 (July): 82–108. Indicates the centrality of the concept of social control in the writings of Thomas, Cooley, Park, Burgess, and others, noting that Park and Burgess asserted that "all social problems turn out to be problems of social control." Contrasts Park and Burgess's earlier perception of the concept with more recent, narrower definitions which view it as a mechanism of conformity.

———. 1978. "Review of Neil Coughlan, *Young John Dewey: An Essay in American Intellectual History*." *AJS* 83 (March): 1280–82. Reviews Coughlan's work on Dewey's life and thought up to 1904 when Dewey left Chicago; Janowitz contends that Dewey stands at the center of the American social science enterprise and calls for a recognition of the multifaceted and profound impact of philosophical pragmatism on sociology. See Coughlan (1976).

Jensen, Howard E. 1947. "Charles Abram Ellwood: 1873–1946." *AJS* 52 (January): 362. A brief memorial review of Ellwood's career and his concern for scholarship, teaching and social reform.

———. 1957a. "Biographical Note on Charles A. Ellwood." *ASR* 22 (October): 586. Notes that contrary to information in Odum (1951a) and Hinkle and Hinkle (1954), Ellwood had no professional experience or employment as a clergyman.

———. 1957b. "Developments in Analysis of Social Thought." Pp. 35–59 in Becker and Boskoff (1957). Postulates that the tendency of American sociologists to neglect social theory before the nineteenth century can be traced, in part, to Small's influence. In emphasizing the development of critical history, political science and economics in nineteenth century Germany, Small neglected the importance of earlier developments (see esp. pp. 37–40).

Joas, Hans. 1980. *Praktische Intersubjektivitat: Die Entwicklung des Werkes von George Herbert Mead*. Frankfurt am Main: Suhrkamp. Outlines Mead's thought, characterizing him as a radical-democratic intellectual, and discussing influences from Hegel and Darwin and the development of Mead's pragmatic approach.

———. 1981. "George Herbert Mead and the Division of Labor: Macrosociological Implications of Mead's Social Psychology." *Symbolic Interaction* 4 (Fall): 177–90. Summarizes Joas (1980), arguing that Mead's work as a whole, and particularly his social psychology, contains an implicit conception of social order that has more clarity than that found in the European classics of sociology. It is not normative integration but communicative coordination that makes human society possible. Discusses the early development of Mead's ideas, his notion of "practical intersubjectivity," influences from Hegelianism and other German theorists, Mead's definition of the psychical, and the meaning of democracy in Mead's political biography. Briefly compares Mead's conception of the social order with that of Durkheim and the utilitarians, and argues for a macrosociological interpretation of Mead that goes beyond Blumer's incomplete treatment, but does not move toward the distortions of the neo-positivists Lewis, McPhail, and Rexroat.

Jocher, Katharine. 1931. "Review of Jane Addams, *The Second Twenty Years at Hull-House*." *SF* 9 (June): 608–609. Discusses Addams (1930) and notes her relationship to the University of Chicago.

John Dewey: The Man and His Philosophy: Addresses Delivered in New York in Celebration of His Seventieth Birthday. 1930. Cambridge: Harvard University Press. A collection of addresses evaluating Dewey's influence in areas of education (E. C. Moore, J. H. Newlon, I. L. Kandel), social welfare (Addams), and liberal thought (J. H. Robinson), and a discussion of the work of Royce, James and Dewey in their American setting by Mead; see Addams (1929) and Mead (1930b).

Johnson, Alvin. 1934. "Thorstein Bunde Veblen." Pp. 234–35 in Seligman and Johnson (1934), Vol. 15. Reviews Veblen's life and work, noting his childhood in a Wisconsin farm community where Norwegian customs prevailed in antagonism to dominant American society, suggesting that that experience affected his later social theories. Concludes that Veblen was an evolutionary social philosopher who saw civilization as characterized by a conflict between the predatory and the industrious.

Johnson, G. David, and Peggy A. Shifflet. 1981. "George Herbert Who? A Critique of the Objectivist Reading of Mead." *Symbolic Interaction* 4 (Fall): 143–55. Takes issue with Lewis (1972, 1976, 1979), Lewis and Smith (1981), and McPhail and Rexroat (1979) for their interpretations of Mead as a realist whose theories are convergent with objective, experimentalist methods differing from Blumer's interpretation. Indicates that the objectivist reading of Mead contains two errors: (1) a faulty conceptualization of epistemology forcing the dichotomy of realism and nominalism; and (2) a misrepresentation of Mead's epistemological concerns as a narrow, prescriptive methodology.

Johnson, Charles S. 1922. *The Negro in Chicago: A Study of Race Relations and a Race Riot*. Chicago: University of Chicago Press. Report of the Chicago Commission on Race Relations.

———. 1944a. "Robert Park." Pp. 26–31 in Ames et al. (1944). Outlines Park's career, his interest in racial issues and social reform, his work with Washington at Tuskegee, his study of public opinion, and his efforts toward developing sociology as a science.

———. 1944b. "Robert E. Park: In Memoriam." *Sociology and Social Research* 28 (May-June): 354–58. Examines Park's careers in journalism and sociology, influences by James, Royce, Santayana, Simmel, Windelbrand and Booker T. Washington. Assesses his impact on the study of race and human ecology, and his efforts to make sociology an objective social science.

Johnson, Guy B. 1925. "Recent Literature on the Negro." *SF* 3 (January): 315–19. Includes discussion of *The Negro in Chicago* (C. Johnson 1923), suggesting that it is primarily a study of the Negro community in Chicago and secondarily a study of the race riot of 1919; maintains that the technique of the study is adaptable to other cities.

———. 1957. "Charles Spurgeon Johnson, 1899–1956." *SF* 35 (March): 279.

Recounts Johnson's life, including his work at Chicago with Park and his position as secretary for the Chicago Commission on Race Relations, 1919–21.

Jonassen, Christen. 1949. "A Re-Evaluation and Critique of the Logic and Some Methods of Shaw and McKay." *ASR* 14 (October): 608–614. Recapitulates Shaw and McKay's approach to the study of juvenile delinquency and some of the research it inspired, suggesting that although their interstitial-area and zonal hypotheses may yet be substantiated, they have not yet been proven and should be used with caution. Rejoinder by Shaw and McKay (pp. 614–17).

Jones, Robert A. 1974. "Freud and American Sociology, 1909–1949." *JHBS* 10 (January): 21–39. Includes brief discussions of reactions to Freud by Small, Burgess and others, and reports results of an examination of the influence of Freud and psychoanalytic theory in *AJS* articles.

Jones, Martin. 1969. "George Herbert Mead's Theory of Emergence." Ph.D. thesis, Tulane University. An analysis of the different connotations of the notion of "emergence" and its applications in a theory of reality as expressed in the writings of Mead.

Jorgensen, Danny L. 1980. "Florian Znaniecki's Sociological Theorizing: A Sociohistorical Analysis." *Journal of the History of Sociology* 2 (Spring): 85–107. Surveys the persistent features of Znaniecki's theoretical writings in order to develop a basis for comparing him to other American sociological theorists, especially those contributing to social action theory, symbolic interactionism, and humanistic sociology.

Kallen, Horace Meyer. 1934. "Pragmatism." Pp. 307–11 in Seligman and Johnson (1934), Vol. 12. Briefly introduces pragmatic philosophy, its relation to British and German philosophy and its development in the United States by Peirce, James and Dewey.

———. 1956. "Introduction." Pp. iii–vii in *The Social Dynamics of George H. Mead* by Maurice Natanson. Washington D.C.: Public Affairs Press. Places Mead's work in the context of the "Genteel Tradition" of social thought influenced by social Darwinism, and speaks of the city of Chicago as a representative of the new industrial America; indicates influences on Mead from James, Dewey and others.

———. 1959. "Individuality, Individualism, and John Dewey." *Antioch Review* 19 (Fall): 299–314. Contends that a concern for individuality and its growth pervades all of Dewey's observations regarding society.

Kang, W. 1976. *G.H. Mead's Concept of Rationality: A Study in the Use of Symbols and Other Implements*. The Hague: Mouton. Presents a detailed analysis of Mead's theories of language, symbols, communication, and rationality.

Kaplan, Norman. 1958. "Idle Curiosity." Pp. 39–56 in Dowd (1958). Examines the relation between Veblen's important concept of "idle curiosity" and the development of science.

Karl, Barry D. 1968. "Charles E. Merriam." Pp. 254–60 in Sills (1968), vol. 10. Suggests that Merriam's life represents and reflects many of the changes in political science and American society in the 20th century. Reviews his efforts with the Local Community Research Committee and relations with Lasswell and White (pp. 256–57) and his involvement with Hoover's Research Committee on Social Trends and influence in the New Deal.

———. 1974. *Charles E. Merriam and the Study of Politics*. Chicago: University of Chicago Press. Outlines Merriam's efforts to develop political science at Chicago observing his crucial role in the formation of the Local Community Research Committee (pp. 150ff.) and his relationship to Small, Mead, Dewey, Thomas, Ogburn, Addams, and others.

Karpf, Fay Berger. 1932. *American Social Psychology: Its Origins, Development, and European Background*. New York: McGraw-Hill. Reviews the role of Mead (pp. 318–26), Dewey (pp. 327–50), Thomas and Faris (pp. 351–84), Ellwood (pp. 385–94), Bogardus (pp. 394–400), Allport, Bernard, Young and others (pp. 400–15). Emphasizes the importance of interactional social psychology in establishing the dominant frame of reference for American social psychology. Foreword by Ellsworth Faris.

Kasarda, John D., and Morris Janowitz. 1974. "Community Attachment in Mass Society." *ASR* 39 (June): 328–39. Contrasts and tests two competing models of urban life—Toennies's and Wirth's theory that increased size and density weakens bonds of kinship and friendship, on the one hand, and the quite different "systemic model" of Thomas, Park, and Burgess. A multiple regression analysis of survey provides support for the systemic model but little support for the Toennies-Wirth approach.

Kaufmann, Felix. 1959. "John Dewey's Theory of Inquiry." *Journal of Philosophy* 56 (8 October): 826–36. Examines the place of Dewey's theory of inquiry in the history of philosophy, and his rejection of traditional distinctions between theory and practice.

Keen, Tom Clifton. 1967. "George Herbert Mead's Social Theory of Meaning and Experience." Ph.D. thesis, Ohio State University. Explores the relevance of Mead's theoretical system for the philosophical issue of the nature of meaning in the context of human actions.

Kendall, Patricia L., and Paul F. Lazarsfeld. 1950. "Problems of Survey Analysis." Pp. 133–96 in *Studies in the Scope and Method of "The American Soldier"* edited by Robert Merton and Paul Lazarsfeld. Glencoe, Ill.: Free Press. Assesses implications of survey metholodology evolving from Stouffer et al. (1949a, 1949b).

Kennedy, Gail. 1951. "John Dewey: Introduction." Pp. 327–75 in *Classic Amer-*

ican Philosophers: Peirce, James, Royce, Santayana, Dewey, Whitehead edited by Max Harold Fisch. New York: Appleton-Century-Crofts. Outlines Dewey's thought and his place in American philosophy, suggesting that for Dewey, philosophy is the intellectual expression of a conflict in culture. Indicates that Dewey's philosophy advocated the application of the methods of science to every possible field of inquiry as a means of solving the problems of an industrial democracy.

Kerckhoff, Alan C., and Thomas C. McCormick. 1955. "Marginal Status and Marginal Personality." *SF* 34 (October): 48–55. Reformulates Park's and Stonequist's notion of "marginality" and the "marginal man," addressing Green's (1947) criticisms of the concepts.

Kessler, Herbert. 1940. "Basic Factors in the Growth of Mind and Self, Analysis and Reconstruction of George Herbert Mead's Theory." Ph.D. thesis, University of Illinois.

Killian, Lewis M. 1970. "Herbert Blumer's Contributions to Race Relations." Pp. 179–90 in *Human Nature and Collective Behavior: Papers in Honor of Herbert Blumer* edited by Tamotsu Shibutani. Englewood Cliffs, N.J.: Prentice-Hall. Analyzes Blumer's approach to race relations in terms of the notion of prejudice as a sense of group position which, Killian argues, is a valuable corrective to overindividualistic notions of prejudice. Analyzes Park's influence on Blumer.

Kimball, Solon T. 1979. "W. Lloyd Warner." Pp. 791–96 in Sills (1968), Vol. 18. Reviews Warner's career, his joint appointment in sociology and anthropology at Chicago, and his research on small communities, urban institutions, race and ethnic relations, industrial studies, and social organization. Describes his associations with Malinowski, Radcliffe-Brown, Mayo, Davis, Havighurst, Hughes, Riesman, Gardner, Redfield, and others.

King, Morton B., and Bruce M. Pringle. 1969. "Walter Thompson Watson, 1895–1967." *American Sociologist* 4 (November): 343–44. Observes that Watson (Ph.D. Chicago, 1930) perpetuated the Chicago approach at Southern Methodist University. With his close friend and fellow Chicagoan, Carl Rosenquist at the University of Texas, he worked for the institutionalization of sociology in the Southwest.

Klein, Viola. 1946. *The Feminine Character: The History of an Ideology*. London: K. Paul, Trench, Trubner and Co. Uses a sociology-of-knowledge approach to provide the only major interpretation of Thomas's ideas on the sociology of women. A chapter is devoted to Thomas's work, placing him in a historical and epistemological context of studies of women.

Klein, Malcolm W., and Lois Y. Crawford. 1967. "Groups, Gangs, and Cohesiveness." *Journal of Research in Crime and Delinquency* 4 (January): 63–75.

Kluckhohn, Clyde, and Henry A. Murray, eds. 1948. "Introduction." Pp. xi–

xiv in *Personality in Nature, Society, and Culture* edited by C. Kluckhohn and H. Murray. New York: Knopf. Contends that Thomas's "Outline of a Program for the Study of Personality and Culture" (written in 1933, first published in Volkart 1951, pp. 289–18) forms a major landmark in the growth of organized research on the relationship between individual development and the biological, social, and cultural matrix in which it occurs."

Kobrin, Solomon. 1958. "Clifford R. Shaw, 1895–1957." *ASR* 23 (February): 88–89. A brief review of Shaw's work in the area of juvenile delinquency and his associations with McKay and Burgess.

———. 1959. "The Chicago Area Project—A 25-Year Assessment." *Annals of the American Academy of Political and Social Science* (March): 12–29. Assesses of the Chicago Area Project's work with juvenile delinquency. Kobrin, who worked with the Project, argues that Shaw's perception of the social causes of delinquency has led to a probable reduction of delinquency rates.

———. 1971. "The Formal Logical Properties of the Shaw-McKay Delinquency Theory." Pp. 101–31 in *Ecology, Crime and Delinquency* edited by Harwin L. Voss and David M. Petersen. New York: Appleton-Century-Crofts. An effort to formalize Shaw and McKay's theories, suggesting that their work marked the beginning of efforts in the United States to construct delinquency theories on a foundation of empirical research.

Kolb, William L. 1944. "A Critical Evaluation of Mead's 'I' and 'Me' Concepts." *SF* 22 (March): 291–96. Analyzes Mead's concepts particularly with reference to later research on attitude differentiation, suggesting that a strength of Mead's theory of the self is that it does not pretend to explain everything. Kolb suggests that Mead erred, however, in positing the "I" as a residual category, arguing that it should be broken down into its component elements.

———. 1954. "The Social Structure and Functions of Cities." *Economic Development and Cultural Change* 3 (October): 30–46. Criticizes Park and the human ecologists, arguing that what they take to be *universal* characteristics of cities are in fact characteristics of Chicago in the 1920s. Furthermore, Kolb argues, anyone who believes that value orientations have had a major part in the historical creation of urban industrial society (as in Weber) must find the theoretical orientation of the ecologists deficient. See comments by Hughes (1954), to whom Kolb responds in footnotes.

———. 1956. "Review of Louis Wirth, *Community Life and Social Policy: Selected Papers by Louis Wirth*." *ASR* 21 (December): 788–89. Examines Wirth's work within the context of Chicago sociology in a review of the volume edited by Elizabeth Wirth Marvick and Albert J. Reiss, Jr. (Chicago: University of Chicago Press, 1956). Speaks highly of his 1947 American Sociological Association Presidential address, in which he spoke of the role of the mass media in achieving a new consensus in urban society.

———. 1957. "The Changing Prominence of Values in Modern Sociological Theory." Pp. 93–132 in Becker and Boskoff (1957). Treats sociological analyses of values, including the theory of values in Thomas and Znaniecki's *The Polish Peasant* (1918–19) (pp. 94–97). Describes Faris and Mead's conceptualization of values as elements of the personality (pp.97–99) and a revival of the value-concept by Znaniecki as a dynamic attitudinal variable and as an object of orientation (pp. 102–106). Criticizes Znaniecki's development of definitions of situations as organized attitudes (pp. 104–105).

Komarovsky, Mirra, and Willard Waller. 1945. "Studies of the Family." *AJS* 50 (May): 443–51. Examines Chicago family studies, particularly those by Ogburn, Burgess, Thomas, Znaniecki, H. Mowrer, J. Bernard, Cottrell, and others; notes that E. R. Mowrer related ecological to interactional approaches.

Kornhauser, Ruth. 1953. "The Warner Approach to Social Stratification." Pp. 224–54 in *Class, Status and Power: A Reader in Social Stratification* edited by Reinhard Bendix and Seymour Martin Lipset. Glencoe, Ill.: Free Press. Summarizes the major research findings and conceptual apparatus of Warner's approach and reviews the controversies surrounding his work. Observes problems with his definition of class, his emphasis on prestige and its relevance for general American stratification studies, the accuracy of his portrayal of the status structure, and his methodological limitations and value orientations.

———. 1978. *Social Sources of Delinquency: An Appraisal of Analytic Models*. Chicago: University of Chicago Press. This broad effort to analyze models of delinquency theories includes considerable discussion of social disorganization theory developed by Thrasher (esp. pp. 51–59) and by Shaw and McKay (pp. 61–138), Shaw and McKay's delinquent subculture model, and Sutherland's cultural deviance model, noting that except for strain models, delinquency theory originated at the University of Chicago.

Kuhn, Manford H. 1964. "Major Trends in Symbolic Interaction Theory in the Past Twenty-five Years." *Sociological Quarterly* 5 (Winter): 61–84. Discusses developments at Chicago and elsewhere since the publication of Mead's lectures. Comments on the problem of minimal publishing by Mead, Faris, and others, noting that Dewey's chief formulation of symbolic interaction theory, *Experience and Nature* (1925), has not been widely read by sociologists. Reprinted in Stone and Farberman (1970, pp. 70–87).

Kuklick, Henrika. 1973. "A 'Scientific Revolution': Sociological Theory in the United States, 1930–45." *Sociological Inquiry* 43 (No. 1): 3–22. Observes a resurgence of concerning Chicago sociology, especially concerning problems of conflict and social disorganization which obsessed Chicago sociologists; argues that the subjectivist orientation of the Chicago school is more congenial to contemporary sociologists than it was in the 1940s and 1950s.

———. 1980. "Boundary Maintenance in American Sociology: Limitations to

Academic 'Professionalization.'" *JHBS* 16 (July): 201–19. Argues that the history of sociology in the United States, and its relation to the Chicago sociology department, shows the inaccuracy of sociological models of professionalization. In spite of sociology's early institutionalization, there has been considerable continuing debate over the intellectual boundaries of the discipline, from the early volumes of the *AJS* to later controversies over sociology's status as a science.

Kurtz, Lester R. 1982. "Introduction to Robert Park's *Notes on the Origins of the Society for Social Research*." *JHBS* 18 (October): 332–40. Indicates five themes in Park's notes: Thomas's impact on Chicago sociology, the role of the SSR, the city as a research laboratory, influences on Park's work, and the importance of the pragmatic perspective. See Park (1939).

Lamont, Corliss. 1959. *Dialogue on John Dewey*. New York: Horizon. Transcript of a freewheeling conversation among luminaries who knew Dewey—James T. Farrell, James Gutmann, Alvin Johnson, Horace M. Kallen, Harry W. Laidler, Corliss Lamont, Ernest Nagel, John H. Randall, Jr.; Herbert W. Schneider; Harold Taylor; and Milton Halsey Thomas. See especially discussions of Veblen (pp. 64–65), Addams (p. 73), and Mead and Cooley (pp. 100–104). Lacking any organization or index.

Lander, Bernard. 1954. *Towards an Understanding of Juvenile Delinquency*. New York: Columbia University Press. A work within the tradition of Shaw, McKay, and Burgess on the relationship between urban areas and delinquency rates that critiques aspects of their approach. Suggests limitations of the correlation between delinquency and ecological variables, suggesting that delinquency rates are fundamentally related to *anomie* and community instability, not simply to the socio-economic conditions of an area. A selection is reprinted in Voss and Petersen (1971, pp. 161–74).

Landesco, John. 1929. *Organized Crime in Chicago*. Chicago: Illinois Association for Criminal Justice. Reissued 1968 with an Introduction by Mark H. Haller. Chicago: University of Chicago Press.

Landis, Paul H. 1939. *Social Control: Social Organization and Disorganization in Process*. Chicago: Lippincott. Comments on the role of Chicago sociologists in developing the notion of social control, the relation between individual and society, the application of the interaction concept to the city, and the importance of primary and secondary groups in the interaction process. Emphasizes the work of Dewey, Cooley, Thomas, Znaniecki, Faris, Park, Burgess, Bernard, Veblen, Sumner, and others (see esp. pp. vii, 11, 18, 66–67, 95–99, 277, 419–20, and 426–27).

Landry, Bart. 1978. "A Reinterpretation of the Writings of Frazier on the Black Middle Class." *Social Problems* 26 (December): 211–22. Assesses critics of Frazier's writings on the black middle class, contending that they have tended to distort his ideas and contribution by focusing too narrowly on his criticisms in *Black Bourgeoisie*. Details his other writings, commenting on Frazier's hope that the new black middle class would recognize its historic role as a catalyst for black development; includes an appendix of Frazier's work on the topic.

Landsman, Randolph H. 1957. "The Philosophy of Veblen's Economics." *Science and Society* 21 (Fall): 333–45. Refutes Dorfman (1945), claiming that Veblen's work is much influenced by pragmatism, following along the lines of James, Dewey and Mead, rather than Peirce, who introduced Veblen to philosophy.

Lang, Kurt, and Gladys Engel Lang. 1953. "The Unique Perspective of Television." *ASR* 18 (February): 3–12.

Lasch, Christopher. 1965. "Introduction." Pp. xiii–xxvii in *The Social Thought of Jane Addams* edited by C. Lasch. Indianapolis: Bobbs-Merrill. A discussion of Addams's work, especially on progressivism, pacifism, and the poor, and forces influencing her thought, as well as a brief treatment of her work with Hull House.

———. 1977. *Haven in a Heartless World: The Family Besieged*. New York: Basic Books. Examines the impact of the Chicago school on family studies, notably Burgess, Ogburn and Park, with an emphasis on the effects of urbanization (see "Sociological Study of the Family in the Twenties and Thirties: 'From Institution to Companionship,'" pp. 22ff.).

Lasswell, Harold D. 1929. "Personality Studies." Pp. 177–93 in Smith and White (1929). Analyzes studies of the human personality at Chicago which developed a more or less distinctive orientation due especially to the influence of Mead and Thomas. Describes their work along with efforts by Cooley, Freud, Watson, Bechterev, Znaniecki, Ellsworth Faris, Park, Burgess, Thrasher, Wirth, White, Gosnell, Forthal, Hughes, Durkheim, Shaw, Cavan, Thurstone, Merriam, Claudius Johnson, and others.

———. 1971. "The Cross-Disciplinary Manifold: The Chicago Prototype." Pp. 416–28 in *Search for World Order* edited by Alfred Lepawsky and Edward H. Buehrig. New York: Appleton-Century-Crofts. Discusses the interdisciplinary nature of work at Chicago in the late 1920s, observing that networks cut across departmental lines, with cross-disciplinary leadership coming from Park, Sapir, Merriam, and others. Hypothesizes that those disciplines which were "most dissatisfied with their elite-speciality status" were the most energetic—political science, sociology, and anthropology.

Lazarsfeld, Paul F. 1962a. "Introduction." Pp. xv–xxxi in *Social Research to Test Ideas: Selected Writings of Samuel A. Stouffer* edited by Paul F. Lazarsfeld. New York: Free Press. Reviews Stouffer's career from his graduate years during the "flowering of the Chicago School." Comments on his work with Pearson and Fisher and interest in social trends, his efforts to provide theoretical interpretation of empirical data in *The American Soldier* (1949a, 1949b), his empirical testing of social theory, and his development of formal theory. See the appended bibliography of Stouffer's writings (pp. 301–306).

———. 1962b. "The Sociology of Empirical Research." *ASR* 27 (December): 757–67. Lazarsfeld's ASA Presidential Address includes a section (pp. 761–63) on pioneer efforts by Henderson and Small to create a program of empirical research in 1902, and Henderson's attempts to develop a "bureau of social research" in 1914.

Leavitt, Frank M. 1912. "Review of George Herbert Mead, et al., *A Report on Vocational Training in Chicago and Other Cities*." *AJS* 18 (November): 402–404. A report of a subcommittee of the City Club of Chicago which Mead chaired, which exemplifies Mead's interest in reform.

Lee, Grace C. 1945. *George Herbert Mead: Philosopher of the Social Individual*. New York: King's Crown Press. An analysis of Mead's works and their place in pragmatic philosophy, concluding that the phrase "social individualism" best describes Mead's orientation. Observes that, like James and Dewey, Mead attempted to rid modern thought of the traditional metaphysical tendency to elaborate a concept of the Absolute, advocating instead a philosophy modelled on research.

Lefebvre, Henri. 1968. *Le Droit à la ville*. Paris: Editions Anthropos.

Lengermann, Patricia M. 1979. "The Founding of the ASR: The Anatomy of a Rebellion." *ASR* 44 (April): 185–98. This study based on archival data and interviews calls into question previous interpretations by Kuklick, Martindale and Faris of the reasons behind the rebellion against the Chicago School in the American Sociological Society in 1935. Outlines the issues and characters in the conflict, suggesting that the conflict was caused primarily by personal differences, professional expansion, changes at Chicago, and the move to quantify sociology.

Lerman, Paul. 1967. "Gangs, Networks, and Subcultural Delinquency." *AJS* 73 (July): 63–72. Critiques of Shaw and McKay's subcultural theories of delinquency, insisting that their assumptions hinder theoretical and empirical understanding of deviant youth cultures. See Comment by James F. Short, Jr., *AJS* 73 (January, 1968): 513–15, with a reply by Lerman, pp. 515–17.

Lerner, Max. 1948. "Editor's Introduction." Pp. 1–49 in *The Portable Veblen* edited by Max Lerner. New York: Viking Press. Review of Veblen's ideas and life, including the time he spent in Chicago when, Lerner contends, Veblen wrote the articles that contain most of his important ideas; claims that Veblen was 'the most creative mind American social thought has produced."

Lerner, Daniel. 1950. "The American Soldier and the Public." Pp. 212–51 in *Continuities in Social Research: Studies in the Scope and Method of the*

American Soldier edited by R. Merton and P. Lazarsfeld. Glencoe: Free Press. Reviews and assesses the response of the public to Stouffer et al. (1949a, 1949b), noting its methodological innovations and the breadth of its importance as indicated by response both among scholars and in the larger society.

Leslie, Charles M. 1968. "Robert Redfield." Pp. 350–53 in Sills (1968), Vol. 13. Reviews Redfield's career as an anthropologist and dean of Social Sciences at Chicago and his links with the sociology department. Observes that Chicago sociologists investigated the city in the same way that functionalist anthropologists were then recording the ways of life in exotic cultures.

Levine, Daniel. 1971. *Jane Addams and the Liberal Tradition*. Madison, WI: Madison State Historical Society of Wisconsin. Although only peripherally concerned with Chicago sociology, this biography describes Addams's association with Edith and Grace Abbott, Small (pp. 93, 169), Taylor (pp. 81, 103, 104, 136, 149), Zueblin (p. 169), and especially Dewey (e.g., pp. 93–94, 100, 109–10, 145). Comments on her interest in James's psychology and suggests that her toast to Dewey at his seventieth birthday sums up "the personal and ideological closeness between" her and Dewey (p. 102) (cf. Addams 1929).

Levine, Donald N. 1971. "Introduction." Pp. ix-lxv in *George Simmel on Individuality and Social Forms* edited by Donald N. Levine. Chicago: University of Chicago Press. Includes a discussion of Simmel's impact on Small (pp. xlviii–xlix) and Park (pp. xlix-lviii), noting that Park relied on Simmel in his own eclectic fashion, both giving Simmel's ideas new life and weakening them as a basis for a general analytic theory.

———. 1972. "Note on *The Crowd and the Public*." Pp. xxvii–xxxii in *The Crowd and the Public and Other Essays* by Robert E. Park; edited by Henry Elsner, Jr. . Chicago: University of Chicago Press. Contends that Park's *The Crowd and the Public* (translated here by Charlotte Elsner) has been underestimated because of Park's deprecation of the work and its lack of availability in English. Observes that it is an early attempt to formulate a functional interpretation of crowd behavior which synthesizes Durkheim's and Simmel's conceptions of the social. Maintains that Park's analytical scheme shows a striking parallel to Weber's later typology of types of authority.

Levine, Donald N., Ellwood B. Carter, and Eleanor Miller Gorman. 1976. "Simmel's Influence on American Sociology." *AJS* 81 (January, March): 813–45, 1112–32. Traces Simmel's American influence, including his important influence on Chicago sociology, notably on Small, Park and Burgess, Wirth, Hughes, and Shils.

Levitt, Morton. 1960. *Freud and Dewey on the Nature of Man*. New York: Philosophical Library. Delineates areas of agreement and disagreement in the works of Freud and Dewey, suggesting that similarities outweigh differences. Using much the same constructs, Dewey concentrated more on outer events and Freud more with inner events, taking complementary, not opposing positions.

Lewis, J. David. 1972. "Peirce, Mead, and the Objectivity of Meaning." *Kansas Journal of Sociology* 8 (Fall): 111–22. Argues that Mead and Peirce were united in their opposition to the epistemological individualism that is sometimes found in contemporary sociology of knowledge.

———. 1976. "The Classic American Pragmatists as Forerunners to Symbolic Interactionism." *Sociological Quarterly* 17: 347–59. Contends that Blumerian symbolic interactionism is essentially a continuation of the nominalistic James/Dewey branch of American pragmatism, rather than of Mead's realism (see Lewis and Smith 1980). Claims that Mead's thought, like Peirce's, proved to be too un-American to flourish in America; it was not sufficiently individualistic. See comment by Francis F. Seeburger and David D. Franks, "Husserl's Phenomenology and Meadian Theory," *Sociological Quarterly 19* (Spring):345–47 and Lewis's reply (*ibid.*, pp. 348–50).

———. 1977. "Reply to Blumer." *Sociological Quarterly* 18 (Spring): 291–92. Answers Blumer's (1977) criticisms of Lewis (1976), concluding that aspects of Mead are unrelated to Blumerian symbolic interactionism and have hardly begun to be tapped.

———. 1979. "A Social Behaviorist Interpretation of the Meadian *I*." *AJS* 85 (September): 261–87. Contends that the potential of Mead's social behaviorism remains unrealized after 40 years because of "profound misunderstandings arrived at by some of Mead's interpreters who have tried to squeeze his theory into paradigms that it does not fit." Criticizes both the "residual" (Kuhnian) and "remedial" (Blumerian) interpretation of Mead's concept of the "I" and outlines a social behaviorist interpretation of Mead, although pointing out the distinction between Mead's position and the psychological behaviorism of Watson and Skinner.

———. 1981. "George Herbert Mead's Contact Theory of Reality: The Manipulatory Phase of the Act in the Constitution of Mundane, Scientific, Aesthetic, and Evaluative Objects." *Symbolic Interaction* 4 (Fall): 129–41. Concludes that Mead's identification of ultimate reality with the experience of physical contact is rooted in his studies of animal perception, and that many of his writings can be viewed as an attempt to generalize his theory of the act from an analysis of action toward mundane objects to include other classes of peceptual objects, such as science, aesthetic experiences, and values.

Lewis, J. David, and Richard L. Smith. 1980. *American Sociology and Pragmatism: Mead, Chicago Sociology, and Symbolic Interaction*. Chicago: University of Chicago Press. A key work which calls into question the frequent assumption that Mead was a progenitor of symbolic interactionism and a central figure in Chicago sociology, arguing instead that Chicago sociology was more influenced by the nominalistic pragmatism of James and Dewey than the realistic pragmatism of Peirce and Mead.

Lewis, Oscar. 1952. "Urbanization without a Breakdown: A Case Study." *Scientific American* 75 (July): 31–41. Questions Wirth's characterization of the nature of urban life.

———. 1965. "Further Observations on the Folk-urban Continuum and Urbanization with Special Reference to Mexico City." Pp. 491–503 in *The Study of Urbanization* edited by P. H. Hauser and L. Schnore. New York: John Wiley. Criticizes Redfield's and Wirth's picture of urban life.

Lichtman, Richard. 1970. "Symbolic Interactionism and Social Reality: Some Marxist Queries." *Berkeley Journal of Sociology* 15 (Annual): 75–94. Develops a Marxist interpretation of symbolic interactionism, including discussion of the works of Mead and Blumer.

Lincourt, John M., and Peter H. Hare. 1973. "Neglected American Philosophers in the History of Symbolic Interactionism." *JHBS* 9 (October): 333–38. Discusses major elements in the theories of Mead and the Chicago School that were anticipated by Chauncey Wright, Peirce, and Royce.

Lind, Andrew W. 1937. *An Island Community: Ecological Succession in Hawaii*. Chicago: University of Chicago Press.

Lind, Andrew W., ed. 1955. *Race Relations in World Perspectives*. Honolulu: University of Hawaii Press.

Lindesmith, Alfred R. 1951. "Edwin H. Sutherland's Contribution to Criminology." *Sociology and Social Research* 35 (March-April): 243–49. An outline of Sutherland's contributions, by one of Sutherland's students, notably his concept of differential association and "white collar crime."

Linn, James Weber. 1935. *Jane Addams: A Biography*. New York: Appleton-Century. A general biography with a description of Addams's relationship to Chicago sociology, notably her articles in the *AJS* (pp. 198–99, 243), and her contacts with Small (pp. 160, 163, 190–91, 243), Dewey (esp. pp. 235, 386), Taylor (esp. pp. 190–91), and others. Provides background material on the settlement movement and examines Addams's writing (pp. 242ff.).

Lipset, Seymour Martin. 1950. "Changing Social Status and Prejudice: The Race Theories of a Pioneering American Sociologist." *Commentary* 9 (May): 475–79. Concludes that much of the current understanding of race relations was formulated by Park as early as 1923. Concludes that Park's fundamental hypothesis was that race prejudice "is created when groups or individuals try to resist a change in social organization; changes in status produce conflicts of interest and race hostility." Admits a weakness in Park's assumption that race relations are subject to inevitable cycles, but claims that Park's work still provides a useful source of hypothesis for future research and a model of the kind of writing social scientists should undertake.

List, Peter. 1973. "Mead's Formulation of the Disposition Theory of Meaning." Pp. 107–33 in Corti (1973). Outlines Mead's social theory of meaning, with its "objective relativism," and notes ways in which it contrasts from much meaning theory in contemporary philosophy.

Llewellyn, Emma, and Audrey Hawthorn. 1945. "Human Ecology." Pp. 466–99 in *Twentieth Century Sociology* edited by Georges Gurvitch and Wilbert E. Moore. New York: Philosophical Library. Outlines the principles and history of the human ecology school developed by Park and Burgess, McKenzie and others, noting the interdisciplinary nature of the approach.

Locke, Harvey J. 1948. "Research Methods as Viewed by W. I. Thomas." *Sociology and Social Research* 32 (July-August): 907–10. Claims that Thomas's primary interest was in securing scientific knowledge on how attitudes, values and institutions are changed in modern civilized societies and that his methods were adapted to the attainment of that knowledge. Reviews the sources of data used by Thomas, his use of hypotheses and generalizations, and his emphasis on comparative studies.

———. 1954. "Ellsworth Faris, 1874–1953." *ASR* 19 (April): 226. A very brief obituary noting Faris's role in the change from armchair sociology to "diligent inquiry and a search after data."

———. 1968. "Ernest W. Burgess." Pp. 219–21 in Sills (1968), Vol. 2. Provides an overview of Burgess's work, with a selected bibliography; emphasizes his work on the family and aging. Traces influences from Park, Thomas, and Mead.

Lofland, Lyn H., ed. 1980. "Reminiscences of Classic Chicago: The Blumer-Hughes Talk." *Urban Life* 9 (October): 251–81. A conversation among Blumer, Hughes, and others at a meeting of an informal group called the "Chicago School Irregulars" at the 1969 meetings of the American Sociological Association.

Lohman, Joseph D. 1937. "The Participant Observer in Community Studies." *ASR* 2 (December): 890–97. Discusses participant observation techniques as used by Burgess, Park, Zorbaugh, Reckless, Shaw and others in studying Chicago communities.

Longmoore, Elsa, and Erle F. Young. 1936. "Ecological Interrelationships of Juvenile Delinquency, Dependency, and Population Mobility: A Cartographic Analysis of Data from Long Beach, California." *AJS* 41 (March): 598–610. Reports that in Long Beach a circular pattern as hypothesized in the Burgess zonal hypothesis can be seen only with great difficulty, if at all, although their study provides for some support for the perspective.

Lopata, Helena Znaniecki. 1965. "Florian Znaniecki: His Life." Pp. xiii–xxviii in *Social Relations and Social Roles* by Florian Znaniecki. San Francisco: Chandler. This biographical sketch suggests that Znaniecki's sociology can best be understood as a constant progressive clarification of the scientific problems he considered basic to sociology: the nature of social systems which are its subject and the methodology by which they can be analyzed. Notes his delineation of four social systems: social relations, social roles, social groups, and societies. Traces the growth of Znaniecki's role theories from his work with Thomas to his last work, *The Method of Sociology*. Observes that his wife, Eileen Znaniecki, helped him with his research, including that on *The Polish Peasant* (1918–19).

———. 1975. "A Life Record of an Immigrant." *Society* 13 (November-December): 64–74. Although primarily autobiographical in nature, this article provides some helpful information about the family background and career of the author's father, Florian Znaniecki, and his association with Thomas.

———. 1976. "Florian Znaniecki: Creative Evolution of a Sociologist." *JHBS* 12 (July): 203–15. Examines the evolution of Znaniecki's thought, his efforts to develop a systematic sociology, his work with Thomas and his typology of systems of social interaction: social relations, social roles, social groups, and societies.

Lopez, R. S. 1963. "The Crossroads within the Wall." 27–43 in *The Historian and the City* edited by O. Handlin and J. Burchard. Cambridge: MIT Press.

Lubin, Isador. 1968. "Recollections of Veblen." Pp. 131–47 in Qualey (1968). Provides considerable of information about Veblen's life and thought learned from their personal relationship, noting the simplicity of his home life, their work in the Food Administration under Hoover, and a report they submitted charging government harassment of the Industrial Workers of the World.

Lundberg, George A. 1954. "Comment on 'Methodological Convergence of Mead, Lundberg, and Parsons." *AJS* 60 (September): 182–84. Confirms much of McKinney's (1954) article on the convergence of Lundberg's ideas with those of Mead and Parsons, pointing to some minor differences.

———. 1960. "Quantitative Methods in Sociology: 1920–1960." *SF* 39 (October): 19–24. This paper, read at a session in honor of Ogburn at the American Statistical Association (26 December 1959), reviews the development of quantitative methods in sociological research. Assesses controversies over (1) demographic methods and the quantitative aspects of population; (2) case study methods associated, in part, with Thomas and Znaniecki's *The Polish Peasant* (1918–19); and (3) attitude scales, noting work by Thomas, Bernard, Faris, Thurstone, Stouffer, and others.

Lyman, Stanford M. 1968. "The Race Relations Cycle of Robert E. Park." *Pacific Sociological Review* 11 (Spring): 16–22. Examines Park's notion of the race relations cycle and its major critics, concluding that it nonetheless constitutes a major contribution to sociological thought.

———. 1972. *The Black American in Sociological Thought*. New York: G. P. Putnam's Sons. Contends that Park's notion of the race relations cycle is one of the most important contributions to sociological thought, but that Park's work established the framework for subsequent studies of American race relations within a narrow Aristotelian perspective that focuses on orderly, continuous, cyclical processes. Includes some discussion of work by Thomas (esp. pp. 15, 19–20, 22) and Wirth (esp. pp. 15, 22, 51, 58–60).

Lynd, Staughton. 1961. "Jane Addams and the Radical Impulse." *Commentary* 32 (July): 54–59. Examines Addams's thought, the Chicago context of her work, and controversies over whether or not she was a radical.

McAulay, Robert E. 1977. "Mead and the Ineffable." *Mid-American Review of Sociology* 2 (Spring): 17–28. Critical discussion of Mead's treatment of language and meaning in *Mind, Self, and Society* (1934), examining difficulties inherent in his work that are raised by the ethnomethodological perspective.

McCaul, Robert Lawrence. 1959. "Dewey's Chicago." *School Review* 67 (Summer): 258–80. Reviews the early history of the University of Chicago and Dewey's relation to Chicago life, especially Jane Addams, her friends, and other social reform groups in the city.

———. 1961. "Dewey and the University of Chicago." *School and Society* 89 (March, April, April): 152–57, 179–83, 202–206. A study of the dispute between University of Chicago President Harper and Dewey, and events leading to Dewey's resignation in 1904; based on documents in the Chicago archives. Notes Small's brief involvement, p. 204.

McDermott, John J. 1973. "Introduction." Pp. xv–xxix in *The Philosophy of John Dewey, Volume I: The Structure of Experience* by J. McDermott. New York: G. P. Putnam's Sons. A biographical sketch of Dewey in which McDermott argues that the Chicago years are crucial for an understanding of Dewey and the evolution of his thought. (The introduction is reproduced in volume II, *The Lived Experience*.)

McDowell, Mary E. 1901. *The University of Chicago Settlement*. Chicago: privately printed. Brief description of the history and program of the Settlement including discussion of its relation to the university (with reference to the "laboratory of human experience") and involvement by Zueblin, Dewey, Vincent, Angell and others, including students who work at the settlement.

McElrath, D. E. 1962. "The Social Areas of Rome." *ASR* (June): 389–90.

McGill, Vivian Jerauld. 1939. "Pragmatism Reconsidered: An Aspect of John Dewey's Philosophy." *Science and Society* 3 (Summer): 289–322. Examines Dewey's philosophy from a Marxist perspective, comparing Dewey's resilient optimism to that of Emerson, Whitman and William James. Compares and contrasts Dewey's pragmatism with historical materialism, noting Marx's call to unify theory practice.

McKay, Henry. 1960. "Differential Association and Crime Prevention: Problems of Utilization." *Social Problems* 8 (Summer): 25–37. Examines implications of Sutherland's differential association theory for delinquency prevention programs, concluding that all of the different programs furnish only fair prospects for the control of delinquency in large cities.

McKenzie, Roderick D. 1923. *The Neighborhood: A Study of Columbus, Ohio*. Chicago: University of Chicago Press.

———. 1924. "The Ecological Approach to the Study of the Human Community." *AJS* 30 (November): 287–301. This classic article provides a fundamental outline of the human ecological perspective. Although without much treatment of the historical or critical development of the perspective, it does discuss the relationship to plant and animal ecology and introduces basic terms as suggested "by members of the department of Sociology in the University of Chicago." Reprinted in *The City* (Park, Burgess, McKenzie 1967 [1925], pp. 63–79).

———. 1934. "Demography, Human Geography, and Human Ecology." Chapter 4 in *The Fields and Methods of Sociology* edited by L. L. Bernard. New York: Lang & Smith. Traces the development of the human ecology approach, contrasting it with human geography and demography. Reprinted, pp. 33–48 in McKenzie (1968).

———. 1968. *Roderick D. McKenzie on Human Ecology: Selected Writings*. Edited and with an Introduction by Amos H. Hawley. Chicago: University of Chicago Press.

McKenzie, William Robert. 1972. "Introduction: Toward Unity of Thought and Action." Pp. xiii–xx in Boydston et al. (1972). Introduces the publications of Dewey from 1895 to 1898 while he was in Chicago, suggesting that they reflect an attempt to unite philosophy with sociology and psychology through the use of the scientific method.

McKinney, John C. 1947. "A Comparison of the Social Psychology of G. H. Mead and J. L. Moreno." *Sociometry* 10 (November): 338–49. Compares Mead and Moreno, arguing that Moreno's work and sociometric analyses make a contribution to "Meadian" social psychology (see Moreno 1947).

———. 1954. "Methodological Convergence of Mead, Lundberg, and Parsons." *AJS* 59 (May): 565–74. Compares Mead's methodology to that of Parsons and Lundberg, finding convergences in the categories of "science and research," "the objective world," "uniformities and causal imputation," and "process: structure and function."

———. 1955. "The Contributions of George H. Mead to the Sociology of Knowledge." *SF* 34 (December): 144–49. Concludes that the contribution of

Mead to the sociology of knowledge lies in the fact that he has supplied it with a more adequate social psychology than is found in the European version of the discipline.

McKinney, Fred. 1978. "Functionalism at Chicago: Memoirs of a Graduate Student, 1929–1931." *JHBS* 14 (April): 142–48. Comments on the Chicago Psychology Department, with brief notes on Thurstone and Mead (cf. Thurstone 1952).

MacLean, Annie Marion. 1923. "Twenty Years of Sociology by Correspondence." *AJS* 28 (January): 461–72. Reviews her experience as a correspondence instructor at Chicago, indicating that she taught 799 students in 47 states and 9 other countries (plus Hawaii).

———. 1926. "Albion W. Small: An Appreciation." *AJS* 32 (July): 45–48. A brief personal memorial, written by one of Small's students and colleagues, emphasizing his efforts in founding the Chicago department and inspiring students and colleagues.

McLemore, S. Dale. 1970. "Simmel's 'Stranger': A Critique of the Concept." *Pacific Sociological Review* 13 (Spring): 86–94. This discussion of Simmel's essay on "The Stranger" includes consideration of Park and Burgess's inclusion of it in their *Introduction* and the development of the "marginal man" concept by Park, Stonequist, Rose and others. Notes that the marginality literature confuses, albeit productively, two aspects of research on the stranger: social distance issues and the impact of "newcomers" on social organization.

McPhail, Clark. 1979. "Experimental Research Is Convergent with Symbolic Interaction." *Symbolic Interaction* 2 (Spring): 89–94. Claims that although most symbolic interactionists have eschewed experimental research, choosing instead "naturalistic investigation," Mead's orientation lends itself to the experimental method as developed by Cottrell, one of Mead's students who took quite a different direction in interpreting Mead from Blumer. Of particular interest is a footnote (p. 91) which traces some of the sources of the Chicago and Iowa "schools" of interactionism.

McPhail, Clark, and Cynthia Rexroat. 1979. "Mead vs. Blumer: The Divergent Methodological Perspectives of Social Behaviorism and Symbolic Interactionism." *ASR* 44 (June): 449–67. Indicates a divergence in the methodological perspectives of Mead's social behaviorism and Blumer's symbolic interactionism, claiming that Mead's methodological perspective enables researchers to avoid problems of naturalistic methodology by reducing the scope of behavior to be examined and by increasing control of the investigator's behavior regarding that which is examined.

———. 1980. "*Ex Cathedra* Blumer or *Ex Libris* Mead?" *ASR* 45 (June): 420–30. The authors defend their judgment that Mead's and Blumer's methodological perspectives are divergent, in spite of Blumer's claims to the contrary (see Blumer 1980, McPhail and Rexroat 1979, and Bales 1966).

Madge, John. 1962. *The Origins of Scientific Sociology*. New York: Free Press of Glencoe. Includes extensive discussion of Chicago sociology, with comments on Thomas and Znaniecki's *The Polish Peasant* (1918–19) (pp. 52–87) and "The Chicago School around 1930" (pp. 88–125), emphasizing the impact of Park his colleagues and students, especially Zorbaugh. Maintains that the fame of the Chicago school rests on its characteristic approach and a highly developed interest in the real world. Describes Shils's studies of primary groups in the military (pp. 323–26).

Maines, D. R. 1977. "Social Organization and Social Structure in Symbolic Interactionist Thought." *Annual Review of Sociology* 7 (Annual): 235–59.

Marcell, David W. 1974. *Progress and Pragmatism*. Westport, CT: Greenwood Press. Compares Dewey's work (pp. 196–257) to that of James and Beard and the overall context of pragmatic philosophy.

Markey, John F. 1929. "Trends in Social Psychology." In *Trends in American Sociology* edited by George A. Lundberg, Read Bain, and Nels Anderson. New York: Harper. Examines Bain's critique of Thomas and Znaniecki (see Bain 1928) and Faris's opposing article (1928), noting difficulties of definitions and operationalization in attitude research. Includes brief discussions of Ellwood, Park, Cooley, Burgess, Ogburn, Mead, Young, Bernard, and others.

Martindale, Don. 1957. "Social Disorganization: The Conflict of Normative and Empirical Approaches." Pp. 340–67 in Becker and Boskoff (1957). Evaluates social disorganization theories, noting that whereas some were liberal in their political implications (e.g., Thomas and Znaniecki), others were conservative (e.g., Durkheim); some of them, furthermore, were normative theories disguised as empirical theories. Considers Thomas and Znaniecki (pp. 347– 49), Ogburn's concept of cultural lag (pp. 349–54), and Park and Burgess's ecological approach (pp. 355–57).

———. 1960. *The Nature and Types of Sociological Theory*. Boston: Houghton Mifflin. Within the context of a typology of sociological theory, Martindale includes discussions of the work of Dewey (pp. 301–302), Mead (pp. 353–61), Ogburn (pp. 324–30), Park and Burgess (pp. 252–56), Redfield (pp. 92–96), Sutherland (pp. 203–205), and Veblen (pp. 393–99).

———. 1976. *The Romance of a Profession: A Case History in the Sociology of Sociology*. St. Paul, Minn.: Windflower. A critical history of the University of Minnesota sociology department with discussions of the Chicago department's role in the discipline (esp. pp. 9–12) and its relationship to the Chautauqua movement. Treats Vincent as a Chicago sociologist and president of the University of Minnesota (pp. 20–35).

Marvick, Dwaine. 1977. "Introduction: Context, Problems, and Methods." Pp. 1–72 in *Harold D. Lasswell on Political Sociology* edited by Dwaine Marvick. Chicago: University of Chicago Press. Outlines the career and interests of Lasswell, who taught political science at Chicago (1922–1938), noting similarities in his work with that of Dewey, Mead, and Whitehead. Observes that, as a graduate student at Chicago, Lasswell shared an office with Redfield and Wirth and through them encountered Park, Burgess, and Small. Discusses his relationship with Mead and Dewey, his study with Merriam and his interdisciplinary approach, as well as his contribution to the *AJS*.

Marvick, Elizabeth Wirth. 1964. "Louis Wirth: A Biographical Memorandum." Pp. 333–40 in Wirth (1964). Outlines Wirth's personal and professional life, his immigration to the United States, his study and teaching at Chicago, and his association with Park, Burgess, Thomas, and others.

Marvick, Elizabeth Wirth, and Albert J. Reiss, Jr. 1956. "Introductory Notes." Pp. 7–8, 109, 191, 283 in Wirth (1956). Brief, but informative, introductions to the four sections of Wirth's articles collected in the volume, placing them within the context of his overall contribution to sociology.

Masoero, A. 1931. "Un Americano non edonista." *Economia* 9: 151–72. A discussion of Veblen's institutional economics.

Masuoka, Jitsuichi, and Raytha L. Yokley. 1954. "Essential Structural Requisites in Race Relations." *SF* 33 (October): 30–35. Describes Park's definition of race relations, with its emphasis on race conflict and race consciousness, and suggests a redefinition that emphasizes structural rather than psychological elements, but drawing upon the work of Blumer, Hughes, and others.

Masuoka, Jitsuiki, and Preston Valien, eds. 1961. *Race Relations: Problems and Theory: Essays in Honor of Robert E. Park*. Chapel Hill: University of North Carolina Press. A collection of papers read at the dedication of the Robert E. Park building, Fisk University, most of them oriented around some aspect of Park's contribution to the sociological study of race relations, e.g., his emphasis on margins and frontiers: E. Hughes, "The Nature of Racial Frontiers" (pp. 51–57); Lind, "Race Relations Frontiers in Hawaii" (pp. 58–77); and Masuoka, "The City as a Racial Frontier: With Special Reference to Colonialism and Urbanism in Africa" (pp. 78–98); cf. Burgess (1961).

Mathews, Shailer. 1936. *New Faith for Old: An Autobiography*. New York: Macmillan. Autobiography of University of Chicago Divinity School dean, a friend of Small's at Colby College, an advocate of "Christian Sociology" and a frequent contributor to the *AJS*.

Matthews, Fred H. 1977. *Quest for an American Sociology: Robert E. Park and the Chicago School*. Montreal: McGill-Queen's University Press. An intellectual biography covering Park's career from his college education to his work as a journalist and an agent for social change, (pp. 1–84), through his time at Chicago as an "entrepreneur of research." Includes extensive discussion of the Chicago sociology department at the time of his arrival, the influences of Small and Thomas on Park's thought, and Park's emphasis on investigation and research. Replete with anecdotes from a wide variety of Park's colleagues, students and friends, including Anderson, Bogardus, Bernard, Blumer, and Lasswell.

Matza, David. 1964. *Delinquency and Drift*. New York: Wiley & Sons. Includes an important critique of aspects of subcultural theories of deviance and Sutherland's theory of differential association.

———. 1969. *Becoming Deviant*. New York: Prentice-Hall.

Maus, Heinz. [1956] 1962. *A Short History of Sociology*. New York: Philosophical Library. Contains discussions of American sociology, noting the work of Small (pp. 97–98), Veblen (pp. 100–101), Mead (pp. 101, 105–106), Ellwood (pp. 104–105), and Bernard (p. 107). Maintains that American sociology became differentiated from European sociology from the 1920s onward, beginning with the publication of Park and Burgess's *Introduction* (1921) (pp. 120–21), Thomas and Znaniecki's *The Polish Peasant* (1918–19) (pp. 120–23), and with Park et al. (1925) and the human ecology perspective (pp. 120; 124–29). Briefly mentions contributions by McKenzie, E. Hughes, Anderson, Thrasher, Wirth, Zorbaugh, Shaw, Cressey, Warner, Ogburn, Lasswell, Janowitz, Whyte, Thurstone, Bogardus, Stouffer, and others. Originally published in Ziegenfuss, *Handbuch der Soziologie* (Stuttgart: Enke Verlag, 1956).

Mead, George Herbert. 1917. "Josiah Royce: A Personal Impression." *International Journal of Ethics* 27 (January): 168–70. Acknowledges a debt to Royce, who "opened up the realm of romantic idealism" and taught him the liberating Hegelian dialectic as a means of philosophical inquiry.

———. 1930a. "Cooley's Contribution to American Social Thought." *AJS* 35 (March): 693–706. Includes comparisons of Cooley's thought with Mead's and with the work of Thomas, Park, Burgess, and Faris. Describes Cooley's theories of the social origins of the self, acknowledging Mead's debt to Cooley. Reprinted, pp. xxi–xxxviii in *Human Nature and the Social Order*, by Charles Horton Cooley. New York: Schocken, 1964.

———. 1930b. "The Philosophies of Royce, James, and Dewey in Their American Settings." Pp. 75–105 in *John Dewey: The Man and His Philosophy: Addresses Delivered in New York in Celebration of His Seventieth Birthday.* Cambridge: Harvard University Press. Relates the pragmatic philosophy of Royce, James, and especially Dewey, to the cultural milieu in which it was formulated, particularly noting early influences of English individualism, Puritanism, and the democracy of the town meeting.

———. 1932. *The Philosophy of the Present*. Chicago: Open Court Publishing Co.

———. 1934. *Mind, Self, and Society: From the Standpoint of a Social Behav-*

iorist. Edited and with an Introduction by Charles W. Morris. Chicago: University of Chicago Press.

———. 1936. *Movements of Thought in the Nineteenth Century*. Chicago: University of Chicago Press. This important edition of notes from Mead's classroom lectures contains Mead's views on various movements of nineteenth century thought and, by implication, some of the influences on his own thought. Chapter 15, "Science Raises Problems for Philosophy—Realism and Pragmatism" (pp. 326–59), contains Mead's interpretation of the origin and meanings of pragmatism as a philosophical movement, and its place in the development of modern thought. Mead maintains that the "doctrine" of pragmatism has two outstanding figures, James and Dewey (p. 344), and two sources: behavioristic psychology and the research process or scientific technique.

———. 1938. *The Philosophy of the Act*. Edited and with an Introduction by Charles W. Morris, in Collaboration with John M. Brewster, Albert M. Dunham, and David L. Miller. Chicago: University of Chicago Press.

———. 1964. *George Herbert Mead On Social Psychology: Selected Papers*. Edited and with an Introduction by Anselm Strauss. Chicago: University of Chicago Press.

Mead, Henry C. A. 1931. "George Herbert Mead." Pp. 31–38 in Ames et al. (1931). A brief biographical sketch of Mead, written by his son, with some discussion of intellectual influences, especially Royce and James, up to the time of his going to Chicago. Reprinted, pp. lxxvi-lxxix in Mead (1938).

Meisenhelder, Thomas. 1977. "Symbolic Action, Art, and Social Order: The Sociological Theory of Hugh Dalziel Duncan." *JHBS* 13 (July): 267–73. Examines Duncan's efforts to address the Hobbesian problem of order in an explicit contrast to Parsons, drawing upon the Chicago School, especially Mead, Dewey, as well as Simmel and Burke.

Meltzer, Bernard N. 1959. *The Social Psychology of George Herbert Mead*. Kalamazoo, Michigan: Center for Sociological Research. One of the first major sociological interpretations of Mead's social philosophy.

Meltzer, Bernard N, and John W. Petras. 1970. "The Chicago and Iowa Schools of Symbolic Interactionism." Pp. 3–17 in *Human Nature and Collective Behavior: Papers in Honor of Herbert Blumer* edited by Tamotsu Shibutani. Englewood Cliffs, N.J.: Prentice-Hall, Inc. Contrasts the Chicago school of symbolic interactionism, developed by Blumer and others, with the "Iowa School," developed by Kuhn. Claims that the fundamental point of divergence is methodological, with Blumer combining scientific research with a humanistic approach, and Kuhn arguing for the need to operationalize the key ideas of symbolic interactionism in the search for a standardized, objective process of measurement of significant variables.

Meltzer, Bernard N., John Petras and Larry Reynolds. 1975. *Symbolic Interactionism: Genesis, Varieties, and Criticism*. London: Routledge & Kegan Paul. Analyzes major ideas in Mead (as the perspective's leading figure pp. 27–42), Dewey (pp. 15–21), Thomas (pp. 22–27), James (pp. 3–8), and Cooley (pp. 8–15). Contrasts the Chicago and Iowa schools (pp. 55–67), and describes developments by and critics of Blumer (54–67, 92–93), Goffman (67–75), Faris and Park (p. 55).

Mencken, H. L. 1919. *Prejudices: First Series*. New York: Knopf. Includes a chapter of criticisms of Veblen, particularly his *Theory of the Leisure Class* (1899), lamenting that in 1918 "Veblen dominated the American scene. . . . There were Veblenists, Veblen clubs, Veblen remedies for the sorrows of the world" (pp. 59–82).

Merriam, Charles E. 1929. "The Metropolitan Region of Chicago." Pp. 78–89 in Smith and White (1929). Reviews studies of metropolitan Chicago by members of the Local Community Research Committee, especially those by Jeter, Goode, Duddy, Steadman, and others. Notes ongoing studies which might lead to better cooperation and reorganization.

Merton, Robert K. 1940. "Bureaucratic Structure and Personality." *SF* 18 (May): 560–68. Maintains that "the transition to a study of the negative aspects of bureaucracy is afforded by the application of Veblen's concept of "trained incapacity" and Dewey's notion of "occupational psychosis."

———. 1968 [1949]. *Social Theory and Social Structure*. Enlarged Edition. New York: Free Press. This broad work includes a treatise on "The Thomas Theorem" (pp. 475ff; cf. Mead's formulation, p. 20), Thomas's concept of the definition of the situation, *The Polish Peasant* (1918–19) (p. 116) and Blumer's critique of it (pp. 148–49), and the concept of relative deprivation in James, Baldwin, Mead, Hyman and Stouffer and *The American Soldier*, and its relation to Mead (pp. 279–34; 292–95, 287). Mentions Small's publication of Simmel in the *AJS* (p. 458) and the work of Lasswell, Thurstone, Sutherland, Shils, Shaw, McKay, Thrasher, Wirth, Znaniecki, Hughes, and others.

Merton, Robert K., and Alice S. Kitt. 1950. "Contributions to the Theory of Reference Group Behavior." Pp. 40–105 in Merton and Lazarsfeld (1950). Identifies and discusses the research in Stouffer et al. (1949a, 1949b) which bear upon the theory of reference groups.

Merton, Robert K., and Paul F. Lazarsfeld. 1950. *Studies in the Scope and Method of "The American Soldier"*. Glencoe, Ill.: Free Press. This edited volume of essays examines implications of the massive study by Stouffer et al. (1949a, 1949b). See separate entries under Shils, Merton and Kitt, Speier, Kendall and Lazarsfeld, Stouffer, and Lerner.

Metzger, L. Paul. 1971. "American Sociology and Black Assimilation: Conflicting Perspectives." *America Journal of Sociology* 76 (January): 627–47. Maintains that Park's "assimilationist" theories of race relations overlook the functions which ethnic pluralism may perform in a democratic society.

Milgram, Stanley. 1970. "The Experience of Living in Cities." *Science* 167 (March): 1461–68.

Miller, David L. 1943a. "G. H. Mead's Conception of the Past." *Philosophy of Science* 10 (January): 29–39. Outlines Mead's understanding of the past and comments on his conceptualization of its relation to the present.

———. 1943b. "G. H. Mead's Conception of the Present." *Philosophy of Science* 10 (January): 40–46. Argues that Mead's philosophy of the present gives an anti-metaphysical interpretation of the scientific method and rejects a reductive method of explanation which assumes that in knowing we must assimilate an effect to its cause.

———. 1947. "DeLaguna's Interpretation of G. H. Mead." *Journal of Philosophy* 44 (March): 158–62. Objects to DeLaguna's (1946) interpretation of Mead, arguing that cooperation and communication can exist even when actors have different purposes, and that Mead never intended to suggest that the self can or should identify itself with society.

———. 1967. "George Herbert Mead." Pp. 473–74 in *Encyclopedia Americana* Vol. 18. New York: Grolier. A brief review of Mead's life and work noting his effort to develop a scientific and empirical social psychology and theories of the self.

———. 1973a. "George Herbert Mead: Biographical Notes." Pp. 17–42 in Corti (1973). Reviews influences on Mead's thought and work, including the period at Chicago (pp. 27ff.) by one of Mead's Chicago students.

———. 1973b. *George Herbert Mead: Self, Language, and the World*. Austin: University of Texas Press. A study of Mead's system of thought, including a biographical introduction that examines influences on Mead's thought, his relationships with Dewey, Small, Thomas, Cooley, and his personal traits. Of particular interest are chapters on "Bio-Social Man . . ." (pp. 3–24), "Mead's Intentions and His Basic Terms" (pp. 25–45), "Mead's Theory of the Self: Its Origin and How It Functions in Society" (pp. 46–65), and "Mead's Principle of Sociality" (pp. 188–206). Contends that "Mead's bold statement that the meaning of a sign, a symbol, or a stimulus is the response it evokes (implicitly or explicitly) is at once the beginning of his thesis that minds . . . must be explained in terms of their functional relation to behavior and, more specifically, in relation to acts of adjustment between individuals and their environments." Re-issued by the University of Chicago Press, 1981.

———. 1973c. "George Herbert Mead: Symbolic Interaction and Social Change." *Psychological Record* 23 (Summer): 294–304. Analyzes Mead's theory of the self and its implications for understanding social processes;

maintains that Mead evades phenomenalism, extreme behaviorism, reductionism, dualism, solipsism, and supernaturalism.

———. 1975. "Josiah Royce and George H. Mead on the Nature of the Self." *Transactions of the Charles S. Peirce Society* 16 (Spring): 67–89. Compares and contrasts Royce and Mead on the self, noting Royce's influence on his student Mead. Both agree that the self is social, is not a substance independent of the community, and cannot be known directly. Basic differences concern Royce's idealistic metaphysics as opposed to Mead's pragmatic naturalism.

———. 1981. "The Meaning of Role-Taking." *Symbolic Interaction* 4 (Fall): 167–75. Examines Mead's concept of "role-taking," arguing that although it has been used extensively for 50 years, the full meaning of the term has not been made explicit. Describes the role of the significant symbol as a linguistic gesture that evokes the same response, and therefore a covert, mental response, in the one who makes it as it does in the one to whom it is addressed. Notes the social construction of "objects," the importance of the hand in developing reflective intelligence, and the difference between linguistic and non-linguistic gestures.

Mills, C. Wright. 1939. "Language, Logic, and Culture." *ASR* 4 (October): 670–80. Reviews aspects of Mead's theories and attempts to apply them to the sociology of knowledge. Suggests, however, that the generalized other does not, as Mead contends, incorporate the whole society, but stands for selected societal segments; claims that Mead's statements are functions of an inadequate theory of society and of certain democratic persuasions. Reprinted in pp. 423–38 in *Power, Politics, and People*, edited by Irving Louis Horowitz (New York: Ballantine, 1963).

———. 1943. "The Professional Ideology of Social Pathologists." *AJS* 49 (September): 165–80. A critical assessment of work in the field of social disorganization, including Thomas, Ogburn, Ellwood and Cooley, arguing that the backgrounds and careers of researchers in the field affect their definitions of problems and the results of their research.

———. 1960. "Introduction: The Classic Tradition." Pp. 1–17 in *Images of Man: The Classic Tradition in Sociological Thinking* edited by C. Wright Mills. New York: Braziller. Includes brief, but significant, discussions of Thomas and Znaniecki and Veblen. Suggests that Thomas and Znaniecki provide a framework for a general sociological view of "personality" which is the foremost contribution of American sociology. Concludes that Veblen is "the best social scientist America has produced," concluding that the master clue to his work as a whole is the distinction between pecuniary and industrial employment, a distinction which in many ways parallels and extends Marx's proletariat and bourgeoisie.

———. 1966. *Sociology and Pragmatism: The Higher Learning in America.*

New York: Oxford University Press. Mills's doctoral dissertation on the professionalization of philosophic education in the United States, with a preface and introduction by I. Horowitz. A major critique of pragmatism, this work includes substantial discussions of Peirce (pp. 121–212), James (pp. 215–76) and Dewey (pp. 279–463), as well as comments on Mead and the Chicago school of philosophy. Traces influences on Dewey's thought from Hegel, Mead, James and others (pp. 279–306), with a chapter devoted to his relationship with Addams and her impact on his work ("Hull House and Consequent Writings," pp. 307–24). Includes a chapter on "Social Psychology: Model for Liberals."

Miner, Horace. 1952. "The Folk-Urban Continuum." *ASR* 17 (October): 529–74. Systematically outlines features of Redfield's continuum, its supporters and critics, and discusses its impact on urban sociology. Reprinted, pp. 22–34, in *Cities and Society: The Revised Reader in Urban Sociology*, edited by Paul K. Hatt and Albert J. Reiss, Jr., Glencoe, Ill.: Free Press, 1957.

———. 1959. "Robert Redfield, 1897–1958." *AJS* 64 (January): 405. Brief memorial review of Redfield's life and career, noting his initial study of the law and his development of the "folk-urban continuum," which was even more influential in sociology than in anthropology.

Mintz, Sidney W. 1953. "The Folk-Urban Continuum and the Rural Proletarian Community." *AJS* 59 (September): 136–43. Discusses and criticizes Redfield's "folk-urban continuum," demonstrating how it does not apply to the author's study of a community of plantation employees in the Yucatan.

Misumi, Issei. 1949. "On Mead's Life." Pp. 463–97 in *Behavioristic Psychology* edited and translated by I. Misumi. Tokyo: Hakuyocha. Biographical sketch in Misumi's Japanese translation of Mead's *Mind, Self and Society* (1934).

Mitchell, G. Duncan 1968. *A Hundred Years of Sociology*. London: Duckworth. Broad history of sociology including sections on the Chicago School (pp. 158–64, 224), Thomas and Znaniecki's *The Polish Peasant* (1918–19) (pp. 164–68), Park (pp. 154–57), as well as discussions of the work of Mead (p. 287), Stouffer (pp. 200–204), Thrasher (pp. 158–61), Zorbaugh (pp. 161–63), and Burgess.

Mitchell, Wesley C. 1930. "Research in the Social Sciences." Pp. 4–15 in White (1930). Recalls his experiences studying at Chicago, particularly his encounters with Veblen and Dewey, noting their similarities of thought.

———. 1936. "Thorstein Veblen." Pp. vii–xlix in *What Veblen Taught* edited by W. C. Mitchell. New York: Viking Press. An introduction to Veblen's career and thought by one of his students at Chicago. Notes influences from Darwin, James, and anthropological studies, concluding that "Veblen remains an inveterate doubter even of his own work" (p. xlviii).

Miyamoto, Frank S., and Sanford M. Dornbusch. 1956. "A Test of Interactionist Hypotheses of Self-Conception." *AJS* 61 (March): 399–403. Suggests that Mead's works have been widely acclaimed, but have led to considerable difficulty in formulating research problems. Develops an empirical study of basic assumptions deduced from Mead's work.

Mizruchi, Ephraim H. 1969. "Romanticism, Urbanism and Small Town in Mass Society: An Exploratory Analysis." Pp. 243–51 in *Urbanism, Urbanization and Change: Comparative Perspectives* edited by P. Meadows and E. H. Mizruchi. Reading, Mass.: Addison-Wesley. Maintains that images of the city held by Wirth and many other sociologists are encumbered by what Shils calls "German sociological romanticism," coming especially from Simmel's work.

Mogey, John. 1969. "William Oscar Brown, 1899–1969." *American Sociologist* 4 (November): 341–42. Remarks on Brown and influences Park and Ellsworth Faris (note: although Mogey indicates Robert Faris and Wirth, he later corrects himself in *American Sociologist* 5 [February, 1970]:47). Quotes Brown as saying that "Park was the greatest intellectual influence of my life" despite the fact that his dissertation was a reaction against Park's theories of race relations.

Moore, Edward C. 1961. *American Pragmatism: Peirce, James, and Dewey*. New York: Columbia University Press. Sketches some major characteristics of pragmatism, including a chapter on Dewey (pp. 183–259) who postulates that reality possesses a practical character, as opposed to traditional metaphysics, and that ideas are intellectual instruments for directing activities.

Moore, Harry Estill. 1938. "Two Sociologists?" *SF* 16 (March): 434–36. A review of a book on Comte and two on Veblen. Notes that both of the books on Veblen (Hobson 1937 and Mitchell 1936) are by well-known economists who make a clear case for classifying Veblen as a sociologist.

Moore, Merritt H. 1936. "Introduction." Pp. xi–xxxvii in Mead (1936). Summarizes Mead's ideas about nineteenth-century social thought, particularly his contention that science, with its demand for freedom and the substitution of rational authority for arbitrary authority, is the outstanding fact of all thought since the Renaissance.

Moreno, J. L. 1947. "Sociometry and the Social Psychology of George Herbert Mead." *Sociometry* 10 (November): 350–353. Brief discussion of differences between his own and Mead's work, in commenting on McKinney (1947) comparing the two. Moreno argues that the differences are considerable; although Mead is a keen analytical observer, Mead's social psychology itself would not have led to techniques of sociometry, psychodrama and sociodrama.

Morris, Charles W. 1934. "Introduction." Pp. ix–xxxv in Mead (1934). Places Mead's social psychology of the self within pragmatic philosophy, and outlines its major dimensions, claiming that Mead and Dewey's work was complementary and never in significant opposition; Dewey gives range and vision, Mead analytical depth and scientific precision.

———. 1938. "Peirce, Mead, and Pragmatism." *Philosophical Review* 47 (March): 109–27. Notes striking similarities in Peirce and Mead and outlines changes from the metaphysical idealism of Peirce through the radical empiricism of James to the empirical naturalism of Dewey and Mead. Suggests that whereas Peirce approached problems as a logician, Mead did so as a social psychologist.

———. 1946. *Signs, Language, and Behavior*. New York: Prentice-Hall. Includes substantial interpretations of Mead's work on signs and symbols (esp. pp. 39–49).

———. 1967. "George Herbert Mead." P. 22 in *Encyclopaedia Britannica* Vol. 15. This brief entry suggests that Mead's main contribution to social psychology was to show how the human self arises in the process of social interaction.

———. 1970. *The Pragmatic Movement in American Philosophy*. New York: George Braziller. Study of the pragmatic philosophical movement, with substantial sections on Dewey (esp. pp. 37–40, 62–65, 68–71, 81–89, 157–67) and Mead (esp. pp. 33–36, 71–74, 126–40), as well as Peirce and James, with a section on "The Chicago School" (pp. 174–91).

Morris, Charles W., John M. Brewster, Albert M. Dunham, and David L. Miller. 1938. "Introduction." Pp. vii–lxxiii in Mead (1938). Discusses Mead's "philosophy of the act" and places his thought in the context of pragmatic philosophy, noting his alternative interpretation of the space-time formulas of relativity. "In contrast to a purely mechanistic interpretation of the order of events, Mead acknowledges the oncoming event as a determinant in action and thereby converts sheer action into a process with past, present, and future in it."

Morris, R. N. 1968. *Urban Sociology*. London: Allen and Unwin. Discusses urban sociology and its development, focusing in large part on Wirth's theories of urban life and the debates that it has precipitated.

Morris, Terence. 1958. *The Criminal Area*. London: Routledge & Kegan Paul. Includes a critique of area studies developed by Shaw, McKay, Lind, and others, noting that their theory does not apply to his study of crime in London (see esp. pp. 92–105). Portion reprinted in Wolfgang et al. (1962, pp. 191–98).

Morrison, Philip. 1957. "The Place of Science in Modern Civilization." *Monthly Review* 9 (July-August): 99–105. Extended review of Veblen (1919) including discussion of Veblen on the "instinct of Workmanship," "idle curiosity," and the relationship among science, technology, and production.

———. 1958. "The Ideology of the Engineers." Pp. 237–48 in Dowd (1958). Discusses Veblen's *The Engineers and the Price System* (New York: Viking,

1947), noting Veblen's attention to subjective factors and his view of the role of practitioners of the industrial arts.

Morrison, Theodore. 1974. *Chautauqua: A Center for Education, Religion and the Arts in America*. Chicago: University of Chicago Press. Traces connection between Chicago and sociology via Harper in the Chautaqua movement (pp. 73–78).

Mowrer, Ernest R. 1941. "Methodological Problems in Social Disorganization." *ASR* 6 (December): 839–52. Critiques the social disorganization perspective as developed by Thomas, Znaniecki, Cooley, Ogburn and others, noting particularly subjective aspects of the perspective.

Mueller, John H. 1950. "Edwin Hardin Sutherland, 1883–1950." *ASR* 15 (December): 802–803. Obituary comments discussing Sutherland's research, his merits as a teacher and influences from Henderson, Small, and Thomas.

Mullins, Nicholas C., with the assistance of Carolyn J. Mullins. 1973. *Theories and Theory Groups in Contemporary American Sociology*. New York: Harper and Row. Analyzes the role of Chicago sociology in the development of American sociological theory, with particular attention to symbolic interactionism as "the loyal opposition" (pp. 75–104; note table 4.2, pp. 84–87 on symbolic interactionists).

Murphy, Arthur E. 1939. "Concerning Mead's The Philosophy of the Act." *Journal of Philosophy* 36 (February): 85–103. Outlines problems in Mead's *Philosophy of the Act* (1938) arising from the attempt to specify the philosophical meaning of statements about perceptual and physical objects by referring them to a context which is incongruous with their actual meaning in use.

———. 1959. "Introduction." Pp. xi–xxxv in Mead (1959). Discusses Mead's theory as a philosophy of nature in the present tense which seeks to understand the world as centered in a present. Suggests that the most original feature of the lectures contained in the volume is Mead's extension of "the social" into a philosophy of nature.

Myrdal, Gunnar, with the assistance of Richard Sterner and Arnold Rose. 1944. *An American Dilemma: The Negro Problem and Modern Democracy*. New York: Harper. This massive study of blacks in the United States includes a criticism of Park's approach to racial problems as naturalistic and therefore fatalistic, leading to resistance to social change, with similar critiques of Thomas and Ogburn (see esp. pp. 1049–57).

Nabers, Lawrence. 1958. "Veblen's Critique of the Orthodox Economic Tradition." Pp. 77–112 in Dowd (1958). Reviews the various aspects of Veblen's critique of orthodox economics, including Mill, Smith, Marshall, Ricardo and others. Notes Veblen's dissatisfaction with being classified as an economist.

Nagano, Yoshio. 1960. *The Social Philosophy of John Dewey*. Tokyo: Shunjusha. A Japanese interpretation of Dewey's philosophy.

Natanson, Maurice. 1953. "George H. Mead's Metaphysics of Time." *Journal of Philosophy* 50 (December): 770–82. Examines Mead's contention that reality exists in a present and that both the past and the future are hypothetical, noting implications of that position for his theories of the self.

———. 1956. *The Social Dynamics of George H. Mead*. Washington, D.C.: Public Affairs Press. Attempts to show the developmental character of Mead's theory of social reality, its underlying principles, and its radical implications for philosophy and the social sciences, noting frequent misunderstandings of Mead's work. Introduction by Kallen (1956).

Nef, John U. 1944. "Robert Park." Pp. 15–19 in Ames et al. (1944). Brief memorial statement with some biographical information and discussion of Park's work as a reporter, his study in Germany and his interest in racial issues.

Nelissen, N. J. M. 1973. "Robert Ezra Park (1864–1944): Ein Beitrag zur Geschichte der Soziologie." *Kolner Zeitschrift fur Soziologie und Sozialpsychologie* 25 (September): 515–29. Introduces Park's life and work; aimed at a European audience with discussion of Chicago sociology and its significance for current sociological theory and methods.

Nimkoff, Meyer F. 1948. "Trends in Family Research." *AJS* 53 (May): 477–82. Suggests that research on the family was built upon two theoretical systems: first, the interactional approach developed by Cooley, Mead, and Thomas, and articulated by Burgess, and second, that of social change. Suggests that the interactional viewpoint is difficult to adhere to and that the latter has led to an analysis of family trends by Burgess and others.

———. 1959. "William Fielding Ogburn, 1886–1959." *ASR* 24 (August): 563–65. Memorial comments on Ogburn, who "above all else stood for the development of sociology by scientific methods."

Nissen, Lowell. 1966. *John Dewey's Theory of Inquiry and Truth*. The Hague: Mouton. Short monograph on Dewey's account of inquiry and his efforts to make the methodology of science available to other disciplines.

Noble, David. 1968. "The Theology of Thorstein Veblen." Pp. 72–105 in Qualey (1968). A treatment of the implications of Veblen's work for an understanding of culture and religion.

Nock, David. 1974. "History and Evolution of French Canadian Sociology." *Insurgent Sociologist* 4 (Summer): 15–29. Examines the influence of the Chicago school on sociology in French Canada.

Novack, George. 1975. *An Appraisal of John Dewey's Philosophy: Pragmatism versus Marxism*. New York: Pathfinder Press. Offers a Marxist critique of Dewey's pragmatism; identifies pragmatism as "America's national philosophy"; reviews Peirce, James and the Chicago School; and discusses shortcomings of instrumentalism.

Nye, F. Ivan. 1958. *Family Relationships and Delinquent Behavior*. New York: Wiley.

Oberschall, Anthony D. 1972. "The Institutionalization of American Sociology." Pp. 187–251 in *The Establishment of Empirical Sociology* edited by A. Oberschall. New York: Harper. Traces the transformation of sociology from "the earlier sociological imperialism, system building, and charities and corrections emphasis" (pp. 232–41). Attributes the success of the department to the university's exceptional resources, and the impact of Park, who had the ability to motivate others and to help them organize their research around an integrated series of projects on the same topics—urban sociology, ecology, and the contemporary Chicago scene.

O'Brien, R. W. 1941. "Beatle Street Memphis: A Study in Ecological Succession." *Sociology and Social Research* 26: 439ff. Lends some support to the Burgess zonal hypothesis.

Odum, Howard W. 1951a. *American Sociology: The Story of Sociology in the United States through 1950*. New York: Longmans, Green. An encyclopedic account of American sociology with sketches of several Chicago faculty and students: Small (pp. 94–96), Vincent (pp. 102–105), Hayes (pp. 119–22), Ellwood (pp. 128–31), Park (pp. 131–35), Thomas (pp. 141–44), Ogburn (pp. 147–52), Bogardus (pp. 158–61), Bernard (pp. 161–65), Reuter (pp. 165–67), Burgess (pp. 168–71), Faris (pp. 180–86), Sutherland (pp. 190–94), Queen (pp. 197–201), Sanderson (pp. 201–204), Wirth (pp. 227–33), Frazier (pp. 233–39), Cottrell (pp. 243–46), Steiner (pp. 274–76), Johnson (pp. 280–81), and discussion of the *AJS* (pp. 403–406) and the social settlement movement and its relationship to the Chicago department (Addams, Abbott, Breckenridge, and Henderson, p. 397).

———. 1951b. "Edwin H. Sutherland, 1883–1950." *SF* 29 (March): 348–49. Brief memorial survey of Sutherland's career, his interest in criminology and social theory.

———. 1951c. "Luther Lee Bernard, 1881–1951." *SF* 29 (May): 480–81. Memorial review of Bernard's career, noting his graduate work with "Chicago's great battery of early sociologists," his teaching career and research and professional involvement, including his active role in the founding of the *ASR*.

———. 1954. "Ellsworth Faris, 1874–1953." *SF* 33 (October): 101–103. A tribute to Faris noting his work as head of the Chicago department and his dynamism at professional meetings. Mentions efforts with Thomas, Park, Burgess, Ogburn, Stouffer, Wirth, and Blumer to develop sociology at Chicago.

Odum, Howard W., ed. 1927. *American Masters of Social Science: An Approach to the Study of the Social Sciences Through a Neglected Field of Biography*. Port Washington, N.Y.: Kennikat Press. An edited volume of portraits including Ward, Small (see Hayes 1927), Giddings, and Veblen (see Homan 1927). Odum's introductory chapter discusses the institutionalization of social science in the United States from 1875 to 1925.

Ogburn, William F. 1922. *Social Change: With Respect to Culture and Original Nature*. New York: B. W. Huebsch.

———. 1933. *Recent Social Trends in the United States*. New York: McGraw-Hill.

———. 1935. "Man and His Institutions." *Publications of the American Sociological Society* 29 (August).

———. 1943. *American Society in Wartime*. Chicago: University of Chicago Press.

———. 1964. *William F. Ogburn on Culture and Social Change: Selected Papers*. Edited by Otis D. Duncan. Chicago: University of Chicago Press.

O'Neill, William L. 1966. "Divorce and the Professionalization of the Social Sciences." *JHBS* 2 (October): 291–302. Notes a revolution in approaches to social problems as sociology became professionalized, with an increasing emphasis on the workability of solutions rather than whether or not they validated Christian orthodoxy. Discusses work by Ellwood, Small, Ross, Sumner, and others and conflicts at the 1908 American Sociological Society meetings.

O'Kelly, Charlotte G., and John W. Petras. 1970. "Images of Man in Early American Sociology, Part II: The Changing Concept of Social Reform." *JHBS* 6 (October): 317–34. Postulates that early American sociologists tended to reject Sumner's evolutionary determinism and laissez-faire doctrines, with a section on Small (pp. 323–34) which notes his emphasis on social reform, suggesting that he was not as individualistically oriented as the other sociologists of his era. For Part I, see Petras (1970b).

Oppenheim, Frank M. 1977. "Royce's Community: A Dimension Missing in Freud and James." *JHBS* 13 (April): 173–90. Notes that Royce's work, especially his argument that social consciousness arises from ego-alter contrasts, anticipated ideas developed by his student Mead; contrasts Royce with Freud and James.

Orleans, Peter. 1966. "Robert Park and Social Area Analysis: A Convergence of Traditions in Urban Sociology." *Urban Affairs Quarterly* 1 (June): 5–19. Assesses Park's approach to urban studies, noting his role as a seminal figure but objecting to an "antiurban bias" in his work which is not found in Shevky and Greer's alternative social area analyses. Maintains that "diversity and complexity are not necessarily productive of social organization" (p. 104). Reprinted in *Urbanism, Urbanization, and Change*, edited by P. Meadows and E. Mizruchi (Reading, Mass.: Addison-Wesley, 1969), pp. 96–106.

Oromaner, Mark Jay. 1968. "The Most Cited Sociologists: An Analysis of Introductory Text Citations." *American Sociologist* 3 (May): 124–26. Shows a surprising lack of citations of Thomas, Mead and Park. Persons obtaining five or more citations in four or more textbooks from 1958–1967 are Bendix, Burgess, Cooley, K. Davis, Durkheim, Hollingshead, Linton, Lipset, Merton, Mills, Murdoch, Parsons, Stouffer, Warner, Weber, and Williams.

O'Toole, Richard, and Robert Dubin. 1968. "Baby Feeding and Body Sway: An Experiment in George Herbert Mead's 'Taking the Role of the Other.'" *Journal of Personality and Social Psychology* 10 (Spring): 59–65. Reports on an experiment designed to operationalize and test Mead's basic formulation, "taking the role of the other."

Owen, Mary Bess. 1941. "Alternative Hypotheses for the Explanation of Some of Faris' and Dunham's Results." *AJS* 47 (July): 48–51. Discusses interpretations Faris and Dunham advance for data on the ecological distribution of mental disorders and suggests an alternative explanation. Followed by brief comments from Faris and Dunham (pp. 51–52).

Page, Charles H. 1940. *Class and American Sociology: From Ward to Ross*. New York: Dial. Examines the concept of class in early American sociology, including a chapter (pp. 113–44) on Small, emphasizing his role in the institutionalization of sociology and the importance that the notions of "universal conflict of interests," class structure, and class "consciousness" played in his work.

Pahl, Raymond E. 1970. *Patterns of Urban Life*. London: Longmans, Green.

Palmer, Vivian 1928. *Field Studies in Sociology: A Student's Manual*. Chicago: University of Chicago Press. A handbook prepared by the field director and counselor for many of the "Chicago studies" conducted during the 1920s and 1930s. This textbook helped both Chicago and other students to shape their research strategies.

Parenti, Michael. 1967. "Introduction." In *The Unadjusted Girl* by William I. Thomas. New York: Harper Torchbooks. Discussion of Thomas (1923) for a revised edition.

Park, Robert E. 1904. *Masse und Publikum*. Reissued 1972 as *The Crowd and the Public and Other Essays*, edited and with an Introduction by Harry Elsner, Jr.; "The Crowd and the Public" translated by Charlotte Elsner, and with a note by Donald N. Levine. Chicago: University of Chicago Press.

———. [1915] 1967. "The City: Suggestions for the Investigation of Human Behavior in the City Environment." *AJS* 20: 577–612. A classic statement of Park's research agenda and approach to the city. Reprinted in Park, Burgess and McKenzie (1967, pp. 1–46).

———. [1923] 1975. "Editor's Preface." Pp. xxiii–xxvi in *The Hobo: The Sociology of the Homeless Man* by Nels Anderson. Chicago: University of Chicago Press. Discusses Anderson's study of the hobo as part of an ongoing effort at Chicago "to describe the changes that are taking place in the life of the city and its peoples, and to investigate Chicago's problems in light of these changes. . . ." The purpose of examining Chicago's natural areas, Park argued, was to emphasize the "generic and universal aspects of the city and its life."

———. 1924. "A Race Relations Survey." *Journal of Applied Sociology* 8 (March-April): 195–205. Discusses a 1919 study undertaken and published by the Chicago Commission on Race Relations, *The Negro in Chicago* (C. Johnson 1922), which Park claimed was the most painstaking and complete study of a racial group in the U.S.; researchers used the ecological approach, questionnaires, interviews, and observational techniques.

———. 1928a. "Foreword." Pp. vii–ix in *The Ghetto* by Louis Wirth. Chicago: University of Chicago Press. Contains a brief discussion of Wirth's work in the context of Chicago urban studies, especially of "natural areas."

———. 1928b. "Human Migration and the Marginal Man." *AJS* 33 (May): 339–44.

———. 1929a. "The City as a Social Laboratory." Pp. 1–19 in Smith and White (1929). Argues that social change in modern cities has assumed something of the character of a controlled experiment and discusses efforts to examine that laboratory in Chicago and elsewhere, including work by Addams, Breckinridge, Anderson, Wirth, Zorbaugh, Shaw, Thomas, and others. Discusses early studies on personality (Simmel, Thomas), poverty and delinquency (the Institute for Juvenile Research and the Behavior Research Fund of Herman M. Adler), and institutions, especially political (Merriam and Gosnell) and economic institutions, and the family. Reprinted, pp. 73–87 in Park (1952).

———. 1929b. *The Immigrant Press and Its Control*. New York: Harper & Bros.

———. 1931a. "Human Nature, Attitudes, and the Mores." Pp. 17–45 in *Social Attitudes* edited by Kimball Young. New York: Holt. A statement of Park's social psychological orientation, including a substantial treatment of Thomas and Znaniecki, particularly their development of the concepts of "attitude" and "value" as an alternative to behaviorism.

———. 1931b. "The Sociological Methods of William Graham Sumner and of William I. Thomas and Florian Znaniecki." Pp. 154–75 in *Methods in Social Science: A Case Book* edited by Stuart A. Rice. Chicago: University of Chicago Press. In a comparison of Sumner's *Folkways* and Thomas and Znaniecki's *The Polish Peasant* (1918–19), Park argues that the latter's chief contribution is not a body of fact, but a new approach to sociological problems and a system of concepts; includes an appendix on "the four wishes."

———. [1934] 1966. "Introduction." Pp. ix–xxii in *Shadow of the Plantation* by Charles S. Johnson. Chicago: University of Chicago Press. Park discusses the issues and research in Johnson's study of black peasants of the southern plantations, suggesting that only if such studies help people to overcome their ethnocentrism, they can "be said to have wholly achieved their purpose."

———. 1936. "Human Ecology." *AJS* 42 (July): 1–15.

———. 1937. "Review of W. I. Thomas, *Primitive Behavior: An Introduction to the Social Sciences*." *ASR* 2 (April): 286–90. Suggests that Thomas's (1936) volume was probably undertaken as a revision of his earlier *Source Book for Social Origins*, which first called attention to the importance of the researches of ethnology and anthropology, "those sciences which stand between biology and civilization." Park discusses changes over that 28-year period in sociology and anthropology as well as Thomas's contributions.

———. 1939. "Notes on the Origin of the Society for Social Research." *Bulletin of the Society for Social Research* 1 (August): 1–5. Discusses the Society for Social Research as a forum for the presentation of faculty and student research, as well as the work of visiting scholars. Park notes the importance of Thomas's *Source Book for Social Origins* (1909), in which Park found "a consistent expression in most, if not all, of the subsequent published studies of the students and instructors in sociology at Chicago." Reprinted in Kurtz (1982).

———. 1941. "Methods of Teaching: Impressions and a Verdict." *SF* 20 (October): 36–46. An autobiographical essay on teaching and teachers that influenced his thought and teaching style. Discusses Calvin Thomas, Georg Friedrich Knapp at Strassburg, James, Dewey, Washington, and Royce. Recalls that Dewey's students always had the notion that he and they were engaged in a common enterprise, and concludes that the systematization of knowledge cannot be done successfully by the teacher alone, even with a textbook; the student must do some of the discovery and interpretation.

———. 1950. *Race and Culture*. Edited by Everett C. Hughes. Glencoe, Ill.: Free Press. A collection of Park's essays; see especially "An Autobiographical Note" (pp. v-ix) in which Park claims, "I can trace my interest in sociology to the reading of Goethe's Faust. You remember that Faust was tired of books and wanted to see the world—the world of men." Park describes his work as a journalist, influences from James, Windelband, and Simmel. Originally included in Hughes (1944).

———. 1952. *Human Communities: The City and Human Ecology*. Glencoe, Ill.: Free Press.

———. 1955. *Society: Collective Behavior, News and Opinion, and Sociology and Modern Society*. Edited by Everett C. Hughes. Glencoe, Ill.: Free Press.

———. 1959. "Review of Milla A. Alihan, *Social Ecology*." *Annals of the American Academy of Political and Social Science* 202 (March): 264–65. Reviews the history of the ecological approach, noting that most of the concepts with which ecological writers have operated are borrowed from local community studies. Claims that Alihan has undertaken an important task and that there are other theories that "need to go through the wringer."

———. 1973. "Life History." *AJS* 79 (September): 251–60. Autobiographical sketch noting his career in journalism, influences from Dewey, James, Royce, Santayana, Burgess, Herbert Miller, Small, Thomas, Faris, Burgess and others, claiming that his only systematic instruction in sociology came from Simmel's lectures in Berlin.

Park, Robert, and Ernest W. Burgess. 1921. *Introduction to the Science of Sociology*. Chicago: University of Chicago Press. Park and Burgess's classic textbook which was central to the institutionalization of American sociology. Note especially the preface, which provides a brief statement of the purpose and organizational principles of the book. Acknowledges indebtedness to Small, Faris, Leon Marshall, and especially Thomas.

Park, Robert E., Ernest W. Burgess, and Roderick D. McKenzie. 1925. *The City*. Chicago: University of Chicago Press. Reissued by University of Chicago Press in the Heritage of Sociology Series, 1967, with an Introduction by Morris Janowitz.

Parsons, Talcott, ed. 1968. *American Sociology: Perspectives, Problems, Methods*. New York: Basic Books.

Pearl, Lester S. 1949. "Review of E. Franklin Frazier, *The Negro Family in the United States*." *SF* 27 (May): 450. Suggests that Frazier's volume (Revised edition, New York: Dryden Press, 1948) provides the most inclusive study of the family culture of a group since Thomas and Znaniecki's *The Polish Peasant* (1918–19), arguing that more work of that type should be undertaken.

Perinbanayagam, R. S. 1974. "The Definition of the Situation: An Analysis of the Ethnomethodological and Dramaturgical View." *Sociological Quarterly* 15 (Autumn): 521–41. Dramaturgical analysis, from Mead, and ethnomethodology, from Wittgenstein and Schutz, are compared in terms of their power to explain Thomas's problem of the "definition of the situation" It is concluded that the dramaturgical approach is most salient.

———. 1975. "The Significance of Others in the Thought of Alfred Schutz, G. H. Mead and C. H. Cooley." *Sociological Quarterly* 16 (Autumn): 500–21. Examines the relationship between "self" and "other" as a dialectical and syntactical one in the work of Schutz, Mead and Cooley; emphasizes Mead's concept of the "generalized other" (see esp. pp. 508–10). See a comment by Valieria Ann Malhotra and Mary Jo Deegan (*Sociological Quarterly* 19 [Winter 1978]:141–45) in which they claim that Perinbanayagam has misinterpreted Schutz, who points to a deeper understanding of the "other" not found in Mead and Cooley; Perinbanayagam responds (pp. 146–51).

Perkins, M. Helen. 1960. *A Preliminary Checklist for a Bibliography on Jane Addams*. Rockford, Ill.: Published privately. An extensive list of works by and about Addams including unpublished addresses and essays and libraries in which they can be found (available in the Regenstein Library, University of Chicago).

Perry, Ralph Barton. 1935. *The Thought and Character of William James. Volume II: Philosophy and Psychology*. Boston: Little, Brown. Includes a chapter on "James and Dewey" (pp. 514–53) containing correspondence between the two observing that James felt that differences between his work and Dewey's were minimal, whereas Dewey believed them to be more fundamental and explicit.

Petras, John W. 1966. "The Genesis and Development of Symbolic Interactionism in American Sociology." Ph.D. thesis, University of Connecticut. A study of the emergence of symbolic interactionism as a perspective that shifts the sociological focus from the individual to the group.

———. 1968a. "George Herbert Mead: An Introduction." Pp. 1–23 in *George Herbert Mead: Essays on His Social Philosophy* edited by John W. Petras. New York: Teachers College Press of Columbia University. Observes a shift of interest from social reform in Mead's early work to problems of self development and more common psychological interests such as perception, thought, and the mind. Discusses Mead's strong interest in educational reform and socialization.

———. 1968b. "John Dewey and the Rise of Interactionism in American Social Theory." *JHBS* 4 (January): 18–27. Contends that Dewey was the peer of Mead in the development of symbolic interactionism, noting his emphasis on social interaction and the conditions of the social group.

———. 1968c. "Psychological Antecedents of Sociological Theory in America: W. James and J. M. Baldwin." *JHBS* 4 (April): 132–42. Emphasizes the impact of social theories of the self developed by James and Baldwin on the later work of Faris, Mead, Thomas, and Cooley, as opposed to individualistic theories of motivation chosen by Small, Vincent, Ward, and Giddings.

———. 1970a. "Changes of Emphasis in the Sociology of W. I. Thomas." *JHBS* 6 (January): 70–79. Argues that Thomas moved toward an increasing awareness of the group concept and its role in behavior, with later theories providing a focal point for understanding the contributions of Cooley, Dewey and Mead.

———. 1970b. "Images of Man in Early American Sociology, Part I: The Individualistic Perspective on Motivation." *JHBS* 6 (July): 231–40. Attempts to demonstrate an individualistic bias in early American sociological theory and includes a discussion of Small and Vincent (pp. 234, 236). For Part II, see O'Kelly and Petras (1970).

———. 1973. "George Herbert Mead's Theory of Self: A Study of the Origin and Convergence of Ideas." *Canadian Review of Sociology and Anthropol-*

ogy 10 (May): 148–49. Examines Mead's theory of the self as a convergence of his ideas in biology, educational reform, philosophy, psychology, and sociology.

Pfeutze, Paul E. 1954. *The Social Self*. New York: Bookman. Critiques the nature and structure of the "social self" in the writings of Mead and Buber; suggests revisions of Mead's theories in the direction of Buber; shows applications of the revised theory to crucial problems in religion, social philosophy, psychotherapy and education. Reprinted with revisions as *Self, Society, Existence*. (New York: Harper Torchbooks, 1961).

Philpott, Thomas L. 1978. *The Slum and the ghetto: Neighborhood Deterioration and Middle Class Reform; Chicago 1880–1930*. New York: Oxford University Press. Includes considerable discussion of Chicago sociologists and their study of Chicago communities and racial conflicts.

Piron, Gaetan. 1939. *Les nouveaux courants de la théorie économique aux Etats-Unis: l'institutionalisme*. Paris: Domat Montchrestien. Includes considerable discussion of Veblen's institutional economics.

Pohlman, Edward W. 1968. "Burgess and Cottrell Data on 'Desire for Children': Example of Distortion in Marriage and Family Textbooks?" *Journal of Marriage and the Family* 30 (August): 433–36. Reports misrepresentations of data from E. Burgess and L. S. Cottrell, *Predicting Success or Failure in Marriage* (Englewood Cliffs, N.J. Prentice-Hall, 1939), in marriage and family textbooks.

Polk, Kenneth. 1957–58. "Juvenile Delinquency and Social Areas." *Social Problems* 5 (Winter): 214–24.

Pottino, Gaetano. 1941. *L'analisi sociologica ed il problema della persona nella filosofia di John Dewey*. Palermo: Flaccovio. An examination of Dewey's sociological theories.

Qualey, Carlton C. 1968. "Introduction." Pp. 1–15 in Qualey (1968). Suggests that Veblen was representative of a consensus among intellectuals of the turn of the century (including Dewey, Ward, and others) who were disturbed by a loss of an earlier national virtue and a tendency toward economic inequality, noting that Veblen was a social critic of unusually acute perceptions. Reviews Veblen's career and major contributions, observing the similarities between him and Galbraith.

Qualey, Carlton C., ed. 1968. *Thorstein Veblen: The Carleton College Veblen Seminar Essays*. New York: Columbia University Press. Edited volume of essays on Veblen. See separate entries under Qualey, Friday, Cochran, Noble, Dorfman, and Lubin. Includes a bibliography of Veblen's writings.

Queen, Stuart A. 1931. "Conflict Situations Between Clients and Case Workers." Pp. 208–35 in *Social Attitudes* edited by Kimball Young. New York: Holt. Includes discussion of Thomas and Znaniecki's terms attitudes and values and their applicability to problems in social work. Notes Bain's criticisms, Faris's rebuttal, and developments of their ideas by Park and Burgess, Faris, and Bernard.

———. 1934. "Charles Richmond Henderson." P. 320 in Seligman and Johnson (1934), Vol. 7. Brief entry observing that "although nominally a sociologist Henderson's contributions were to social ethics and social reform."

———. 1940. "The Ecological Study of Mental Disorders." *ASR* 5 (1940): 201–209. A review of ecological studies of mental disorders following Faris and Dunham (1939). Concludes that "it is plain that mental patients are not evenly distributed over the city but are more or less concentrated in limited areas."

———. 1951. "In Memoriam: Edwin H. Sutherland, 1883–1950." *AJS* 56 (January): 359. Brief sketch of Sutherland's career and personal characteristics.

Queen, Stuart A., and Delbert M. Mann. 1925. *Social Pathology*. New York: Crowell. Develops the social disorganization perspective with considerable discussion of Thomas, Znaniecki, Park, Burgess, Lindeman, and others.

Quinn, James A. 1939. "The Nature of Human Ecology: Reexamination and Redefinition." *SF* 18 (December): 161–68. Reviews developments in human ecology, recapitulating its early definition by Burgess, McKenzie and Park, noting contradictory conceptions of the field by Bews, Barrows, and Park and criticisms (e.g., by Alihan). Suggests a redefinition which sees ecology as a way of examining community phenomena through abstractions of ecological interaction and ecological structure.

———. 1940a. "The Burgess Zonal Hypothesis and Its Critics." *ASR* 5 (April): 210–18. A critical review of responses to Burgess's zonal hypothesis suggesting that it has been neither clearly proved nor disproved; argues that it possesses sufficient merit to warrant extensive testing.

———. 1940b. "Human Ecology and Interactional Ecology." *ASR* 5 (October): 713–22. Discusses varieties of human ecology, including a section on ecology as a sociological perspective developed by Park and McKenzie; notes the formation of the Division on Human Ecology in the American Sociological Society.

———. 1940c. "Topical Summary of Current Literature on Human Ecology." *AJS* 46 (September): 191–226. Provides an extensive bibliography and a review of the field of human ecology, critiques of the approach, and summaries of research in the area from 1925 to 1939. Comments on the diversity of definitions and approaches within the field and discusses writings by Park, Burgess, McKenzie, Wirth, Anderson, Mowrer, Duncan, Frazier, Zorbaugh, Hollingshead, and others, suggesting that support for the approach was increasing.

Quinney, Richard. 1964. "Crime, Delinquency, and Social Areas." *Journal of Research in Crime and Delinquency* 1: 149–54.

Raiser, Konrad. 1971. *Identität und Sozialität: George Herbert Meads Theorie der Interaktion und ihre Bedeutung für die theologische Anthropologie.* Munich: Kaiser. Analyzes Mead's theories of interaction and their meaning for "theological anthropology."

Randall, John Herman, Jr. 1953. "John Dewey, 1859–1952." *Journal of Philosophy* 50 (January): 5–13. Memorial tribute at Columbia University summarizing Dewey's contribution, suggesting that his *Experience and Nature* (1925) may be the most enduring work.

Raphelson, Alfred C. 1973. "The Pre-Chicago Association of the Early Functionalists." *JHBS* 9 (April): 115–22. Argues that the social psychology which developed at Chicago can be better understood by taking into account intellectual experiences Dewey had at Johns Hopkins (influences from Peirce, G. Stanley Hall and George S. Morris), and their subsequent development at Michigan, where Dewey, Mead, and Angell interacted.

Ratner, Joseph. 1939. "Introduction to John Dewey's Philosophy." Pp. 3–241 in *Intelligence in the Modern World: John Dewey's Philosophy* edited and with an Introduction by Joseph Ratner. New York: The Modern Library. A lengthy introduction to various aspects of Dewey's philosophy, observing his basic argument that theory in philosophy, as in science, must submit to the test of practice and experience.

Ratner, Sidney. 1951. "The Evolutionary Naturalism of John Dewey." *Social Research* 18 (December): 435–48. Discusses Dewey's early work, *The Influence of Darwin on Philosophy* (1916), and Dewey's later theory of evolutionary naturalism.

Raushenbush, Winifred. 1979. *Robert E. Park: Biography of a Sociologist.* Durham, N.C.: Duke University Press. A biography rich with quotations from letters and papers by Park, discussing his early life, his newspaper career, his work with Washington and the Tuskegee Institute, his encounter with Thomas, his career at Chicago, and his concern with race relations and urban problems.

Raymond, Jerome H. 1895. "American Municipal Government." Ph.D. thesis, University of Chicago.

Reck, Andrew J. 1963. "The Philosophy of George Herbert Mead (1863–1931)." *Tulane Studies in Philosophy* 12 (Annual): 5–51. Comments on Mead's thought and its context in American philosophy and pragmatism, suggesting that the "Chicago tradition" in social science stems in large measure from Mead's writings.

———. 1964a. "Introduction." Pp. xiii–lxix in *George H. Mead: Selected Writings* edited by Andrew J. Reck. Indianapolis: Bobbs-Merrill.

———. 1964b. *Recent American Philosophy: Studies of Ten Representative Thinkers*. New York: Pantheon. Includes a chapter "the Constructive Pragmatism of George Herbert Mead" (pp. 84–122) suggesting that Mead has not been fully appreciated because he was overshadowed by Dewey; Mead rendered pragmatism scientifically precise, imputing to it philosophical depth.

Reckless, Walter. 1940. *Criminal Behavior*. New York: McGraw-Hill. Outlines a sociological approach to the study of criminal behavior, with an historical sketch that highlights the work of Henderson and Shaw.

Redfield, Robert. 1945. "Foreword." Pp. vii–xi in Gottschalk, Kluckhohn, and Angell (1945). Places Thomas and Znaniecki's *Polish Peasant* (1918–19) in the context of an ongoing debate over the use of personal documents in research, sponsored by the Social Science Research Council. See separate entries under Gottschalk, Kluckhohn, and Angell (1945).

———. 1947. "The Folk Society." *AJS* 52 (January): 293–308.

———. 1948. "The Art of Social Science." *AJS* 54 (November): 181–90. In suggesting that social science is something of an art, Redfield discusses Thomas and Znaniecki's *Polish Peasant* (1918–19), Veblen's *Theory of the Leisure Class* (1899), as well as de Tocqueville and Sumner. Bernard responds to the substance of Redfield's remarks in "The Art of Science: A Reply to Redfield" *AJS* 55 (July 1949), pp. 1–9.

Redfield, Robert, and Milton Singer. 1954. "The Cultural Role of Cities." *Economic Development and Cultural Change* 3 (October): 53–77.

Reeves, Floyd W., Nelson B. Henry, Frederick J. Kelly, Arthur J. Klein, and John Dale Russell. 1933. *The University of Chicago Survey. Volume III: The University Faculty*. Chicago: University of Chicago Press. A survey of the university provides information on activities within the sociology department vis-à-vis other departments in the university, especially during the period 1924–1929; note especially the reports on research projects (table 42, p. 228) showing the sociology department to be more active than other departments, and the appendixes on faculty, publications, degrees, honors, etc. (pp. 286ff.).

Reichenbach, Hans. 1939. "Dewey's Theory of Science." Pp. 157–92 in Schilpp (1939). Analysis of Dewey's pragmatic approach to science and his understanding of scientific method which requires eliminating any conception of science as a system of absolute truths.

Reiss, Albert J., Jr. 1949. "Review of Robert E. L. Faris, *Social Disorganization*." *AJS* 54 (May): 561–62. Suggests that although Faris's *Socal Disorganization* (New York: Ronald Press, 1958) introduces excellent substantive materials, his theoretical framework is defective. In his treatment of the concepts of social organization, social disorganization, personal disorganization, and social reorganization, it is difficult to discern what is meant by the concept of "function" which underlies them.

———. 1951. "Delinquency as the Failure of Personal and Social Controls." *ASR* 16: 196–207.

———. 1955. "An Analysis of Urban Phenomena." Pp. 41–51 in *The Metropolis in Modern Life* edited by R. M. Fisher. N.Y.: Doubleday. Critiques Wirth's view of urban life.

———. 1956. "The Sociology of Urban Life: 1946–1956." Pp. 107–13 in *Sociology in the United States of America* edited by Hans L. Zetterberg. New York: UNESCO. Reviews the history of the field, noting that the major outlines were laid down by students of Park and Burgess at Chicago and that between 1946 and 1956 efforts focused on the study of ecological organization. Reprinted, pp. 3–11 in *Cities and Society: The Revised Reader in Urban Sociology*, edited by P. Hatt and A. Reiss, Jr. (Glencoe, Ill.: Free Press, 1957).

———. 1964. "Introduction." Pp. ix–xxx in Wirth (1964). Outlines Wirth's ideas, observing that his theoretical writings center around the problem of consensus as the basis of social order; Wirth analyzed social organization in terms of social structure or forms and social processes. Includes an appended bibliography and a biographical memorandum by Marvick (1964).

Reissman, Leonard. 1964. *The Urban Process: Cities in Industrial Societies*. New York: Free Press of Glencoe.

Reuter, E. B. 1940. "Racial Theory." *AJS* 50 (May): 881–93. Suggests that Park's concept of the "marginal man" marked the great turning point in racial theory away from "biological modes of thought" to a strictly sociological analysis.

Reynolds, Larry T. and Bernard N. Meltzer. 1973. "The Origins of Divergent Methodological Stances in Symbolic Interactionism." *Sociological Quarterly* 14 (Spring): 189–99. Suggests that current methodological differences in symbolic interactionism can be traced to institutional ties of those holding the divergent stances, particularly differences between those institutionally connected to the University of Chicago and those connected to the University of Iowa.

Rice, Stuart A. 1931a. "Behavior Alternatives as Statistical Data in Studies by William F. Ogburn and Ernest W. Burgess." Pp. 586–613 in *Methods in Social Science* edited by S. Rice. Chicago: University of Chicago Press. Discusses methodological implications of two studies by Ogburn and one by Burgess which examine voting behavior as indices of attitudes and opinions.

———. 1931b. "Hypotheses and Verifications in Clifford R. Shaw's Studies of Juvenile Delinquency." Pp. 549–65 in *Methods in Social Science: A Case Book* edited by Stuart A. Rice. Chicago: University of Chicago Press. Discusses Shaw's research method, particularly his use of the case method, and influences on Shaw's work from Burgess.

Richards, Robert O. 1976. "The Sociology of Robert Park: An Ideological Legacy." *Western Sociological Review* 7: 79–89. Contends that Park's sociology, especially his emphasis on ecological processes and structure, contains an implicit ideology, i.e., that inequities such as race discrimination must be seen as intrinsic to the social order and will be eliminated only through gradual evolutionary processes.

Riesman, David. 1953. *Thorstein Veblen: A Critical Interpretation*. New York: Scribner's. Somewhat unsympathetic interpretation of the social criticism and social theory developed by Veblen, including discussion of his life and work at Chicago (pp. 11ff., 14ff., 38, 100ff.). Riesman suggests that it was at Chicago that Veblen had his most sympathetic and stimulating colleagues and where most of his best work was done (pp. 18–19).

Ritzer, George. 1975. *Sociology: A Multiple Paradigm Science*. Boston: Allyn and Bacon. Sketches the development of symbolic interactionism at Chicago in the work of Mead, Thomas, Blumer (and Cooley), in an effort to outline sociology's three paradigms: the social facts, social definition (see pp. 96–108 on symbolic interactionism) and social behavior paradigms.

Robbins, Richard. 1971–1972. "The Shadow of Macon County: The Life and Work of Charles S. Johnson." *Journal of Social and Behavior Sciences* 18 (Fall and Winter): 20–26. Discusses three contributions made by Johnson: "the strengthening of the social science tradition by black social scientists, the development of the ethnographic case study method in the rural South, and the implicit rebuke to white racist mythology about the *Negro problem*."

———. 1974. "Charles S. Johnson." Pp. 56–84 in *Black Sociologists: Historical and Contemporary Perspectives* edited by James E. Blackwell and Morris Janowitz. Chicago: University of Chicago Press. Sketches Johnson's sociological career, including his graduate study at Chicago and work with the Chicago Commission on Race Relations, the Chicago Urban League and the National Urban League, as well as his research on blacks in the United States, particularly in the South.

Robins, Lee N., Robin S. Jones, and George E. Murphy. 1966. "School Milieu and School Problems of Negro Boys." *Social Problems* 13 (Spring): 428–36.

Robinson, W. S. 1950. "Ecological Correlations and the Behavior of Individuals." *ASR* 15 (June): 351–57. Criticizes the "ecological correlation," concept as used by Shaw, Gosnell, Ogburn, and others. Concludes that ecological correlations cannot be validly used as substitutes for individual correlations, calling into question a number of important studies. Reprinted in Voss and Petersen (1971, pp. 147–58).

Rochberg-Halton, Eugene. 1982. "The Real Relation Between Pragmatism and Chicago Sociology." *Contemporary Sociology* 11 (March): 140–42. A review of Lewis and Smith (1980) which concludes that the common theme shared by the pragmatists that meaning is determined by its consequences may be more significant than the "great divide" suggested by Lewis and Smith between nominalism and realism.

Rock, Paul. 1979. *The Making of Symbolic Interactionism*. Totowa, N.J.: Rowman and Littlefield. An exposition on symbolic interactionism tracing its roots to Chicago sociology, Simmel, and pragmatism; outlines its principle contributions and difficulties.

Rogow, Arnold A., ed. 1969. *Politics, Personality and Social Science in the Twentieth Century: Essays in Honor of Harold D. Lasswell*. Chicago: University of Chicago Press. A collection of essays including, among others, Leo Rosten, "Harold Lasswell: A Memoir" (pp. 1–13), a chapter on philosophical underpinings by Heinz Eulau (pp. 15–40); sections on Lasswell's social psychology by Roy R. Grinker (pp. 107–22), Rogow (pp. 123–46), and Arthur J. Brodbeck (pp. 225–60) and one on world politics by William T. R. Fox (pp. 367–82). See separate entries Janowitz, Shils, and B. Smith.

Ropers, Richard. 1973. "Mead, Marx and Social Psychology." *Catalyst* 7 (Winter): 42–61. Analyzes similarities between Mead and Marx, particularly their common view of humans as thoroughly social beings. Suggests that Meadian concepts of mind, consciousness, language and self may be helpful in developing a Marxist social psychology and in explicating the dialectic between social structures and psychological reality.

Rose, Arnold. 1950. "Review of Robert Park, *Race and Culture*." *SF* 29 (December): 212–13. Reviews the collection of Park's essays on racial and cultural relations (1950), outlining major ideas and suggesting that the reader finds "the seminal mind of a scientist at work here" despite the lack of charts, tables, questionnaires and sociodramas.

———. 1955. "The Contributions of Ernest W. Burgess to Sociology." *Midwest Sociologist* 16 (Winter): 7–13. Summarizes and evaluates Burgess's work, his association with Park, McKenzie, Shaw, McKay, Locke, and others, and influences from Thomas and Znaniecki.

Rosen, Lawrence, and Stanley H. Turner. 1967. "An Evaluation of the Lander Approach to Ecology of Delinquency." *Social Problems* 15 (Fall): 189–200. A critique of Lander (1954) and a discussion of the relationship between ecology and delinquency, arguing that widely used statistical methods are inappropriate for the task he and others have undertaken.

Rosenberg, Bernard. 1956. *The Values of Veblen: A Critical Appraisal*. Washington, D.C.: Public Affairs Press. Analyzes Veblen's scholarship, suggesting that he stands equidistant between Marx and Weber, that many of his incidental ideas do not bear scrutiny at all, but that his "conglomeration of hunches, insights, philosophies and impressions . . . stands up remarkably well." Notes the importance of Veblen's marginal status and his "imaginative dissatisfaction."

———. 1963. "Introduction." Pp. 1–14 in *Thorstein Veblen* edited by B. Rosenberg. New York: Thomas Y. Crowell. A review of Veblen's work, emphasizing its uniqueness. Although often admired by Marxists and socialists, Veblen dismissed Marx as a Romantic philosopher with untenable theories and he denounced socialists as having "succumbed to jingoism and militarism."

Rosenthal, Sandra B. 1969. "Peirce, Mead, and the Logic of Concepts." *Transactions of the Charles S. Peirce Society* 5 (Summer): 173–87. Comments on Mead's elaboration of Peirce's recognition of the inadequacy of an essentially sensory theory of thought and mind, and the importance of habit.

Ross, Frank Alexander. 1933. "Ecology and the Statistical Method." *AJS* 38 (January): 507–22. Warns against statistical dangers encountered by ecologists, particularly the use of insufficient cases, the failure to account for such variables as sex and age, and the possibility of overlooking the importance of differential population mobility. Critiques R. E. L. Faris's study of insanity and makes recommendations for the statistically-sound use of the ecological perspective.

Rossides, Daniel W. 1978. *The History and Nature of Sociological Theory*. Boston: Houghton Mifflin Company. Treats pragmatism (pp. 393–403) and its influence on social theory via Dewey, with a chapter on Thomas, emphasizing his insistance on empirical research and his ahistorical pragmatism (cf. Bogardus 1959).

Rucker, Darnell. 1969. *The Chicago Pragmatists*. Minneapolis: University of Minnesota Press. Gives a detailed account of the Chicago School of pragmatic philosophy. A chapter on "Sociology, Economics and Political Science: Applied Pragmatism" (pp. 132–157) discusses the impact of Mead and Dewey on the sociology department and its faculty, including Small, Henderson, Thomas, Park, Faris, Ellwood, and others.

Russell, Bertrand. 1945. *A History of Western Philosophy and Its Connection with Political and Social Circumstances from the Earliest Times to the Present Day*. New York: Simon and Schuster. Includes a chapter (pp. 819–28) on Dewey which claims he is the leading living philosopher of America; assesses his instrumentalism and his conception of thought as an evolutionary process. Considers influences from Hegel, and Dewey's harmony with the age of industrialism and collective enterprise; cf. the chapter on James (pp. 811–18).

Sanders, Marion K., ed. 1970. *The Professional Radical: Conversations with Saul Alinsky*. New York: Harper & Row. Includes critical comments about the Chicago sociology department and Alinsky's experiences studying there.

Santayana, George. 1939. "Dewey's Naturalistic Metaphysics." Pp. 245–61 in Schilpp (1939). Analyzes Dewey's attempt to unite the two seemingly-contradictory systems of metaphysics and naturalism, commenting on his quasi-Hegelian tendency to dissolve the individual into social functions as well as everything substantial or actual into something relative or transitional.

———. 1953. "Three American Philosophers." *American Scholar* 22 (Summer): 281–84. Comments on Dewey's, James's, and his own philosophy, contending that "it is only Dewey who genuinely represents the mind of the vast mass of native, sanguine, enterprising Americans."

Satariano, William A. 1979. "Immigration and the Popularization of Social Science." *JHBS* 15 (October): 310–20. Brief discussion of Chicago social scientists who provided the most important opposition to restrictive immigration laws in the 1920s and 1930s (e.g., in *AJS* articles), when popular journals and magazines were supporting immigration restrictions.

Savitz, Leonard. 1970. "Delinquency and Migration." Pp. 473–80 in *Sociology of Crime and Delinquency* edited by M. E. Wolfgang, L. Savitz, and N. Johnston. 2nd Edition. New York: Wiley.

Scheffler, Israel. 1974. *Four Pragmatists: A Critical Introduction to Peirce, James, Mead, and Dewey*. New York: Humanities Press. Portrays major themes of the four main pragmatists, with biographical sketches of each (see chapters on Mead, pp. 149–84 and Dewey, pp. 187–255), arguing that the Chicago school stressed the social dimension of human action (pp. 150–51). Chapters on Peirce and James also provide insights into pragmatism and, by implication, its influences on sociology.

Schilpp, Paul Arthur, ed. 1939. *The Philosophy of John Dewey*. Evanston, Ill.: Northwestern University Press. A collection of essays on Dewey's philosophy, some of which pertain to his influence on Chicago sociology; see separate entries under Jane Dewey, Reichenbach, Allport, Geiger, and Santayana.

Schmid, Calvin F. 1963. "Jesse Frederick Steiner, 1880–1962." *ASR* 28 (October): 815–16. Discusses Steiner's career, including his study under Park at Chicago and his work with the Chicago City Club and Chicago United Charities, as well as his teaching at North Carolina and Washington.

Schmitt, Raymond L. 1974. "SI and Emergent Theory: A Reexamination." *ASR* 39 (June): 453–56. Takes issue with Huber (1973a, 1973b) suggesting that her treatment of interactionism and the Chicago school is inadequate, and contending that she has not attended to the weaknesses of traditional testing procedures.

Schneider, Eugene V. 1968. "Howard Becker." Pp. 40–41 in Sills (1968), Vol. 2. A brief recapitulation of Becker's work and influence, and the relationship between his work and that of Park, Mead, Weber, and von Wiese.

Schneider, Herbert Wallace. 1946. *A History of American Philosophy*. New York: Columbia University Press. Includes discussions of Dewey and Mead (passim, esp. pp. 390ff., 532ff., 550ff.); see chapter 33, "Genetic Social Philosophy" (pp. 380–95), esp. the discussion of Small, Dewey, Mead, Thomas, Veblen and Tufts (pp. 289ff.).

Schneider, Joseph. 1944. "Cultural Lag: What Is It?" *ASR* 6 (December): 786–91. Contrasts Ogburn's treatment of the concept of "cultural lag" with definitions and examples of the term in an effort to show the importance of the concept and its correct usage.

Schneider, Louis. 1948. *The Freudian Psychology and Veblen's Social Theory*. Morningside Heights, NY: King's Crown Press. Compares Veblen's work with Freud's, emphasizing their relevance to an analysis of the social order and the relationship between institutions and the individual, and that between sociology and psychoanalysis. Summarizes Freudian and Veblenian perspectives on rationality and social cohesion.

Schnore, Leo F. 1965. "On the Spatial Structure of Cities in the Two Americas." Pp. 347–98 in *The Study of Urbanization* edited by Philip M. Hauser and Leo F. Schnore. New York: Wiley and Sons. Review of Chicago sociologists' study of spatial patterns, Burgess's zonal hypothesis of city growth, and later studies.

———. 1966. "The City as a Social Organism." *Urban Affairs Quarterly* 1 (March): 58–69. Includes comments on developments by Park and the Chicago school of the notion of "the city as a social organism," with two faces, the symbiotic and the consensual; comments on earlier developments of the organismic analogy, especially in Spencer.

Schuessler, Karl. 1973. "Introduction." Pp. ix–xxxvi in *Edwin H. Sutherland on Analyzing Crime* edited by Karl Schuessler. Chicago: University of Chicago Press. Analyzes Sutherland's career and his contribution to criminology, particularly his *Principles of Criminology*, his theory of differential association, and his concept of white-collar crime.

Schwendinger, Julia, and Herman Schwendinger. 1971. "Sociology's Founding Father: Sexists to the Man." *Journal of Marriage and the Family* 33 (November): 783–99. Includes discussion of Thomas's theories (esp. pp. 786–90), arguing that although he objected to assumptions that women were inferior, Thomas nonetheless developed sexist social theories that relied on biological analogies, instinct theory, natural law concepts and an historical interpretation of evolutionary change that saw women as standing "nearer to plant processes than man."

———. 1974. *The Sociologists of the Chair: A Radical Analysis of the Formative Years of North American Sociology (1883–1922)*. New York: Basic Books. A radical critique of Chicago and American sociology with comments on influences from Durkheim (pp. 254ff.) and Small's efforts to undermine Marx's influence (pp. 280–83). Contends that much of the early American sociologists' work was sexist and racist (pp. 290ff.; cf. Schwendinger and Schwendinger 1971). Finds assumptions complementary to monopoly capitalism in Thomas, Park, Ogburn's psychoanalytic assumptions (pp. 335–82) and in Park and Burgess's concepts of social change (pp. 383–409). Scrutinizes Park and Burgess's theories of competition, conflict and accommodation (pp. 412ff.), Mead on reform (pp. 453–57), Ogburn on cultural lag (pp. 457–63, 469–71), and Chicago urban sociology (pp. 476–89), with criticisms of Thrasher, Anderson, Cressey, Zorbaugh (pp. 482–87). Assesses Bemis's dismissal (pp. 491–94), Small, Vincent and the *AJS* (pp. 232–53; pp. 508–11), and Veblen on universities (pp. 511–20).

Scott, Clifford H. 1976. *Lester Frank Ward*. Boston: Twayne. Ward's biography; treats Ward's relations with Small and the *AJS* (pp. 33–34, 132–33), his visiting professorship at Chicago (p. 39), and his contacts with Dewey (p. 63).

Seckler, David. 1975. *Thorstein Veblen and the Institutionalists*. Boulder, Colo.: Colorado Associated University Press. A detailed examination of Veblen and the institutional economists resulting from a "lifelong obsession with Veblen." Notes two wings of institutional economics, one associated with Veblen and the other with Commons. Describes Veblen's relations with Laughlin and the University of Chicago (pp. 29ff.) and includes a chapter on Mitchell, a student and admirer from Chicago.

Seeman, Melvin. 1971. "The Urban Alienations: Some Dubious Theses from Marx to Marcuse." *Journal of Personality and Social Psychology* 19 (August): 135–43.

Seligman, E. R. S., and Alvin Johnson, eds. 1934. *Encyclopedia of the Social Sciences*. New York: Macmillan.

Shanas, Ethel. 1945. "*The American Journal of Sociology* through Fifty Years." *AJS* 50 (May): 522–33. Recapitulates the journal's role as a vehicle for the expression of sociological thinking, for technical professional discussions, in combating provincialism in American sociology, and in helping to delineate the field of sociology.

Shaw, Clifford R. 1930. *The Jack-Roller: A Delinquent Boy's Own Story*. Chicago: University of Chicago Press. Reissued 1966, with Introduction by Howard S. Becker.

———. 1939. *The Natural History of a Delinquent Career*. Chicago: University of Chicago Press.

———. 1945. "The Case Study Technique: Value of Delinquent Boy's Own Story." In *The Jack-Roller* by C. Shaw. Chicago: University of Chicago Press. Evaluates life history and case study techniques in social research, noting the role of Thomas and others in developing the approach. Reprinted in Wolfgang et al. (1962, pp. 101–107).

Shaw, Clifford R., and Jesse A. Jacobs 1940. "The Chicago Area Project." Pp. 508–16 in Reckless (1940). Presents a summary of the underlying principles, philosophy, and characteristic features of the Chicago Area Project; notes Burgess's role as an advisor and contributor to the project.

Shaw, Clifford R., and Henry D. McKay. 1942. *Juvenile Delinquency and Urban Areas: A Study of Rates of Delinquents in Relation to Differential Char-*

acteristics of Local Communities in American Cities. Chicago: University of Chicago Press.

Shaw, Clifford R., Harvey Zorbaugh, Henry D. McKay, and Leonard S. Cottrell. 1929. *Delinquency Areas*. Chicago: University of Chicago Press.

Sheldon, Eleanor Bernert. 1968. "Louis Wirth." Pp. 588–89 in Sills (1968), Vol. 16. Argues that Wirth's lasting impact on the social sciences as policy sciences derives from his insistence that knowledge cannot be separated from social action. Discusses influences from Small, Park, Burgess and Thomas, his work on human ecology and urban life.

Shevky, Eshref, and Marilyn Williams. 1949. *The Social Areas of Los Angeles*. Berkeley: University of California Press. Presents an approach to the study of the city through social area analysis that is both an extension of and a departure from Park.

Shibutani, Tamotsu. 1961. *Society and Personality: An Interactionist Approach to Social Psychology*. Englewood Cliffs N.J.: Prentice-Hall. An effort to develop an interactionist social psychology developed by a Chicago student who studied with Blumer, Hughes, Thomas and Wirth. Draws upon and discusses their work, as well as that of Mead, Dewey, Park, Sapir, and others (*passim*).

———. 1968. "George Herbert Mead." Pp. 83–87 in Sills (1968), Vol 10. Reviews Mead's analysis of the "act" and the self, his pragmatics, and his efforts to account for the emergent properties of humans—thinking in abstractions, self-consciousness, and purposive and moral conduct.

———. 1970. "Foreword." Pp. v–viii in *Human Nature and Collective Behavior: Papers in Honor of Herbert Blumer* edited by Tamotsu Shibutani. Englewood Cliffs, N.J.: Prentice-Hall. Briefly assesses Blumer's work and influences from Cooley, Dewey, Thomas, and Park, with a bibliography of Blumer's writings.

Shils, Edward A. 1948. *The Present State of American Sociology*. Glencoe, Ill.: The Free Press. Includes substantial discussion of Chicago sociology, including the work of Park (pp. 9–11, 15–16, 25–27, 40), Thomas (pp. 6, 15–16, 25–26), Wirth (pp. 9, 12, 26, 29), Burgess (pp. 11, 32, 40), Warner (pp. 17–19, 44, 47), Hughes (pp. 16, 29, 44), Lasswell (pp. 34–39, 59), and others, especially in the areas of urban sociology, ethnic groups, and stratification. Assesses efforts by Thrasher (pp. 10, 40), Zorbaugh (p. 10), Landesco (p. 10), Cressey (pp. 10, 20), Shaw (pp. 17, 41), McKay (p. 17), Bogardus (P. 27), Thurstone (p. 27), Frazier (pp. 26, 28), Stonequist (pp. 26–27), Ogburn (p. 31), Mowrer (p. 31), Whyte (p. 44), and Znaniecki (p. 56).

———. 1950. "Primary Groups in the American Army." Pp. 16–39 in Merton and Lazarsfeld (1950). Examines studies of primary groups reported in Stouffer et al., (1949a, 1949b), noting their original purposes and their evolution.

———. 1963. "The Contemplation of Society in America." Pp. 392–410 in *Paths of American Thought* edited by A. Schlessinger, Jr., and M. White. Boston: Houghton Mifflin. A brief discussion of Chicago sociology (esp. pp. 393–94) in the context of the development of the social sciences in the U.S. Suggests that the fundamental outlook of Park, Thomas, Cooley, Dewey and Mead has been assimilated into the intellectual line of succeeding decades and that Dewey's conception of humans, developed from a Darwinian inspiration, has continued at the center of American social science. An enlarged version of this essay is in Shils (1980).

———. 1969. "Reflection on Deference." Pp. 297–345 in *Politics, Personality and Social Science in the Twentieth Century* edited by A. Rogow. Chicago: University of Chicago Press. Focuses on Lasswell's treatment of deference as an example of his exceptional ability to combine a macrosociologial view with attention to personality functions; mentions influences from Marx, Weber, Pareto, and Freud.

———. 1970. "Tradition, Ecology, and Institution in the History of Sociology." *Daedalus* 99 (Fall): 760–825. Explores the Chicago department's role in the development of sociology as a discipline from the outbreak of the First World War until the end of the Second. Observes the department's dependence upon the major intellectual personalities of Thomas and Park and the early focus on urban and ethnic studies; comments on its publications (esp. the *AJS*), as well as contributions by Small, Thomas, Park and Burgess, Ogburn, Stouffer, Hughes, and others (see esp. pp. 183–88, 215–20). A revised version of this essay is included in Shils (1980).

———. 1980. *The Calling of Sociology and Other Essays on the Pursuit of Learning*. Chicago: University of Chicago Press. A collection of essays with a number of references to Chicago sociology, including a revised and enlarged version of Shils (1963) and a revision of Shils (1970).

———. 1981. "Some Academics, Mainly in Chicago." *American Scholar* (Spring): 179–96. Reminisces about Shils's years as a student at Chicago, discussing the teaching, research, and personal styles of Park, Burgess, Wirth, Lasswell, and Knight. Discusses a seminar on Weber's *Wirtschaft und Gesellschaft* taught by Knight, Burgess's course based on his and Park's *Introduction* and his work with Wirth. Recalls taking Park's last course and visits to Chicago by Parsons.

Short, James F., Jr. 1960. "Differential Association as a Hypothesis: Problems of Empirical Testing." *Social Problems* 8 (Summer): 14–25. Concludes that much support has been found for the principle of differential association only if the liberties taken in the process of its operationalization are granted, commenting on types of further research needed to reform and operationalize the theory.

———. 1963. "Introduction." *The Gang: A Study of 1,313 Gangs in Chicago* by Frederick M. Thrasher. Chicago: University of Chicago Press. Analysis of Thrasher's classic study (1927) and its impact on the study of crime and delinquency.

———. 1969. "Introduction to the Revised Edition." Pp. xxv-liv in *Juvenile Delinquency and Urban Areas* by Clifford R. Shaw and Henry D. McKay. Chicago: University of Chicago Press. Shaw and McKay's impact on the study of criminology and their relation to Chicago sociology are assessed, as are subsequent developments in the field, particularly concerning issues initiated by Shaw and McKay. An addendum treats "The Chicago Area Project as a Social Movement" organized around Shaw's vision and charismatic abilities in the service of political and social self-determination by local neighborhoods and communities as well as broader sociological interests.

———. 1971. "Introduction." Pp. xi–xlvi in *The Social Fabric of the Metropolis: Contributions of the Chicago School of Urban Sociology* edited by James F. Short, Jr. Chicago: University of Chicago Press. Traces the development of urban studies in Chicago especially from the 1920s, including the development of research methods, social organization, social psychology of city life, structure and change, communication, social worlds, and social problems. Discusses Small's role in organizing social science studies at Chicago (p. xiii); Park and Burgess's contributions (pp. xiv–xv); the use of surveys and statistics by Park, Burgess, Wirth, Ogburn, Shaw, and McKay (pp. xv–xviii); and the importance of concern over social issues.

———. 1982. "Life History, Autobiography, and the Life Cycle." Pp. 135–52 in Snodgrass (1982). Examines implications for research and theory from Shaw (1930) and Snodgrass (1982).

Short, James F., Jr., and Fred L. Strodtbeck. 1965. *Group Process and Gang Delinquency*. Chicago: University of Chicago Press. Observes changes that have occurred in gangs from the time of classical studies by Thrasher, Shaw, and McKay, and suggests that lower-class gangs frequently support convention as well as deviant values.

Shott, Susan. 1976. "Society, Self and Mind in Moral Philosophy: The Scottish Moralists as Precursors of Symbolic Interactionism." *JHBS* 12 (January): 39–46. Outlines antecedents to symbolic interactionism as found in the eighteenth century Scottish moralists, noting that some aspects of Mead's theory are foreshadowed by Adam Smith and others, despite divergences in their treatment of emotion, communication, political structure, and the origin of sympathy.

Sills, David L. 1968. *International Encyclopedia of the Social Sciences*. New York: Macmillan and Free Press.

Simkhovitch, M. K. 1943. "Neighborhood Planning and the Settlements." *Survey* 79 (June): 174–75. Includes discussion of Addams and the *Hull-House Maps and Papers* (Addams 1895).

Simpson, George L., Jr. 1946. "Review of William Fielding Ogburn, ed., *American Society in Wartime*." *SF* 25 (December): 235–36. Review of a collection of lectures (Ogburn 1943) at the University of Chicago on the character of American society during the war, including Ogburn, Burgess on the family, Wirth on the urban community, Sutherland on crime, Warner on the American town, Redfield on Japanese-Americans, Stouffer on use of social science in the army, Park on racial ideologies, Faris on the role of the citizen, Blumer on morale, and Lowry Nelson on farming.

Simpson, Jon E., and Maurice D. Van Arsdol, Jr. 1967. "Residential History and Educational Status of Delinquents and Nondelinquents." *Social Problems* 15 (Summer): 25–40.

Singelmann, Peter. 1972. "Exchange as Symbolic Interaction: Convergences Between Two Theoretical Perspectives." *ASR* 37 (August): 414–23. In an effort to identify convergences between exchange theory and symbolic interactionism, Singelmann includes considerable discussion of the work of Mead, Blumer, and others.

Singer, Milton B. "George Herbert Mead's Social Behavioristic Theory of Mind." 1936. Master's thesis, University of Texas at Austin. An unpublished examination of Mead's theory of mind.

———. 1950. "The Social Sciences." Pp. 123–48 in *The Idea and Practice of General Education: An Account of the College of the University of Chicago, by Present and Former Members of the Faculty* edited by Milton B. Singer. Chicago: University of Chicago Press. Provides a sketch of undergraduate education in the social sciences at Chicago, including the reading lists for social science course sequences.

———. 1959. "Comparative Urban Sociology." Pp. 334–59 in *Sociology Today* edited by Robert K. Merton. New York: Basic Books. Discusses the Chicago School in the context of a broader survey, noting the impact of and problems with the human ecology approach that takes the city as an independent variable; notes its development by Park, Wirth, Redfield, Hawley, Zorbaugh, and others (pp. 340–44). Suggests that Wirth and Redfield have overstated their case and that city life, as suggested by Whyte, Oscar Lewis, and others, can be highly organized.

Sjoberg, Gideon. 1953. "Review of Robert Redfield, *The Primitive World and Its Transformations*." *AJS* 59 (November): 277–78. Suggests that Redfield's *The Primitive World and Its Transformations* sets the stage for a partial critique of his own folk-urban continuum, noting that a distinction must be made between folk and peasant societies.

———. 1960. *The Pre-Industrial City: Past and Present*. Glencoe, Ill.: Free Press. This classic study of the pre-industrial city includes a critique of prevailing theories of urban life, including the approach taken by Wirth and Redfield (esp. pp. 13–16), as well as opposing orientations which stress either (a) cultural or social values (Firey, Kolb, and Weber) or (b) social power arrangements. Argues that Wirth's and Redfield's overemphasis on secularization and disorganization have led to neglect of much of the organization of the city; Furthermore, their folk-urban comparison blurs the distinction between folk societies and peasant communities. Despite criticisms of the "Wirth school," the city can be seen as a factor in "determining" selected types of social phenomena.

———. 1965. "Theory and Research in Urban Sociology." Pp. 157–89 in *The Study of Urbanization* edited by Philip M. Hauser and Leo F. Schnore. New York: Wiley & Sons. A critical appraisal of urban sociological theory with considerable discussion of the Chicago School: the "urbanization school," as developed by Wirth and Redfield (pp. 159–64); the "subsocial school," with its emphasis on temporal and spatial dimensions, developed by Park and Burgess (pp. 165ff.); and the "ecological complex (or sustenance) school," inspired by Park and Burgess and developed by McKenzie, Hawley, and others.

Sjoberg, Gideon, and Walter Firey. 1982. "Issues in Sociocultural Ecology." Pp. 150–64 in *Urban Patterns: Studies in Human Ecology* edited by George A. Theodorson. Revised Edition. University Park: Pennsylvania State University Press.

Small, Albion W. 1895. "The Era of Sociology." *AJS* 1 (July): 1–15. Outlines the "platform" of the *AJS* within the context of Small's perception of sociology as a science.

———. [1915] 1975. "An Autobiographical Letter by Small (1915)." Pp. 201–204 in *The Legacy of Albion Small* by Vernon K. Dibble. Chicago: University of Chicago Press. Autobiographical sketch from childhood through the period at the University of Chicago.

———. 1916. "Fifty Years of Sociology in the United States, 1865–1915." *AJS* 21 (May): 721–864. Recapitulates developments during the period, with a section on Chicago (pp. 204ff.), noting the importance of its founding and the role of Harper in the institutionalization of sociology. Includes a discussion of the founding of the *AJS*. Reprinted, *The American Journal of Sociology: Index to Volumes 1–52*, Chicago: University of Chicago Press, 1947, pp. 177–269.

Smith, Bruce Lannes. 1969. "The Mystifying Intellectual History of Harold D. Lasswell." Pp. 41–105 in Rogow (1969). Traces influences on Lasswell's thought, including Small, Henderson, Thomas, Park, Dewey, Mead, and Merriam (esp. pp. 49ff.).

Smith, Charles U. 1972. "Contributions of Charles S. Johnson to the Field of Sociology." *Journal of the Social and Behavioral Sciences* 18 (Spring): 26–31. From an examination of the few items written about Johnson and from a survey of sociologists who knew or worked with him, Smith discusses the importance of his contributions to research in race relations (esp. C. Johnson 1934), and his development of the sociology department at Fisk.

Smith, Dusky Lee. 1965. "Sociology and the Rise of Corporate Capitalism." *Science and Society* 29 (Fall): 1–18. In arguing that the founding fathers of American sociology were ideological protagonists for corporate capitalism, Smith contends that Small's commitment to capitalism changed from time to time, but only as matter of degree. Reprinted, pp. 68–84 of *The Sociology of Sociology*, edited by Larry T. Reynolds and Janice M. Reynolds (New York: David McKay, 1970).

Smith, James Ward. 1952. "Pragmatism, Realism, and Positivism in the United States." *Mind* 61 (April): 190–208. A systematic discussion of relationships among Peirce, James, and Dewey; pragmatism, realism, and positivism.

Smith, Joan K. 1979. *Ella Flagg Young*. Ames, Iowa: Educational Studies Press and the Iowa State University Research Foundation. Analyzes Dewey's leadership of the Laboratory School and the controversy over his departure from Chicago.

Smith, M. Brewster. 1968. "Samuel A. Stouffer." Pp. 277–80 in Sills (1968), Vol. 15. Evaluates Stouffer's role as a founder of large-scale quantitative social research and his 1949 study of *The American Soldier* as a model of mass production in research, with an emphasis on quantitative evidence, avoidance of theoretical speculation except in close contact with the data, and a close connection with applied problems. Outlines influences from Thurstone, Ogburn, Pearson, and Fisher.

Smith, Michael P. 1979. *The City and Social Theory*. New York: St. Martin's. Scrutinizes the Chicago school of urban sociology (pp. 1–48), the ecological social disorganization perspectives, and the work of Park and Wirth. Notes Wirth's advocacy of urban planning and attention to processes of mass communication and social control, criticizing his "lack of perspective concerning the limitation of rational-comprehensive urban planning and the continuing vitality of urban neighborhoods" as well as his failure to "recognize that community organization and political conflict are often the only means available to organize the interests of the lower strata of society."

Smith, Richard L. 1977. "George Herbert Mead and Sociology: The Chicago Years." Ph.D. thesis, University of Illinois at Champaign-Urbana. Explores the nature and extent of Mead's actual influence on sociology in general and Chicago sociology in particular, claiming that there was limited and differential recognition of Mead among Chicago sociologists (cf. Lewis and Smith 1980).

Smith, T.V. 1931. "The Social Philosophy of George Herbert Mead." *AJS* 37 (November): 368–85. Suggests that there is a discrepancy between Mead's robust personality and his available writings and that the most significant aspects of Mead's speculation include an empirical account of the genesis and nature of the self, the cathartic and aesthetic function of intelligence in the social field, the significance of ideals, and a faith in the worthwhileness of thought.

———. 1932. "The Religious Bearings of a Secular Mind: George Herbert Mead." *Journal of Religion* 12 (April): 200–13. Postulates that despite Mead's rejection of his early religious orientation, much of his social psychology—notably his social view of the self—have their roots in Christianity.

———. 1934. "George H. Mead." Pp. 241–42 in Seligman and Johnson (1934), Vol. 10.

Smith, T. V., and Leonard D. White, eds. 1929. *Chicago: An Experiment in Social Science*. Chicago: University of Chicago Press. Assesses the first five years of the Local Community Research Committee, with appendixes that list publications growing out of the studies and the names of research assistants on the various projects and their occupations in 1929; cf. Park (1916), White (1929a, 1929b), Burgess (1929a, 1929b, 1929c), Merriam (1929), Gosnell (1929), Lasswell (1929), Breckinridge and White (1929).

Snodgrass, John. 1972. "The American Criminological Tradition: Portraits of Men and Ideology in a Discipline." Ph.D. thesis, University of Pennsylvania. Traces Sutherland's career and work in chapter 5, "The Gentle and Devout Iconoclast."

Snodgrass, Jon. 1973. "The Criminologist and His Criminal: The Case of Edwin H. Sutherland and Broadway Jones." *Issues in Criminology* 8: 1–17.

———. 1976. "Clifford R. Shaw and Henry D. McKay: Chicago Criminologists." *British Journal of Criminology* (January & July): 1–17, 289–93. Introduction to the work by Shaw and McKay as early figures in the field of criminology.

———. 1982. *The Jack-Roller at Seventy: A Fifty-Year Follow-Up*. Lexington, Mass.: D.C. Heath. An examination of Shaw's *The Jack-Roller* (1930) in which Snodgrass contacts "Stanley," the subject of Shaw's life history account, to see what has happened to him in the ensuing years. Evaluates Shaw's work and notes that Shaw was unaware of the extent of his own impact on Stanley.

———. 1983. "The Jack-Roller: A Fifty-Year Follow-Up." *Urban Life* 11 (January): 440–60. Summarizes and explores Shaw (1930) and Snodgrass (1982).

Somjee, Abdulkarim Husseinbhoy. 1968. *The Political Theory of John Dewey*. New York: Teachers College Press. Presents a systematic treatise on Dewey's political theory in the context of his broader philosophy, noting Dewey's belief that society had been disorganized as a consequence of industrialization, and, on the other hand, his optimism in the possibility of building a new community.

Sorokin, Pitirim A. 1928. *Contemporary Sociological Theories: Through the First Quarter of the Twentieth Century*. New York: Harper & Row. A broad discussion of sociological theory, with considerable discussion of Park, Thomas, Burgess, Small, Ogburn, Znaniecki, Hayes, and Ellwood, and some discussion of Veblen, Faris, and Sutherland (see esp. pp. 508–11, 642–45).

Sorre, Max. 1952. *Les fondements de la géographie humaine*. 3 vols. Paris: A. Colin. This broad historical, comparative survey includes some discussion of Chicago urban studies, notably Burgess's concentric zone theory (esp. pp. 332ff., 435).

Sorrentino, Anthony. 1959. "The Chicago Area Project after Twenty-five Years." *Federal Probation* (June): 40–45. A retrospective analysis of the Chicago Area Project founded by Shaw to combine research with a practical program for social change.

Speier, Hans. 1950. " 'The American Soldier' and the Sociology of Military Organization." Pp. 106–32 in Merton and Lazarsfeld (1950). Indicates contributions to the sociology of organization and of knowledge made in Stouffer et al. *The American Soldier* (1949a, 1949b).

Sprietzer, Elmer, and Larry T. Reynolds. 1973. "Patterning in Citations: An Analysis of References to George Herbert Mead." *Sociological Focus* 6 (Winter): 71–82. An analysis of references to Mead in the *AJS* and the *ASR* and in introductory sociology textbooks, finding that references to Mead were most frequent in journal articles during the 1956–1960 period, although the frequency has remained almost constant since then. Although most articles citing Mead were written by sociologists with an interactionist orientation, there is an increasing tendency for others to quote Mead, although perhaps resulting in a distortion of his basic concepts.

Stefania, Vergati 1976. "Louis Wirth e la scuola di sociologia di Chicago (Louis Wirth and the Chicago School of Sociology)." *Critica Sociologia* 38: 164–72. Reviews Chicago sociology and Wirth's place in it. Assesses his efforts to overcome biological determinism in the ecological perspective and his interest in sociopsychological aspects of Jewish social organization.

Stein, Maurice R. 1964. *The Eclipse of Community: An Interpretation of American Studies*. New York: Harper Torchbooks. Assesses Park's interest in social organization and institutions, social control, "natural areas," and urban processes (pp. 13–46). Comments on Burgess, Shaw and McKay, Thrasher, Warner (pp. 70–93), Zorbaugh, Davis, Gardner and Gardner on "Deep South" (pp. 153–74), Stouffer on military communities (pp. 175–98), Whyte on suburbia (pp. 199ff.), Park's influence on anthropological theories, especially Redfield's, as well as work by Wirth, and the symbolic interactionists (Hughes, Mead, Goffman, and Strauss).

Steiner, Jesse F. 1929. "An Appraisal of the Community Movement." *SF* 7 (March): 333–42. Examines the development of community studies, with their origins in work by Booth and others in England and with the *Hull House Maps and Papers*. One of the first volumes to contain community studies was Small and Vincent's 1895 introductory text, although Vincent's efforts did not have much impact. Examines work by McKenzie, Bushnell, and Park.

———. 1930. "Is the Neighborhood a Safe Unit for Community Planning?" *SF* 8 (June): 492–93. Although Steiner supports most conclusions made by Burgess and the Local Community Research Committee, he questions whether large cities other than Chicago have such well-defined natural communities. Furthermore, even in Chicago they are changing too rapidly to be used as units for agency administration.

Stern, Bernard J., ed. 1932. "Giddings, Ward, and Small: An Interchange of Letters." *SF* 10 (March): 305–18. These letters, with an introduction by Stern, provide insight into conflicts between Small and Giddings, especially over the nature of sociological method and Giddings's *Principles of Sociology*.

———. 1933. "The Letters of Albion W. Small to Lester F. Ward." *SF* 11 (November): 163–73. Further letters (see Stern 1932), with an introduction by Stern in which he points out that Ward had been on the verge of abandoning sociology as hopeless until Small's public endorsements of his writings. Notes how their diverse attitudes toward religion, their disparate personalities, social philosophies and world views led to strains in the relationship.

———. 1935. "The Letters of Albion W. Small to Lester F. Ward: II." *SF* 13 (March): 323–40. Additional letters, without any introduction by Stern, covering a variety of topics, including Ward's publications in the *AJS*. Small mentions reading Giddings, discusses Dewey, and invites Ward to teach at Chicago in the summer, with a comment that "Ross is making a strong impression" on students at Chicago while teaching there (summer of 1896).

———. 1936. "The Letters of Albion W. Small to Lester F. Ward: III." *SF* 15 (December): 174–186. Provides information about developments in the Chicago department, Ward's coming to Chicago in 1897, and Small's invitation to Giddings to teach in the summer of 1898 "not because I believe in his methods, but because I want to disarm any possible suspicion that I am afraid of it."

———. 1937. "The Letters of Albion W. Small to Lester F. Ward: IV." *SF* 15 (March): 305–27. The final installment of letters edited by Stern. "Apparently we are due for a scrap," Small writes 22 March 1910. "You should have found better evidence than you have cited before you advertise me or any one else as a traitor to sociology."

Stevens, Edward. 1967a. "Bibliographical Note: G. H. Mead." *AJS* 72 (March): 551–57. A bibliography in four sections: (I) Published Sources (by Mead); (II) Reliability of Published Sources; (III) Unpublished Sources and Their Evaluations; (IV) Select Secondary Works on Mead Evaluated in the Light of This Survey. Argues that the posthumously published sources are ideologically comprehensive and reliable, historically and genetically deficient, and have had too predominant an influence on later interpretations of Mead's work.

———. 1967b. "Sociality and Act in George Herbert Mead." *Social Research* 34 (Winter): 613–31. Systematically examines an aspect of Mead's work, presenting a scheme which represents the relationship between act and sociality; argues that for Mead, structural sociality can be expressed in terms of the social constitution of the self over against the generalized other.

Stewart, Robert L. 1981. "What George Herbert Mead Should Have Said: Exploration of a Problem of Interpretation." *Symbolic Interaction* 4 (Fall): 157–66. Stewart takes the role of Mead in examining debates over his writings on role-taking, stimulus-response patterns, etc. Postulates that Mead's approach helps account for both convergences and divergences of interpretations of Mead. Concludes that his work should be put to practical use.

Stocking, George. 1968. *Race, Culture and Evolution*. New York: Free Press. Discusses Thomas and Dewey on the study of race (pp. 245–50), noting Thomas's development of thought and his later lack of emphasis on innate differences in racial temperament, and discussing influences from Boas on Thomas's thought (pp. 260–63).

Stoetzel, Jean. 1941. "La psychologie sociale et la théorie des attitudes." *Annales sociologiques* Serie A (Fasc. 4): 1–24. Reviews social psychological studies of attitudes; includes discussions of Ellwood, Thomas, Veblen, Bogardus, and Thurstone.

Stone, Gregory P. 1954. "City Shoppers and Urban Identification: Observations on the Social Psychology of City Life." *AJS* 60 (July): 36–45.

Stone, Gregory P., and Harvey A. Farberman. 1967. "On the Edge of Rapprochement: Was Durkheim Moving Toward the Perspective of Symbolic Interaction?" *Sociological Quarterly* 8 (Spring): 149–64. Examines Durkheim's lectures on "Pragmatism and Sociology" delivered at the Sorbonne in 1913 and 1914 (see Durkheim 1964) and his interest in the work of Peirce, James, and Dewey, arguing that he was moving toward a symbolic interactionist perspective. Traces similarities between Durkheim's thought and that of the pragmatists, concluding that the social theory of mind toward which Durkheim was moving "appears full blown" in Mead. Reprinted in Stone and Farberman (1970, pp. 100–12).

Stone, Gregory P., and Harvey A. Farberman, eds. 1970. *Social Psychology*

Through Symbolic Interaction. Waltham, Mass.: Xerox. A collection of readings on the symbolic interactionist perspective, with introductory sections that discuss Mead, Thomas, and others, as well as reprints of Desmonde (1957), Kuhn (1964), Blumer (1966).

Stone, Gregory P., David R. Maines, Harvey A. Farberman, Gladys I. Stone, and Norman K. Denzin. 1974. "On Methodology and Craftsmanship in the Criticism of Sociological Perspectives." *ASR* 39 (June): 456–63. Criticizes Huber's (1973) attack on interactionism, raising questions about methodology, field techniques, biases in interactionism, and matters of craftsmanship, placing her work within a context of the debate over positivism.

Stonequist, Everett V. 1937. *The Marginal Man*. New York: Scribner's. Extends Park's concept of the "marginal man," with a comment in the preface about Park's introducing him to the concept (pp. vii ff.) and with references to Park, Simmel, Lind, and others.

Storr, Richard. 1966. *Harper's University: The Beginnings*. Chicago: University of Chicago Press. A history of the early days of the university, including some brief, but informative, discussions of the role of Small (as dean of the Graduate School of Arts and Literature), Dewey, and Mead in the general administration and formation of the university.

Stouffer, Samuel A. 1930. "An Experimental Comparison of Statistical and Case History Methods of Attitude Research." Ph.D. thesis, University of Chicago.

———. 1950. "Some Afterthoughts of a Contributor to 'The American Soldier.'" Pp. 197–211 in Merton and Lazarsfeld (1950). This retrospective essay assesses contributions and problems in Stouffer et al. (1949a, 1949b), noting applied aspects of the research, and methodological implications.

Stouffer, S. A., E. A. Suchman, L. C. DeVinney, S. A. Star, and R. M. Williams, Jr. 1949a. *The American Soldier, Vol. I: Adjustment During Army Life*. Princeton: Princeton University Press.

Stouffer, S. A., A. A. Lumsdaine, R. M. Williams, Jr., M. B. Smith, I. L. Janis, S. A. Star, and L. S. Cottrell, Jr. 1949b. *The American Soldier, Vol. II: Combat and Its Aftermath*. Princeton: Princeton University Press.

Strauss, Anselm. 1951. "Review of John Dewey and Arthur F. Bentley, *Knowing and the Known*." *AJS* 57 (September): 200. Suggests that, although written by philosophers, the book can be recommended to sociologists. Argues that "as a reminder of the bankruptcies of dualistic thinking, Dewey is without peer," but that "his concepts seem not to be so specifically fruitful and stimulating to social psychologists as those of his fellow-pragmatist, Mead."

———. 1964. "Introduction." Pp. vii–xxv in Mead (1964). Analyzes Mead's work and his influence on sociology, arguing that his position was radically different from that of most social psychologists and sociologists, who have emphasized his concepts of the "generalized other" and the socialized self, ignoring his processual view of social organization. Notes influences from Darwin and on Dewey; suggests that Faris provided the link between Mead and the Chicago sociology department. Observes that interest in Mead has unfortunately been restricted primarily to *Mind, Self and Society* (1934).

Street, Elwood. 1930. "Some Community Uses of Sociological Studies." *SF* 8 (June): 496–97. Notes contributions made by Burgess and other Chicago sociologists and divergences between their perspectives and those of community agencies in St. Louis and Washington, suggesting that the different positions point to the same thing.

Strong, Samuel M. 1939. "A Note on George H. Mead's *The Philosophy of the Act*." *AJS* 45 (July): 71–76. Outlines major ideas in Mead's *The Philosophy of the Act* (1938), which contains a synthesis of much of Mead's earlier thought as well as an emphasis on experimental scientific techniques and the possibilities for research around the concept of the "generalized other" and the process of "role-taking."

Stryker, Sheldon. 1980. *Symbolic Interactionism: A Social Structural Version*. Menlo Park, Cal.: Benjamin/Cummings. Assesses the connections between more general sociological theory and symbolic interactionism. Contains a discussion of the early developments, noting contributions from Dewey, Cooley, Thomas, Mead and, later, Blumer and Kuhn with the Chicago and Iowa "schools." Notes another wing somewhat independent of the Blumer wing, building from Thomas through Park and Hughes to more recent generations of students. Contends that Park and Hughes paid more attention to the link, through the concept of role, between self and social structure, and that Hughes was responsible for moving Chicago students to participant observation as a principal research form.

———. 1981. "Symbolic Interactionism: Themes and Variations." Pp. 1–29 in *Social Psychology: Sociological Perspectives* edited by Morris Rosenberg and Ralph H. Turner. New York: Basic Books. Essentially an abbreviated version of Stryker (1980). See especially pp. 5–13, which provides a summary of the development of symbolic interactionism at Chicago and elsewhere.

Stuart, Johannes. 1936. "Mobility and Delinquency." *American Journal of Orthopsychiatry* 6: 286–93.

Surie, H. G. 1970. "De Marginale Mens." *Sociologische Gids* 17 (July-August): 306–19. Reviews Park's and Stonequist's concept of marginality and attempts to clarify it by proposing a model placing it in a structural context and relating it to Merton's reference theory.

Sutherland, Edwin H. 1929. "Edward Cary Hayes, 1868–1928." *AJS* 35 (July): 99–99. Discusses Hayes's life and work, including a story of Small's telling Hayes as a young scholar, "I believe you are one of the men who can help to create a science of sociology."

———. 1937. *The Professional Thief.* Chicago: University of Chicago Press.

———. 1945. "Social Pathology" *AJS* 50 (May): 429–35. Reviews developments in "social pathology" over a fifty-year period, discussing the work of Spencer, Ward, Henderson, Wirth, Thomas, Znaniecki, Dewey, Mead, Cooley, Small, Blumer, Vincent, Ogburn, and others. Discusses the social disorganization perspective, theories of cultural lag, and the human ecology approach.

———. [1942] 1973. "Development of The Theory [of Differential Association]." Pp. 13–29 in *Edwin H. Sutherland on Analyzing Crime* edited by Karl Schuessler. Chicago: University of Chicago Press. Sutherland's personal account of his development of the hypothesis that criminal behavior is caused by differential association, noting influences from Henderson, Thomas, Park, Burgess, McKay, and others. Originally an address given as retiring president of the Ohio Valley Sociological Society, April, 1942.

Suttles, Gerald D. 1976. "Introduction to the Paperback Edition." Pp. vii–xx in *The Nature of Human Nature* by Ellsworth Faris. Abridged Edition. Chicago: University of Chicago Press. Examines Faris's life and work, his relation to Mead and his role as chair of the sociology department and editor of *AJS*. Comments on his social psychology which embraced both psychology and sociology, as well as his interest in social control and the primary group.

———. 1968. *The Social Order of the Slum.* Chicago: University of Chicago Press.

Swanson, Guy E. 1961. "Mead and Freud: Their Relevance for Social Psychology." *Sociometry* 24: 319–39. Compares and contrasts the complementary social psychologies of Mead and Freud, observing ways in which social psychologists consider Mead to be theoretically fundamental but empirically unfruitful, and Freud as empirically provocative but theoretically wrong.

———. 1968. "Symbolic Interaction." Pp. 441–45 in Sills (1968), Vol. 4. Surveys interactionism as initiated especially by Mead, with influences from Dewey, Peirce, James and Blumer.

Sweezy, Paul M. 1957. "The Theory of Business Enterprise and Absentee Ownership." *Monthly Review* 9 (July-August): 105–12. Postulates that a comprehensive theory is needed to coordinate the basic elements and trends discussed by Veblen—depression, monopoly, waste, salesmanship, and relations between business and militarist politics; there is more inspiration and guidance in Veblen's *Business Enterprise* and *Absentee Ownership* than in all the rest of American social science put together. (See Huberman and Sweezy 1957.)

Sykes, Gresham M., and David Matza 1957. "Techniques of Neutralization: A Theory of Delinquency." *ASR* 22 (December): 664–70. Critiques Sutherland's theory of differential culture, suggesting that the juvenile delinquent is at least partially committed to the dominant social order as evidenced by shame or guilt he or she frequently expresses.

Taggart, Richard V. 1932. *Thorstein Veblen*. Berkeley: University of California Publications in Economics, vol. 9, no. 1.

Talbot, Marion. 1936. *More Than Lore: Reminiscences of Marion Talbot, Dean of Women, The University of Chicago, 1892–1925*. Chicago: University of Chicago Press. Recalls her appointment by President Harper to teach "sanitary science" courses in the early social science department (pp. 2–5), and provides a thorough documentation of the work of early women at the University of Chicago. In particular, Talbot provides evidence of an organized protest by the women, resulting in several promotions.

Tappan, Paul W. 1947. "Who is the Criminal?" *ASR* 12 (February): 96–102. Attacks Sutherland's concept of "white collar crime," suggesting that it creates confusion and contending that it is better to study crime as legally defined.

Taylor, Graham. 1915. "Charles Richmond Henderson." *Survey* 34 (10 April): 55–56. A brief memorial to Taylor's colleague and his contribution to sociology at Chicago.

———. 1920. "Jane Addams's Twenty Years of Industrial Democracy." *Survey* 25 (December 3): 405–409.

———. 1930. *Pioneering on Social Frontiers*. Chicago: University of Chicago Press. This autobiographical volume discusses social and religious reform movements in Chicago, and "The Developing Sociological Teaching" (pp. 385–406), with brief treatments of Addams, Small, Henderson, and Ellwood.

———. 1936. *Chicago Commons Through Forty Years*. Chicago: Chicago Commons Association. An autobiographical examination of the Chicago Commons and its relation to the Chicago School of Civics and Philanthropy at the University (esp. pp. 154–59). Recalls his first encounter with Harper (p. 155) and relations with Addams, Dewey, Henderson, and Lathrop.

Taylor, Ian, Paul Walton, and Jock Young. 1973. *The New Criminology: For a Social Theory of Deviance*. New York: Harper & Row. A radical critique of criminology with considerable discussion of Chicago sociology.

Thayer, Horace S. 1968. *Meaning and Action: A Critical History of Pragmatism*. Indianapolis: Bobbs-Merrill. A critical and historical approach to pragmatic philosophy, with chapters on Dewey (pp. 165–204) and Mead (pp. 232–68) as well as a chapter on Dewey's notion of "continuity" and its foundations in the philosophies of Hegel and Darwin (pp. 460–870).

Thomas, Evan A. 1978. "Herbert Blumer's Critique of *The Polish Peasant*: A Post Mortem on the Life History Approach in Sociology." *JHBS* 14 (April): 124–31. Reviews Blumer's critique (see Blumer 1938), which occurred at a time when most sociologists were skeptical of the value of personal document research. Discusses Thomas and Znaniecki's *The Polish Peasant* (1918–19) and their "Methodological Note," suggesting that there has been recent renewed interest in that method as an approach to the study of the subjective meaning of concrete social life.

Thomas, Jim. 1983a. "Chicago Sociology: An Introduction." *Urban Life* 11 (January): 387–95. Reviews the work done at Chicago by way of introduction to a special issue of *Urban Life* entitled "The Chicago School: The Tradition and the Legacy."

———. 1983b. "Toward a Critical Ethnography: A Reexamination of the Chicago Legacy." *Urban Life* 11 (January): 477–90. Discusses the ethnography of the Chicago school and suggests that it provides a powerful tool that could be used to revitalize current theory and develop a "critical ethnography" which addresses broader issues of social structure.

Thomas, John L. 1950. "Marriage Prediction in *The Polish Peasant*." *AJS* 55 (May): 572–77. Criticizes Thomas and Znaniecki's *The Polish Peasant* (1918–19) because their predictions of marital instability among American Poles were inaccurate. Claims that the problem lay in their lack of statistical verification of the representativeness of their data, their simplification of reality by not recognizing the manifold "values" forming an "attitude," and because they did not fully consider the possibility of a conflict of "attitudes" resulting in ambivalence. Znaniecki responded (pp. 577–58), conceding the validity of some of the criticisms, but redefining them and suggesting that "a defective theory is scientifically more useful than no theory."

Thomas, Milton H. 1962. *John Dewey: A Centennial Bibliography*. Chicago: University of Chicago Press. A listing of Dewey's prolific published writings from the earliest in 1882 to 1960 (pp. 1–153), and a large selection of writings about Dewey (pp. 155–293). Thomas's preface contains a few brief remarks about Dewey and the compilation of the bibliography in consultation with Dewey.

Thomas, William I. 1907. *Sex and Society: Studies in the Social Psychology of Sex*. Chicago: University of Chicago Press. A collection of articles, reprinted primarily from the *AJS*.

———. 1909. *Source Book for Social Origins: Ethnological Materials, Psychological Standpoint, Classified and Annotated Bibliographies for the Interpretation of Savage Society*. Chicago: University of Chicago Press; Boston: Richard G. Badger.

———. 1923. *The Unadjusted Girl: With Cases and Standpoint for Behavior Analysis*. Boston: Little, Brown, and Co.

———. 1936. *Primitive Behavior: An Introduction to the Social Sciences*. New York: McGraw-Hill.

———. 1939. "Comment by W. I. Thomas." Pp. 82–87 in Bain et al. (1939). Evaluates his and Znaniecki's methodology in *The Polish Peasant* (1918–19), suggesting that their lack of the use of statistical methods and controls was a defect of their method and materials, and yet "it is evident that statistical studies of the behavior of populations will have a limited meaning so long as the statistical data are not supplemented by individual case histories." See also Blumer (1939b).

———. 1966. *W. I. Thomas on Social Organization and Social Personality: Selected Papers*. Edited and with an Introduction by Morris Janowitz. Chicago: University of Chicago Press.

———. 1973. "Life History." *AJS* 79 (September): 245–50. An autobiographical sketch (see Baker 1973) with a cover letter to Luther Bernard, in which Thomas notes the influence of Mead and Cooley (although suggesting that he was not significantly influenced by Dewey), as well as Small, Henderson, Booker T. Washington, Znaniecki, Bernard, Burgess, Thrasher, Zorbaugh, and Shaw.

Thomas, William I., Robert E. Park, and Herbert A. Miller. 1921. *Old World Traits Transplanted*. New York: Harper & Brothers. Although published under the authorship of Park and Miller because of the controversies surrounding Thomas's forced resignation from the University of Chicago, this work was authored primarily by Thomas (see Volkart 1951:59, 259).

Thomas, William I., and Dorothy Swaine Thomas. 1928. *The Child in America: Behavior Problems and Programs*. New York: Knopf.

Thomas, W. I., and Florian Znaniecki. 1918–19. *The Polish Peasant in Europe and America*. 5 vols. Boston: Badger. Vols. I and II originally published by University of Chicago Press, 1918. Second edition, 2 vols., New York: Knopf, 1927; reprinted, 2 vols., New York: Dover, 1958. Thomas and Znaniecki's classic study, which significantly influenced the type of research done at Chicago by subsequent generations of sociologists.

Thrasher, Frederick M. 1927. *The Gang: A Study of 1,313 Gangs in Chicago*. Chicago: University of Chicago Press. Reissued 1963, with Introduction by James F. Short, Jr.

Thurstone, Louis L. 1952. "L. L. Thurstone." Pp. 295–321 in *History of Psychology in Autobiography* edited by Edwin G. Boring et al. Worcester Mass.: Clark University Press. Includes a comment by Thurstone that he had been highly influenced by Mead's social psychology courses as a graduate student.

Thurstone, L. L., and E. J. Chave. 1929. *The Measurement of Attitudes*. Chicago: University of Chicago Press.

Tilly, Charles. 1964. "Review of Ernest W. Burgess and Donald J. Bogue, eds., *Contributions to Urban Sociology*." *ASR* 29 (December): 928–29. Review of the volume edited by Burgess and Bogue (University of Chicago Press, 1964) suggesting that the selections from Chicago theses reflect both the limitations and the "features that account for the great accomplishments of the Chicago school."

Timasheff, Nicholas S. 1955. *Sociological Theory: Its Nature and Growth*. New York: Random House. A general treatment of sociological theories with sections on Small (pp. 66–68), Veblen (pp. 91–92), Thomas (pp. 149–59), Ogburn (pp. 206–208), Znaniecki (pp. 248–50), and a chapter on human ecology which evaluates the work of Park, Burgess, McKenzie, Thrasher, Shaw, Zorbaugh, Hawley, Hauser, and Duncan (pp. 212–15).

Tims, Margaret. 1961. *Jane Addams of Hull-House: 1860–1935*. London: Allen & Unwin. Discusses Addams's ideas and activities, including a brief discussion of Chicago sociology (p. 62) and the urban research Addams facilitated.

Tolman, Frank L. 1901–1903. "Study of Sociology in Institutions of Learning in the United States, Parts I-III." *AJS* 7–8 (May, July, September, January): 797–838, 85–121, 251–72, 531–58. Includes discussions of Chicago sociology and a description of the Chicago department's program and course offerings (see esp. Vol. 8, pp. 115–21). Describes the Sociology Club (pp. 120–21) and lists courses by Dewey and Mead in philosophy and by Mitchell and Veblen in the political economy department.

Tonnes, A. 1932. "A Notation of the Problem of the Past—With Especial Reference to George Herbert Mead." *Journal of Philosophy* 29 (27 October): 599–606. Delineates Mead's treatment of the past, making a distinction between metaphysical and epistemological aspects; Mead denies the existence of a past as a metaphysical entity independent of the present.

Traywick, Leland Eldridge. 1942. "Parallelisms in the Economic Ideas of Karl Marx and Thorstein Veblen." Ph.D. thesis, University of Illinois. Raises doubts about Veblen's originality, suggesting that much of Veblen's contribution can be found in Marx, despite differences in their thought.

Tremmel, William C. 1957. "The Social Concepts of George Herbert Mead." *Emporia State Research Studies* 5 (June): 3–36. An introduction to Mead's basic works and ideas, arguing that although Mead's work is somewhat difficult to follow, it is extremely rich and deserves more careful attention than it has received.

Troyer, W. L. 1946. "Mead's Social and Functional Theory of Mind." *ASR* 11 (April): 198–202. Postulates that an outline of Mead's position should culminate rather than begin with his understanding of mind, noting that the natural order of Mead's thinking seems to have been "society-self-mind" rather than the reverse.

Tudor-Silovic, Neva. 1973. "Thomasova Studija o Prostituciji-Obrazac Primjene Kvalittetnih Metoda na Temel ju Dobro Razradene Teorije." *Revija za Sociologiju* 3 (3–4): 3–4, 99–102. Reviews Thomas's study of prostitution and his typology of the four wishes, arguing that much of what Thomas wrote is valid in contemporary Yugoslav society.

Tufts, James H. 1931. "George Herbert Mead." Pp. 24–30 in Ames et al. (1931). Comments at Mead's memorial service recollecting their meeting in

Berlin, Mead's background and efforts as a stimulating teacher, and his broad interests in the arts. Comments on his efforts at social reform, suggesting that "the three causes nearest his heart were the University of Chicago Settlement, the City Club of Chicago, and the Vocational League."

Turner, Jonathan. 1974. *The Structure of Sociological Theory*. Homewood, Ill.: Dorsey. Develops a substantial section on "Interactionist Theorizing" (pp. 309–390), discussing Mead's role in bringing the concepts of James, Cooley, and Dewey together into a coherent theoretical perspective (pp. 316–21); briefly examines Park's role theory (p. 322), and examines differences between the Chicago and Iowa schools (pp. 326–46).

Turner, Ralph H. 1967. "Introduction." Pp. ix–xlvi in Park (1967). Assesses Park's ideas and his impact on sociology, including his notion of the nature and tasks of sociology, the importance of the concept of social control, and his development of the concepts of symbiosis and socialization, and human ecology, as well as his study of collective behavior.

Ueda, Seiji. 1946. *The World of Act*. Tokyo: Riso-Sha. Contains a chapter entitled "The Summit of American Behaviorism" that includes references to Mead (pp. 105–231).

———. 1956. *Philosophy of Sign Analysis*. Tokyo: Kigensha Shuppan. Has a substantial treatment of Mead's analysis of signs and symbols in a chapter entitled "George Herbert Mead."

———. 1961. *Foundations of Pragmatism*. Tokyo: Waseda University Press. Includes eight short articles on Mead as part of a larger discussion of pragmatism.

Valien, Preston. 1958. "Sociological Contributions of Charles S. Johnson." *Sociology and Social Research* 42 (March-April): 243–48. Outlines accomplishments of Johnson as a sociologist and president of Fisk University, his contributions to the study of race relations, and influences on his career from his study as a graduate student at Chicago with Thomas, Mead, Burgess, and especially Park.

———. 1968. "Charles S. Johnson." Pp. 262–63 in Sills (1968), Vol. 8. A review of Johnson's career which emphasizes his apprenticeship under Park and his study with Thomas and Faris, as well as his sociological contributions in the area of race relations and his presidency of Fisk University.

Van Wesep, Hendrikus B. 1960. *Seven Sages, The Story of American Philosophy: Franklin, Emerson, James, Dewey, Santayana, Peirce, Whitehead*. New York: Longmans, Green. Examines American philosophers including a section entitled "John Dewey: Promethean Instrumentalist" (pp. 179–247) which outlines Dewey's ideas and career. See especially chapter four, "The Social Element," which van Wesep claims is the all-pervasive feature of Dewey's thinking and is related to Dewey's close association with Mead.

Van Wyk, A. W. 1974. "Stedelikheid as Lewenswyse—'n Kritiese Evaluasie van die Siening van Wirth." *Die Suid-Afrikaanse Tydskrif vir Sosiologie [South African Journal of Sociology]* 10 (September): 91–99. Criticizes Wirth's "Urbanism as a Way of Life" article, arguing that primary groups must be regarded as an integral part of an urban community.

Vatter, Barbara. 1964. "Veblen, the Analyst and His Critics." *American Journal of Economics and Sociology* 23 (April): 155–64. Summarizes Veblen's provocative theories and some of his critics.

Veblen, Florence. 1931. "Thorstein Veblen: Reminiscences of His Brother Orson." *SF* 10 (December): 187–95. An informative biographical piece, but with no mention of Chicago, except that Veblen married Ann Fessenden Bradley, who had been one of his students at Chicago.

Veblen, Thorstein. 1899. *The Theory of the Leisure Class: An Economic Study of the Evolution of Institutions*. New York: Macmillan. Veblen changed the subtitle in 1912 to *An Economic Study of Institutions*.

———. 1914. *The Instinct of Workmanship*. New York: Macmillan.

———. [1918] 1969. *The Higher Learning in America*. New York: Hill and Wang. Veblen's scathing critique of American universities based on his experiences at Chicago as well as Stanford and Missouri.

———. 1919. *The Place of Science in Modern Civilization*. New York: W. B. Huebsch.

Vergati, Stefania. 1976. "Louis Wirth e la scuola di sociologia di Chicago." *Critica Sociologica* 38: 164–72. Brief review of Chicago sociology is followed by an analysis of the life and work of Wirth and his place in Chicago sociology. Discusses Wirth's efforts to overcome biological determinism in the ecological perspective, and his interest in sociopsychological aspects of Jewish social organization.

Vianello, Miro. 1961. *Thorstein Veblen*. Milano: Edizioni de Conunita. Studi e Ricerche di Scienze Sociali 109. An introduction to Veblen's institutional economics and social theory, including a discussion of "La Posizione del Veblen nel pensiero sociologico" (pp. 283–97).

Victoroff, David. 1952. "La Notion d'émergence et la catégorie du social dans la philosophie de G. H. Mead." *Revue Philosophique* 142 (October-December): 555–62. An introduction to Mead's work, suggesting that the notions of emergence and the social are the two poles around which his philosophical system is oriented; agrees with Dewey that Mead is a seminal mind of the very first order.

———. 1953. *G.H. Mead: Sociologue et philosophe*. Paris: Presses Universitaires de France. Analyzes Mead's social psychology and philosophy and his writings on the history of philosophy, noting the importance of Mead's rejection of the false antimony between the individual and society. Briefly discusses Mead's influence on French social thought (pp. 3ff.).

Vinokur, Annie. 1969. *Thorstein Veblen et la tradition dissente dans la pensée économique américaine*. Paris: R. Pichon et R. Durand-Auzias. Examines Veblen's approach to economics, his critique of orthodox theories, his evolutionary point of view, and his analysis of American culture and capitalism.

Voget, Fred W. 1954. "The Folk Society—An Anthropological Application." *SF* 33 (December): 105–13. A critique and reformulation of Redfield's notion of the folk society contending that Redfield has written of folk society more in the spirit of a social philosopher and historian than as sociologist or anthropologist.

Vold, George. 1951. "Edwin Hardin Sutherland: Sociological Criminologist." *ASR* 16 (February): 2–9. A memorial review of Sutherland's career as "America's best known and singularly consistent sociological criminologist" who always viewed crime from the standpoint of social processes and the impact of social organization and cultural heritage. Includes a picture and a bibliography of Sutherland's published works.

Volkart, Edmund H. 1951a. "Biographical Note." Pp. 323–24 in *Social Behavior and Personality* edited by Edmund H. Volkart. New York: Social Science Research Council. Brief sketch of Thomas's life and work, including a discussion of the circumstances surrounding his forced departure from the University of Chicago.

———. 1951b. "Introduction: Social Behavior and the Defined Situation." Pp. 1–32 in *Social Behavior and Personality: Contributions of W. I. Thomas to Theory and Social Research* edited by Edmund H. Volkart. New York: Social Science Research Council. Elaborates the essential elements of Thomas's approach to sociological research, emphasizing his concern with "the situation" and the "definition of the situation" and his commitment to examining both the objective and subjective aspects of human life.

———. 1953. "Aspects of the Theories of William I. Thomas." *Social Research* 20 (Autumn): 345–57. Argues that Gisela Hinkle's efforts to find a unifying theory in Thomas's work offer unnecessarily narrow interpretations of his writings, that they underestimate the amount of personal evolution experienced by Thomas and have overestimated the number of his fixed ideas. See Hinkle (1952) and her rejoinder (1953).

———. 1968. "W. I. Thomas." Pp. 1–6 in Sills (1968), Vol. 16. Claims that Thomas was one of the most influential social scientists of the century; examines his work on *The Polish Peasant* (1918–19), cultural evolution and social change, the "definition of the situation," and the "four wishes." "He helped to lead sociologists out of the armchair and into the field and laboratory by establishing the tradition of empirical research for doctoral degrees in sociology."

Volkman, Rita, and Donald R. Cressey. 1963. "Differential Association and the Rehabilitation of Drug Addicts." *AJS* 69 (September): 129–42. Reviews

Sutherland's theory of differential association and its implications for rehabilitation programs as suggested by Cressey and applied in Synanon.

Von Haselberg, Peter. 1962. *Functionalismus und Irrationalität: Studien über Thorstein Veblens "Theory of the Leisure Class."* Frankfurt: Europäische Verlagsanstalt. Frankfurter Beiträge zur Soziologie. A study of functionalism and irrationality in Veblen's *Theory of the Leisure Class* (1899).

Voss, Harwin L., and David M. Petersen, eds. 1971. *Ecology, Crime, and Delinquency*. New York: Appleton-Century-Crofts. An important selection concerning the relationship between ecological theories and theories of crime and delinquency (see separate entries under Bordua 1958, 1939; Lander 1954; Robinson 1950; Jonassen 1949; Kobrin 1971; Chilton 1964; Conlin 1967; Gordon 1967; and Rosen and Turner 1967). In their introduction Voss and Petersen argue that "the significance of Shaw and McKay's position for subsequent theoretical developments in the area of delinquency can scarecely be overestimated," noting links from them to Sutherland, Cohen, Cloward and Ohlin (see esp. pp. 13–24).

Wacker, R. Fred. 1975. "Race and Ethnicity in American Social Science, 1900–1950." Ph.D. thesis, University of Michigan. A critical analysis of the work of Park, Thomas, Kallen, and others in the area of race and ethnicity in America. The author highlights the disparity between the approach to race relations taken by Park and Kallen, and the views of most "liberal" sociologists of the era.

———. 1976. "An American Dilemma: The Racial Theories of Robert E. Park and Gunnar Myrdal." *Phylon* 32 (June): 117–25. Outlines conflicting perspectives on race relations of Park and Myrdal; postulates that Park was less optimistic than Myrdal because of Park's belief that racism in the United States was deeply rooted in the history and customs of American society, and in its frontier heritage.

Wade, Louise. 1964. *Graham Taylor: Pioneer for Social Justice, 1851–1938*. Chicago: University of Chicago Press. Study of life and work of Taylor, who taught in the department from 1902 to 1906 as a part-time instructor (he was also at the Chicago Theological Seminary).

Wallace, David. 1967. "Reflections on the Education of George Herbert Mead." *AJS* 72 (January): 396–408. Reprints some early letters to and from Mead and analyzes them in terms of the development of Mead's thought.

Wallas, Graham. 1916. "Review of Thorstein Veblen, *Imperial Germany and the Industrial Revolution*." *Quarterly Journal of Economics* 30 (November): 186. An English sociologist, Wallas, although irritated by Veblen's irony and obscure language, thinks that he is a thinker comparable to Jeremy Bentham.

Walther, Andreas. *Soziologie und Sozialwissenschaft in Amerika*.

Ward, Paul William. 1930. "The Doctrine of the Situation and the Method of

Social Science." *SF* 9 (October): 49–54. A systematic treatment of Dewey's notion of the situation underlining its importance for research in the social sciences, but with no discussion of its relationship to the work of Thomas and Mead.

Ward, Lester R. 1900. "Review of *Theory of the Leisure Class* by Thorstein Veblen." *AJS* 5 (May): 829–37. A lengthy, positive review of Veblen's work which defends it from its critics, pointing out that its subject is an economic study in the evolution of institutions rather than a simple attack on existing institutions.

Warner, W. Lloyd. 1940. "Introduction: Deep South—A Social anthropological Study of Caste and Class." Pp. 3–14 in *Deep South: A Social Anthropological Study of Caste and Class* by Allison Davis, Burleigh B. Gardner, and Mary R. Gardner. Abridged Edition. Chicago: University of Chicago Press. Discusses Davis, Gardner, and Gardner's study of class and caste in the social organization of the South, noting how they employed a theoretical perspective of social organization developed by Warner and his colleagues in their study of Yankee City.

Warner, W. Lloyd, Marchia Meeker, and Kenneth Eels. 1949. *Social Class in America: A Manual of Procedure*. Chicago: Science Research Associates.

Waskow, A. I. 1967. *From Race Riot to Sit-In: 1919 and the 1960's*. New York: Doubleday.

Waterman, Willoughby C. 1926. "Review of Robert E. Park and Ernest W. Burgess, *The City*, and William Kenneth Boyd, *The Story of Durham*." *SF* 5 (September): 195–96. Suggests that Park and Burgess (Chicago: University of Chicago Press, 1925), have provided a study that differs from surveys of urbanization of the past in that it is more than a description of city life—rather, "it is a scientific analysis of the forces and elements that go to produce our urban civilization," noting particularly Burgess on "The Neighborhood" and Park on the newspaper.

Watkins, Myron W. 1958. "Veblen's View of Cultural Evolution." Pp. 249–64 in Dowd (1958). Observes Darwinian influences in Veblen's work, noting particularly his emphasis on cultural evolution and his orientation toward reality as constantly changing. Suggests that Veblen drew heavily upon James, Dewey, Loeb, and McDougall.

Watson, Goodwin. 1949. "John Dewey as a Pioneer in Social Psychology." *Teachers College Record* 51 (December): 139–43. Suggests that Dewey's social psychology was seen by Dewey as a basis for attacking world problems and that he forecast later trends in social psychology, such as the formation of social norms, the findings of the Hawthorne experiments, Allport's studies on participation and ego-involvement, and studies in group dynamics, among others.

Weeks, H. Ashley. 1956. "Review of Robert Park, *Society: Collective Behavior, News and Opinion, Sociology and Modern Society*." *ASR* 21 (April): 234. Notes the importance of Park's collected papers, edited by Hughes (Glencoe, Ill.: Free Press, 1955) and suggests that they reflect Park's anti-provincial nature, with references to many who are not sociologists. Suggests that Park "has made one of the clearest statements of sociology's place in the social sciences."

Weigert, Andrew J. 1975. "Substantival Self: A Primitive Term for a Sociological Psychology." *Philosophy of the Social Sciences* 5 (March): 43–62. Combines symbolic interaction and phenomenological perspectives, comparing work by Blumer, Mead, and others with Schutz, Psathas, Tiryakian and others. Contains considerable discussion of Mead, noting his emphasis on concomitant awareness and reflexivity.

Wells, Harry K. 1954. *Pragmatism: Philosophy of Imperialism*. New York: International Publishers. A Marxist critique of pragmatism arguing that it is the reactionary subjective idealist view of life of a bankrupt capitalist class; includes substantial sections on Dewey (esp. pp. 77–186).

Werner, M. R. 1939. *Julius Rosenwald: The Life of a Practical Humanitarian*. New York: Harper and Bros. A biography of the Chicago businessman and philanthropist who gave approximately $63 million to various causes, including the University of Chicago and reform organizations in Chicago (pp. viii–x, 279). Notes his relationship with Johnson (pp. xii, 136, 338, 367, and esp. 273–74) and the Commission on Race Relations, Addams and Hull House (pp. 91–93, 279ff.), Taylor and McDowell (pp. 90, 123) and others.

White, Leonard D. 1929a. "Co-operation with Civic and Social Agencies." Pp. 33–46 in Smith and White (1929). Reviews the relationship between the Local Community Research Committee and various institutions with whom the LCRC cooperated or from whom it received funds. Particularly helpful is a table (pp. 36–38) listing agencies and the amount of research funds received from each from 1924–1929, notably the Commonwealth Club, the Union League Club, the Chicago Historical Society, the Association of Community Chests and Councils, the Chicago Council of Social Agencies, the Chicago Urban League, the Institute of Meat Packing, and Julius Rosenwald (of Sears).

———. 1929b. "The Local Community Research Committee and the Social Science Research Building." Pp. 20–32 in Smith and White (1929). Discusses the Local Community Research Committee and the contributions of Small, Cooper-Cole, Lasswell, E. Abbott, White, Merriam, Gossnell, and others, the building of the Social Science Research building, and funds obtained from the Laura Spelman Rockefeller Memorial.

White, Leonard D., ed. 1930. *The New Social Science*. Chicago: University of

Chicago Press. A collection of addresses delivered at the dedication of the Social Science Research Building at Chicago, 16–17 December, 1929, which assessed the achievements of the Local Community Research Committee at the University and looked at the future of research in social science generally. See separate entry under W. C. Mitchell (1930).

White, Morton G. 1943. *The Origin of Dewey's Instrumentalism*. New York: Columbia University Press. Provides a chronicle of Dewey's ideas on the nature of inquiry and related subjects, particularly his shift from idealism to instrumentalism.

———. 1947. "The Revolt Against Formalism in American Social Thought of the Twentieth Century." *Journal of the History of Ideas* 8 (April): 131–52. Compares the work of Dewey (pp. 139–42) and Veblen (pp. 142–48) to that of Holmes, Robinson, and Beard, suggesting that they were united in a common revolt against formalism which culminated in an emphasis on historical and cultural factors.

———. [1947] 1957. *Social Thought in America: The Revolt Against Formalism*. Revised Edition. Boston: Beacon. Expands themes in White (1947) and analyzes liberal social thought in America with substantial emphases on Dewey's "instrumentalism" (see esp. pp. 18–21, 128–54, 242–46), Veblen's "institutionalism" (esp. pp. 21–27, 76–93, 97–100, 196–99, 206–12), and pragmatism (e.g., differences between Dewey and James, pp. 142–46). Reprinted as *Social Thought in America: Original Sin, Natural Law, and Politics* (Boston: Beacon, 1957).

Whitley, R. L. 1932. "The Case Study as a Method of Research." *SF* 10 (May): 567–73. Discusses values of the case study as found in his own work in cooperation with Thrasher (in his Boys' Club Study at New York University) and with Nels Anderson in connection with his Studies in Care of the Homeless of the Research Bureau of the Welfare Council of New York City.

Whyte, William Foote. 1943. *Street Corner Society: The Social Structure of an Italian Slum*. Chicago: University of Chicago Press. This study, originally a dissertation, finds evidence of an implicit social organization in a low-income Italian neighborhood. The preface details the research process and mentions debts to Warner, Hughes and others.

———. 1967. "On *Street Corner Society*." Pp. 156–68 in Burgess and Bogue (1967). Evaluates the impact of Whyte (1943) on urban sociology, theories of group processes and social psychology, and methodologies of social research. Notes the trend from moralistic to "an objective or scientific approach" in the sociology of slum districts, discussing work by Booth, Woods, Park, Miller, and Wirth as representing the objective approach. Discusses participant observation and community studies and the importance of immersing oneself in the situation.

Wilensky, Harold L., and Charles N. Lebeaux. [1958] 1965. *Industrial Society and Social Welfare*. New York: Free Press. Distinguishes between urbanization and industrialization, arguing that Wirth's and Park's picture of "urbanism as a way of life" confuses the two.

Wiley, Norbert. 1979a. "Notes on Self Genesis: From Me to We to I." Pp. 87–105 in *Studies in Symbolic Interaction: A Research Annual* edited by Norman K. Denzin. Vol. 2. Greenwich, Conn.: JAI Press. Argues that the "I-me problem in social psychology" has not received sufficient attention, noting that James and Mead translated Kant's insight into the Hegelian dialectic. Subsequent discussions, however (Kolb 1944; Lewis 1976) buried the issue as a false one, and Blumer has replaced the formulation with looser notions of "communication with oneself," etc. Combines elements of pragmatism (Mead) and phenomenology (Schutz) for a theory of self genesis.

———. 1979b. "The Rise and Fall of Dominating Theories in American Sociology." Pp. 47–79 in *Contemporary Issues in Theory and Research* edited by W. E. Snizek, E. R. Fuhrman, and M. K. Miller. Westport, CT: Greenwood Press. Recapituates the rise and decline of the Chicago School (pp. 54–63), suggesting some reasons for both. The Chicago department combined the right faculty with a monopoly of the means of intellectual production until the mid-thirties, when competing centers (e.g., Columbia) and a focus on quantitative methods facilitated a rebellion against Chicago within the discipline.

Wilken, Paul H. 1973. *The Evolutionary and Ecological Approaches: A Comparison and Analysis of the Possibility of Synthesis*. Chapel Hill: University of North Carolina Press.

Willhelm, S. M. 1964. "The Concept of the Ecological Complex: A Critique." *American Journal of Economics and Sociology* 23: 241–48.

Williams, Robin M., Jr. 1976. "Sociology in America: The Experience of Two Centuries." Pp. 77–111 in *Social Science in America: The First Two Hundred Years* edited by Charles M. Bonjean, Louis Schneider, and Robert L. Lineberry. Austin: University of Texas Press. This broad review of the development of sociology and its influences in American thought includes several references to the Chicago department (esp. pp. 87ff.).

Williams, William Appleman. 1957. "The Nature of Peace." *Monthly Review* 9 (July-August): 112–17. Discussion of Veblen's work on the intimate connection between foreign policy and domestic policy as part of a tribute to Veblen (See Huberman and Sweezy 1957).

Willie, Charles V., and Anita Gershenovitz. 1964. "Juvenile Delinquency in Racially Mixed Areas." *ASR* 29: 740–44.

Wilson, Edmund. 1958. *American Earthquake*. Garden City: Doubleday & Company. Includes a discussion of "Hull-House in 1932," pp. 447–64.

Wilson, H. H. 1957. "The Higher Learning in America." *Monthly Review* 9 (July-August): 117–22. Delineates Veblen's study of the "conduct of universities by business men," drawing upon his experiences at Chicago, Stanford, and Missouri (see Huberman and Sweezy 1957).

Wilson, Robert A., and David A. Schulz 1978. *Urban Sociology*. Englewood Cliffs, N.J.: Prentice-Hall. An overview of the field of urban sociology with considerable discussion of Chicago sociologists throughout the volume.

Wilson, Thomas P. 1970. "Normative and Interpretive Paradigms in Sociology." Pp. 57–79 in *Understanding Everyday Life* edited by Jack D. Douglas. Chicago: Aldine. Contrasts the "normative paradigm" (e.g., Skinner, Homans, Parsons and Shils) with the "interpretive paradigm" developed by Blumer, Mead, Turner, and others.

Wirth, Louis. 1928. *The Ghetto*. Chicago: University of Chicago Press.

———. 1934. "Albion Woodbury Small." Pp. 98–99 in Seligman and Johnson (1934), Vol. 14. Briefly recapitulates Small's accomplishments indicating that he was "effective in mediating the results of European (especially German) thought and in challenging the provincial, separatist and dogmatic spirit of the older and academically respectable social science." Comments on Small's belief in sociology as an objective science, but one which was a means for the orderly improvement of social life and contends that he was a "critical and sympathetic student of Marx but advocated gradual, orderly and constitutional reform. . . ."

———. 1938. "Urbanism as a Way of Life." *AJS* 44 (July): 1–24.

———. 1944. "Robert Park." Pp. 20–25 in Ames et al. (1944). These comments at Park's memorial service emphasize Park's accomplishments as a scholar, notably his study of human ecology, race relations, and the human community. Notes his "passion for social reform" and disregard for "crusaders who ignored reality" and discusses the apprentice-master relationship which Park cultivated as a teacher.

———. 1945. "Human Ecology." *AJS* 50 (May): 483–88. Traces the history of the ecological approach as borrowed from plant and animal ecology and developed by Park, Burgess, McKenzie, and others. Contends that it has contributed much but provides only a segmental view of human group life and should be examined in cooperation with students of social organization and social psychology.

———. 1947. "American Sociology, 1915–1947." Pp. 273–81 in *American Journal of Sociology: Index to Volumes 1–52* edited by Herbert Blumer et al. Chicago: University of Chicago Press. This sequel to Small (1916) examines topics in *AJS* articles, noting a transformation from a more or less undifferentiated body of ideas into a set of highly specialized interests, and mentions the creation of the *ASR* and other periodicals as well as Park and Burgess's *Introduction*.

———. 1953. "The Social Sciences." Pp. 33–82 in *The Twentieth Century* edited by Merle Curti. Cambridge: Harvard University Press. Brief but significant discussions of Chicago sociology which argue that Small was influential in turning sociology from speculation in the abstract to rigorous study of interpersonal and intergroup relations (pp. 75–76); emphasizes distinctive contributions made by Park and Burgess (pp. 78–79) in their empirical studies and introductory textbook, and by Thomas and Znaniecki (p. 79) in setting a new standard for the systematic analysis of sociological data. Reprinted, pp. 55–106 in Wirth (1956).

———. 1956. *Community Life and Social Policy: Selected Papers by Louis Wirth*. Edited by Elizabeth Wirth Marvick and Albert J. Reiss, Jr. Chicago: University of Chicago Press.

———. 1964. *Louis Wirth on Cities and Social Life: Selected Papers*. edited by Albert J. Reiss, Jr. Chicago: University of Chicago Press. See Reiss (1964); Marvick (1964).

Wirth, Louis, ed. 1940. *Eleven Twenty-Six: A Decade of Social Science Research*. Chicago: University of Chicago Press. Proceedings of the tenth anniversary celebration of the Social Science Research Building at Chicago, with papers by Merriam, Redfield, Wirth (pp. 51–63), Ogburn (pp. 64–77), and Thurstone (pp. 78–112). Includes an extensive bibliography (pp. 296–486) of works published by, among others, Burgess (pp. 308–10), Faris (pp. 327–28), Hughes (p. 343), Ogburn (pp. 376–80), Park (pp. 380–84), Shaw (pp. 402–403), Smith (pp. 405–407), Stouffer (pp. 408–409), Thurstone (pp. 409–10), and Wirth (pp. 418–20).

Wolfgang, Marvin E., Leonard Savitz, and Norman Johnston. 1962. *The Sociology of Crime and Delinquency*. New York: Wiley. An edited volume with a number of key articles on crime and delinquency. See separate entries under Cressey (1960), Shaw (1945), Glueck (1956), Cloward and Ohlin (1961), Bordua (1961), and Morris (1958).

Wood, Arthur Lewis. 1951. "Discussion of Cressey's *The Criminal Violation of Financial Trust*." *ASR* 16 (February): 97–98. Briefly discusses positive and negative attributes of a paper by Cressey (*ASR* 15 (December, 1950): 738–43), suggesting that its limitations lie in efforts to discover universal generalizations concerning *individual* behavior which is virtually impossible, because individuals are unique.

Wood, Margaret Mary. 1934. *The Stranger: A Study in Social Relationships*. New York: Columbia University Press. A broad application of Simmel's concept of the stranger, with discussions of Park, Burgess, Wirth, Thomas, Znaniecki, Thrasher, Zorbaugh, Small, and others.

Woodard, James W. 1934. "Critical Notes on the Cultural Lag Concept." *SF* 12

(March): 388–98. Systematically explores Ogburn's concept of cultural lag, claiming that it is very useful, although one must be aware of subjective aspects of its application, particularly when referring to changes one wishes to see take place.

Woodard, James W. 1936. "A New Classification of Culture and a Restatement of the Cultural Lag Theory." *ASR* 1 (February): 89–102. Attempts a more precise statement of the culture lag theory of Ogburn, MacIver and others, calling for the elimination of the distinction between material and non-material culture. Discussion by H. S. Becker (pp. 102–104).

Woods, Robert A., and Albert J. Kennedy. 1911. *Handbook of Settlements*. New York: Charities Publication Committee. General Review of the settlement movement in the United States; see descriptions of Hull House (pp. 53–64), with discussions of Addams and Ellen Gates Starr, and the University of Chicago Settlement (pp. 69–72) and Mary McDowell.

Wright, Helen. 1954. "Three Against Time: Edith and Grace Abbott and Sophonisba P. Breckinridge." *Social Service Review* 28: 41–53. Discusses work of Edith Abbott as an instructor in the sociology department, dean of the Social Service Administration, and important developer of methods of collecting and analyzing information about urban situations.

Yablonsky, Lewis. 1959. "The Delinquent Gang as a Near-Group." *Social Problems* 7: 108–17.

Yamamoto, Haruyoshi. 1963. *Pragmatism after the First World War*. Tokyo: Aoki Book Store. Includes a chapter on the "Social Psychology of Dewey and Mead" (pp. 133–47).

Yarros, Victor S. 1932. "Philosophy in the Light of Science, Professor G. H. Mead's *Philosophy of the Present*." *Open Court* 46 (November): 787–91. Observes that Mead's *Philosophy of the Present* (Cf. Murphy 1959) provides a summary of some fundamental and fruitful aspects of Mead's contribution to American philosophy. Maintains that Mead's most original and daring generalization concerns "sociality as a principle."

Young, Donald. 1951. "Foreword." Pp. v–vi in *Social Behavior and Personality: Contributions of W. I. Thomas to Theory and Social Research* edited by Edmund H. Volkart. New York: Social Science Research Council. Observes the lack of life history documents on Thomas and discusses efforts by D. Young, Blumer, Sellin, D. Thomas, and Volkart to make his out-of-print and unpublished work available.

———. 1961. "Samuel Andrew Stouffer, 1900–1960." *ASR* 26 (February): 106–7. Brief memorial highlighting Stouffer's contributions to quantitative methods and his participation in major studies such as *The American Soldier* and Myrdal's *The American Dilemma*. Suggests that Stouffer was "an exceptionally influential instructor."

———. 1971. "Introduction to the Republished Edition." *Old World Traits Transplanted* by William I. Thomas together with Robert E. Park and Herbert A. Miller. Montclair, N.J.: Patterson Smith. Discusses the reasons for Thomas's not being identified as the author of *Old World Traits Transplanted* when it was first published in 1921 (it was published under Park and Miller's names shortly after Thomas was forced out of the University). Outlines Thomas's use of various concepts such as "attitude," "value," "fundamental wishes," "definition of the situation," and "primary group," noting that some of his theoretical conceptualizations and terminology may now seem old-fashioned. Argues that it still remains an important work, an early example of applied sociology and social psychology. Furthermore, its call for mutual adaption of values and attitudes of immigrants and the older population is still unheeded by many.

Young, Earle F. 1944. "A Sociological Explorer: Robert E. Park." *Sociology and Social Research* 28 (July-August): 436–39. A memorial tribute which comments on Park's unusual contributions to a wide variety of research fields.

Young, Kimball. 1924. "Review of W. I. Thomas, *The Unadjusted Girl*." *SF* 2 (September): 747–49. Contends that only recently (1924) the standpoint in social psychology for which Thomas contended has begun to be accepted and that Thomas was one of the first Americans to recognize the importance of Freud, "with whom he had come in contact during his research on the Polish peasant in Europe." Observes that the volume may provide the most thorough theoretical account of the place of wishes and attitudes in his writings, and remarks on the method of the case study.

———. 1927a. "Review of Charles A. Ellwood, *The Psychology of Society: An Introduction to Sociological Theory*." *SF* 5 (June): 669–70. Claims that the volume (New York: Appleton, 1925) is the most comprehensive work that Ellwood has published. Comments that while Ellwood draws heavily on individual psychology, he believes the province of sociology and social psychology to be the group. Insists that there is a "genuine methodological problem as to whether the science of sociology must rest essentially on biology and psychology," or "construct its own science in terms of group phenomena."

———. 1927b. "Topical Summaries of Current Literature: Personality Studies." *AJS* 32 (May): 953–71. Briefly discusses Thomas and Znaniecki, Faris, Park, Burgess, Anderson, Reckless, Shaw, Zorbaugh, and Krueger, in the context of his review of the literature and methodological debates in personality studies.

———. 1931a. *Social Attitudes*. New York: Holt. An edited volume dedicated to Thomas, whom Young claims first made the study of social attitudes prominent. See the introduction (pp. vii–x) which notes that the contributors were all associated with Thomas as students or collaborators (Bernard, Bogardus, Burgess, Faris, McKenzie, Herbert A. Miller, Park, Queen, Reuter, Steiner, Sutherland, Thrasher, Erle Fiske Young, and Znaniecki). (See separate entries under Faris, Park, and Queen.)

———. 1931b. "Frederik M. Thrasher's Study of Gangs." Pp. 511–27 in Rice (1931c). Explores the methodological implications of Thrasher's *The Gang* (1927), with references to the human ecology approach, Park, Burgess, Thomas, Shaw, and others.

———. 1932. "Method, Generalization, and Prediction in Social Psychology." *Publications of the American Sociological Society* 27 (Annual): 20–34. Assesses methodological debates within social psychology, with particular discussion of problems and possibilities of both statistical methods and historical or case study approaches. Discusses work by Mead, Thurstone, Thomas, Znaniecki, and others.

———. 1948. "William I. Thomas: 1863–1947." *ASR* 13 (February): 102–104. Reviews Thomas's work and suggests that although Thomas never regarded himself as essentially a theorist, his empirical research represented a shift away from armchair philosophizing toward concrete research, the findings of which must eventually be systematized into a comprehensive theory.

———. 1962–1963. "The Contribution of William Isaac Thomas to Sociology." *Sociology and Social Research* 47 (October, January, April, July): 3–24, 123–37, 251–72, 381–97. Traces Thomas's contribution to sociology as broad and significant and maintains that he was basically an empiricist rather than a theorist. Looks at Thomas's research in five periods: (1) 1896–1907: topics in folk psychology (*Sex and Society*, 1907); (2) 1908–1910: social psychology of cultural (institutional) origins (*Source Book for Social Origins*, 1909); (3)1911–1926: his magnum opus, *The Polish Peasant* (1918–19); (4) 1927–1936: critique of current research on child behavior (*The Child in America*, 1928); and (5) 1937–47: collection of sociological and anthropological materials on nonliterate societies.

Young, Michael, and Peter Willmott. 1957. *Family and Kinship in East London*. Baltimore: Penguin.

Young, Pauline V. 1932. *The Pilgrims of Russian Town*. Chicago: University of Chicago Press.

———. 1944. *Scientific Social Surveys and Research: An Introduction to the Background, Content, Methods and Analysis of Social Studies*. New York: Prentice-Hall. Refers to efforts to develop survey methods by Burgess, Park, Ellwood, Faris, Shaw and McKay, McKenzie, Ogburn, W. I. Thomas, Dorothy Swaine Thomas, Thrasher, Thurstone, Wirth, Znaniecki, Zorbaugh, and others. Indicates that "there is perhaps no other sociologist who has so profoundly influenced American field research students as has Dr. Thomas" (p. 78), and notes the importance of Chicago research (esp. pp. 73ff.).

Zeitlin, Irving M. 1973. *Rethinking Sociology: A Critique of Contemporary Theory*. New York: Appleton-Century-Crofts. In an effort to develop a new synthesis of sociological theory, Zeitlin critiques functionalism, social exchange theory, conflict theory, phenomenology and ethnomethodology, and symbolic interactionism. After substantial reviews of the work of Mead, Goffman, and Blumer (pp. 191–242), he develops a synthesis of Marx, Mead, and Freud.

Zentner, Henry. 1951. "Morale: Certain Theoretical Implications of Data in *The American Soldier*." *ASR* 16 (June): 297–307. Declares that the most systematic conception of "morale" was developed by Blumer and that data in Stouffer et al., *The American Soldier* (1949a, 1949b), imply that Blumer's conceptualization is "grossly inadequate." Blumer responds (pp. 308–309) that Zentner has failed to test any of his propositions and Zentner makes a rejoinder (pp. 309–10).

Znaniecki, Eileen. 1945. "Polish Sociology." Pp. 703–17 in *Twentieth Century Sociology* edited by Georges Gurvitch and Wilbert E. Moore. New York: Philosophical Library. Includes a discussion of Florian Znaniecki as one of the six most influential persons in the development of sociology in Poland, indicating that it is doubtful that the full range of his thinking will ever be fully appreciated since half of his work is published in English and the other half, distinctly different, in Polish.

Znaniecki, Florian. 1939. "Comment by Florian Znaniecki." Pp. 87–98 in *Critiques of Research in the Social Sciences, I: An Appraisal of Thomas and Znaniecki's "The Polish Peasant in Europe and America"* by Herbert Blumer. New York: Social Science Research Council, Bulletin 44. Indicates problems with *The Polish Peasant* (1918–19), admitting that a major difficulty was that he and Thomas took stability for granted when dealing with the problem of change, whereas in fact the world of culture is in ceaseless and apparently chaotic flux. He defends their efforts to test sociological theory in human documents. See also Blumer (1939b).

———. 1940. *The Social Role of the Man of Knowledge*. New York: Columbia University Press.

———. 1948. "William I. Thomas as a Collaborator." *Sociology and Social Research* 32 (March-April): 765–67. Personal recollections of Znaniecki's relationship with Thomas, emphasizing his wide sympathetic interest in the vast diversity of sociocultural patterns and a genius for understanding the uniqueness of human personalities. Insists that their divergent intellectual interests did not create conflict in their personal and intellectual relationships. Finally, he discusses Thomas's interest in Freud's theories.

———. 1969. *Florian Znaniecki on Humanistic Sociology: Selected Essays*. edited by Robert Bierstedt. Chicago: University of Chicago Press.

Zorbaugh, Harvey W. 1929. *The Gold Coast and the Slum: A Sociological Study of Chicago's Near North Side*. Chicago: University of Chicago Press. Reissued in 1976; see Chudacoff (1976).

INDEX

Note: References to the introductory material are by page number, and to the annotated bibliography by author and date.